WORKERS' CONTROL

A Reader on Labor
and Social Change

WORKERS' CONTROL

A Reader on Labor and Social Change

Edited by **Gerry Hunnius,**
G. David Garson and John Case

Vintage Books
A Division of Random House
New York

VINTAGE BOOKS EDITION 1973
First Edition

Copyright © 1973 by The Cambridge Policy Studies Institute
All rights reserved under International and Pan-American Copyright
Conventions. Published in the United States by Random House, Inc.,
New York and simultaneously in Canada by Random House of Canada
Limited, Toronto.

Library of Congress Cataloging in Publication Data

Hunnius, Gerry.
  Workers' Control.

  Bibliography: p.
  1. Employees' representation in management—United States—Ad-
dresses, essays, lectures. 2. Employees' representation in management—
Addresses, essays, lectures. I. Garson, G. David, joint author. II. Case,
John, joint author. III. Title.
[HD5660.U5H8 1973b]   331.8   72-8864
ISBN 0-394-71862-3 (pbk)

Manufactured in the United States of America

PERMISSIONS AND ACKNOWLEDGMENTS

"Know thy enemy . . ." was first published in England as a political
poster by *The Black Dwarf* in November 1968. It is reprinted here by
permission of C. Logue. Copyright © 1968 by C. Logue.

"Living with Automation in Winnipeg" is reprinted with the permission
of Ian Adams from his book *The Poverty Wall,* McClelland and Stewart,
Ltd., Toronto, 1970.

"Rebellion in American Labor's Rank and File" originally appeared, in
part, in the June 1967 issue of *International Socialist Journal,* edited by
Maurice Zeitlin, under the title "U.S.A.: The Labor Revolt." Copyright
© 1967 by Stanley Weir. This is a much revised and expanded version of
that article.

"The Subversion of Collective Bargaining" by Daniel Bell first appeared
in the March 1960 issue of *Commentary* magazine. It is reprinted here,
in slightly shortened form, by permission of Daniel Bell.

"A Trade Union Strategy in the Common Market" is taken from a book
by the same title edited by Ken Coates and published in England by
Spokesman Books, the Bertrand Russell Press, Nottingham. It is reprinted
by permission of the publisher.

"On the Relevance and Future of Workers' Management" by Paul Blumberg is a slightly revised form of the first four pages of his book *Industrial*

Know thy enemy,
He does not care what color you are
provided you work for him;
he does not care how much you earn
provided you earn more for him;
he does not care who lives in the room at the top
provided he owns the building;
he will let you say whatever you like against him
provided you do not act against him;
he sings the praises of humanity
but knows machines cost more than men;
bargain with him he laughs and beats you at it;
challenge him
and he kills;
sooner than lose the things he owns
he will destroy the world.

Editors' Note

Workers' control means democratizing the workplace: the office, the factory, the shop, the company or institution. It means that a firm's management should be accountable to its employees. And it means, conversely, that the workers—blue- and white-collar alike—should bear the responsibility for running the enterprise's operations. Workers' control suggests both an ultimate goal—of a self-managing, publicly responsible economy—and a strategy for reaching that goal.

It is an idea which for many years has been lost to Americans and Canadians. The historic notion that workers should manage their workplaces, termed "industrial democracy" in its early formulations, has been buried by the all-pervasive, U.S.-dominated corporate economy, and by its attendant ideology of private enterprise, the profit motive, chain-of-command efficiency, and management rights. By now, ideas of workers' control too often conjure up visions of obscure revolutionary sects, or the academic theories of some nineteenth-century reformer.

This, of course, need not be the case. The example of Yugoslavia, described later in this book, demonstrates that workers' self-management can be a practical system for operating a fast-developing industrial economy. Experience in Western Europe —Sweden, Norway, Germany, Great Britain—while more limited, indicates that workers' control can be a prime topic of concern among large numbers of workers in countries very much like our own. Moreover, there are beginning signs of a revival of the issue in North America. The Canadian Labour Congress recently went on record in favor of "industrial democracy." Industrial unions such as the United Auto Workers have shown an increased interest in moving beyond the traditional limits of collective bargaining to issues associated with workers' control, such as pricing policies and production processes. Several major Canadian unions, such as the Pulp and Paper Workers' Brotherhood, are moving in the same direction.

Perhaps most important in this context has been the growth of a movement for "participatory democracy" in the United States and Canada. As a rallying cry for students, ghetto blacks, young professionals, and ordinary citizens who feel estranged from the processes of government, the idea of participation has been a common theme in the various movements for change of the past decade. When this movement is combined with a growing disaffection from established unions and from labor-management policies as described in later sections of this book, there is a firm foundation for anticipating major changes in the workplace and in the economic system.

But what exactly might these changes be, and how might they come about? In a sense, this book is designed to fill a vacuum. Very little on the subject of workers' control has been published or is available in North America. The book therefore contains basic information for readers unfamiliar with the issues of self-management. It reviews the problems faced by workers, and the inadequacies of present union policies. It explains the urgent need to transcend the system of collective bargaining. It describes the experience in other countries with alternative models of workers' participation and self-management, and explores the possibilities of workers' control as a strategy for change in our own societies. It is directed toward all those concerned with a strategy for labor and with social change: toward radical activists seeking to define a program and a vision for political action; toward students and professionals in industrial relations; toward unionists, workers, and citizens. The book provides no definitive answers. Rather, it seeks to begin what could be an immensely important dialogue about the nature of democracy and the corporate system in the United States and Canada.

This book is the product of a collective effort by two collaborating groups: the task force on workers' management of the Cambridge Policy Studies Institute in Cambridge, Massachusetts;

and the task force on workers' control of Praxis: Research Institute for Social Change in Toronto, Ontario. Praxis was born in the winter of 1968 and began operating the following summer. From the beginning, Praxis has attempted to make research and analysis directly relevant to action for social change, through a variety of projects and organizing efforts aimed at the grass roots of the community and the workplace. The Cambridge Policy Studies Institute organized in the fall of 1968 as a private, nonprofit agency of applied research. The Institute has undertaken task forces and specific research projects to grapple with questions of program and strategy for change. It has worked closely with activist organizations and community groups, in Boston and throughout the nation, to test theory by social action.

Although half of the present volume represents original work emanating from these two groups, the editors would like to thank the authors and publishers who kindly gave permission to reprint the previously published articles which are interspersed throughout. And we would particularly like to thank participants in both task forces who, though they may not have contributed an essay, were immensely helpful in the discussions which gave shape and direction to this book. Responsibility for the final product is, of course, our own.

Gerry Hunnius
G. David Garson
John Case

Cambridge, Massachusetts
Toronto, Ontario
June 1972

Contents

I. The Management of Work: Dissenting Views

II. Beyond Collective Bargaining

III. Contemporary Models of Worker Participation and Self-Management

IV. Workers' Control: Strategies for Change

WORKERS' CONTROL

Foreword:
Capitalism and Workers' Self-Management

David Ellerman

The purpose of this essay is to examine the property-theoretic basis of capitalism. What is the moral basis of property? How is property rightfully appropriated? Certainly chattel slavery violated inalienable natural rights. Does capitalism do the same? If so, how can these rights be satisfied?

Let's approach these questions with a concrete example. Suppose that a criminally inclined entrepreneur hires a number of people at a fixed wage to rob a bank. Suppose that he rents a car to escape in and that the car owner is not otherwise involved. The car owner is not a co-conspirator or co-worker with the entrepreneur and his employees. After the crime, the bank robbers are caught. In court, the hired criminals assert that they are just as innocent as the car owner. They inform the judge that they and the car owner are owners of certain services (labor services in the one case and the services of the car in the other) which they sell as commodities on the market and which will then be used by the buyer. If the buyer uses these services to commit some crime, that is not the fault of the original factor owner.

Naturally the judge would reject this defense and hold that, unlike the car owner, the hired workers were responsible for the crime together with the entrepreneur. Why the distinction? The car owner, like the others, is a moral agent, but he only sold the entrepreneur the services of a natural agent (his car) and he was not involved himself as a moral agent. The hired workers, on the other hand, sold the entrepreneur the services of moral agents, i.e., themselves. The labor contract does not somehow turn the workers into machines like the car which can be used by others and which would have no responsibility for the results of the services provided. Thus the judge would correctly look beyond the superficial labor contract and hold that all those human agents who committed the crime were responsible for it. We might also suppose that, as a last resort, the hired criminals produced another contract they had made with the entrepreneur which "absolved" them of all responsibility for their actions and "transferred" it to the entrepreneur. The judge would, no doubt, be unmoved by this final gesture and would point out that their responsibility resulted directly from the fact that they deliberately performed the actions. Moral responsibility for one's actions cannot be "transferred" or "alienated" by consent or contract.

All this is clear and obvious in the case of hired criminals, but how, from the moral viewpoint, can it be any different in the case of ordinary hired labor? When the employees of an ordinary productive enterprise produce something of net positive value, do they *then* suddenly become like machines which are "used" by their employers and have no responsibility for the results of their services? Or is this case of productive hired labor simply the case where the propertied class finds it profitable to treat the workers as if they were such machines by instituting a special capital-ist property system which gives the *legal* responsibility for the results of productive labor to the owners of capital?

Property Appropriation

The above example makes a number of points which we may now explore at a more abstract and general level. The basic principle is that people have the moral responsibility for the positive and negative results of their deliberate actions. If certain people act cooperatively as a group, then they have as a group the responsibility for the results of their actions. When their actions result in the creation of material goods, then their responsibility for these goods means, in property-theoretic language, that they rightfully appropriate the goods. If they are responsible for using up or destroying certain goods, then they rightfully are liable for those goods. These are the property-theoretic consequences of their moral responsibility for their actions, and thus these rights of appropriation are moral or natural rights. The legal rights assigned to people in a specific legal property system may or may not coincide with their natural rights. In any case, people have the natural right to the results of their actions, i.e., to the assets and liabilities that they create. Furthermore, since these natural property rights result from the agents' moral responsibility, they are inalienable, because moral responsibility cannot be "transferred" or "alienated" by consent or contract (as we noted in the example). Of course, material goods that have been rightfully appropriated can then be exchanged or transferred, but it was one's nontransferable responsibility which accounted for one's rightful appropriation of the goods in the first place.

Consider a human enterprise such as an economic firm (or an institution such as a university or a hospital). All who work in the enterprise—whether they are called "white-collar," "blue-collar," "management," or "labor"—cooperatively perform the work of the enterprise. The legal role assigned by the legal system to "employees" does not somehow turn them into automata which are "used" by their "employers" and which have no responsibility for their actions. Thus, regardless of the legal superstructure: (1) all those who work in an enterprise have, as a group, the moral responsibility for their productive activities. If they utilize and create material goods, then these material results of their activities can be represented by a list of positive and negative quantities $X = (x_1, x_2, \ldots, x_n)$, where the positive quantities represent the amounts of the commodities produced and the negative quantities represent the amounts of the commodities used up by the enterprise during a given time period. We will call list X the *whole product* of the enterprise during the given time period; the positive quantities will be called the *assets produced* while the negative quantities will be called the *liabilities incurred*. One must be careful to note that *both* the assets and liabilities created in production are included in the whole product. This whole product is the material result of the productive activities of the workforce in the enterprise. Since they have the moral responsibility for the results of these activities, (2) the workforce has the natural right to appropriate the whole product of production. Furthermore, for the reasons given above, these natural rights are inalienable. If a legal property system is not to violate these moral rights, then it must recognize and guarantee in law: (1') that the workforce in an enterprise has the collective legal responsibility for its productive activities, i.e., that the workers have the right to self-manage their work, and (2') that the workforce in an enterprise has the legal right to appropriate its whole product. This form of production might be called *laborist production, labor-management,* or *workers' self-management.*[1] If the means of production or any of the material goods used in production are owned by absentee owners (e.g., by the workers who produced intermediate goods or by the community in the case of land and natural resources which are not the products of labor), then the workforce of the enterprise will have to satisfy its prospective liabilities by obtaining the owners' consent. This would usually require the payment of rent, interest, use tax, or simply purchase price.

The natural rights of an enterprise workforce to the self-management of its work and to its whole product are not even recognized, much less guaranteed, in the capitalist property system. The legal rights to the management of production and to the whole product are essential components in the bundle of legal rights called the "firm." In the capitalist system, these legal rights are typically attached directly to capital. In a corporation,

---

[1] The property theory sketched here is essentially a development of the classical labor or natural rights theory of property. See for instance: Richard Schlatter, *Private Property: The History of an Idea* (Rutgers University Press, 1951); or, Anton Menger, *The Right to the Whole Produce of Labour: The Origin and Development of the Theory of Labour's Claim to the Whole Product of Industry* (London: Macmillan and Co., 1899; also reprinted by Augustus Kelly, N.Y.). The labor theory of property was the foundation of the classical libertarian critique of capitalism by Proudhon and the early laborist school of "Ricardian socialists." This laborist tradition continued in the cooperativist, guild socialist, and anarcho-syndicalist movements.

the owners of the "firm" are the owners of the capital assets of the enterprise—the stockholders. These extra "divine rights of capital"—the rights to management and to the whole product—vastly extend the usual legitimate rights to receive rent or interest for the use of one's capital and they are the defining characteristic of the peculiarly capital-ist property system.[2]

These natural rights of an enterprise workforce are also not recognized in a state capitalist or state socialist system where the government legally appropriates the whole product and manages production. Under state socialism, the workers, far from being self-managing producers, are essentially changed from being privately owned commodities rented on the labor market to being socially owned resources drafted into the industrial army. Many socialists seem to implicitly accept the capitalist principle that the legal rights to the management of production and to the whole product are correctly attached to the ownership of the means of production. They are only against the *private* ownership of the means of production." This form of left-wing statism is against both the private management of an enterprise by capital and the private self-management of an enterprise by the people who work in it.

Professor Jaroslav Vanek, in his excellent book *The General Theory of Labor-Managed Market Economies* (Cornell, 1970), correctly isolates the capitalist principle that is shared by state socialists. He shows the inadequacy of the usual "spectrum" of "possible economic systems," where they are classified according to the degree of state intervention, but where they all assume the capitalist principle:

> It is interesting to note that the almost universally accepted principle is that the right to manage—or more broadly, to control—an economic enterprise derives from the ownership of the capital

---

[2] Analogous remarks apply to nonprofit institutions. For instance, the legal rights to the management of a university are typically attached to those who have trusteeship over the capital assets of the university. The natural right of all those who work in a university (i.e., the faculty, students, and staff) to the self-management of their work is not recognized by the legal system. But in spite of these private economic and educational oligarchies based on "property rights" and "legal charters," most legal systems now acknowledge the inalienable right of the whole community to the self-management of its *public* affairs.

assets used by the enterprise. The principle is equally applicable in western capitalism where the owners are private individuals; in Soviet-type socialist countries where the owner is society, or more operationally the state; and even in many traditional producer cooperatives where control has been linked to shares of joint ownership of the participants. The principle of labor management is entirely different, not having anything to do with ownership of productive assets. Rather, it postulates that in a productive activity where a group of men cooperate in a joint effort, the right to control and manage that effort rests with all the members of the group.

It is important to note that the principle of labor management is in conflict with the principle of control and management by capital—i.e., by the owners of capital—but not with the principles of private or social ownership of productive assets. Capital assets still can be owned by individuals or anybody else outside the enterprise, but the owners cannot decide on the complex of human activities which constitute the production. The owners can only expect an adequate compensation for the use of the assets, established through market forces or in any other manner (pp. 4–5).

Capitalism and Chattel Slavery

In order to elucidate the relationship between the systems of capitalism and chattel slavery, we will present a parallel analysis and comparison of the systems. Sane adults are morally responsible for their deliberate actions. As they have this responsibility, it is their natural right to make their own decisions. This is the person's natural right to individual self-management and self-determination. As this moral responsibility cannot be "transferred" by consent or contract, the right is inalienable. A legal system can violate peoples' inalienable rights in two ways: by not recognizing them at all and by recognizing them only as alienable rights. Chattel slavery involved both violations, since certain persons' natural rights were not recognized at all, much less guaranteed: they were legal chattel. The legal rights to own and govern this chattel were not even initially held by the slaves but by other persons who had satisfied certain legal prerequisites. This was the historical case of involuntary chattel slavery.

A more illuminating case, from the theoretical viewpoint,

would be a system of voluntary chattel slavery. In such a system, certain individuals' right to self-determination would be recognized only as an alienable right. By undertaking a certain voluntary legal performance, e.g., by voluntarily signing a certain "chattelhood contract," one could for a specified period of time extinguish one's legal agency and become, in the eyes of the law, a chattel under the government of another person. One should, of course, distinguish this sort of "contract" from an ordinary contract wherein one does not give up one's legal personality but chooses to bind oneself to exercise it in a particular fashion. As noted before, such "contracts" which would purport to "transfer" inalienable rights would be moral nonsense. The signing of contracts, the solemn pronouncements of judges, and the establishment of an entire legal superstructure to enforce the extinction of the slave's legal personality would not change the reality of the slave's moral agency, i.e., his capacity for moral responsibility. A person is not somehow changed into a brute beast even though he voluntarily enters into such concocted "chattelhood contracts." Of course, there can be social systems in which a certain segment of the population is maintained in such a state that they will voluntarily enter into that type of "contract." However, these "contracts" would provide no more of a sufficient moral reason for a legal system to extinguish their legal personality than would the color of their skin. Chattel slavery, voluntary or involuntary, constitutes a legally sanctioned institutionalization of kidnapping and murder—not the murder of biological individuals but the annihilation and transformation of legal persons into legal chattel.

The capitalist property system is entirely comparable. It does to "labor" (i.e., to the workforce of each enterprise during its time of productive work) what involuntary chattel slavery did to certain persons. The capitalist property system does not recognize even as alienable rights the workforce's natural rights to the self-management of its work and to the ownership of the whole product, much less guarantee them as inalienable rights. The corresponding legal rights are not attached to the workforce in an enterprise and they may be acquired by anybody who has satisfied certain legal prerequisites (e.g., the acquisition of corporate stock). Since these legal rights are not attached, even initially, to labor, labor enters a productive enterprise on par with the productive services provided by machines and animals—i.e., as a "productive service" sold to the owners of the whole product by the "factor owners." Thus labor becomes legally a commodity—a marketable productive service—just as the slave was legally a chattel. The wage contract sets the terms of the market transactions in the commodity "labor," just as the contracts on the slave market set the terms of the traffic in persons.

"But," it will be protested, "the worker is a free man who sells his own labor by voluntary contract, whereas the slave is owned and sold by others against his will." Yes, capitalism and chattel slavery are not identical. The essential difference derives from the fact that *all* the natural rights of the slave were legally denied. His whole person was thus considered legal chattel and he had no residual legal personality eligible to own that chattel. Thus the slave was legally owned and sold by *other* persons. In the case of the worker in a capitalist enterprise, it is only his natural rights resulting from his work which are legally denied, so it is only his labor that becomes a legal commodity, not his whole person. He can maintain a residual legal personality as a "factor owner" of his labor-commodity (and, of course, as a consumer and a citizen). The two legal roles of "commodity-owner" and "commodity," which were of necessity held by different people under chattel slavery, are held by the same person under capitalism.

This difference between the systems has had enormous apologetic and obfuscatory consequences. It is a veritable mainstay of capitalist thought (not to mention so-called "right-wing libertarianism") that the moral flaws of chattel slavery have not survived in capitalism since the workers, unlike the slaves, are free people making voluntary wage contracts. But it is only that, in the case of capitalism, the denial of natural rights is less complete so that the worker has a residual legal personality as a free "commodity-owner." He is thus allowed to voluntarily put his own working life to traffic. When a robber denies another person's right to make an infinite number of other choices besides losing his money or his life and the denial is backed up by a gun, then this is clearly robbery even though it might be said that the victim is making a "voluntary choice" between his remaining options. When the legal system itself denies the natural rights of working people in the name of the prerogatives of capital, and this denial is sanctioned by the legal violence of the state, then the theorists of "libertarian" capitalism do not proclaim institutional robbery, but rather they celebrate the "natural liberty" of working people to choose between the remaining options of selling their labor as a commodity and being unemployed.

As before, we can hypothetically consider a voluntary form of the institution. In "voluntary capitalism," the natural rights of the workforce in each enterprise to the self-management of its work and to its whole product would be legally recognized, but only as alienable rights. These rights would not be attached to capital at the outset, and capital would have to depend on its bargaining power to transfer these rights in its direction. The legal transfer would be accomplished by means of a new "commodityhood contract" (analogous to the previously considered "chattelhood contract"). As in the case of voluntary chattel slavery, this "contract" would annihilate the legal personality of the party in question, which in this case is the workforce of the enterprise. The legal agency of the enterprise work-community would be extinguished and they would be transformed, in the eyes of the law, into an assemblage of "commodity-owners" who sell their labor-commodity to the new owners of the "firm." Such a "commodityhood contract" is quite different from an ordinary contract. When a self-managing workforce made an ordinary contract, it would not be annihilating its legal agency. Rather the workforce would be choosing to bind itself to *exercising* its self-management rights in the particular fashion specified by the contract. For instance, it might choose to sell part of its future produce to retailers at a specified price as insurance against price fluctuations, or it might contract to produce certain goods in a specific "custom-made" manner.

"Voluntary capitalism," like voluntary chattel slavery, is a hypothetical system of only theoretical interest. It is of interest because some economists have inexplicably held that a "commodityhood contract" is "implied" in the wage contract. It is said rather vaguely that the workers "give up" their rights to the ownership of the product in exchange for the "security" of a wage. One is left in the dark as to the identity of these legal rights to the product which the workers are said to "give up." This is, to say the least, a rather willful interpretation of the wage contract, since it can hardly be said that the managerial rights of stockholders are "transferred" to them by labor in the wage contract. However, for the sake of argument, we have considered a hypothetical system of "genuinely" voluntary capitalism. It, like voluntary chattel slavery, flounders on the rock of *inalienable* natural rights. The moral agency of human action (whether the agents be productive workers or criminals, as in our opening example) cannot somehow be annihilated by a legal performance like the signing of a "commodityhood contract." Moral responsibility cannot be alienated by consent or contracts. This being the case, there is no sufficient moral reason for a legal system to recognize and enforce such concocted "contracts" by annihilating the corresponding legal agency of the one contracting party and by transferring their legal responsibility for their actions to the other party. That is why the rights are inalienable.

As the capitalist property system does not recognize or guarantee the inalienable rights of the workforce to the appropriation of its whole product and to the self-management of its work, the system constitutes a legally sanctioned institutionalization of theft and tyranny in the workplace. In short, as Proudhon pointed out in his famous passage, slavery is murder and the capitalist property system is theft, "the second proposition being no other than a transformation of the first." Chattel slavery was abolished by recognizing and guaranteeing the inalienable natural rights of each person to individual self-determination, so that all people became free self-governing agents. Similarly, capitalist production would be abolished by recognizing and guaranteeing the inalienable natural rights of the work-community in each enterprise so that all enterprises would become free associations of self-managing producers.

Capitalist Political Economy

We can now consider the highpoints of preclassical, classical, and neoclassical capitalist political economy as represented, respectively, by John Locke, John Stuart Mill, and John Bates

Clark. Locke is often considered the originator of the labor or natural rights theory of property, but that opinion does not stand up under critical scrutiny. The labor theory is a theory of appropriation and Locke did not even have a theory about the creation of property rights. Instead, he assumed an "original position" of *existing* property rights, with human labor treated as one form of property among others (owned by the agent in the original position), which could then be transferred by voluntary exchange. One could exchange one's labor with Nature for the "fruits of one's labor," or one could exchange one's labor for a wage so that the new owner could then enjoy the fruits of "his" labor. Note that this involves the play on words between "one's labor" in the morally relevant sense of "one's moral agency," and "one's labor" in the sense of a commodity that was bought.

> Thus the Grass my Horse has bit; the Turfs my Servant has cut; and the Ore I have digg'd in any place where I have a right to them in common with others, become my *Property*, without the assignation or consent of any body. The *labour* that was mine, removing them out of that common state they were in, hath *fixed* my *Property* in them.[3]

If Locke rents a horse (i.e., buys its services from its owner) and uses these services to produce something, then he has the sole moral responsibility for the results, as the horse is not a moral agent at all and the agency of the original owner is not involved. Locke also thinks that he may rent a man (i.e., buy his services from their owner) and that the fruits of these services will be the fruits of the *"labour* that was mine," i.e., Locke's. However, as the man is a moral agent, these fruits are not the result of only Locke's moral agency (unlike the case of the horse). Locke's gambit is to treat human labor as another form of property that can be bought on the market like the services provided by animals and machines and that can be used by others without the original owners' incurring any moral responsibility for the results of the services. Locke's gambit is the commoditization of labor. Locke's "natural right" is the

---

[3] John Locke, *Two Treatises of Government,* ed. Peter Laslett (Cambridge, 1960), section 28 of the second treatise, lines 24–30.

"natural right" of each person to the original ownership of his labor-commodity.

The classical tradition tried to preserve a rather vague form of the labor theory of property and it is instructive to consider the attempts to reconcile it with capitalism. John Stuart Mill begins with a brief statement of the labor theory—i.e., the foundation of property is "the right of producers to what they themselves have produced"—but he immediately sees that there may be a difficulty involved in the capitalist property system:

> It may be objected, therefore, to the institution as it now exists, that it recognizes rights of property in individuals over things which they have not produced. For example (it may be said) the operatives in a manufactory create, by their labour and skill, the whole produce; yet, instead of its belonging to them, the law gives them only their stipulated hire, and transfers the produce to some one who has merely supplied the funds, without perhaps contributing anything to the work itself, even in the form of superintendence.

After such a clear statement of the peculiar prerogatives of those who have "merely supplied the funds," one would expect Mill to give a justification of these specific features. Instead he only argues for the usual right to have something paid for the capital funds and capital goods used in production, i.e., for the "fruits of previous labour."

> If the labourers were possessed of them, they would not need to divide the produce with any one; but while they have them not, an equivalent must be given to those who have, both for the antecedent labour, and for the abstinence by which the produce of that labour, instead of being expended on indulgences, has been reserved for this use.[4]

Although Mill considers this a sufficient "answer" to the objection, it is inadequate, since capitalism is not the system in which laborers appropriate "what they themselves have produced" and

---

[4] John Stuart Mill, *Principles of Political Economy* (Penguin Books, 1970), p. 368 (Book II, chapter II, section I).

in which they "need to divide the produce" in order to satisfy
the liabilities they have incurred. Instead, capitalism is the
system in which *"the law* gives them only their stipulated hire,
and *transfers* the produce to some one who has merely supplied
the funds" [italics added]. Mill does not attempt to justify these
peculiar prerogatives of capital, which are quite additional to
the usual right to receive interest, and which are given to capital
by "the law" in the capitalist property system.

Mill's strategy is to misrepresent the laborist argument as
holding that the laborers should receive as *net* income the total
revenues from the assets produced and should somehow not
also be responsible for the liabilities incurred in production.
Hence he can "answer" the laborist straw man by showing that
interest, rent, or purchase price would have to be paid for the
funds and goods used in production. But the labor theory
implies with perfect symmetry that, for exactly the same reason,
labor is also responsible for the costs incurred—the intermediate
ate goods used up—in production, and the theory hardly implies that the workers who produced these intermediate goods
are supposed to give away their product—the "fruits of previous labor"—free. Thus Mill's apology fails and the plain logic of
the libertarian principle that natural property rights are created
only by labor (and transferred only by voluntary exchange)
drives one to the conception of production wherein the workers
appropriate "what they themselves have produced" and wherein
they "need to divide the produce" in order to cover the liabilities they themselves have incurred, i.e., the logic drives one to
the conception of laborist production. The consistently libertarian economists of Mill's time, such as William Thompson,
Thomas Hodgkins, and the others in the laborist school, drew
essentially that logical conclusion.

The modern neoclassical treatment of the difficulties involved
in the capitalist property system is very simple and yet quite
sophisticated. Basically the idea is to completely *evade* property-
theoretic questions in favor of concentrating solely on price-
theoretic questions. There is associated with the whole product
list $X = (x_1, \ldots, x_n)$ the list of product and factor prices $P = (p_1, \ldots, p_n)$. The property-theoretic part of political economy should consider the question: "How is and how should the

appropriation of the whole product X be determined?" Price theory considers the question: "How is and how should the magnitude of P be determined?" Orthodox economic theory typically begs the property-theoretic question by assuming the prerogatives of capital and the status of labor as a marketable productive service, and then it concentrates on price theory. But it is the answer to the logically prior ownership question which determines whether labor may be treated as a factor at all—to be bought at a certain price by capital—or whether labor should always take the form of self-managing producers renting or owning the capital they use. Also the orthodox treatment of the problems of "distribution" does not consider the basic structure of the distributive process as determined by the capitalist property system (i.e., who appropriates the whole product and controls industry, and thus who does the distributing). Instead, capitalist economists treat, in great detail, the "allocative efficiency" of the price system and, sometimes, they voice individual opinions about the "equity" of the final distribution of property ownership. Reforms, such as effective progressive taxation, lump-sum redistributions, and a guaranteed minimum income, are suggested which will upset the final distribution of ownership without questioning the capitalist principle embodied in the basic structure of the distributive process. Property theory is the unopened Pandora's box of capitalist political economy.

While the fundamental strategy of modern capitalist theory is a strategy of evasion of basic property questions (banalities about "the" private property system notwithstanding), this does not mean that price theory is free of ideological content. John Bates Clark, the American developer of marginal productivity (MP) theory, tried to give an appropriation-theoretic interpretation to the MP theory of factor prices. Clark, like Locke, Mill, and many others, wanted to develop a theory which would apologize for capitalism and, at the same time, co-opt the intuitive moral force of the labor theory of appropriation. Clark's ploy was to take the labor theory and for "moral agent" substitute "productive agent" (i.e., anything that is causally efficacious in production—moral agents *and* natural agents such as machines, animals, raw materials, etc.), for "responsibility" substitute "productivity" (causal efficacy), and for "actions by moral agents" (labor) substitute "productive services of productive agents." Clark assumed, of course, that the whole product was appropriated by capital (not to mention the status of labor as a commodity) and then he interpreted the factor payments made to the owners of the productive agents as their appropriation of their contribution (as measured by the productivity of the services they sell). The factor owners would be paid according to the principle: "to each what he [sic] creates." It is the "natural law of distribution." This theory has now become a solid part of the "conventional wisdom" or "folklore" engendered by capitalist economic theory.

Naturally there are a few difficulties involved in this "marginal productivity theory of appropriation." First, not all productive "agents" are moral agents and it is absurd to attempt to derive normative consequences from the causal efficacy of natural agents, e.g., to impute the blame for a crime to both the criminal and the "tools of his trade"—to each according to "his" productivity. The human owner of a natural agent incurs no responsibility if he is not in any other way involved than as owner. His ownership only implies that those who are involved in the productive activities are liable to him for the use of his property. Second, even if we restrict consideration to the moral agents involved, their responsibility is not determined by their "marginal productivity." For instance, criminals cannot avoid all responsibility for their actions by using redundant labor (so that the marginal productivity of their labor would be zero). They share, as a group, the responsibility for the results of their actions, and, of course, the same holds for other, more productive, cooperative human activities. Third, the MP theory of appropriation does not answer the ownership question even if it could be given a moderately plausible interpretation. That is, it does not determine who is to be the owner of the whole product and, thus, who is to be the residual claimant. The theory only tries to *paste* an appropriation-theoretic interpretation onto the factor payments made by the owners of the whole product in order to justify the specific magnitudes of the factor prices in the price list P. Evidently the only way that working people can be wronged is to be paid too low a price for their labor-commodity. Aside from the implausibility of the interpretation itself, this is rather like trying to close the barn door after capital has already walked off with the legal rights to the whole product and the management rights over production.

Although Clark's ploy fails, he had some awareness of the problem:

> A plan of living that would force men to leave in their employers' hands anything that by right of creation is theirs would be an institutional robbery—a legally established violation of the principle on which property is supposed to rest.[5]

Quite so—but one should note that even this manner of posing the possibility of institutional robbery maintains the usual ideological subordination to the capitalist principle, i.e., it is a matter of how much the workers "leave in their employers' hands."[6]

The Dehumanization of Labor

One can consider a hypothetical system in which labor has been suitably dehumanized so that the legal treatment of labor as a commodity—a marketable productive service—would be permissible. In order to do this, we must borrow from science fiction some scheme wherein electrodes would be inserted in the brains of working people so that computers could drive them independently of their volition and cause them to perform their normal tasks. During nonworking hours they would be "unplugged" so that they could lead their usual lives as consumers, citizens, and labor sellers. In such a system, human labor would

[5] John Bates Clark, *The Distribution of Wealth* (New York: Macmillan and Co., 1899), p. 9.

[6] For a slightly more detailed treatment of capitalist economics, see my "Introduction to Normative Property Theory," *Review of Radical Political Economics,* vol. IV, no. 2, Summer 1972.

genuinely be devoid of moral agency. Labor would then truly be a commodity, like the services provided by a machine or animal which can be bought from its owner and used by others without the original owners' incurring any moral responsibility for the results of the services. Although labor would then be devoid of moral agency, the causal efficacy of these services need not be changed, so the concepts of marginal productivity theory would still be applicable. Since a worker would only be run as a human tool on a part-time basis (during the work hours), he would maintain a residual moral personality as an owner of these labor services, as a consumer, and as a citizen. Since this residual agency is all that the capitalist legal system recognizes in the first place, that legal system would then be adequate. Since the original owners of these labor services would no longer have the moral responsibility for their use or the results of their use, the capitalist property system's denial of the rights of labor would then be accurate. The labor sellers would still, of course, combine into unions to bargain collectively about the wage rate and to set up grievance procedures for the workers who didn't like the way their labor was being used. Labor law would scrupulously guard the usual rights of labor sellers and it would humanely curb abuses of labor by the employers. Philosophers would celebrate the natural right of each individual to the original ownership of his labor services. Slavery would be abolished and each person would exercise his natural liberty to sell his own labor services by voluntary contract to the highest bidder on the labor market.

In short, this system would be the same as normal capitalism, except that it would not violate the humanity of people during their working lives since that humanity would have been suspended. By turning working people into part-time human tools (or "worked people"), labor would be rendered morally safe for capitalism. Since this system, which employs actually dehumanized labor, requires the same institutions as normal capitalism, it shows why normal capitalism is intrinsically dehumanizing. The basic legal and property structure of the actual capitalist system treats working people *as if* they already were such part-time human tools—just as the system of chattel slavery treated the slaves *as if* they were full-time or complete human tools. That being the case, it is no surprise when the workers in this system feel alienated from their product as if it were not the result of their actions and when they think of their work as if it were just so many hours taken out of their lives. The attempts, by apologetic economists and philosophers, to describe the status of "free labor" in the capitalist system in terms of the ideals of humanism and libertarianism does not require further comment.

> Many persons talk of admitting working-people to a share in the products and profits; but in their minds this participation is pure benevolence: they have never shown—perhaps never suspected—that it was a natural, necessary right, inherent in labor, and inseparable from the function of producer, even in the lowest forms of his work.[7]

These words are as true today as when they were written—two decades before America had even abolished chattel slavery. Today, a century and a quarter later, we have an abundance of "new" participation, profit sharing, and job enrichment programs. These programs may help to mitigate the dehumanizing impact of capitalist production, just as similar programs might have helped the "attitude" and "productivity" of "maladjusted" and "alienated" slaves. But most reformers have never realized—"perhaps never suspected"—that capitalism, like chattel slavery, *structurally* violates the inalienable natural rights of working people. Chattel slavery was legalized kidnapping and murder; the capitalist property system legalizes theft and tyranny in the workplace. As in the one case, so in the other; the institutional wrongs can only be righted by basic changes in the property system. This requires the abolition of the unnatural prerogatives of capital and the refounding of private property appropriation on the natural basis of labor. It requires that the legal system recognize and guarantee in law the inalienable natural rights of the working people in each enterprise to the self-management of their work and to the appropriation of their whole product. All enterprises would then be free associations

[7] P.-J. Proudhon, *What Is Property?*, trans. Benjamin Tucker (New York: Dover Publications, Inc., 1970), p. 112.

of self-managing producers. All people could have human dignity and sovereignty in their working lives as well as in their lives as consumers and citizens. Then justice would mean more than "a fair day's wage for a fair day's work." And democracy would no longer stop at the factory gates.

I

The Management of Work: Dissenting Views

Introduction
to Section I

The book you are reading is partisan. The editors believe that the present system of management of work is more than inefficient, it is dehumanizing. Marx saw this when he wrote that people are by nature productive, taking joy and deriving meaning in life from their work and creation, a nature inconsistent with the organization of labor under capitalism. Workers' control is not an obscure point in labor relations but is at the heart of socialist theory. It is central to participatory democracy and the criticism of existing institutions launched by new movements on the left in Canada and the United States during the last decade.

Workers' control is emerging as a focal point of social criticism largely because of the changing nature of the workforce; the new generation of young blue-collar workers is less ready to accept the autocracy of the factory, and the new class of human service workers tends to have humanistic priorities. As yet, the changing nature of the workforce is obscured by liberal "human relations" rhetoric widely accepted by the workers themselves. "The trouble with you academics," a union official said to one of us recently, "is that you don't understand the human aspect of the problem. Oh, we have money problems like always—our members have a harder time than I did to buy a house! But do you know what it's like down in the plant? Guys who came into the union back in the 1930s had a different attitude, but now the younger guys won't take all that crap. They won't raise their hand to get permission to go to the john. They won't take the foreman being on their backs all the time. But what can we do? We need a new way of working—I don't know what it is, but we need a different system."

We believe that that different system lies in the direction of workers' control combined with other forms of participatory democracy. Readings in this first section, however, are directed toward showing the sources of discontent with the prevailing system of work. There are many, often contradictory, bases of this discontent. Some managers are interested in the greater productivity associated with worker participation, as in the Scanlon Plan companies in the United States. Government may follow the European lead in seeking in worker participation a way to smooth over rising wildcat strikes, slowdowns, absenteeism, and sabotage, and to replace the conflict system of labor relations with the merger of labor into the existing coalition of big business and government as in the German system of co-determination. Radical interest is sparked by spontaneous takeovers of factories in France and Italy, where control seems to have appeared as an immediate and practical working class need. Within academia, the concept of economic democracy has been central to the attack on the dominant "pluralist" celebration of American democracy. Even men like Robert Dahl, heretofore a chief academic apologist for the capitalist system, have been forced to move toward advocacy of some form of industrial democracy.

Whether born of the needs of workers, management, government officials, or university intellectuals, the concept of workers' control has reached the intellectual agenda of advanced capitalist countries. Some form of economic democracy is part of the platform of social democratic parties in Britain and Sweden, a demand of the German federation of trade unions, a key part of the agenda of the trade union group of the Common Market. Movements for workers' control have appeared in several countries and the Canadian movement has made industrial democracy part of the platform of the Canadian Labour Congress.

This general interest obscures many differences, of course. The editors argue for control, not participation; for community control, not workers' control in isolation; for workers' control in the context of government planning, not in an unregulated market. Other questions include the relation of workers' control to nationalization; to establishment of new structures from above or from below; change by spontaneous seizure, voluntary agreement, or government action; relation to the trade union movement. There is no general solution to these questions. Emphasis is on implications of alternatives rather than definition of a single strategy for labor.

The first section begins with a definition of the problem of work organization from the points of view of the union and the worker. In discussing dissenting views about work organization, the readings describe the immediate experience of one worker at the point of production, then present more general data showing that this experience, far from being untypical, only begins to suggest the depth of the problem of undemocratic management of work. Later readings in the first section narrate how, in conjunction with this general experience, unions still oriented toward a workforce of another generation are undergoing the beginnings of a rank-and-file revolt that would have been unthinkable in the 1950s, both in the United States and Canada. A final reading discusses the future of trade unionism, relating these trends to workers' control.

Living with Automation in Winnipeg

Ian Adams

Most people work in jobs they dislike. Although Adams describes work in a factory, most other work situations have their own forms of oppression. Typing, keypunching, or trying to process scores of welfare cases is not a humanizing experience, either. The common thread is the alienating nature of working at the bottom of a hierarchy, lacking control over what one does, much less over the product of one's work. In a volume edited by Perry Anderson and Robin Blackburn titled *Towards Socialism,* Andre Gorz has described the nature of this work.

"At the confines of a civil society which is formally free," Gorz writes, "industry maintains a despotic and authoritarian society, under a hierarchy and discipline of military character, which demands of its workers both unconditional obedience and active participation in their own oppression. . . . [I]ts ideal social model is the man who is active, but submissive and narrow-minded, and whose skills, however extensive, are solely employed in the technical field. In fact, the majority of wage claims are revolts against this kind of oppression—revolts against the systematic mutilation of the worker's personality, against the stunting of his professional and human faculties, against the subordination of the nature and content of his working life to technological developments which rob him of his powers of initiative, control, and even foresight. . . . Wage claims express a demand for as much money as possible to pay for the life wasted, the time lost, the freedom alienated in working under these conditions. . . . In short, the worker—even the highly paid worker—tries to sell himself as dearly as possible because he cannot avoid having to sell himself. And conversely, whatever the price he manages to get for his freedom, that price will never compensate him for the human loss he has suffered; however much he squeezes out of his employers, it will never give him control of his working life, never give him the freedom to determine his own situation."

Hear it! The crunching smash of twenty-four bottles of beer, all splintering against each other as I misdeal on the packing machine. Smell the stink of the warm beer pouring over my clothes, washing over the sour sweat of my body. I can feel the unheard curse as I toss the wet, mangled carton down the rollers for some poor bastard to sort out. And back to the mother-eating machine where the bottles are already starting to pile up on the conveyor belt. The ten-second delay bell starts ringing. The jangling vibrations echo in my skull, and the foreman comes running over, screaming incoherently. How the hell can I hear him over the roar of four acres of machinery and the teeth-jarring rattle of 25,000 bottles, all clinking against each other as they ride down the hundred yards of clanking metal conveyor belts.

But don't try to figure out what the foreman's yelling, you'll only lose more time. The bottles will back up all the way to the pasteurizer, the thirty-second delay hooter will start whooping like an air-raid siren, then they'll pull you off this job for sure and send you down to the washers, so forget him and just keep moving. With your left hand crush the right hand corner of the next empty carton and ram it on the hydraulic lift. Kick your heel down on the pedal to send the drawer up. The bottles drop through the metal leaves this time with a nice *thonk,* thank God! And even as they are hitting the bottom of the box, stab the pedal with your toe to bring the drawer back down. Before it stops, spin off the loaded carton with your right hand to send it in the direction of the sealing machine. Don't wait for it to clear the drawer, reach for the next empty carton with your left hand. But you have to waste time, reaching in to push the "filler" down flat. And without even looking at him, you scream at the filler man, "Look what you're doing, you son-of-a-bitch! Can't you even put these lousy pieces of cardboard in straight?" He, seeing only your lips curling, snarls obscenely back. Never mind him either. He's been here fourteen years, paying his union dues, kissing the foreman's ass. Look at the zombie, pot-bellied on all the free beer, draggy-eyed from a lifetime of night shifts, skin like a corpse, embrace your fellow industrial worker!

A group of tourists are coming through the brewery. Cowed by the noise, they shy away from the machines, cringing behind the protective eyeglasses issued at the front office. They stop to wonder at the frantic activity around the packing machine. And we, the sweat running down our faces, our shirts soaked, our hands and feet doing five different things at once, turn smiling and scream the crudest of obscenities at the women. And they, unhearing, smile and mouth thank you, then walk on with another uncertain smile for the monkeys in the freak show.

All this ten hours a day. Surrounded by four or five other

workers who endlessly fold cardboard cartons in a bored blur of hand movements. Their hands turn flat shapes into square boxes, insert handles and fillers that will keep the bottles separated from each other. Behind them on scores of wooden platforms await thousands of unfolded cardboard cartons. They are literally unfolding a forest of trees between their hands. Other men tend the monotonous machines. One feeds thousands of bright little labels into slots; each label costs one cent, but that's more than the beer inside the bottle is worth. "Everything else is taxes and profit," that's what the brewmaster said. Another man sits dreamily beside a lighted yellow panel. In hypnotic progression, each bottle passes briefly in front of this panel before being filled with beer. The man tries to catch the ones that are still jammed with trapped mice, cigarette butts, and old safes, even after going through the washers.

All the men are wearing the same dingy uniforms, green work pants and shirts. They are my brotherhood, and we are men of our time, working in feverish, mute activity, unable to communicate, drowned out by the roar of our age, the ass end of this industrial epoch. Run this packing machine, you slob. Pack twenty-four bottles of beer every six seconds. Ten cases every minute, six hundred in an hour, six thousand in a ten-hour shift. Fill all those empty bottles full of beer so all the leisure programmed people in this country can drink their beer in creepy bars and dirty, men only beer parlors. Pack so the whores on Main Street can tease their fancy men over a couple, so the businessmen can pull on a three o'clock beer and ease a contented fart. And you, you sad bastard, work! Work to fill up those empty boxes with bottles of beer so that all those beautiful people out there can piss it away.

Don't waste time thinking about the absurdity of this effort. Just pack and think about the $125 a week you're clearing. Pack and forget about the bills you can't pay. Pack and don't look at the man going around giving out pink slips. Just keep packing, you dummy. Because while you're sitting there running that machine, with the sweat running down into your eyes, with your hands and feet going like an epileptic's, they're already building a machine to do your job. And brother, nobody can hear a word you're screaming.

The Factory as an Oppressive and Non-Emancipatory Environment

Charles Hampden-Turner

The experience described by Ian Adams is not an isolated one, nor can it be easily forgotten about during one's "leisure time." The simple fact is that there is a direct relationship between the nature of work and the development of human personality. The relations of work entrench themselves in the mind and reappear as social relations, including the relations of leisure time. When discussing workers' control, the issue is not merely economic reform, but laying the basis for more fulfilling personality development and changed social relations. If these goals seem utopian, it is only a reflection of the prevailing system's emphasis on materialism, consumerism, and quantitative growth without structural change. Workers' control is a fundamental human issue transcending economics, as the following article illustrates.

Perhaps the most detailed and perceptive study ever made of the condition of American workers was that of Arthur Kornhauser (1964) who studied Detroit automobile plants along with other smaller factories in the area. He used a measuring index of "Mental Health." Those with "Low" Mental Health typically suffered at least two psychosomatic symptoms. They had low self-esteem, periodic feelings of depression, poor social relationships, uncontrollable anxiety reactions, strong hostilities, chronic distrust, and poor life satisfaction. The absence of such symptoms, plus a positive feeling of self-worth and strong friendships, constituted "High" Mental Health. Only 34 percent of the sample of young factory workers (nineteen to twenty-nine) were found to have "High" Mental Health. (Only those with at least three years' steady work were included in the sample.) Since "High" and "Low" are relative terms, we need comparison groups in order to judge whether the large factory is a much more neurotic, tense, and depressed environment than are other places of work. The comparisons made by Kornhauser are illustrated below.

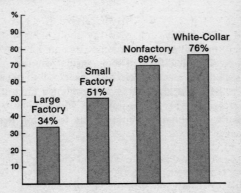

Clearly the Large Factory is the worst place for the young worker. The white-collar worker, of equivalent education and socioeconomic class, is over twice as likely to have "High" Mental Health, and so is the nonfactory worker, in this instance public service employees of gas and electric utilities.

Mental Health indices are very important measures, not only because they are sensitive indicators of the "quality of life" human beings enjoy (which is supposed to be what our civilization is about), but because Low Mental Health accompanies a host of problems that plague industry. Workers with Low MH were by far the highest in turnover, absenteeism, dispensary visits, and industrial accidents. Argyris (1964) summarized half a dozen studies which found Low MH associated with the rate of grievances, with sabotage, stealing from work, "horseplay," and the mental exhaustion of low-level supervisors.

Kornhauser found most large factory workers were segregationist, prejudiced, and antidemocratic in their sentiments. Nearly half showed hostility to the "dangerous ideas" discussed in universities and advocated the limiting of free speech. However, the Low MH group were considerably *more* bigoted, with the young *less* tolerant than the old. Although this study was completed before the Vietnam War captured the headlines, over 50 percent of the workers and nearly three quarters of those low in MH had nothing good to say for foreigners. Subsequent surveys have found blue-collar workers overwhelmingly "hawkish."

The Low MH group was clearly miserable. Eighty-two percent could find only negative things to say about their own characters. Seventy percent know of *no one* they could count upon, 88 percent agreed that "I often boil inside without showing." Eighty-six percent regard their lives as close to meaningless. Even when the Highs and Lows were combined the total picture was dismal. Taking his total sample of young workers in large Detroit plants, Kornhauser reported the following percentages of agreement:

"Most people are out for themselves and don't care what happens to others." (53%)

"These days a person cannot know who to count upon." (45%)

"I feel restless, wanting to do something but not knowing what." (52%)

"I feel no optimism about the future." (51%)

Thus far the data presented, grim though they appear, give a much *rosier* picture than that faced by "hard-core" minority group members. With the exception of the questions on segregation and foreigners, the answers made by workers referred mostly to *other white workers*. Hence those "out for themselves" and those difficult "to count upon" were preponderantly white. Given the majority of racist opinion (and where there is a dominance of any sentiment those who disagree usually keep quiet) one can only imagine the distrust and hostility had these questions been asked about black workers.

A second reason why these figures are rosy is that the High MH group were mostly *skilled* workers, all with more than six years of steady employment and relatively secure seniority rights. The average hard-core recruit would need at least six (and probably ten) years of steady, increasingly skilled work in order to win the status, seniority, and companionship of the "healthier" skilled workers. It is among the *semi*skilled workers, 70 percent of the total workforce at Detroit, that the hard-core trainee would spend the first decade of his employment (assuming he stuck it out). Below we see the degrees of mental health associated with different skill levels.

Degrees of Skill and Mechanization	*Proportion with "High" Mental Health*
Skilled	58%
Semiskilled	35
Repetitive semiskilled	10
Repetitive, machine-paced, semiskilled	7

These differences are *not* accounted for by social background or education, since only those with very similar prejob characteristics were used in making this comparison. We see that mental health drops precipitously as a result of a combination of low skills and mechanical dictation of the pace of work. The "soul" is destroyed in proportion to the domination of the machine. To put it mildly the implications of these figures are appalling. It means that 93 percent of those in machine-paced repetitive, semiskilled work are more likely than not to report each of the long catalogue of ills and miseries mentioned so far.

Concerned that his Detroit study was unrepresentative, Kornhauser examined samples of repetitive workers in a number of plants. The percentage of those with High MH is given below:

Percentage of Repetitive Workers with High Mental Health

All Small Plants	29%
All Large Plants	18
Large plants with many repetitive jobs	16
Large plants with "poor" industrial relations	12
Large plants with "fair" or "good" relations	28

Here we see that Detroit does seem to be among the worst plants (although a few of the repetitive workers were skilled, making direct comparison with *semi*skilled Detroit workers difficult). Nevertheless the chance of *any* repetitive worker in *any* kind of plant achieving High Mental Health *is less than 30 percent*. In the average large plant it is less than 20 percent. The percentage of "healthy" white-collar workers of almost comparable education and background is *over four times higher* (75%) than the percentage of healthy repetitive workers in large plants (18%).

Even *these* figures are rosier than is the predicament faced by the hard-core recruit to a large plant. We have not yet taken into account the effect of early emotional disturbance, discrimination, poor education, financial poverty, and fatherless homes. *The factory system wears down the weak before the strong.* Together, a disadvantaged background *and* a repetitive semiskilled job "add up," and together they form an almost insuperable barrier.

For example, the chance of "the average worker" in a repetitive job having High Mental Health was one in five, but the chance of a poorly educated, low-income worker having High Mental Health was one in ten. Add to this condition a history of rejection and a fatherless family and the chance of good health was virtually nil. Kornhauser did not include discrimination or minority group membership but it seems likely that these would just push the hard-core farther through the bottom of the scale.

The table below shows how just two factors, low-skilled repetition and low childhood self-confidence can combine to sap the health of workers:

Percentage of those with High Mental Health who have:

	Low Childhood Self-Confidence	High Childhood Self-Confidence
High Skilled	38%	51%
Semiskilled	26	33
Repetitive Semiskilled	7	15

Among those with low childhood self-confidence there are fewer workers with any degree of health to impair, yet the factory system seems to impair the survivors more thoroughly. Among those with low self-confidence, repetitive work reduces the ranks of the healthy by over 80 percent. Among those with high self-confidence repetitive work reduces the ranks of the healthy by less than 70 percent. Thus handicaps do more than "add up" like a succession of blows. They make the individual more vulnerable to an additional blow and more likely to be floored by it. One is tempted to observe that all the hard-core need is a good dose of semiskilled, repetitive work in a large factory, and *that will finish them!*

We need to examine the proposition that the system is oppressing the workers with far greater care. Actually two rival explanations are commonly used to explain the same set of facts. Douglas McGregor (1964) called these Theory X and Theory Y. I will call them *conservative* and *radical* hypotheses, respectively, for that is what they amount to. Consider the following facts. Low Mental Health correlates with high turnover/absenteeism/sabotage/stealing, etc., which correlates with an oppressively simple and structured system of control, which correlates with Low Mental Health and so around. When arguing about cause and effect we have the perennial "chicken or egg" problem. Of course it is fruitless arguing which came first, the only question is *where shall we intervene?* Radicals say, alter the system and man's natural virtues and repressed abilities will manifest themselves. Thus in the vicious circle below:

A. The Simple, Controlled
    System

                    B. Low Mental Health

        C. Dissatisfied and
            Unmotivated Workers

Radicals seek to alter A, the overly simple system, that constrains workers.

Conservatives, and these predominate among lower-level supervisors and often higher ones, too, assume that the Controlled System is needed to discipline the dissatisfied and unmotivated workers. Insofar as conservatives hope to improve things at all, they give "pep talks" to workers and make moral judgments about their laziness in an attempt to intervene at Point C. Predictably enough, this is the attitude taken by *Fortune* magazine toward hard-core recruits to JOBS programs. Complaining that recruits often report sick rather than continue with tedious work, *Fortune* adds, "the malingering, of course, is the result of little experience in living by the clock, bad housing, and the dogmatic boredom that seems to afflict all the unmotivated."

Robert Goodman, a professor at M.I.T. with a different political outlook, comments on the *Fortune* article, "Why 'living by the clock' is a good way to live, why 'good housing' should make tedious work attractive, and why anyone in his right mind should not be dogmatically bored by tedious work is never touched on."

The trouble with *both* radical and conservative outlooks is that their respective advocates can go an entire lifetime without testing their ideas. The conservative, by *assuming* that workers are an idle rabble, helps to *create the fact,* and by never letting up on an oppressive system prevents himself from discovering that it could have been otherwise. Workers infuriated by the conservative's oppression *behave just as "badly" as he always said they would,* and in their "bad behavior" convince him how right he was to restrain them in the first place!

The radical says you must "change the system," but because it is often very difficult to change he can easily spend an entire lifetime advocating change and never successfully practicing it. If the system changes are modest but still ineffective, he will tell you that much *larger* changes are needed, but really his ideas cannot be confirmed until there is a revolution, and so we must wait!

Blue-collar workers and hard-core recruits to their ranks have to contend, however, with a conservative ideology which assumes that every system failure *reflected* in the personalities of workers is first and foremost a failing of that particular worker and his character. He is called upon to be "responsible" by managers who themselves take little or no responsibility for the system they have designed and which they operate.

Even the mental health figures I have quoted here are subtly disparaging to the workers. Just to label their affliction "poor mental health" assumes some disease which is "inside them," some permanent mark or affliction that can be used to justify paternal or custodial treatment. A manager might even admit that the workplace had made the workers that way, but he could still say, "As of now I am sane and they are unstable. I must exercise close control."

Dozens of research studies have connected close control and managerial directiveness with poor worker morale and lack of productivity. Fleishman and Harris (1961) found that turnover varied with the amount of compliance to orders demanded by supervisors and the extent to which tasks were structured in advance. Argyle, Gardner, and Coffee (1958) found that absenteeism varied within the same plant, being higher among those groups with "directive" supervisors who attempted close and detailed control over their men. Lindquist (1958) found that "poor job adjustment" was a function of being directed and controlled. Peterson (1960) found that accidents and absenteeism increased wherever employees felt themselves subject to "arbitrary discipline." Argyris (1964) found that alienation and low morale accompanied management's praise for the *reliable* worker rather than the *enterprising* one.

One suspects that there *is* an aspect of neurosis in this situation but that it is the neurotic *relationship* between management and worker which is at the root of the trouble. You see, managers would answer to the above research findings, "close and directive supervision is *necessary* because some work groups are simply less motivated than others. If we did not hound them, they would do no work at all!"

If this assumption is false, we have a classic neurotic pattern, with management *making what it fears come true by overly defensive precautions*. It is a variant of the tragic predicament of war, in which the stronger of two combatants insists that he must defend himself, and the weaker sees this "defense" as aggression, and insists he must defend himself. Each sees the other's "defensive precautions" as "basic aggression."

There is an increasingly influential theory of insanity and neurosis which claims that for every person labeled "sick" there is at least one other who helped to make him that way and has succeeded in blaming the sick *relationship* upon just *one party* to that relationship, the weaker one. Thus Laing (1968) and Cooper (1969) contend that the "medical analogy" is misleading. Most poor mental health derives from wounds inflicted in a human jungle, not from "mental poison" somewhere inside the heads of sufferers.

In arbitrating between the usefulness of radical and conservative positions, the mere correlation between highly controlled systems and Low Mental Health among workers is *not* decisive. If we wish to show that the conservative assumption about management-worker relationships is neurotically self-fulfilling, then we need to establish:

1. That the needs of workers which are unfulfilled by the system are "productive needs" rather than "lazy" or "destructive needs."

2. That the symptomatology plaguing the factory is correlated with the frustration of productive motivations and not with the fulfillment of destructive motivations.

3. That the system actually diminishes the ambition and motivation which young workers bring with them when entering the system, and that those who retain any hope after years of factory work nourish that hope *outside* the system.

Let us take these one by one.

1. *The needs of workers unfulfilled by the system are "productive needs" rather than "lazy" or "destructive needs."*

Canarius (1962) asked all levels of management from the board down to the foremen, as well as workers, what their "unfulfilled needs" were. The results are given below.

UNFULFILLED NEEDS

Needs	Top Mgt.	Middle Mgt.	Fore-men	Workers
Making the most of my capacities	39%	47%	49%	45%
Chance to learn new things	34	33	50	54
Chance for greater responsibility	27	47	55	42
Recognition when I do well	32	46	52	55

	All Management Categories	
Work that is interesting	21	46
Wanting to pitch in	31	44
Variety in the work I do	13	29

The first surprise is how remarkably similar the needs of the highest and lowest persons in the organization are. The contention that the workers are "different," that self-fulfillment is a value of researchers, not workers, that passive repetitive jobs are the only answer for passive, repetitive people—none of these receives support here. The main difference between managers and workers is the degree to which the latter are denied satisfaction relative to the former, and the increasing degree of denial at the lower levels of the corporation. Karsh (1957) reviewed seven studies of worker satisfaction and dissatisfaction. In each case worker satisfaction corresponded with high productivity, while dissatisfaction corresponded with poor productivity. (Any evidence that workers "enjoy goofing-off" has never yet come to my attention.) Karsh concluded that satisfaction is bound up with the degree to which the worker can exercise his own judgment on his job and the extent to which he can control the conditions affecting his work.

2. *The symptomatology plaguing the factory is correlated with the frustration of productive motivations and not with the fulfillment of destructive motivations.*

According to a study by Chinoy (1955) some 50 percent of blue-collar workers "think of becoming foremen" with various degrees of intensity, yet only ten vacancies occurred in this same plant every year among six thousand workers. It says something of the sheer courage and resilience of the human spirit that half the workers can still hope for an annual chance of 600 to 1 of being promoted, or 1 chance in 12 in a fifty-year worklife. In other studies realistic hopes seem to have been crushed. Berger (1960) reported that 94 percent of workers regarded their jobs as permanent, but 32 percent "still hoped to become foreman some day."

Kornhauser (1964) found that 40 percent of the *younger* workers still had hopes of "getting on" but in the older workers it had all but died. That the mental health of younger workers was slightly worse than that of older workers was traced by Kornhauser to the much higher levels of *frustrated energy*. The steadiness of older workers could be explained by the virtual absence of "a purposeful life-style" which had been replaced by a "resigned stability." Simple Gallup Polls which asked workers if they were satisfied with their jobs often achieved a 60 percent "yes" answer, but probing revealed the resignation. "I'm satisfied. I *have* to be! What's the use?"

Perhaps a better question is: "If you start all over again, would you take this job and live this life?" Seventy-eight percent of Kornhauser's sample said "no," and nearly all wanted something different for their children.

There is considerable evidence that many of the "labor problems" the organization suffers from (notice how our habitual language has already assigned the blame) are in fact connected to the crippling of self-expression. Argyris (1958) reviewed a series of studies showing that absenteeism varied directly with the degree to which the "absent worker" felt that his personally valued skills went unused by the organization. Had the absenteeism *itself* been an expression of idleness one would have expected "happy absentees," but they were not satisfied at all. They were bitter that their talents were ignored. Some newspaper stories have revealed that managers now visit hard-core recruits who are absentees and roust them out of bed! So now one gets insulted at work *and* at home. Psychologically this "damned if you do" and "damned if you don't" dilemma is known as the *double-bind*. According to Grier and Cobbs (1968) dilemmas such as this produce "Black Rage," their term for the very high rate of paranoid psychosis among ghetto inhabitants.

If workers often resist change it is because it leaves them vulnerable to earning less pay for equal effort and because once simple hand movements have been learned by rote one can often converse or daydream while doing the job. Any change will often mean a period of intense concentration upon essentially *simple* hand movements until they once again become habitual, and this is a very irritating way to lose piecework earnings.

Work that is *genuinely* more varied and challenging is generally appreciated, however, even after initial suspicion and resistance. Thus, Mann and Williams (1962) found that installation of data processing equipment encountered resistance followed by the intense pleasure of those persons whose jobs had been enlarged. But several persons experienced reduced job challenge and they were angry.

In his Detroit study Kornhauser addressed himself directly to the question of whether *the jobs themselves,* or *the people in the jobs* were the chief cause of the very poor mental health in semiskilled and machine-timed occupations. He concluded:

> Mental health, as here defined, is poorer among factory workers as we move from more skilled, responsible and varied types of work to jobs lower in this respect. . . . [This] relationship is not due in any large degree to any differences in pre-job background or personality of the men who enter and remain in the several types of work. The relationship of mental health to occupation, in other words, appears "genuine"; mental health is dependent on factors associated with the job.

In fact this conclusion is virtually unavoidable. Are we to believe that the differences between semiskilled workers (10% High Mental Health) and non-factory public service workers (69% High Mental Health) is due to some magnetic lure by which the factory attracts the sickly, while public utilities attract the proud and free?

3. *The system actually diminishes the ambition and motivation which young workers bring with them when entering the system. Those who retain any hope after years of factory work nourish that hope outside the system.*

Before comparing blue-collar employment to white-collar employment, in order to get some idea of the relative deprivation, let us compare the white-collar employment of workers with a high school education with that of those from high school who go on to college. Once again the two groups have been matched for IQ and social class. Trent and Craise (1967) compared the two groups four years after high school. They found that the "college group" had far outstripped the "corporate group" on measures of Social Maturity, Creativity, Concept Mastery, Nonauthoritarianism. This much might be expected. They also found that *the white-collar corporate group had regressed on nearly all measures since their last year at school.*

With all the rude things being said about American high schools it is ironic to reflect that white-collar employment in large corporations begins to erode whatever little the high schools have achieved. Up to this point my report has pictured white-collar employment (71% High Mental Health) as a paragon of virtue compared to repetitive work in large factories (28% to 10% High Mental Health). Now there are figures to suggest that even low-level white-collar work produces an atrophy of human capacities. What blue-collar employment must do to high school leavers makes one shudder.

There is much scattered evidence to keep us shuddering. In an early study Baake (1940) reported,

> Many a working class family was integrated around the effort to provide children with educational and training equipment which would make possible a non-working class life. This desire was shared by the children, *until they took their first job.* Very few ambitions to get out of the working class apparently survived the actual experience of having made a start as a worker.

Friedman (1961) followed a group of workers through their early years of employment. At first they were "restless and distressed," constantly scheming to change jobs, to go into business for themselves, to "beat the system." Later they settled down into steady work without hope of improvement. Chinoy (1955) found that "The American Dream" still flickered behind the frustration of the younger workers, but as time went on their plans of escape became less and less realistic and workers would listen to one another's "escape fantasies" with a soothing disbelief.

Form and Aeschweider (1962) found that the most unhappy group among the older workers were those who had been unable to cast off their middle class aspirations. A few of these were enraged with the system, but the large majority blamed themselves and were full of self-contempt. The system's final triumph over individual aspiration appears to lie in its capacity to induce each worker to blame himself for not getting that one foreman's job per six hundred workers. Few question a system with 599 annual "losers" for every "winner." The system is designed by graduate engineers and assorted experts with skills beyond the workers' comprehension. It gets more technical, baffling, and "scientific" every year. Like the vast majority of less educated people who inhabit this globe, workers assume their environment to be "natural," like water to a fish. If they fall short of their aspirations they ruefully admit "I am not good enough at competing."

Herzberg *et al.* (1957) summarized the results of twenty-three studies of fluctuations in worker morale over extended periods of employment. Seventeen of these studies indicated:

—that morale is high before and/or very shortly after the young worker is employed, and

—that morale drops sharply over the first six years. This drop is associated with experienced monotony, frustration, and insecurity. Morale starts to rise again in middle life and levels off. The rise is associated with increasing security and adjustment to a condition of life regarded as inevitable.

A more recently completed study, which followed up those workers who were fired when the Packard Motor Company closed, suggests that there are worse things than being unemployed, and among these are low-skilled employment and being fired a second time. Aiken, Ferman, and Shepard (1968) looked at the degree of alienation and political extremism among the labor force once employed at Packard. Twenty-five percent had never found another job, a statistic which is significant in itself, and helps to explain the factory worker's preoccupation with security. The bottom rungs of the ladder are extremely slippery. If you slip off just once, *your life may be too short to gain or regain the security that comes from seniority*. The "last hired, first fired" rule subjects the worker to a cruel dilemma. Either he must hang grimly on to a repetitive, dead end job, or face a lifetime of short term employment and layoffs. Not for him is the middle class youth's search for identity, and the leisurely trying out of a number of roles. The young worker is arbitrarily assigned a place in the machinery. He has one, possibly two, chances to hold the job. The scrapheap is inches beneath his dangling feet.

The Packard study showed that a further 15 percent of that workforce had found work for a few years or months, *only to be laid off again.* Taking four groups, those who were still unemployed, the reemployed and refired, the reemployed at low-skill level and the reemployed at high-skill level, the most alienated and extreme were the "refired," followed by the low-skilled, *followed by the unemployed,* with only the higher skilled subscribing to anything approximating democratic norms and attitudes.

We must, however, view with caution the conclusion that being unemployed is less alienating than low-skilled employment, since the unemployed group was much older on the average than the reemployed groups. More research is needed in this area, but the claim that low-skilled employment is some kind of emancipation for the unemployed seems totally without foundation.

We may conclude, then, that there is overwhelming evidence that the factory system is unworthy of the motivation and spirit that workers initially bring to their tasks. The system breaks the man or at best reduces him to a state of quiet resignation. If we accept the vicious circle:

A. The Simple Controlled
   System

                    B. Low Mental Health

   C. Unmotivated Workers

then clearly the conservative strategy of intervening at point C, denouncing the worker and urging him to mend his ways, is not workable and will not break him out of the circle. Since the worker often suffers from chronically low self-esteem, criticizing him in terms of personal morality would probably make things worse. He has been on the receiving end of blame most of his life.

On the other hand, if the system could be altered there would seem to be a veritable store of unused human capacities yearning for an opportunity for expression. The circle and its viciousness might be modified by radical interventions at point A.

Rebellion in American Labor's Rank and File*

Stanley Weir

Beyond the dehumanized conditions that affect the individual worker, the present system of organization of work leads to acts of collective resistance, both spontaneous and planned. The undemocratic organization of work places the union in the position of trading "control of the membership" for contract gains. Rank-and-file support of union leadership, however strong at contract negotiation time, deteriorates in the long stretches between contracts when the union finds itself committed to keeping its members "in line" to uphold its end of the contract. At the same time, the union lacks control over the workplace to meet the changing demands of its membership. The long term decline in the rapport between rank and file and union leadership is rooted in this imbalance be-

* The first part of this article was originally published in the June 1967 issue of the *International Socialist Journal,* edited by Maurice Zeitlin. It has been revised and extended by the author.

tween the responsibility for labor management that unions have accepted on the one hand, and their relative lack of control over the management of work on the other.

The following article by Stanley Weir outlines the development of the labor revolt that has grown out of this dilemma. Since Weir's widely noted article first appeared, much additional evidence has accrued supporting its arguments. In 1967, the same year Weir's article appeared, the Fraternal Association of Steelhaulers was founded as a national movement in the trucking industry, now the largest of several rank-and-file organizations of truck drivers protesting against the leadership of the International Brotherhood of Teamsters. Most publicized of the insurgent groups has been the Detroit Revolutionary Union Movement (DRUM) and similar black workers' caucuses, some of which joined in an interindustry Black Workers' Congress in 1970. Equally important has been the development of a strong rank-and-file movement against Tony Boyle of the United Mine Workers, involving organizations ranging from workers' black lung groups to the rank-and-file journal The Miner's Voice. Traditional Left groups have successfully organized a militant rank-and-file conference, drawing on many of these new insurgent groups. Within the steel industry there are now several active insurgent caucuses, the first and largest of which is the National Ad Hoc Committee of Concerned Steelworkers. Nor is activity confined to the industrial sphere. The Social Welfare Workers' Movement, insurgent caucuses within teachers' unions, and militant activities of health workers illustrate this, as well as militant rank-and-file activity in the postal union.

The rank-and-file union revolts that have been developing in industrial workplaces since the early 1950s are now plainly visible. Like many of their compatriots, American workers are faced with paces, methods, and conditions of work that are increasingly intolerable. Their union leaders are not sensitive to these conditions. In thousands of industrial establishments across the nation, workers have developed informal underground unions. The basic units of organization are groups composed of several workers, many of whom work in the same plant area and are thus able to communicate with one another and form a social entity. Led by natural on-the-job leaders, they conduct daily guerrilla skirmishes with their employers and often against their official union representatives as well. These groups are the power base for the insurgencies from below.

Widespread Revolt Begins in Auto

The General Motors Corporation employs as many workers as all other auto manufacturers combined. In 1955, the United Auto Workers' president, Walter Reuther, signed a contract with GM which did not check the speedup or speed the settlement of local shop grievances. Over 70 percent of GM workers went on strike immediately after Reuther announced the terms of his agreement. A larger percentage "wildcatted" after the signing of the 1958 contract because Reuther had again refused to do anything to combat the speedup. For the same reason, the auto workers walked off their jobs again in 1961. The strike closed every GM and a number of large Ford plants.

The UAW ranks' ability to conduct a nationwide wildcat strike is made possible by a democratic practice that has been maintained by GM workers since the thirties. Every GM local sends elected delegates to Detroit to sit in council during at least part of national contract negotiations. Thus ideally each local can instruct its negotiators and confer with them as the bargaining progresses. Again, ideally the council and negotiators arrive at an agreement on the package that the latter have been able to obtain from the employer and both the rank-and-file delegates and leaders recommend ratification by the ranks and the local union level. In 1961, when the council unanimously recommended rejection and strike, Reuther notified the press that the strike was official, that he was leading it and that it would continue until all grievances concerning working conditions had been settled in separate local supplemental agreements rather than in the national contract. He thus maintained control. The ranks were outmaneuvered and angered.

Just prior to the negotiation of the 1964 contract a development took place in the UAW that is unique in American labor history. Several large Detroit locals initiated a bumper sticker campaign. In all cities across the country where UAW plants are located the bumpers of auto workers' cars pushed the slogan: HUMANIZE WORKING CONDITIONS. Lacking the support of their official leaders, these workers were attempting to inform the public of the nature of the struggle they were about to conduct, and that its primary goal would be to improve the condition of factory life rather than wages.

Their attempt to bypass Reuther failed. Contrary to established practice he opened negotiations with Chrysler, the smallest of the Big Three auto makers. He imposed the pattern of this contract on the Ford workers and then announced that the Chrysler-Ford agreements would be the pattern for the GM contract. The dialogue between GM workers and their president was brief. They struck every GM plant for five weeks and were joined by thousands of Ford workers. They returned to work under a national contract no better than those signed with Ford and Chrysler. Their strike won the settlement of a backlog of local grievances; created pride in the knowledge that it was primarily and publicly directed against Reuther's maneuver, and made possible the further development of rank-and-file leaders. They demonstrated that they would not give ground in their efforts to make their national contract a weapon against the speedup and to rid themselves of a grievance procedure that allows the settlement of individual grievances to take up to two years.

Aware that the ranks would be continuing their fight and seeking revenge, at the UAW's September 1966 convention in Long Beach, California, Reuther sought issues that could be used to divert their wrath. In early 1965 the ballot count in the election between incumbent International Union of Electrical Workers (IUE) President James B. Carey and his challenger Paul Jennings was in doubt. Reuther issued a statement to the press announcing his offer to merge the IUE with the UAW. The merger might have salvaged Carey's reputation and employment in the labor movement. It could also have been used as a major agenda item necessitating extended discussion at the UAW convention, but Carey rigidly turned down Reuther's offer, claiming that he had learned of it only hours before it was made public.

The Long Beach UAW convention in May of last year [1966] was the first labor convention experience for over 60 percent of the delegates. Many of the faces that had become familiar to Reuther during previous conventions were absent. None of the delegates got a chance to discuss what was the main issue for the ranks that elected them—their demands for the 1967 contract; that point on the agenda was postponed to a special conference in April 1967. Reuther won more than a breathing spell at Long Beach. In the months preceding the convention the rebellion in the UAW's 250,000-man Skilled Trades Department had reached crisis proportions. Their wages had fallen behind those of craft union members doing comparable work in other industries. They threatened to disaffiliate and join the rival International Society of Skilled Trades (independent). The convention amended the UAW constitution to give the Skilled Trades Department, containing less than 20 percent of the UAW's members, veto power over all national contracts. They do not work under the same conditions as the semiskilled who buck the assembly lines and who are the majority and now second class citizenry of the UAW. Reuther has obtained an aristocratic power base and laid the foundation for another and more violent rupture in the UAW.

For more than a decade it has been absolutely clear that the UAW ranks demand top priority be given to the fight to improve working conditions. Their efforts to make Reuther lead this fight have been herculean. At this late date it is almost paradoxical that he remains rigid in his refusal to make that fight. And so he must try to go into the April conference equipped with a diversionary tactic of gigantic proportions—based on more than a transparent maneuver that will only further enrage his ranks. His recent resignation as first vice president of the AFL-CIO and his open split with that body's president, George Meany, has, among other things, armed him with such a diversion. The question of total withdrawal from the AFL-CIO is the first point on the agenda of the April conference, which is now scheduled to last only three days.

Leaflets circulated by UAW members in Detroit auto plants prior to the split ridiculed Reuther for his inability to stand up to Meany. They were picked up by the national press and significantly hurt Reuther's prestige. Evidence mounts to indicate that Reuther was finally driven to sever his distasteful relationship with Meany for two principal reasons: (1) the demands of the UAW's revolt and internal struggle, (2) the widespread revolts throughout the labor movement, particularly in the unions that form Reuther's domain in the AFL-CIO (Industrial Union Department). The latter may include a third principal factor. The revolts are numerous enough to have given Reuther the vision that the revolts in the 1930s gave to John L. Lewis—the formation of a powerful new labor confederation through the organizational centralization of the unions that are in rebellion—a confederation that could now include white-collar, professional, service, and farm workers.

The wildcat strike of UAW-GM Local 527 in Mansfield, Ohio, in February [1967], revealed the depth of the liberal stance Reuther has taken in his fight with Meany. The total walkout at Mansfield occurred because two workers were fired for refusing to make dies and tools ready for shipment to another plant in Pontiac, Michigan. GM has long followed a policy of transferring work out of plants where workers have established better working conditions or are conducting a struggle to improve them, to other plants with less militant workforces. The Mansfield workers had long observed this practice in silence. To be forced to participate in the transferral and their own defeat was the final indignity.

Mansfield is a key GM parts feeder plant and their strike idled 133,000 men in over 20 shops. Instead of utilizing this power to win his men's demands, Reuther declared the strike illegal. Moreover, he threatened to put the local into trusteeship and suspend local democracy. In an all-day session on February 22 his leadership pressured Local 727 leaders into asking their men to return to work without winning a solution of their grievances. The local leaders were told that the strike was poorly timed because it came on the eve of the UAW's big push for annual salaries and profit sharing in 1967 bargaining. These two demands are to be given preference over all others. It is probable that the Mansfield strike has prematurely revealed the argument that Reuther will use in the April Conference against rank-and-file demands that the big push be to eliminate the speedup and inoperable grievance machinery.

The above probability is reinforced by the February 8 UAW Administrative Letter issued to elaborate Reuther's position on his split with Meany. It contains a long and detailed "Outline of UAW Program For The American Labor Movement." Under its section on collective bargaining it stresses the "development of a sound economic wage policy." No mention or hint is made of the need to improve working conditions, which to this moment is the cause of the major crisis for Reuther's leadership.

Under "Aims and Purposes of a Democratic Labor Movement" the February 8 letter stresses collective bargaining and "appropriate progressive legislation" as the methods to be used to advance the interests of union members and their families. But Reuther's current policies insure that direct action, including wildcat strikes and minor acts of sabotage in the plants, will daily continue to interrupt production. His program's concessions to the revolt can only encourage the fight against conservative union leadership and do not include goals that will enable him to lead and contain it. His failure to champion an improvement of working conditions will create a consequent dimming of enthusiasm and support for Reuther's new program for American labor, both within the UAW ranks and in the ranks of unions whose support he hopes to win. His actions will tend also to undercut the possibility of success for the many good policies the program contains.

Longshoremen and Steelworkers

In 1964 the ranks of the International Longshoremen's Association (East and Gulf Coasts) conducted a strike/revolt against both their employers and union officials that was identical to and almost simultaneous with that accomplished by the UAW rank and file. The stevedoring companies and ILA officials had negotiated what appeared to be an excellent contract. It contained, by past standards, a significant wage increase. It guaranteed every union member a minimum of 1,600 hours of work per year and minor economic fringe benefits. The dockers struck immediately upon the announcement of the terms. Their president, Thomas W. Gleason, hurriedly toured all locals at the request of George Meany on a mission called "Operation Fact." Gleason claimed his ranks wildcatted because they didn't understand the contract. They understood only too well. In return for the recommended settlement the number of men in each work gang was to be cut from 20 to 17. The employers originally demanded a gang size reduction to 14 men, a size more nearly in line with manning scales negotiated by International Longshoremen's and Warehousemen's Union President Harry Bridges for West Coast longshoremen. The ILA ranks did not give in to this or the many other undercutting pressures. President Johnson declared a national emergency and invoked the 80-day "cooling off" period under the provisions of the Taft-Hartley Act.

Wildcat strikes resumed on December 21, one day after the "cooling off" period ended, and continued through January. All ports were on strike at the same time for over 18 days, and longer in Southern and Gulf ports where separate and inferior contracts were offered. Longshoremen in New York and northern East Coast ports returned to work having lost on the main issue of gang size, but their defeat in this battle was not accompanied by a deep demoralization. Their union has long been unofficially divided into separately led baronies. For the first time in the history of the ILA the entire membership initiated and conducted an all-union strike.

The United Steelworkers Union revolt deserves special attention because it demonstrates how long it takes in some instances for a revolt to develop. In 1946 the steelworkers conducted a 26-day strike; in 1949, 45 days of strike; in 1952, 59 days; in 1956, 36 days. All of these strikes were conducted with only reluctant or forced support from the international leadership.

In 1957, an obscure rank-and-file leader named Ronald Rarick ran against USW President David MacDonald. Rarick, a conservative who has since become a reactionary, based his entire program on opposition to a dues increase and increase in the salaries of officials. As the campaign for the presidency developed, the rank-and-file could see that Rarick was not a militant unionist. Militants couldn't vote for Rarick with enthusiasm. His candidacy was used in the main to record opposition to MacDonald. He beat MacDonald in the Pennsylvania region by a slight margin, but lost nationally. The vote ran 223,000 for Rarick, 404,000 for MacDonald. I. W. Abel, running for Secretary-Treasurer, got 420,000 and his opposition got 181,000. In effect, Rarick disappeared after the election, but the vote he received alarmed the leaders of the large unions.

Four years later, MacDonald ran unopposed and received only 221,000 votes. It was obvious that MacDonald had been able to win a large vote against Rarick because he was able to utilize the treasury and resources of the International. To beat MacDonald a candidate had to be recruited from inside the International who also had access to its facilities.

As early as the Special Steelworkers Conference of 1952, the regional and local union leaders of the USW had warned Mac-Donald that he would have to do something about the deterioration of working conditions in the plants. They further warned that the resulting rank-and-file anger was threatening their position and they might have no other alternative than to transmit this pressure to him.

Twelve years later many of these same secondary and tertiary leaders realized that they could not survive under MacDonald's leadership. They picked I. W. Abel, a man who had not worked in a mill for twenty-five years, to challenge MacDonald. After a long dispute over the ballot count, Abel was declared the winner. Under his leadership a significant democratization of the negotiation process has begun. Delegates to the 1966 USW convention terminated the union's participation in the joint employer/union Human Relations Committee whose function was to study plant working conditions and to determine how they could be changed in order to cut the costs of production and speed the automation process. The union's 165-man Wage Policy Committee, which had the power to ratify contracts, was also completely stripped of its power. A new and somewhat liberalized method for allowing the ranks a voice in negotiations was instituted. The policy of last minute "shotgun" bargaining a few days prior to contract expiration was substituted for Mac-Donald's practice of beginning negotiations a year in advance of deadline.

Electrical Workers and Their Secondary Leaders Unite

James B. Carey, President of the International Union of Electrical Workers, was removed from office in a struggle similar to that which deposed David MacDonald. By 1953 he had been out of contact with his membership for many years. He had failed to lead them in a fight for improved working conditions against the General Electric and Westinghouse corporations. He had been less successful than Reuther or even MacDonald in obtaining wage increases to ease his ranks' anger. However, he felt the pressure of coming rebellion and sought to oppose rather than appease it. He proposed a constitutional change for his union that would have had the employers collect union dues and send them directly to the union's Washington, D.C., headquarters, which would in turn dispense to the locals their stipulated share.

The secondary leaders recognized the danger to themselves inherent in this policy, and in 1964, with the backing of the ranks, organized an opposition to Carey. In Paul Jennings of the Sperry local in New York they found a candidate with a good union reputation. Jennings beat Carey, but a majority of the ballot counters were Carey supporters and they declared Carey the winner. Jennings forces challenged the count and Carey supporters readied a second set of ballots to show the challengers. They would have given Carey the victory. Because of the ease with which Carey made enemies, even among men like George Meany, the supporters of Jennings were able to obtain aid in a world unfamiliar to the union's ranks. The U.S. Department of Labor impounded the original ballots before a ballot switch could be made.

The struggle for rank-and-file autonomy in the IUE did not end with Jennings's 1964 part-coup victory. In a very short time Jennings did more to improve wages than his predecessor, but he too neglected the fight for working conditions. Under his leadership the IUE engineered a united effort of eleven unions in the 1966 negotiations and subsequent strike against GE. A showdown was long overdue. GE had a 1965 volume of $6.2

billion, up one billion over 1964. It spent $330 million for capital expansion and still netted $355 million after taxes. Profits after taxes for the 1960–1965 period were up 52 percent. They had grown accustomed to docile union negotiators. The IUE-led united front broke GE's Boulwarist approach to bargaining, i.e., GE's practice of making their first settlement offer their last settlement offer under Board President Boulwaris's chairmanship. It also broke President Johnson's 3.2 percent wage guideline and obtained a 5 percent wage increase. However, after the contract was signed, major locals of all unions in the front, including thousands of workers of the IUE, UAW, International Brotherhood of Electrical Workers, and the independent United Electrical Workers, stayed out on strike. Jennings and the leaders of the other unions had failed to negotiate an improvement of grievance machinery and working conditions. A Taft-Hartley injunction was necessary to end the strike of those involved in defense production.

Carey and MacDonald were not the only leaders of large industrial unions to be felled since 1964. In that year O. A. "Jack" Knight, President of the Oil, Gas, and Atomic Workers, retired three years early in the face of a developing rank-and-file revolt. During the Miami convention of the United Rubber Workers Union in September 1966 the widespread unrest and revolts in the local unions that had preceded the convention forced incumbent President George Burdon to withdraw his candidacy for renomination. In an emotional speech he conceded the "serious mistakes" made during his administration. The major criticisms leveled against him were: loss of touch with the ranks, lack of personal participation in negotiations, and an attempt to have the union pay his wife's personal traveling expenses. Veteran vice-president Peter Bommarito was swept into office by acclamation. He immediately pledged to take a tougher position against the employers.

[A lengthy section is omitted here in which Weir discusses in similar terms the situation of the coal miners, West Coast longshoremen, maritime workers, airline mechanics, teamsters, painters, and pulp and paper workers.]

What of the future of the rank-and-file union revolts, which so far have occurred mainly in the mass production and transportation industries? One of their principal strengths arises from the consciousness that motivates them: large numbers of industrial workers are simply no longer willing to tolerate the conditions under which they are expected to produce the goods and services that in major part maintain this society. Their major strength, however, lies in the organizational base on which they are founded, the primary or informal work groups. The groups are created by production technology which puts from three to ten workers in regular face to face communication with one another during each work turn. They have naturally selected informal leadership. They are able to maintain control and discipline over their members through use of the social weapon, first by the "chill" treatment, then ridicule, then worse. They can effect the speed and efficiency of production of goods or services. They are the micro-organizational units which create the phantom unions that are behind all wildcat strikes, slowdowns and withdrawals of efficiency. They are the only organizations that cannot be taken away from the ranks and that cannot be bureaucratized.

A third strength of these revolts is the fact that they have broken out at a time when there is deep dissatisfaction in other large specific segments of the labor force and in the population generally. This was far less true in the 1930s. At that time there were no large scale radicalizations as such among racial or ethnic minorities, students and professionals—that is, that had very definite independent and separate identities of their own. There were no hints of a growing radicalization among women. Public workers were not ignoring antistrike laws and forming massive unions. In short, the CIO revolution, although dramatic, did not occur in as widespread an atmosphere of social change. Even though it has yet to manifest itself as dramatically, today's struggle against the "life that is" is far more general than in the 1930s.

The fourth major strength is a historical first—intellectuals now have potential means for building their own independent base inside organized labor. This opportunity exists as a result of the organization of unions by teachers, social workers, and professionals in many career categories. During the 1930s, intellectuals obtained access to the labor movement mainly by invitation from union officials in need of assistance. They came as outsiders. Paid and unpaid they worked as staffers and consultants. They remained until they were no longer of use or until they differed openly with their employers or sponsors on serious policy issues. They can now participate as equals, as card carrying members, in large numbers and with memberships of their own to back them. And because professionals are now getting their own unions, blue-collar workers are in position to give direct and immediate aid to a large segment of the new middle class. In return, and not as a gift, blue-collar workers can have available to them, by a much more direct process, the cultural sophistication and technical and intellectual skills that a class conscious economic, social, and educational system denies to so many of them and which are so necessary to their struggle.

The rank-and-file revolts have one overall general weakness: thus far they have been waged mainly around immediate issues within separate workplaces that involve large numbers of supporters for only brief crisis periods. Between those periods their active supporters tend to dwindle to a small number of militants who are then faced with the problem of defending themselves from their employers and top union officials while seeking to maintain a core of key rebel leaders in wait for the next crisis issue that will enable them to again put large numbers into motion.

The problem of how to attract the support of a critical mass in each place of work and then retain it reveals three major and specific weaknesses: First, though not necessarily most important, the revolts have been unable to overcome their organizational isolation from one another. The sense of isolation in itself has a demoralizing effect upon the rebels. And because the revolts have been conducted within separate local unions representing separate workplaces, their opponents have been allowed to deal with them in the same way, thereby avoiding the necessity of making major concessions. There are no large rebel caucuses or committees. There are no organizational vehicles to unite rebelling local unions in different workplaces owned by the same employer, to unite locals in the United States and Canada within the same industry or international union, or to unite rebel groups across industrial lines within the same city or region. Among other things, this makes it impossible for the rebels to challenge directly the offices of top union officials who are unresponsive to the needs of the ranks.

The second specific and major weakness of the revolts is directly related to the fact that their stated demands have thus far been limited to a series of slogans for single and relatively immediate goals. No rank-and-file group has yet come forth with an overall program or long range perspective statement. Thus, to those not involved in their groups, either in or outside industry, it appears that the rebels seek only piecemeal reform within their unions and within the present institution of collective bargaining. But in order to obtain any one or more of certain specific demands—for example, funded pensions after thirty years of labor regardless of age, a 30-hour week with 40 hours' pay, the right to place limitations on production paces and work loads, the right of the ranks to choose collective bargaining goals as well as to ratify what has been negotiated by union negotiators, increased job and skill upgrading opportunities for black and brown workers—requires far more than a concerted drive to rally the ranks around slogans. For one thing, drives that are limited to the winning of one or a series of popular demands seldom produce a stable organization, if they produce one at all. As a result the drives are unable to sustain themselves at the needed momentum for more than brief periods. They do not bring together broad groupings of labor. They are unable to bank the change in consciousness level of the participants. Too often, rank-and-file militants find themselves facing a new outbreak of mass militancy in their workplaces with little more organizational development to handle it than existed at the beginning of the previous outbreak.

Ongoing organizations with any kind of mass participation and following are those that have developed a "world view" or context that supports their popular demands. They have been able to attract larger than elite core numbers because they have been able to overcome the skepticism and pessimism that exists in the majority because of their inability to see a successful alternative to doing things as they are presently done. In most instances, today's outbreaks of mass dissatisfaction whether in ghettoes, on campuses, or inside industrial workplaces are momentary acts of desperation against "things as they are." The sense of hopelessness about accomplishing progressive change is only temporarily overcome. Failure to obtain quick results in response to popular demands brings a return of the feeling that it is hopeless to try to win the demands because the powerful employers are opposed to them and the union officials aren't interested in making the fight. This demoralization is fed primarily by two things: (1) the failure of the rank-and-file leadership to project a vision of union democracy wherein bureaucratic officials could not so easily frustrate rank-and-file drives for worklife improvements and (2) the failure to propose the concrete, democratic structural-governmental union reforms necessary for fulfillment of the vision. The present crisis in the Auto Workers Union provides an excellent example of this. The ranks of that union are now, as they have been for years, interested in exercising limitations on the production speeds set by the employers. They are able to use a formalized grievance process in order to protest the speedup, but have found it ineffective in stopping it. In addition to poor collective bargaining contract language, the ratio of union representatives to workers on the shop floor is as high as one to four hundred. Grievance committee men and women are unable to give ample representation to the workers they are supposed to represent and moreover, are strangers to most of them. In the face of this problem, leaflets have recently been distributed by rebel groups in Detroit General Motors UAW locals calling for union representation on the shop floor equal to that of management's, which is often as low as one to fifteen. Such a ratio for the union would mean that every worker would work within eyesight of his or her union representative who also labors "on the line." What if working shop stewards of this sort formed plant-for-plant committees and city, regional, and national councils based upon the committees? Pyramiding of this sort from elementary units of representation that are based in the work process might be an alternative basis for UAW government, far superior to the present elite executive board elected at biannual conventions held in places far removed from the workplace. The demand for a better union representation ratio is a good one, but it is improbable that large numbers in the ranks will mobilize around it until they see it as more than a simple and immediate reform of the grievance handling process.

To be able to envisage a new union structure that does not immediately and bureaucratically conservatize new militants who are elected to official positions is prerequisite for successful rank-and-file rebel mobilization. Present union governmental structures and practices cause new leaders to immediately lose direct contact with the people who elected them. The institution of the monthly local union meeting has failed as a method of maintaining that contact. The automobile population explosion and the disappearance of cohesive neighborhoods of industrial workers near the factories makes attendance at local meetings too great a chore. Few locals get attendances of over five percent of their membership. This factor alone cuts the vast majority out of the union decision-making process. It is difficult to arouse sustained enthusiasm for immediate reforms if the system that has frustrated the fulfillment of previous reforms continues to operate unchanged.

The third major weakness of the rank-and-file revolts also results from the limitations of the stated goals held by those that lead them. Between 1937 and 1940, five million semiskilled American workers established industrial unions. The momentum which made the CIO possible came from far more than a desire for union recognition and collective bargaining contracts —over and above the practical demands was the dream of a whole new life expressed in idealistic terms. This momentum was lost during World War II and the bureaucratized unions that emerged from the war make demands that, if won, do no more than provide workers with the material wealth necessary to enable them to continue to produce, and under conditions that are deteriorating rather than improving. It is not that the vision of a new and better life is dead. The revolts are proof that the dream still exists. A generation of relative full employment has meant that millions of workers have spent lifetimes doing murderously repetitive work without interruption or relief. They have found that work whose only reward is the ability to pay bills has no meaning; that work to create products that cannot be identified with brings a quality of meaninglessness to their entire existences. They want to make quality products in which they can take pride, which are built to last. They want to produce quality services without sacrifice of what is creative in their personalities. The older workers do not want to finish out their work lives in monotony and boredom. The young do not want to be shuffling drudges by the time they reach forty, sapped to a point where they have little energy left after a day's work for anything but momentary escape. The general public will one day be shocked to learn that there is not an auto or rubber worker who doesn't curse or look the other way when they see their products rolling down the street; that there is not an electrical appliance worker who likes to have at home one of the products he or she helps to make; and that there is not a steel worker who is not angered by employer-imposed conditions that cheat a run of steel of its potential quality. It is the same for all workers regardless of industry. Beneath the crust of cynicism created by work done under conditions that deny responsibility is the old dream. Workers want to be able to participate in the making of the decisions that affect their work lives. But until they make their angers and desires known beyond the areas behind the timeclocks, the public will continue to believe that the official pronouncements of the unions represent the true feelings of the workers and that their major interests do not go beyond the purely material. But how is it possible to break away from the limitations of present official union practices and ideologies without open presentation of alternatives to their equally narrow goals? This is the biggest of the tasks that history has placed upon the rank-and-file unionists who lead the revolts.

Trade Unionism and Workers' Control

Stanley Aronowitz

Given the alienating nature of work and the resulting discontent that manifests itself in challenges to both management and the unions, it is hardly surprising that much attention has been paid to the "crisis of American labor." But it is only rarely appreciated how thoroughgoing that crisis is, how much discontent the prevailing system of collective bargaining has engendered, and how strictly the ideological confines of capitalist mentality keep us from even considering alternative systems of work. The following article by Stanley Aronowitz steps outside of these rigid confines to speculate on possible future development of trends noted in the earlier essays. The crisis of collective bargaining is examined in greater detail in the next section, which follows Aronowitz's article.

The configuration of strikes of the past four years is unprecedented in the history of American workers. Since 1967, there have been more strikes, rank-and-file rejections of proposed union settlements with employers, and wildcat walkouts than in any similar period in the modern era.

The most notable feature of the present situation is that the unions are no longer in a position of leadership in workers' struggles; they are running desperately to catch up to their own membership. In many cases, union sanctions for walkouts have followed the workers' own action. In others, the leadership has attempted to thwart membership initiative and, having failed, has publicly supported the strike while sabotaging it surreptitiously. There are few instances in the current strike wave where the union heads have actually given militant voice to rank-and-file sentiment.

For the most part, union national bureaucracies have sided with employers in trying to impose labor peace upon a rebellious membership. What is remarkable is that the rebellion has been largely successful despite enormous odds. The unions are afraid to oppose the rank and file directly. Their opposition has taken the form of attempting to channel the broad range of rank-and-file grievances into bargaining demands which center, in the main, on wages and benefits. The huge backlog of grievances on issues having to do with working conditions remains untouched. Rank-and-file militancy has occurred precisely because of the failure of the unions to address themselves to the issues of speedup, plant removal, increased workloads, technological change, and arbitrary discharges of union militants.

Wages have also been an enormously important factor in accounting for the present rash of strikes. Since 1967, workers have suffered a pronounced deterioration in living standards. Despite substantial increases in many current settlements, real wages for the whole working class have declined annually; that is, wage increases have simply failed to keep pace with the cost of living. In many contracts, the first year increase is equal to the cost of living increases as tabulated by the Bureau of Labor statistics for the previous year. But the second and third year increases are usually not as great. During the second and third years workers' real wages deteriorate. There are few contracts which provide for cost of living increases in addition to the negotiated settlements. Even where cost-of-living clauses have been incorporated into the contracts, there is usually a ceiling on the amount of increase to which the company is obligated.

Long term contracts, which have become standard practice in American industry, have robbed the rank and file of considerable power to deal with its problems within the framework of collective bargaining. Workers have been forced to act outside of approved procedures because they know instinctively that the union has become an inadequate tool to conduct struggles, even where they have not yet perceived the union as an outright opponent of their interests.

For most workers, the trade unions remain the basic organizations for the defense of their immediate economic interests against employers. Despite the despicable performance of labor leadership during the past thirty years, and especially in the last two decades—including its adherence to the imperialist policies of the successive Democratic and Republican administrations from Truman to Nixon and its collaboration with the large corporations to discipline the workers against their own interests—blue- and white-collar workers regard their unions as their only weapon against the deterioration of working conditions and the rampant inflation responsible for recent declines in real wages.

In part, trade unions retain their legitimacy because no alternative to them exists. In part, workers join unions because the unions give the appearance of advancing workers' interests, since they must do so to some extent to gain their support. A union bureaucracy can betray the workers' elementary economic demands for a considerable period of time. However, the last decade has been studded with examples of rank-and-file uprisings against the least responsible of the labor bureaucrats. In nearly all cases of rank-and-file revolts aimed at replacing union leadership, however, the new group of leaders has reproduced the conditions of the old regime. In the steel, rubber, electrical, and government workers' and other important unions one can observe some differences in the style of administration in the leadership's willingness to conduct strike struggles and in the political sophistication of the bureaucracy. But these unions are neither radical nor have they made sharp breaks from the predominant policies of the labor movement in the contemporary era.

Some radicals explain this phenomenon in a purely idealistic way. According to conventional wisdom, the weakness of the factional struggles within the unions over the past decade has been that they have been conducted without an alternative ideological perspective. The left has been largely irrelevant to them. Therefore, if the new leadership merely recapitulates "the same old crap" (Marx's words), we should blame our own failure to concentrate our political work within the working class. Presumably, a strong Left could have altered the kind of leadership and the program of the rank-and-file movements.

There is undoubtedly some truth in these assertions. Yet the disturbing fact is that the Communist Left was part of the trade unions' leadership for many decades prior to 1950. In some unions there are remnants of the Left still in power. There is a tendency to explain the failure of the old Communist Left by reference to its "revisionist" policies. Such superficial explanations assume that if only the politics of radical labor organizers had been better, the whole picture would have been qualitatively different. This will be shown not to be the case.

If the trade union remains an elementary organ of struggle, it is also a force for integrating the workers into the corporate capitalist system. Trade unions have historically fought to determine the price of labor power on more favorable terms to the workers. But inherent in the labor contract is both the means to insure some benefit to the workers and to provide a stable, disciplined labor force to the employer. The union wins both rights and assumes obligations in the collective bargaining agreement.

Under contemporary monopolistic capitalism, these obligations include: 1) the promise not to strike, except under specific conditions, or at the termination of the contract; 2) a bureaucratic and hierarchical grievance procedure consisting of many steps during which the control over the grievance is systematically removed from the shop floor and from workers' control; 3) a system of management prerogatives wherein the union agrees to cede to the employer "the operation of the employer's facilities and the direction of the working forces, including the right to hire, suspend, or discharge for good cause and . . . to relieve employees from duties due to lack of work"[1]; and 4) a "checkoff" of union dues as an automatic deduction from the workers' pay checks.

The last provision, incorporated into ninety-eight percent of union contracts, treats union dues as another tax on workers'

---

[1] Collective Agreement between Oil, Chemical, and Atomic Workers International Union with Gulf Oil Co., Port Arthur, Texas, 1966–9.

wages. It is a major barrier to the close relations between union leaders and the rank and file. Workers have come to regard the checkoff as another insurance premium. Since workers enjoy little participation in union affairs, except when they have an individual grievance or around contract time, the checkoff of union dues—designed originally to protect the union's financial resources—has removed a major point of contact between workers and their fulltime representatives. This procedure is in sharp contrast to former times when the shop steward or business agent was obliged to collect dues by hand. In this period, the dues collection process, however cumbersome for the officials, provided a means for workers to voice their complaints as well as a weapon against the abuses of bureaucracy.

The modern labor agreement is the heart of class collaboration between the trade unions and the corporations. It mirrors the bureaucratic and hierarchical structure of modern industry and the state. Its provisions are enforced not merely by law, but by the joint efforts of corporate and trade union bureaucracies. Even the most enlightened trade union leader cannot fail to play his part as an element in the mechanisms of domination over workers' rights to spontaneously struggle against speedup or *de facto* wage cuts, either in the form of a shift in the work process or by inflationary price increases. The unions' hands are tied by law as well by the contract.

The role of collective bargaining today is to provide a rigid institutional framework for the conduct of the class struggle. This struggle at the point of production has become regulated in the same way as have electric and telephone rates, prices of basic commodities, and foreign trade. The regulatory procedure in labor relations includes government intervention in collective bargaining, the routinization of all conflict between labor and the employer on the shop floor, and the placing of equal responsibility for observing plant rules upon management and the union.

The objective of this procedure is to control labor costs as a stable factor of production in order to permit rational investment decisions by the large corporations. The long term contract insures that labor costs will be a known factor. It guarantees labor peace for a specified period of time. The

agreement enables employers to avoid the disruption characteristic of stormier periods of labor history when workers' struggles were much more spontaneous, albeit more difficult.

An important element in the labor contract is that most of
the day-to-day issues expressing the conflict between worker
and employer over the basic question of the division of profit
are not subject to strikes. In the automobile and electrical
agreements as well as a few others, the union has the right to
strike over speedup, safety issues, or a few other major questions. In the main, however, most complaints about working
conditions and work assignments are adjusted in the final step
of the grievance procedure by an "impartial" arbitrator selected
by both the union and management. In industries where the
strike weapon is a permitted option, the union leaders usually
put severe pressure on the rank and file to choose the arbitration route since strikes disrupt the good relations between the
bureaucracy and management, a situation valued highly by
liberal corporate officials and union leaders.

With few exceptions, particularly in textile and electrical
corporations, employers regard labor leaders as their allies
against the ignorant and undisciplined rank-and-file workers.
This confidence has been built up over the past thirty-five years
of industrial collective bargaining.

The trade unions serve corporate interests in America today.
This is not merely the result of the conservative consciousness
of the leadership. The trade unions have become an appendage
of the corporations because they have taken their place as a
vital institution in the corporate capitalist complex. Their role
as an organ of struggle has deteriorated, but has not entirely
vanished. If union leaders are compelled to sanction and often
give militant voice to worker demands, it is due to the fact that
the union is a political institution, much like the electoral
system which selects legislative officials.

The democratic foundations of the trade unions have been
undermined almost universally, however. The Left understood
that the old craft unions were essentially purveyors of labor
power. The terror and violence of craft union leadership against
the rank and file was only the most extreme expression of their
monopoly over the labor force. They controlled both the supply

of skilled labor and its price. Since the old unions were defined narrowly by the economic functions and by their conservative ideology, the assumption of Socialists and Communists who helped build industrial unions which included the huge mass of unskilled and semiskilled workers was that these organizations would express broader political and social interests, if not radical ideologies.

The new industrial unions organized in the past forty years were to be organs of rank-and-file power. The workers would have an opportunity to participate in union affairs on all levels of decision making. On the whole, despite corruption and bureaucratic resistance to the exercise of membership control, many unions in the United States have retained the forms but not the content of democracy. It is possible to remove union leaders and replace them, but it is not possible to transcend the institutional constraints of trade unionism itself.

Trade unions have fallen victim to the same disease as the broader electoral and legislative system. Just as the major power over the state has shifted from the legislative to the executive branch of government, power over union affairs has shifted from the rank and file to the corporate leaders, the trade union officials and the government. Trade unions are regulated both in their relations with employers and in their internal operations by the state. Moreover, the problems of union leadership have been transformed from political and social issues to the routines of contract administration and internal bureaucratic procedures such as union finances. The union leader is a business executive. His accountability is not limited to the membership—it is extended to government agencies, arbitrators, courts of law, and other institutions which play a large role in regulating the union's operations.

The contradiction between the role of trade unions as an organ of struggle and integrator of the labor force is played out at every contract negotiation in major industries. Over the past several years the chasm between the leadership and membership has never been more exposed. During this period, a rising number of contract settlements have been rejected by the rank and file. In 1968, nearly thirty percent of initial proposed settlements were turned down by union memberships. The rank and file has veto power, but no means of initiative in contract bargaining. In the first place, many major industries have agreements which are negotiated at the national level. There is room for local bargaining over specific shop issues, but the main lines of economic settlements are determined by fulltime officials of the company and the union; many rank-and-file bargaining committees are relegated to the role of bystander, window dressing, or advisor in union bargaining. One reason for this concentration of power in fulltime officials is the alleged technical nature of collective bargaining in the modern era. Not only leaders and representatives of the local membership sit on the union's side of the bargaining table, but lawyers, insurance, and pension experts and sometimes even management consultants as well. The product of the charade which is characteristic of much of collective bargaining today is a mammoth document which reads more like a corporate contract of a mortgage agreement than anything else. In fact, it is a bill of sale.

I would argue that the specialization of functions within the trade unions is only partially justified by the needs of the membership. Insurance and pension plans do require the employment of specific talents, but the overall direction of worker–employer relationships has been centralized in the hands of experts as a means of preventing the direct intervention of the rank and file. More, the domination of specialists within the collective bargaining process signals the removal of this process from the day-to-day problems of the workers. The interpretation of provisions of the agreement is beyond the intervention of the rank and file. The special language of the contract, its bulk, and its purely administrative character help perpetuate the centrality of the professional expert in the union hierarchy.

In this connection, it is no accident that the elected union official has limited power within the collective bargaining ritual (and, in a special sense, within the union itself). Few national union leaders make decisions either in direct consultation with the membership or with fellow elected officials. The hired expert, particularly the lawyer, holds increased power in union affairs because of the businesslike character of labor relations, the legal constraints upon union as well as rank-and-file initiatives and the specialized content of all union agreements.

But the union official is not distressed by the growing need for experts. He has employed the expert as a buffer between officialdom and the restive rank and file. As in other institutions, experts have been used to rationalize the conservatism of the leadership in technical and legal terms leaving the official free to remain politically viable by supporting the sentiments expressed by the membership while, at the same time, rejecting their proposed actions.

During the past decade in the auto, steel, rubber, and other basic manufacturing industries, the critical issues of working class struggle have been those related to control over the workplace. The tremendous shifts in plant location, work methods, job definitions, and other problems associated with investment in new equipment, expansion, and changing skills required to operate new means of production have found the union bureaucracies unprepared. The reasons for trade union impotence at the workplace go beyond ideology. They are built into the sinews of the collective bargaining process.

Many important industries have national contracts between the union and the companies covering most monetary issues, including wages. In the electrical, auto, and steel industries, negotiations are conducted with individual companies, but in reality there is "pattern" bargaining. A single major producer is chosen by the union and corporations to determine wage and fringe benefit settlement for the rest of the industry. All other negotiations stall until the central settlement is reached.

The national leadership of the union always poses the wage demands as the most important negotiating issues. Problems such as technological changes, work assignments, job classifications, and pace of work are negotiated at the local level after the economic package has been settled. And by the time the local negotiations begin—often conducted between rank-and-file leaders and middle managers—the national union has lost interest in the contract. Its entire orientation is toward the narrowly defined "economic" side of the bargaining. Although many agreements stipulate that resumption of work will not take place before the resolution of local issues, the international representatives and top leaders of the union put enormous pressure on the membership to settle the local issues. It is at the plant level that the sellouts take place. The local feels abandoned, but rank-and-file resentment is diverted to the failure of the shop leadership rather than the top bureaucracy because the national union has "delivered the goods."

After every national auto settlement, a myriad of local walkouts are called over workplace issues. These strikes are short lived and usually unsuccessful in preventing the company's attack on working conditions. In the main, young workers and black workers are the spearhead in struggles against speedup. The impatience of the bureaucracy with this undisciplined action is expressed in long harangues to local leaders and the rank and file by international representatives, employees of the national union. When persuasion fails, the local is sometimes put into receivership and an administrator is sent from the head office to take over the local until the revolt is quelled and order is restored.

The conventional wisdom of today is to admit the conservative character of trade unions in the era of monopoly capitalism —their integration and subordination to the large corporations. At the same time, many radicals stress the important defensive role trade unions perform during periods when growing capitalist instability forces employers to launch an offensive against workers' living standards and working conditions.

Despite the conservative ideology of labor leaders, rank-and-file pressure is forcing unions to lead the fight against employer efforts to transfer to the working class the burdens of the present recession. In this sense, some believe that unions still play a major part in providing protection against the arbitrariness of capital, especially with respect to economic issues.

A recent illustration was provided by the General Electric strike. The conjuncture of inflation, deteriorating working conditions, and the arrogant bargaining posture of the company produced the first unified strike in the electrical industry in twenty-three years. It does not matter that the leaders of the AFL-CIO unions representing most of the workers did not want the strike or unity with the independent United Electrical Workers. Rank-and-file pressure within the largest AFL-CIO union, the IUE, was sufficient to threaten the hegemony of the leadership and reverse the timid collective bargaining strategies of past contract negotiations. Repeated offers by the unions for arbitration of outstanding issues were rejected by the company. GE attempted to win a clearcut victory in order to break the emerging solidarity of the workers and set a pattern for other industries. The company sought a return to the old divide and conquer practice of separate agreements with each union. It encouraged back to work movements, but with little success.

Yet it would be a mistake to infer from the GE experience that temporary trade union militancy, borne of employer opposition, signals an end to class collaboration or the institutional constraints of collective bargaining on workers' autonomy. In fact, the GE strike points sharply to the persistence and dominance of these constraints. The call by the unions for arbitration and acceptance of the good offices of "neutral" political figures such as Senator Javits to intervene in a fact finding investigation was an indication that the leadership lacked confidence in the ability of the workers to win their own struggle and sought to end the strike as soon as possible. The trade union movement with its tremendous financial resources and twenty million members did not effectively mobilize support for the strike. The boycott did not catch fire.

The weakness of the strike was not a lack of willingness by workers to fight. Despite the sellouts, paternalism, and anti-Communism used for years as weapons to split their ranks, GE workers exhibited tremendous courage and a capacity for organized struggle in defending their living standards. But the workers—locked within the apparatus of bureaucratic unionism—were unable to widen the struggle beyond the quantitative economic terms framed by the leadership. The unions offered to settle the strike on the basis of agreement on wages and cost-of-living clause and defer all other demands to arbitration and discussion.

The militant rhetoric of top union leaders in reaction to President Nixon's announced wage freeze in 1971 illustrates the fact that union leaders operate partly as political men, in the sense that they cannot simply support the government and corporate efforts to discipline the workforce. Officials from all "wings" of organized labor attacked the freeze, declaring that it amounted to a windfall to big business. The conservative President of the AFL-CIO, George Meany, led the barrage of invective against the administration, threatening a rash of strikes if the freeze was maintained. Leonard Woodcock, the head of the million-and-a-half member United Auto Workers, declared that the union would cancel its contracts with auto makers unless the freeze was rescinded or the government took steps to place severe enforceable restrictions on prices at the same time. The grand old man of labor's decimated independent "left-wing" unions, Harry Bridges of the West Coast Longshoremen, refused to end the coastwide strike in progress at the time.

Behind the threats of mass strikes and scorn for the wage freeze demand, however, were factors which revealed the real positions of the unions. In the first place, the unions would have risked another blow to their declining prestige among the rank and file if they had refused to give militant voice to the blatant inequality contained in the President's order. Second, Meany himself had been proposing a wage-price freeze since 1969. Union leaders were willing to suspend the strike weapon and wage increases if the administration was prepared to impose similarly stringent controls over prices. In effect, the union leaders were prepared to accept another step in the direction of government regulation of labor relations if the corporations would agree to the principle of "equality of sacrifices." Third, unions warmly cooperated with two previous freezes imposed by Democratic administrations during the Second World War and again during the Korean War. There was much suspicion that the unions would not have reacted so firmly to the order of a Democratic President.

Even during the 1950s union leaders were often forthright in their criticism of the big business orientation of the Eisenhower administration, particularly with respect to economic policies. But one must recall the feeble response of unions to the enactment of the Landrum-Griffin Act in 1959 to keep the infrequent evidence of rhetorical militancy in perspective. Although the bill to extend controls over labor's financial affairs was introduced by a Republican and a Southern Democrat, it had genuine bipartisan support, including the active backing of Senator John F. Kennedy. Union lobbyists welcomed Kennedy's participation in the formation of the legislation because they appreciated his efforts to moderate the extent of controls. Only the Teamsters Union and the handful of other independent unions really opposed the bill. The union leaders were unwilling to militantly oppose the legislation because they felt that it was inevitable. Moreover, many of their loyal congressional supporters convinced the union leaders that outright rejection of the idea of reporting and disclosing union finances would merely provoke a movement for stronger requirements. The unions offered tepid opposition because they would not risk hurting Democratic chances in the 1960 elections.

Until the recent strike wave in response to the decline of real wages, economic issues were not sufficient to spur workers to undertake protracted strikes. The 116-day steel strike in 1959 was fought over the right of the company to change work rules and institute technological changes without consulting the union. The two year-long oil strikes in 1963 were conducted over the question of layoffs and job security in the wake of technological innovations. Most auto walkouts in recent years have been over speedups and other working conditions issues. Even the lengthy GE strike was fought against the arbitrariness of the company; its attack was against working conditions as much as wages.

But the trade union structure has become less able to solve elementary defensive problems. Higher wages for organized workers since the end of World War II have been purchased at a high price. One result of the close ties between unions and corporations has been the enormous freedom enjoyed by capital in transferring the wage increases granted to workers in the shop to the shoulders of the workers as consumers. Wage increases have been granted with relative ease under these circumstances.

Equally significant has been the gradual increase of constraints in the collective bargaining agreement on the workers' freedom to oppose management's imposition of higher production norms, labor-saving technologies, and policies of plant dispersal. (This left millions of textile, steel, auto, shoe, and other workers stranded in the forties and fifties.) The bureaucratization of grievance procedures has robbed shop stewards of their power to deal with management on the shop floor. The inability of workers to change their working conditions through the union has had two results: workers limit their union loyalty to the narrow context of economic struggle, and they go outside the union to solve their basic problems in the plant. Thus the wildcat strike has become not only a protest against the brutality of industrial management, but also against the limits imposed by unionism. The conditions pertaining to the role of trade unions during the rise of industrial capitalism in the United States no longer apply in the monopoly epoch.

The Rise of the Industrial Union in the United States

A little more than fifty years ago, in 1919, the first national strike among unskilled workers in a mass production industry ended in defeat. Judge Elbert Gary, the last of the patronate in the steel industry, defeated the efforts of the 350,000 workers by a combination of tenacity borne of the immense resources of the U.S. Steel Corporation, divisive propaganda to sever the fragile unity of skilled and unskilled workers, and plain scab-herding and other more blatant forms of strikebreaking. Some oldtimers and trade union historians claim that the real cause of the defeat lay in the old AFL craft type of organization which dominated the strike.

Although the strike was not successful, it was remarkable for the fact that workers stayed out for over three months to gain union recognition. Their chief demand was the right to bargain collectively with the giants of the steel industry. The employers agreed that they would unilaterally meet many of the other demands of the strikers, including a cut in the number of work hours (U.S. Steel actually reduced the twelve-hour day to eight hours, with an accompanying twenty-five percent wage increase the following year), but they would never deal with outside representatives of their employees. The open shop was a sacred principle of Judge Gary and his fellow steelmen. After the strike the union withered until the great industrial union movement fifteen years later.

However, the corporation heads of the steel industry and other mass production industries were by no means unified on the question of collective bargaining. The older production men heading the large corporations were haunted by memories of the great homestead steel strike of 1894, the national strikes in mining and in railroads at the turn of the century, and the development of the Socialist party into an important force in American politics. They were in genuine fear that a unionized workforce would lead to radical social change.

The kernel of their objections to unionization was not that unions would elect more representatives to public office or even that they would provide organized pressure for wage increases and more social benefits. Gary himself was one of the leading proponents of corporation sponsored "welfare capitalism," a phrase denoting the recognition by the corporations of their obligation to make provisions for the nonwage needs of the workers. The near monopoly position of the giant industries in the American economy was already making them more receptive to economic demands.

The old robber barons who headed the major corporations were afraid that unions would intrude on the prerogatives of management to run their business. The unions represented a threat to the control by the corporations of production and the direction of the labor forces. This is not to say that employers would hesitate to cut wages or lay off workers during periods of economic crisis, or that they would gladly accede to the wage demands of workers without the intervention of unions. On the contrary. The history of American labor is a constant battle against efforts of employers to make workers pay for crises by taking cuts in direct wages or by indirect wage decreases in the form of higher prices.

But a newer group of corporation directors had made their appearance about 1910. They were not cut out of the mold of the self-made man or the production manager. They were sales experts and financial wizards. Charles Schwab, Gary's successor, was a professional fund raiser and organizer who reorganized several faltering corporations prior to his assumption of the position of chief executive officer of U.S. Steel. Gerard Swope, the head of General Electric, also did not function as a production manager.

These men were interested in lower production costs and

uninterrupted production. They were keenly aware of the costs of the long steel strike to industry. As early as 1915, Swope was prepared to entertain the possibility of dealing with labor organizations. He even went so far as to suggest to Sam Gompers, the president of the AFL, that GE could be organized. Swope, undoubtedly influenced by the mass strikes in the garment trades, mining, and textiles during the previous five years, was looking for ways to stabilize labor relations—to make labor a known cost factor as well as delimit the influence of unions to make claims on the pace of work and the direction of the workforces. In the same year, a member of the Employers Association of the Chicago Men's Clothing Industry praised the leader of the Amalgamated Clothing Workers Union, Sidney Hillman, who later would become a major force in the CIO. "We regard Sidney Hillman very highly," he said. "We believe him honest, high minded and capable. . . . With Hillman dead or dethroned we would be in the hands of the old grafting pirates who would not enforce an agreement, who would foment shop strikes . . ."[2]

To be sure, most corporation leaders did not look to the AFL as the solution to the labor problem, even though Gompers had become a junior crony in the National Civic Federation—an early attempt to find a meeting ground between labor, management, and the public in the interest of advancing American capitalism. Instead, the main direction of their efforts was to establish employee representation plans. During the First World War, hundreds of company unions were ordered formed by government edict. In many cases, including the steel and packing industries, the union militants succeeded in taking over these organizations and the companies were forced into primitive collective bargaining under pressure of the government's resolve to insure continuous production of war materiel.

Despite the reluctance of some sectors of industry (notably, the recalcitrant Judge Gary), the "works councils" or employee associations strengthened the belief of many corporate liberals that collective bargaining provided the best hope to control the

[2] Matthew Josephson, *Sidney Hillman: Statesman of American Labor,* New York, Doubleday & Co., 1952, pp. 124–5.

labor force and dissipate the more radical elements in the unions.

On the other hand, in labor's ranks the idea of collective bargaining itself was not a universally accepted strategic goal of labor struggle. Most AFL leaders, Socialist and non-Socialist, accepted the notion that unions were necessary means to improve wages and working conditions. But these demands were by definition reformist, since they attempted to wrest concessions from employers without fundamentally changing power within the factory or in society. For the craft-minded AFL, the ability to win depended on the skill of the workers as much as on their degree of organization or their economic conditions. Whenever unskilled or semiskilled workers had flocked to the unions, as in the garment or mining industries, it was explained as an aberration. The AFL leaders held that the skilled craftsmen in these industries, such as cutters or weighers, were the soul of the struggle. Without their support, union organization was out of the question. By themselves, unskilled workers could not carry through a successful battle, even if they could be organized—a doubtful prospect in any case.

Around the turn of the century, revolutionary syndicalism had begun to take root in America. Long regarded as a doctrine whose origins were to be found among workers in underindustrialized countries such as Spain and Italy, the spread of syndicalist ideas was remarkable for its popularity among native-born American miners as well as Italian shoe and textile workers and Jewish garment workers. Unlike the socialists who believed that the struggle for liberation from capitalist oppression must be preceded by a prolonged period of reformist struggles, especially through collective bargaining and peaceful parliamentary activity, the syndicalists advocated the formation of revolutionary unions whose object was to capture power in the factories, smash the state as it attempted to protect property, and establish a society controlled directly by the producers.

Between 1905, the year of the formation of the Industrial Workers of the World (IWW), and the Depression of the 1930s, the syndicalist spirit continued to be an influence among American workers, even when the fortunes of the IWW were low. The

IWW never succeeded in generating a national strike. Its most dramatic activities were confined to individual strikes in mass production industries. But it showed that unskilled workers were capable of sustaining long strikes and were potentially, at least, a force to be reckoned with by both employers and reformist-minded unions.

The IWW abhorred collective bargaining. They believed that the uprising of a group of workers within a particular industry was produced by their grievances and could only end when the grievances were removed. The employers could restore a wage cut, slow the pace of work, or grant other concessions to the workers. The workers should decide whether to return to work or spread the struggle to other industries. The IWW hoped for the general strike which would bring down the system of industrial slavery and capitalist governments. In any case, they refused to sign contracts guaranteeing labor pace. If the workers returned to their jobs, they reserved their right to strike at any time.

Labor history is usually written as if the IWW and the AFL were antagonists vying for the support of the rank and file. The IWW was more of a movement than an organization. Its bureaucracy was fairly loose, its organizers undisciplined. In many industries such as the garment trades, IWW sympathizers belonged to the established union but agitated consistently for no compromises with employers, for the general strike, and for flash strikes against grievances.

Sidney Hillman of the Amalgamated Clothing Workers of America and the leaders of the International Ladies Garment Workers Union ruthlessly opposed the efforts of anarchists and syndicalists within their unions. The Amalgamated was particularly hostile to the idea of revolutionary unionism. By 1914 the Amalgamated had embarked on a course from which it was never to depart. It proclaimed the era of permanent labor management cooperation in the men's clothing industry as a result of its victory in the Hart Schaffner and Marx strike the same year. Industry boards regulating piecework rates, establishing welfare programs, and consulting on industrial conditions were established on a bipartite basis.

The union remained militant with respect to the unorganized

sector of the industry, however. Indeed, the subsequent twenty
years were marked by strikes and energetic organizing campaigns to consolidate union power in the industry. But the
socialist leaders of the union were clear about the separation of
politics from economics. Socialism was a doctrine to be
preached in the union publications and in educational programs.
But it had no place around the bargaining table. Although the
socialists who were active in unions disagreed with Gompers on
many ideological issues, including the necessity for unions to get
involved in politics (the ACWA supported Socialist candidates
until 1936), their disagreements with the AFL president on
trade union matters were limited to tactics. The Amalgamated
was not a crude union in business matters as many AFL craft
unions were. It had become a sophisticated purveyor of business
interests as the best insurance of its own members' welfare.

It is interesting to compare the role of Gompers during the
First World War with that of Hillman during the Second. Each
became the labor spokesman within the government as well as
the government spokesman within labor's ranks. The presumed
antagonism between industrial unionists and Socialists within
the AFL and the business-minded leadership of Sam Gompers
and his successors revolved around methods and not goals. The
AFL sponsored the steel strike of 1919 and gave it direction. Its
goals were fully consistent with AFL philosophy. The fact that
the strike was lost may have been a function of the incompe-
tence and venality of the old type craft organizations who spent
more energy jockeying for jurisdictional positions than working
to win the strike. But its object, collective bargaining for unskilled as well as skilled workers, prefigured essentially the
program of the CIO.

The employers may have discussed the ideology of labor
peace, but it was not until the 1930s that they were willing to
listen carefully. The 1920s witnessed the near destruction of the
most powerful of industrial and craft unions and the end of the
growth of unionism in some basic industries such as steel and
packing where beachheads had been established during the war.
The ten-year period following World War I was a return to the
prewar conditions of wage cuts, arbitrary firing of working class
militants, and attempts by conservative trade union leaders to

make bargains with employers in order to insure the survival of the union and their own leadership within it. The prosperity of the 1920s had its reflection in rising wages, but it cannot be said that the trade union was instrumental in determining the wage level.

After the 1929 crash, most of the corporation leaders and their government allies were in confusion and disarray. Big business had no program to deal with the economic and social crisis beyond measures to transfer the burdens of shrinking employment, profits and production to the workers, farmers, small businessmen, and other countries. Only a minority of those with power sought to prepare a broader program for economic revival.

The remnants of the AFL leadership were caught in the interstices of the big business offensive and their own desire for institutional survival. They held tenaciously to a keyhole vision of the crisis. With their organizations reduced in numbers and their political influence at a low ebb, the stolid guardians of the "House of Labor" whined their litany of complaint but firmly rejected mass struggle. Only the ex-socialist Sidney Hillman of the ACWA and the United Mine Workers president, John L. Lewis, leaders of the two most important industrial-type unions in the Federation, were able to take advantage of the deep resentment of the workers.

The Amalgamated, the International Ladies Garment Workers Union, and the Miners were able to recover somewhat from the dismal union decline of the 1920s and to organize thousands of new members. But most craft unions shrank to skeletal size as building construction ground to a near-halt, industrial production declined nearly fifty percent, and millions of skilled workers joined the ranks of the unemployed.

John L. Lewis and Sidney Hillman were old AFL men. Both believed in the strike as an ultimate weapon to force employers to deal with unions over the bargaining table. Both opposed the radicals within their ranks until the radicals came over to their way of thinking. When the radicals proved loyal to trade union objectives, they were permitted to join the effort to organize workers in mass production industries into the CIO. In some cases, they were even permitted to lead unions, provided they represented no sharp departures in *practice* from the policies of the central organization. Autonomy was permitted to international unions on all matters not specifically covered by CIO policy. When left-wingers veered on questions of foreign policy during the organizing upsurge, they were slapped on the wrist but not opposed outright. Later, after the upsurge was spent, the Left was unceremoniously removed.

In the 1930s, shorn of their genuine radical wing, the trade unions moved rapidly to cement their alliance with both employers and the government. The union drive against General Motors was militant because the company, still ensconced in the old ways, refused to recognize the union. A week after the sitdown strike at GM resulted in union recognition, Schwab of U.S. Steel concluded an agreement with John L. Lewis recognizing the Steel Workers Organizing Committee as bargaining agent for its employees. Between 1933 and 1937 the bulk of the workers in basic industries were organized by the CIO or its rival AFL.

Popular explanations for the rapid victory of industrial unionism rely heavily on the economic crisis. But this explanation is not good enough. The wave of union organization actually occurred during an economic upswing, not in the depth of the crisis. Between 1929, when there were two important textile strikes in the South, and 1933, the year of the mass strike among miners and the general strike in the garment trades, both union organization and strike struggles were at their ebb.

Beginning in 1933, the companies started to hire again. Most of the new workforce was made up of young men who had had steady employment throughout the thirties. The hardest hit section of the workforce were the older workers, recently displaced agricultural workers and minority group workers. The resentment of the young workers was connected to their refusal to shoulder the heavy burdens of exploitation. The injustice of the situation was evident to those who continued to be employed, even though it was only by selling their labor at low prices and enduring speedup, stretchout, and other measures designed to increase profits.

Strikes in the mid-thirties occurred as much because of

speedup and the authoritarianism of management as they did because of declines in real wages either due to wage cuts or price increases engendered by the government's policies of providing investment incentives. Between 1933 and 1935 general strikes broke out in the mines, the garment industry, textiles, and, in San Francisco and Minneapolis the entire cities were paralyzed by general strikes arising from walkouts of workers in important transportation industries. Flash strikes broke out in auto, steel, electrical, and rubber plants, but these were local struggles and failed to encompass the whole industry until several years later. The outbreak of mass strikes corresponded to the economic upturn of the 1933–6 period. In this recovery period, corporations and smaller employers felt particularly bold both because of the persistence of large-scale unemployment in the midst of the upturn and because of the protection afforded by the government's policy of assuring business high rates of profit through artificially stimulated prices.

The general strike in San Francisco, the Minneapolis teamster strike, and the national textile strike of more than 250,000 workers, took place in 1934, a year before the passage of the Wagner Act. The organization of these struggles occurred mainly outside the framework of the AFL or other branches of organized labor. They were led by young workers, some of whom were Communists. And the strikes took place in part as a revolt against the conservative policies of the AFL unions who held formal jurisdiction in these industries. Although the unions —both the AFL and the short-lived Communist variety— sought to thwart or channel these struggles, they were not the "organizers" of them. Organization always takes place from the inside. Outside organizers are, at best, catalysts; at worst, they channel the struggle into bureaucratic paths. In most of the labor struggles of the thirties, the militants were defeated in the end. Suffused with uncompromising spirit, if not syndicalist ideology, they opposed settlements, refused to sign no-strike agreements, and became oppositionists even in the so-called left-wing unions.

If the necessary condition for the success of industrial unionism of the thirties was the revolt of young workers, it did not prove sufficient to determine the character of the labor movement or labor relations. The sufficient condition to explain the development of United States trade unionism was that the historical tendency both within employer and trade union ranks to formalize and regulate labor relations found its soil in the development of state capitalist forms during the New Deal period.

The condition for economic expansion of modern capitalism is the close integration of the state and the corporations. But the same policies responsible for attempting to synchronize the activities of the government and of private corporations to guarantee recovery and sustain economic growth were responsible for developing the means to make labor a stable factor of production, that is, to predict its price with a degree of accuracy sufficient to undertake corporate and state planning. When corporate and government leaders understood the critical importance of coordinating their efforts to prevent disaster in the economic crisis of the early 1930s, they immediately recognized the importance of bringing unions into partnership. For, if workers were to continue to struggle around their needs without regulation, the whole enterprise of state capitalist planning could be disrupted. From the point of view of the national economic and political leadership, the economic crisis was an emergency akin to war. The first New Deal measures after the ascent to power by the corporatists (whose national coordinator was Roosevelt) were not addressed to problems of hunger or disease. Rather, Congress was asked to delegate to the executive powers to restore the banks, stimulate investment, regulate wages, and increase prices. The National Recovery Act was the agency charged with the task of dealing with trade, of which labor relations were regarded as a dependent variable.

The first attempts at government regulation of labor relations were somewhat crude. Unions represented on the industry boards responsible for setting wages and prices were too weak to influence the decisions of these bodies except in the scattered instances, as in the clothing industry, where they had managed to preserve some of their pre-Depression strength. For the most part, union leaders cooperated with the Roosevelt program of massive state intervention to save the tottering social and economic system, hoping for some crumbs from the corporate table. But the significance of their agreements was limited by their weakness. The price of cooperation, Section 7A of the National Recovery Act which guaranteed the right of workers to join unions of their own choosing, was neither legally enforced by the government nor capable of practical implementation by the unions whose financial resources remained meager and whose moral stature among workers had been damaged by the degrading company unionism of the 1920s. In a few instances, the NRA provisions assisted viable labor organizations to recruit new members. In the main, the workers remained outside the traditional trade unions during the early years of the New Deal.

But the failure of the unions to win the support of workers in mass production and transportation industries did not mean that workers remained passive. It was no easy task to impose a partnership on the rank and file even if the discredited labor leadership was eager to be absorbed in the emerging state capitalist Roosevelt coalition. In the first two years of the New Deal, prior to the enactment of the Wagner Labor Relations Act (which was the first serious attempt to bring the class struggle under the aegis of government regulation), unprecedented mass strikes occurred in many important industries. In most cases the strikes had a spontaneous quality in their immediate causes, although they were preceded by considerable agitation, partial walkouts, and organizational activity conducted by radicals and labor organizers. Where unions captured leadership of these strikes and were able to direct them into acceptable collective bargaining channels, this was accomplished after the strikes had already begun.

The Communist party and other left-wing groups—except the Socialist party—viewed the early New Deal with open hostility. In the radical view, the New Deal was created to achieve economic, social and political stability for the continued domination of the country by the giant corporations, not for the interests of workers, black people, and farmers. The Left denounced the NRA as an attack on workers' living standards. They described Section 7A as a chimera designed to lull the working class into false security.

Historically, there had been disagreements on the Left over

the application of the rule of law to trade unionism. The traditional IWW position, shared by many other radicals, was that workers should not seek union contracts, since they limit or prohibit the right to strike and narrow the possibility of militant struggle against onerous working conditions. The Communist party, which dominated most of the radical movement after 1931, never took a clearcut position on these questions of trade union practice. In 1936 the Wagner Act established government machinery for regulating trade unions to assure their subordination to the capitalist state. While the Communist party supported the Wagner Act and other state capitalist measures affecting workers, it did so without explaining or justifying its position.

In the period from the onset of the Depression in 1929 to 1935, the Communist party labor policy in this country had pursued two paths. The main thrust was to form independent, dual unions. But it also urged its members to "penetrate the fascist mass organizations like the AFL."[3] In cases where the leadership of established AFL unions was both powerful and so repressive that militants were barred from effective functioning, such as in the United Mine Workers, the Communist party formed dual "revolutionary unions." At times, as in the case of the auto industry, party militants were no weaker than their AFL counterparts. In these instances, the party leadership was often forced to bend the wishes of its own rank and file to countenance the formation of independent unions. In industries such as the electrical or maritime industry, where there was barely the shell of an AFL affiliate, the Communist party helped form independent unions, sometimes under its own domination but sometimes in coalition with other independents.

Prior to 1935, the party wielded its two tactics in a flexible manner. Many of its leading trade union cadre were AFL stalwarts, especially those in the building trades. Even though the party policy was officially inclined toward dual unionism for much of the 1929–35 period, it permitted deviations from this line when the realities of the situation did not permit dual organization.

[3] Earl Browder, Speech at Extraordinary Conference, July 1933, Communist Party of the United States in *The Communist*, Summer 1933.

During the early days of the New Deal industrial unionism was seen by the AFL as a radical product. Most effective unionism during the period prior to the enactment of the Wagner Act took place outside the AFL. John L. Lewis and Sidney Hillman recognized that the New Deal, combined with the persistence of the economic crisis, presented a new opportunity for the rise of union organization among unskilled and semiskilled workers. They were acutely aware of unrest among these workers and vainly attempted to convince Gompers' successors of the necessity of establishing leadership over the new industrial union movement.

Both men were close to the Roosevelt administration and did not hesitate to use the prestige of the administration to assist recruiting drives within their own industrial jurisdictions. Hillman saw a rejuvenated labor movement as an important ally to Roosevelt's coalition. The evidence of his activity points to the distinctly political character of the Amalgamated's interest in helping to form a committee for industrial organization within the AFL.

It was plain to Lewis and Hillman that unless the AFL acted decisively to control the developing mass upsurge among industrial workers, the Left could pose a serious threat to conservative and liberal leaders of the unions and upset the emerging Roosevelt coalition. An ardent supporter of NRA Section 7A, Lewis was convinced that workers would never join unions as long as they appeared to be radical and subversive. But, according to Saul Alinsky, Lewis's best biographer, the miners' president "could read the revolutionary handwriting on the walls of American industry" in the 1934 strikes. After several years of futile appeals, Lewis finally convinced the AFL to set up the committee on industrial organization to thwart the threat from the Left, and insure that workers would be firmly ensconced within the AFL House of Labor.

The year 1935, however, brought a sharp reversal in Communist party policies. Instead of attempting to form independent, dual unions under their own leadership, the Communists were now committed to collaborate with the Socialists and trade union leaders within the mainstream of political and trade union organizations. The Seventh World Congress of the Communist International of 1935 heard its General Secretary, George

Dimitrov, proclaim the end of the period when Communists would attack Socialists and the bourgeoisie with merciless equanimity. Now the crucial task of the working class was to oppose fascism. The defense of liberal capitalism and civil liberties was the basic precondition of revolutionary action in the future. The Communist policy of branding Socialist and liberal forces as "social fascists" had backfired severely in Germany and Italy. Now fascism threatened to overthrow the Spanish Republic, was establishing its rule in France, and was even bidding for power in the United States. According to the new policy of the world Communist movement, the time had come to put aside sectarianism and join forces with all democratic organizations to prevent Hitler's bid for world domination. The Soviet regime made proposals at the League of Nations for collective security against Hitler. The new policy meant that the Communists were no longer to be found in the opposition to the liberal state and the social democratic labor leaders.

Within the United States, Communists were obliged to abandon their virulent attacks on the Roosevelt administration and on the liberal wing of the AFL. The Trade Union Unity League, the Communist party instrument in the labor movement, dissolved, and militants were urged to merge with AFL unions in their industry. In many basic industries, the CP and TUUL organizations were transformed into nuclei for the CIO organizing drive. In his report to the 1936 convention of the party, Communist party general secretary Earl Browder declared:

> The Committee for Industrial Organization has taken up the task of organizing all mass production industries in America in industrial unions. The success of this effort is a basic necessity upon which depends the future of the American labor movement in all other respects. The CP unconditionally pledges its full resources, moral and material, to the complete execution of this great project.[4]

The Communist party remained somewhat critical of Roosevelt, but supported his reelection in 1936. They also supported the state capitalist measures of his administration, including the

[4] Earl Browder, *The People's Front,* New York, International Publishers, 1938, p. 40.

National Labor Relations Act, which simultaneously widened government intervention into the collective bargaining process and protected the right of workers to join unions. The party and most radicals never perceived the dangers inherent in greater government regulation of labor relations. They were dedicated and tireless organizers within the "center-Left" coalitions led by Lewis.

In 1935–6 Communist party trade unionists in New York, Michigan, Wisconsin, and elsewhere worked for the formation of local labor parties, patterning themselves after the Minnesota Farmer-Labor Party which had succeeded in electing its candidate, Floyd Olson, governor in 1934. The strategy underlying Communist party support of the Farmer-Labor Party movement was twofold: on the one hand, it would provide a mass basis for the defeat of the ultra-Right in American politics and mitigate its influence over liberal capitalists such as Roosevelt. On the other hand, it would represent the political expression of the developing trade union and farmers movement, providing at the same time a wider political base for Communist influence. The Communist party also attempted to influence the leaders of the newly emerging CIO, which was then regarded as the main force for worker organization.

Although Communist party leadership urged its rank and file to build the party as the mass party of the American working class, these appeals were subordinated to the main task of building "the people's front against fascism" and its core organization, the CIO. In effect, the party became a pressure group on the Democratic party and the CIO. The Farmer-Labor parties, particularly the American Labor Party in New York state, which represented the political center-Left coalition within labor's ranks, were little more than another line on the voting machine to harness labor's support for the Democrats. In the tradition of the British Labour Party, it had a dual structure. On the top were the leaders of the key industrial unions, particularly of the garment trades and transport workers. In the neighborhoods, the left-wing activists, members of the Communist party or its periphery, performed social services for constituents, organized rent strikes, consumer protests, and election campaigns.

After 1937, the modest criticisms of Roosevelt and the CIO

leaders still evident at the 8th Communist Party Convention during the previous year all but disappeared. In the July 1937 issue of *The Communist,* the party's chief theoretical organ, its editor, Alexander Bittleman, vehemently defended both Roosevelt and Lewis. Against the charge that Lewis had become a "labor dictator with great power," Bittleman replied, "The crime of the CIO is not that it is a dictatorship but on the contrary that it is a progressive labor movement seeking to build itself up on the basis of inner union democracy as well as a force for democracy in the country."[5] He went on to say, "The CIO is already one of the chief fortresses of democracy, its brightest home and promise of realization. That is the message Communists must spread widely among the masses."[6]

The defense of Roosevelt was made against those who criticized his court proposals and the Chicago massacre of steel workers. In the same issue of *The Communist* Bittleman dismissed these charges on the ground that the steel barons were responsible for the massacre, not the administration. The court issue was part of the "unfolding of the central struggle of the day between reaction and progress on both the economic and political fields."[7]

By 1939 Communists had become entrenched in the top echelons of several important CIO and, to a lesser extent, AFL organizations. At one point it was estimated that a third of the CIO membership belonged to unions euphemistically called "left wing." In practice, they were progressive, close to or in the Communist party. The unions included electrical workers, auto workers, West Coast longshoremen, maritime workers, transport workers, metal miners, packinghouse workers, furniture workers, distributive and department store workers, fur workers, white-collar and public workers.

Among AFL unions, Communists did not play leadership roles on national levels, but were important in local and district organizations of painters, carpenters, hotel and restaurant

---

[5] Alexander Bittleman, Review of the Month in *The Communist,* July 1937, p. 583.

[6] Ibid., p. 584.

[7] Ibid., p. 585.

workers, railroad brotherhoods and some others. In a remarkable article written for *The Communist* in November 1939, William Foster, the secretary of the AFL committee directing the 1919 steel strike and now a leading American Communist, wrote a retrospect on Communist party trade union policy. The article represents the perspective of a man who had renounced dual unionism more than twenty-five years earlier. The two key points of the article are that Communists must now work for AFL-CIO unity, basing themselves on the tactic of pressuring the decent elements in both the federation and the government, and that the party should no longer maintain factions within the CIO. On the first point, Foster wrote:

> Roosevelt in his unity efforts reflects the desires of the great majority of New Dealers. Lewis speaks for the solid unity sentiment of the entire CIO. . . . Tobin expresses the unity [sic] will of a big majority of AFL members, and Whitney undoubtedly does the same for the bulk of railroad unionists.[8]

And on the second, he stated:

> The organizational forms of Communist trade union work have changed radically to correspond to the present period [of center-Left unity]. Party members do not now participate in groupings or other organized activities within the unions. The party also discountenances the formation of progressive groups, blocs, and caucuses in unions; it has liquidated its Communist factions, discontinued its shop papers and is now modifying its system of industrial branches. Communists are policy making and administrating on an unknown scale . . . building the highest type of trade union leadership based on efficient service and democratic responsibility to the rank and file.[9]

Not only did the Communist party abandon "dual unionism" and subordinate its organizing thrust to the CIO under Lewis, it abandoned its own political identity. Important trade union

[8] William Z. Foster, "Twenty Years of Communist Trade Union Policy," in *The Communist,* November 1939.
[9] Ibid.

cadre became trade union bureaucrats for whom an independent rank and file was anathema.

Communist trade unionists became indistinguishable from their liberal colleagues during World War II. Left-wing leaders of the new mass industrial unions in auto, electrical, and other basic industries put the objective of winning the war ahead of the workers' interests and voluntarily gave up the right to strike. Communists joined their liberal allies and urged workers to abandon their traditional hostility to piecework schemes and incentive pay. In some industries where company efforts to introduce these methods of speedup had been the catalyst for union organization—in the packing, steel, and electrical industries, for example—day work systems gave way to incentive pay geared to productivity or even to outright piecework. In the auto industry, the assembly line was simply speeded up, while workers were asked to maintain their no-strike pledge and wage freeze.

Wildcat strikes were frequent in the auto industry, shipbuilding, and other areas of mass production. In many cases, the deep resentment of the workers was corralled by opportunist leaders like Walter Reuther, who used the occasion to attack the "center-Left coalition" which led the UAW. After the war, Reuther easily defeated the Thomas-Addes leadership of the union which was supported by the Communist party.

When the U.S.S.R.-United States alliance was erased by the Cold War, the combination of rank-and-file resentment against "red company unionism," open red-baiting and repression by the corporations and the government, and the sectarian policies of the Communists themselves sealed the isolation of the Left from the mass of industrial workers. Some radicals in the unions survived the Cold War. They were trade unionists who functioned as open Socialists, who vigorously fought with workers against the deterioration of working conditions, and who refused to become part of the trade union bureaucracy. They included members of all radical tendencies. Their distinguishing feature was not their political affiliation; it was their radical sensibility.

Following a period of rhetorical militancy, the articulate former Socialist Walter Reuther engineered a five-year contract with the auto industry in 1950. The contract signaled the end of an era in industrial unionism. Saddled with a no-strike provision which permitted the company to speed up the assembly line without effective counteraction within the framework of collective bargaining, the rank and file was forced to act outside the union structure. The wildcat movement in the auto industry during 1953–5 embraced all major companies and sections of the country. Thousands of workers participated in flash walkouts as the companies tried to increase production from 48 to 50 cars per hour to more than 60 cars an hour. Often the walkouts were initiated by the body shop workers, who do the heaviest and dirtiest jobs in the plant, or by the workers in wet sanding departments, most of whom were black.

The extent and frequency of the walkouts forced the union to restore the right to strike in the next contract and to cut down the contract duration. But strikes were permitted only when management changed the pace of work or for safety reasons. Even then, workers were not permitted to walk out at the point of the change. They were obliged to select the strike weapon after enduring a long period of aggrievement through the procedure established by the contract. In one stroke, Reuther bowed to the realities of the situation and tried to cool workers' militancy by placing strings on the strike weapon.

In 1955 the UAW and other industrial unions became concerned with the problem of automation and other forms of major technological change. During the year, it sponsored a large conference on the shorter work week to coincide with the opening of negotiations of a new contract. The result of the UAW demand for a shorter work week to counteract anticipated joblessness among its members was the agreement with companies to provide supplementary unemployment benefits to laid-off workers. Shortly thereafter, the steel industry followed suit and the shorter work week was dead.

Although the wildcat strikes of the early 1950s were smashed, the challenge to the unions did not abate. The next phase of the rank-and-file attempt to capture control over their own conditions was the mushrooming of rank-and-file movements to replace the old leadership. After a 166-day steel strike to protect basic work rule rights in 1959, steel workers witnessed the deterioration of their job conditions and relative wage rates. Beginning in the late fifties and early sixties, there was a parade of electoral challenges to the leaders of many key industrial unions. Although most of the pretenders to the thrones were middle-rank leaders, they rode to power on the strength of membership discontent. Such contests took place in the Steelworkers Union, in the Rubber Workers, Textile Workers, Oil and Chemical Workers, Teachers, State County and Municipal Workers, the Electrical Workers, and in many locals of the Auto Workers where each collective bargaining defeat was followed by the defeat of a raft of local union incumbents.

Another manifestation of the emergence of rank-and-file discontent in the sixties was the rise of the Teamsters Union as a major challenger to traditional union jurisdictions. The apparent militancy of this "outlawed" union meshed neatly with rank and file disgust with the softness of the now middle-aged CIO labor statesmen. The merger of the AFL and the CIO had prevented workers from seeking alternative representation when their unions revealed company union practices. The expulsion of the Teamsters from the House of Labor in 1957 provided disgruntled workers with a powerful alternative to the old labor unions.

But by the late sixties the initial enthusiasm of the workers for competitive unionism and internal union reform had ebbed. Real wages declined each year since 1967 and, after a period of economic growth due to the Vietnam War, the economy began to slow down. The first effects of the slowdown were reflected in rising layoffs and the elimination of overtime which took the gloss from pay envelopes. But the slowdown in production and employment did not have its concomitance in the movement of prices, which kept rising.

The last two years of the sixties and the opening of the 1970s were marked by the reawakening of rank-and-file militancy. This militancy took different forms in different sectors of the workforce. Among public workers and workers in voluntary institutions such as hospitals, a wave of union organizing and strike movements took place. This wave was led by teachers and hospital workers. The impact of public employee organizing was peculiar because every strike of this group of workers is, perforce, a strike against the state. In many places, the pent-up frustration of these workers who had borne the worst effects of the inflation and the fiscal crisis of the public sector caused widespread disrespect for laws prohibiting strikes of public employees and court injunctions aimed at enforcing the law. In many cities, particularly on the Eastern seaboard, the leaders riding the crest of the wave of militancy became important political figures and were ultimately absorbed by the municipal governments as warm allies and important sources of political power. Although the fiscal crisis afflicting all public organs prevents a secure alliance of the workers with government authority, the unions do represent a newly discovered power of the membership.

Another manifestation of this militancy has been the reappearance of the wildcat strike. The wildcat strike of postal workers in 1970 took place over the heads of the union leadership and became a national strike without central coordination or direction. The strike was preceded by the twenty-year efforts of the national postal union leadership to operate within approved legislative channels through lobbying methods and political pressure on the administrative directorate. Even more dramatic than the postal rebellion was the extraordinary wildcat strike by 100,000 teamsters in the Midwest and on the West Coast in rejection of the contract negotiated by their national leaders. The vaunted authority of the union over the membership, its reputation for militancy and toughness at the bargaining table, its myth of invincibility, collapsed beneath the insurgent rank and file which acted independent of the bureaucracy for the first time.

The Present State of Unions and the Future of Workers

The bureaucratization of the trade unions; their integrative role within production; their conservative political ideology; and their dependence on the Democratic party are not primarily the result of the consciousness of the leading actors in the rise of industrial unionism. To the extent that the Left participated in redefining the trade unions as part of the corporate system, it must now undertake merciless critique of its own role before a new working class strategy can be developed.

It is not enough to admit bureaucratic tendencies in the unions or in their Left leadership, however. The strategy flowing from this focus is to reform the unions from within in order to perfect their fighting ability and rank-and-file class conscious-ness. This line of thinking categorically denies that the unions are mainly dependent variables within the political economy.

One of the important concepts of Marxist orthodoxy is that economic crisis is an inevitable feature of capitalist develop-ment, and that the tendency of employers will be to reduce and attack the power of trade unions during periods of declining production. The government-employer attempts to circumscribe workers' power by restricting trade union functions will produce rank-and-file pressure confronting the leadership with the choice of struggle against capital or their own displacement. Thus the unions become objectively revolutionary despite their conserva-tive leadership.

However, strategies for rank-and-file reform ignore the bu-reaucracy and conservatism inherent in the present union struc-ture and function, as well as the role of the unions in the division of labor. The growth of bureaucracy and the decline of rank-and-file initiative is built into the theory and practice of collective bargaining.

During periods of crisis or stagnation the union bureaucracy seeks an accommodation with management on the basis of sectoral interests of its immediate constituency. This practice can be observed in the settlement of the 1969 GE strike, where the unions agreed to a long-term contract which partially pro-tected workers from inflationary pressures, but made no sub-stantive advances. But the forty-month contract provision of the agreement is a sign that the leadership was prepared to settle for consolidating its gains in the wake of the recession in the economy. Long-term agreements have been viewed traditionally as a management demand to stabilize production and labor costs. Militant unionism has always fought for one-year con-tracts based on its view of contracts per se as a limitation on workers' power to deal effectively with problems on the job.

GE workers were forced to strike against inflation and the

attempt of the company to make gains against wages and working conditions. The attack was repulsed. But the struggle is not won to prevent the company from making up for wage increases by other devices. In this area, top leadership of the unions permitted the company to raise prices and increase productivity without protest and resistance. Local struggles to deal with the problems of women workers, production norms, and new machinery were fragmented. All unions, except IUE, agreed to drop their demands for an end to discriminatory wages for women and Southern workers. The IUE, the largest union in the coalition, provides for contract ratification by its top committees. This means the rank and file had no genuine voice in accepting or rejecting the settlement except through elected representatives.

The strategy of trade union reform also ignores the fact that the last thirty-five years of industrial unionism has failed to effect any substantive change in the distribution of income. Trade unionism under conditions of partial unionization of the labor force cannot do more than redistribute income within the working class. Workers in heavily organized industries such as auto, rubber, and steel have relatively high wages compared to workers in consumer goods industries such as garments and shoes (which have migrated to the South), retail and wholesale workers, and most categories of government and agricultural workers.

The high wages of certain categories of industrial workers depend as much on the high proportion of capital to living labor and the monopoly character of basic industries as they do on trade union struggle. The tendency for employers in heavy industry to give in on union wage demands presupposes their ability to raise prices and productivity. In competitive industries such as light manufacturing, the unions have been transformed into stabilizers of industrial conflict in order to permit high rates of profits where no technological changes can be introduced. The result has been low wages for large numbers of blacks, Puerto Ricans, and poor whites locked into these jobs.

The self-protective orientation of trade unionism conceived as demands based on industry or occupation is partially responsible for racism. Racist ideology is not rooted in the "privileges" of white workers. On the contrary, it is based upon their economic and social insecurity and their industrial and trade union consciousness. High wages are not the same as white skin privileges because the latter are determined by the historical level of culture. Nor have the relative wage and occupational advantages of whites meant an end to their exploitation.

Since advanced capitalism requires consumerism both as ideology and as practice to preserve commodity production, its payment of high wages to large segments of the working class, and minimum income to those excluded from the labor markets, is not objectively in the workers' interest. It is a means to take care of the market or demand side of production.

The ability of workers to purchase a relatively large quantity of consumer goods is dependent on the forces of production, which include the scale and complexity of technology and the productivity and skill of the labor force. Technological development, in turn, is dependent on the availability of raw materials and the degree of scientific and technical knowledge in society.

The most important issue to be addressed in defining the tasks ahead is not the question of inflation, wages, or general economic conditions. No matter how inequitable the distribution of income, no matter how deep the crisis, these conditions will never, by themselves, be the soil for revolutionary consciousness.

Revolutionary consciousness arises out of the conditions of alienated labor, which include economic conditions but is not limited to them. Its starting point is in the production process. It is at the point of mental and manual production, where the world of commodities is produced, that the worker experiences his exploitation. Consumption of waste production, trade union objectives in the direction of enlarging wages and social benefits, and the division of labor into industries and sections are all mediations which stand between the workers' existential exploitation at the workplace and their ability to comprehend alienated labor as class exploitation.

Radicals have tended to address the problem of consciousness from the wrong end. We assume that racism, trade unionism, or conservatism will either be dissolved by discussion and exhortation alone, or that "objective" conditions will force new understandings among workers. The notion that ideologies can be changed through ideological means or that capitalistic contradictions will change consciousness with an assist from ideologically correct lines or education is a nonrevolutionary position: in both cases, the role of practice is ignored. Nor will workers' struggles against economic hardship necessarily raise political consciousness.

In this connection one must reevaluate the rise of industrial unionism in the 1930s. Many radicals and labor historians have interpreted the failure of the CIO to emerge as an important force for social change as a function of the misleadership of its officials and the opportunism of the Communist party and other radical parties who participated in its formation. According to a recent work on the development of the CIO by Art Preis, a contemporary labor reporter writing from a Trotskyist position, the 1930s were a prerevolutionary period. Preis writes: "The first stage of awakening class consciousness was achieved, in fact, with the rise and consolidation of the CIO. The second stage will be marked by a further giant step, the formation of a new class party based on the unions."[10]

No important left-wing critique exists of unionism. Unions are, for most orthodox Marxists, the preliminary step workers must take on the way to achieving political class consciousness. That is, the recognition by a decisive section of the working class that the solutions to its immediate problems as well as long run ills resides in its assumption of power over the whole society and the transformation of all social relations. Marxists assume that the bonds of solidarity forged in the course of trade union struggles can, with the proper ideological leadership within the working class and the proper systemic crisis, produce political consciousness.

Evaluations of the 1930s, therefore, find the economic crisis a necessary condition for the development of class consciousness, but blame the Communist and Socialist policies for the failure of a significant radical force among the mass of workers.

I would dispute this theory since there is no genuine evidence

[10] Art Preis, *Labor's Giant Step,* New York, Pioneer Publishers, 1964, p. xvi.

that the CIO could ever have become an organized expression of a new class politics in America, or that trade unionism in the era of state capitalism and imperialism can be other than a force for integrating workers. After the disappearance of the IWW from the labor scene, there was no significant force within the working class offering a radical alternative. The trade union activists who belonged to Marxist parties functioned, in the main, as instruments for liberal union leaders. Their political thrust was dissipated by two factors. First, they were unwilling to become pariahs within the working class by opposing the rise of industrial unionism within the liberal consensus. Instead, they hoped to gain an operational foothold into the mass industrial unions from which to develop radical politics later on. Second, gradually, radical politics became more rhetorical than practical for the left-wingers who entered the CIO. And it did not matter whether the left-winger was in the Communist party or anti-Communist party; the central thread was the same. Most radicals were all too willing to follow John L. Lewis. To them, he was performing the necessary preparatory work for socialism, later—despite his pro-capitalist bias, now.

Most non-Communist radicals within the labor movement refused to follow the CIO leadership into the New Deal coalition. It was the one distinguishing feature separating their politics from those of the Communist party. But insofar as they supported the CIO itself and subordinated themselves to its program, they could not help but aid the despised Democratic party.

In sum, radical ideologies and organizations played virtually no independent role in the trade unions after 1935. The few dissenters were swiftly cast aside in the triumphant march of industrial unionism.

One hundred years ago workers fought desperately for their right to form unions and to strike for economic and social demands. Unions arose out of the needs of workers. In the period of the expansion of American capitalism they were important means for restraining the bestiality of capital. Even into the twentieth century, long after the labor movement as a whole stopped reflecting their interests, workers fought for unions. But their hope was not to become new agents of social transformation. Industrial workers joined unions in the twentieth century seeking a share in the expansion of American capitalism, not its downfall.

Since the 1920s, the ideology of expansion has permeated working class consciousness. On the one hand, many workers have no faith in the corporations to provide for their needs unless forced to do so by powerful organizations. On the other, American expansion abroad, and the intervention of the government into the operation of the economy, has convinced workers that the frontier of economic opportunity was not closed to them. The persistence of the idea of individual mobility amidst recognition of the necessity for collective action is partially attributable to the immigrant base of a large portion of the industrial working class in the first half of the twentieth century. The comparative advantages of American capitalism to the semifeudal agrarian societies of Europe in the early part of this century remained vital influences on workers' consciousness despite the Great Depression. For the minority of radical immigrant workers who didn't buy the expansionist ideology, corporations and the government reacted with consistent deportments, jail terms and attempts at demoralization.

Thus the violence of American labor struggles has been a two-pronged factor in the development of working class consciousness. On the one hand, it indicates the militancy with which workers have been prepared to conduct their struggles. But the readiness of employers and the government to use methods of severe repression to break strikes and cleanse the working class of its most militant elements has become an object lesson for workers. Working class consciousness is suffused with the awesome power of the corporations over American life. They have sought and helped create unions which mirror the hierarchical structure of corporations and can compete with them in marshaling resources to bargain effectively with them. James Hoffa was a hero to many workers because he represented not a challenge to the robber baron but the labor equivalent of it. Hoffa was seen as a formidable opponent to the corporations precisely because the Teamsters were the quintessential business union.

Strikes in the United States are of longer duration than in any advanced capitalist country. Workers know that large corporations cannot be immediately crippled by walkouts and that their resources are usually ample to withstand months of labor struggle. Moreover, in some industries employers have created strike insurance plans to protect themselves. Similarly, unions have long developed institutional forms of strike insurance. The largest unions boast of huge strike funds. During the 1970 auto strike, however, the multimillions in the United Auto Workers strike chest was exhausted within a few months, even though benefits never exceeded $25 a week for the several hundred thousand GM workers. At the same time, thousands of workers lost their savings to pay for the strike. The companies drove home another lesson to the workers: despite unions, strikes are expensive. Although the threat of starvation is no longer an immediate deterrent to militancy, the legitimacy of labor unions among workers is reinforced by their ability to raise money and to render concrete assistance to strikers' families.

In 1946, the workers in most large American industries conducted a mass strike for a substantial wage increase. The strike was largely successful since workers had been forced to endure a wage freeze for the entire period of the Second World War. Neither union leaders nor corporate opposition could thwart the resolve of industrial workers to walk out. Neither the union leaders nor the corporations were anxious for the strike. Its resolution, however, did have an important influence on the course of the postwar economy. The companies finally acceded to the workers' demands, but exacted a major concession from the union leaders. The immediate consequence of the wage settlement was the announcement of the steel companies of a significant price increase. Union leaders remained mute, thus giving tacit support to the companies. Together, unions and corporations imposed the pattern of wage-price spiral on the whole society. Organized workers learned that their power was sufficient to make gains in real wages, provided they did not make social demands—that is, challenge the profits of the companies. Further, they were impressed by the importance of the growing international role of the United States, particularly in rebuilding Europe, for their economic well-being. The 1946 mass strikes ended in reinforcing the ideology of expansion among workers. Consciousness was fragmented, since the workers could separate their role as producers from their role as citizens and consumers.

When the Communists, following the lead of the Soviet Union and the world Communist movement, opposed the extension of United States hegemony abroad, they were not supported by the workers. Of course, it is true that the Communist party lost much prestige by its wartime support of repressive labor policies of the Roosevelt administration and the labor leaders. But deeper than its discredit, workers watched while the government aided by liberal union leaders put Communists in jail for violating the non-Communist affidavit required by the Taft-Hartley Act because they perceived the opposition to United States foreign policy as a threat to their own welfare.

It cannot be denied that working class militancy has generally been ambivalent in the United States. Workers are no less anti-employer than any other working class in the world. Strikes are bloodier, conducted for longer periods, and often manifest a degree of solidarity unmatched by any other group of workers. But working class consciousness is industry-oriented, if not always job-oriented. Workers will fight their unions and the companies through wildcat strikes and other means outside the established framework of collective bargaining. But they are ideologically and culturally tied to the prevailing system of power, because until now it has shown the capacity to share its expansion with a large segment of the working class.

Black workers, women and youth have historically been excluded from these shares. But since 1919 it is not accurate to claim that black workers are not integrated at all into the industrial workforce. They are excluded from unions representing skilled construction workers. But blacks constitute between one-third and two-fifths of the workforce in the auto and steel industries, and smaller but significant proportions of other mass production industries. They are more militant than older white workers because they are not given the relatively easier jobs in the plants, but are forced to work in the dirtiest, lowest-paid occupations. Moreover, they are underrepresented within the top echelons of union leadership. At best, tokenism characterizes most union responses to the large numbers of black workers in the shops.

Discrimination against blacks and, to a lesser extent, young white workers, has led to the formation of caucus movements inside the unions based on specific sectoral demands of these groups. Some black caucuses seek more union power and, at the same time, demand upgrading to better paying skilled jobs. Youth caucuses have been organized within the UAW making similar demands, but have gone further to suggest that the rigidity of industrial labor be relaxed. Some caucuses have asked that the uniform starting time of most workplaces be rescinded, that supervision be less severe, and that ways be found to enlarge job responsibility so that the monotony and meaninglessness of most assembly line tasks be erased. Young workers are groping for ways to control their own work, even though they are making piecemeal demands. Black workers are demanding liberation from the least satisfying of industrial tasks and more control over union decision-making processes.

But these are only tentative movements toward a different kind of working class consciousness. They are still oriented toward making demands on companies and unions, and do not aim autonomously at taking control over their own lives. Within the American working class, no significant movement or section of workers defines itself as a class and sees its mission to be the same as the liberation of society from corporate capitalist social relations.

Such consciousness will never arise in America from abject material deprivation. The position of the United States in the world has become more precarious since the end of World War II, but workers know that American capitalism has not reached a dead end. However, the consciousness that most work in our society is deadening and much of it unnecessary has permeated the minds of young people, including the new entrants into the factories and offices. The growing awareness of the need for new forms of labor manifests itself in spontaneous ways. Corporations are becoming more concerned that young workers are not sufficiently disciplined to come to work on time or even every day. The new plans for shorter number of work days, even if they propose to retain the forty-hour work week, are not likely to catch fire in the near future. But they indicate that corporations are searching for new methods of coping with the manifest breakdown of industrial discipline among the millions of workers who have entered the labor force in the past decade and have not experienced the conservatizing influence of the Depression. After all, if poverty is not really a threat for large numbers within our society, how can they be expected to endure the specialization of work functions and their repetitive character? The specter that haunts American industry is not yet the specter of Communism, as Marx claimed. It is the specter of breakdown leading to a new conscious synthesis among workers.

It is the practice of trade unions and their position within production which determines their role in the social process. The transformation of the working class from one among many competing interest groups to capitalism's revolutionary grave-digger depends on whether working class practice can be freed from the institutions which direct its power into bargaining and participation instead of workers' control.

The trade unions are likely to remain both a deterrent to the workers' initiative and a "third party" force at the workplace, objectively serving corporate interests both ideologically and in the daily life of the shop, and remaining a diminishing instrument of workers' struggles to be employed selectively by them. But the impulse to dual forms of struggle—shop committees, wildcat strikes, steward movements—may become important in the labor movements of the future.

The rise of new instruments of workers' struggle would have to reject the institutionalization of the class struggle represented by the legally sanctioned labor agreement administered by trade union bureaucracies. Workers would have to make conscious their rejection of limitations on their freedom to take direct action to meet their elementary needs at the workplace. Although many wildcat strikes are implicitly caused by issues which go beyond wage demands, these remain hidden beneath the more gross economic struggles. Labor unions are not likely to become formally committed to the ideas of workers' control over working conditions, investment decisions, and the objects of labor. On the contrary, they will remain "benefits"-oriented, fighting incessantly to improve the economic position of their own membership in relation to other sections of the workforce rather than relative to the employers. They will oppose workers' efforts to take direct action beyond the scope of the union agreement and to make agreements with the boss on the informal basis of power relations on the shop floor.

The forms of anti-union consciousness within the working class are confused by the fact that they partially reflect the inability of these workers to organize collectively to defend their interests on an independent basis. Trade unionism still appears as a progressive force among the mass of working poor, such as farm and hospital workers, who labor under conditions of severe degradation. At first, unionization seems to be a kind of deliverance from bondage. But after the initial upsurge has been spent, most unions fall back into patterns of class collaboration and repression. At the point when grinding poverty has been overcome and unions have settled into their conservative groove, the bureaucratic character becomes manifest to workers.

We are now in the midst of a massive reevaluation by organized industrial workers of the viability of the unions. It is an action critique, however, rather than an ideological criticism of the union's role and the legal implications of it. In the end, the spontaneous revolt will have to develop its own alternative forms of collective struggle and demands. It is still too early to predict their precise configuration in the United States. But the European experience suggests that workers' councils and committees, that is, autonomous creations of workers at the point of production, will not replace the unions immediately, but will exist side by side with them for some time.

II

Beyond
Collective Bargaining

Introduction
to Section II

The problem of work is perhaps most easily understood at the level of the worker as an individual, his discontent and its manifestations on his job and in his union. Fundamentally, however, this is not an individual problem, a union problem, or even (as social scientists misleadingly label it) a "labor problem." The problem of work is a problem of the whole system of labor, the core institutions of which are "free enterprise" and "collective bargaining." Collective bargaining is almost sacrosanct at present, praised by unions and management alike. Section II of this volume seeks to puncture the lofty mystique of the bargaining system, to call an end to the assumption that it represents the end of history, the final stage of labor-management development.

In the readings that follow, it is argued that collective bargaining has served a crucial historic role, that it will continue to have a role, but that its limitations and failures are so severe that alternative systems involving workers' control as a strategy for labor are now urgent matters. The initial article details some of the more fundamental limitations and failures of the present system, while the second article, by Daniel Bell, details the crisis of collective bargaining in a particular industry. This is followed by three articles in which a Canadian unionist, a Common Market labor organization, and an American sociologist note how the issue of industrial democracy emerges from the crisis of collective bargaining.

Beyond Collective Bargaining

G. David Garson

It is a long way from 1824, when collective bargaining with respect to wages and hours was recognized in English law, yet today many people talk of this system as if it were an eternal whole rather than an historical artifact with a past and a future. In the previous section the need for change in the industrial order was discussed at the level of the worker and of the union. The question raised here is whether the traditional importance of collective bargaining as a weapon in labor's protracted conflict with management has not obscured certain important trends which have eroded its effectiveness.

The diminishing returns of collective bargaining are everywhere apparent. Far from representing some imagined "post-modern" resolution of the economic problem, the bargaining system is now yielding fewer and fewer real gains. Unions find themselves on an economic treadmill, forced to run ever faster simply to protect gains already won. Labor economists have long agreed that the collective bargaining system has left the share of labor in the national income quite unchanged in this century. More recently, real wages have approached a standstill while profits continued to mount. The American Federation of Labor–Congress of Industrial Organizations, for example, recently reported that in real wages a worker with three dependents earned a dollar less in July 1970 than he had five years earlier. As James

O'Connor noted, real income of state employees has actually been declining since 1965, in spite of the great increase in unionism in the public sector. It may be objected that these trends injurious to the workingman are not due to collective bargaining per se, but to government policy, the War, economic conditions—in short, to the state of the capitalist order. Such an objection, of course, misses the central point: it is precisely because collective bargaining has been unable to advance the share of the worker against the tendencies of the prevailing political economic system that discontent abounds!

Although remuneration is at the heart of the established system of business unionism, the failure in this area is not the fundamental cancer devitalizing collective bargaining. Here one must consider the failure of collective bargaining to alter the basic social relations of production and the consequent continuing assault on the mental health and opportunity for self-fulfillment of the worker. That to talk of such objectives seems lofty and remote from current forms of unionism is indicative of the limited nature of the dominant bargaining system.

In July 1970, *Fortune* magazine ran an article titled "Blue-Collar Blues on the Assembly Line," analyzing how "young auto workers find job disciplines harsh and uninspiring," venting "their feelings through absenteeism, high turnover, shoddy work, and even sabotage." From the union point of view, dissatisfaction is shown in the increase in wildcat strikes and the diminution of union loyalty of members, particularly among young workers. Perhaps of more importance, psychological studies compiled by Charles Hamden-Turner in a recent report for the Center for Community Economic Development (Cambridge, June 1970) show that mental ill health and dissatisfaction become prevalent as one descends the ladder of industrial occupations. Matthew Dumont has documented in his recent article on "The Changing Face of Professionalism" how discontent with traditional forms of worker association and with bureaucratic work organization is leading to the formation of new insurgent coalitions in medicine, social work, education, and other fields.

The failure to change the social relations of work is evident in many ways. In his recent study, *Blue-Collar Life,* Arthur Shostak has examined these issues, concluding that reform is essential: 1) reforms to help workers deal more effectively with problems of health, housing, education; 2) reforms which would "grapple with the workingman's sense of powerlessness in confrontation with anonymous and authoritarian bureaucracies"; 3) reforms "addressed to the workingman's loss of the meaning of work." Shostak notes, "Increasingly technology undermines the conviction that it is through his labor that a man establishes his identity and his relationships both to his neighbor and to God." The problem is not that the collective bargaining labor system causes the problems that beset the worker; it is rather, of course, that it is inadequate to deal with them. In fact, these problems have become so severe that an important Republican advisory group has urged President Nixon to exploit for the traditional enemies of unionism the opportunity created by just this inadequacy.

The Advantages and Limits of Bargaining

This is not to say that unionism is merely form without content, of no real advantage to workers. Nothing could be further from the truth. Consider, for example, the following data released in 1970 by the United States Bureau of Census:

WAGES OF UNIONIZED WORKERS COMPARED
WITH UNORGANIZED WORKERS IN SELECTED
OCCUPATIONAL GROUPS, 1966

	Organized	*Unorganized*
Construction craftsmen	$8,580	$5,955
Mechanics and repairmen	7,954	5,943
Metal craftsmen	8,240	7,526
Assemblers, checkers, examiners, and inspectors in mfg.	5,929	4,821
Drivers and deliverymen	7,843	5,518
Clerical workers	5,867	4,572
Male service workers	5,183	4,149
Female nonhousehold service workers	3,913	2,603

The clear advantage in wages of union workers is due to organization, even after such factors as lack of unionism in small, traditionally poor-paying firms is taken into account. Striking examples abound as, for instance, the recent accomplishment of the new New York City hospital workers union in raising wages thirty percent to fifty percent above previous rates (and above rates in cities such as Boston) in a few short years.

Nor has the bargaining system been limited to wages: one could cite extensive programs achieved through collective negotiations for pensions, health and welfare benefits, unemployment compensation and job retraining, and job security, as well as union-initiated housing, recreation, and social service projects. Thus George Meany could hold, at the 1965 convention of the AFL-CIO, that "Far from being obsolete or on its way out—as some of our 'way-out' friends on the sidelines predict—[collective bargaining] is being extended and expanded into new and broader areas of employment and in the resolution of new issues confronting workers in their relations with their employers." One could cite, for example, the 1970 campaign of the auto workers for extremely progressive health care benefits, forcing companies to favor national health insurance as a way of transferring costs to the public sector.

In spite of these gains, there are certain limits to the bargaining system. To be sure, one can imagine and even find historical examples of American unions under the collective bargaining system which have transcended customary limits, managing to act as if they were also workers' councils, preempting managerial decisions. Worker self-management is not a matter of replacing one form (unions) by another (councils); it makes no essential difference if existing unions take on new functions and structures or if alternative associations arise to fill new needs. In fact, the European record suggests that government-established workers' councils ordinarily come to work closely with existing unions, often augmenting their effectiveness and acting as a catalyst for the spread of labor organization to unorganized plants.

To say the bargaining system has limits is not at all to say that it is obsolete. On the contrary, most advocates of worker self-management have stressed the necessity of preserving free, independent unions to protect worker interests even when these are antagonistic to those of government or industry. But after this is duly noted, it is still possible to observe tendencies in the prevailing bargaining system that restrict labor interests and prevent effective dealing with the basic problems of workers suggested at the outset:

1. Collective bargaining generally neglects involvement of the shop-level worker.

Apart from occasional crises the union is remote from the rank-and-file worker, even when it is valued. Low attendance at union meetings occurs even in democratic, responsive unions not because workers aren't organizationally minded or because union leaders are unfamiliar with the techniques of making participation attractive, but because the bargaining system itself makes the selection of the bargaining team leadership the only essential decision apart from strike votes. Nor, from the leadership point of view, is there much real need to contact members apart from referenda on contract offers (even here, many unionists feel they know member interests and have no real need to consult). While attempts to reinvigorate union democracy are commendable and may at times succeed, the tendency of the present labor system is to make participation seem irrelevant. Needless to say, this neglect of the shop-level worker undermines the extent to which the union can mobilize his support.

2. Collective bargaining cannot significantly alter the distribution of the economic surplus accruing to the working class.

As innumerable liberal (Galbraith) and radical (Baran) economists have shown, the increasing concentration of industrial control has so severely undercut the "free competition" capitalist model that labor cost increases are generally passed on to the consumer (that is, back to the worker). Under these conditions it has been impossible for the union movement, as effective as it has been in particular cases, to increase the share of wages in national income. Only as worker organizations begin to acquire power over price decisions, with or without coordinate government planning, can the vicious cycle that has trapped the labor movement for the last century be broken and the consumer interest protected.

Again, price control could conceivably be effected through bargaining, but the tendency of the collective bargaining system is against this possibility: 1) because of the present "legal rights" of capital under the existing labor relations system; 2) because in any given instance the union will find it preferable to trade price control demands for more direct economic gains; and 3) because the highly uneven development of American unionism prevents price control from even being attempted on a national basis through voluntary, concerted efforts of unions.

3. Collective bargaining serves only a minor section of those who work.

There is a modern liberal equivalent to the old ideology of rugged individualism which places on social movements the burden of remedying the systematic evils of prevailing institutions, rather than also insisting on the change of those institutions themselves. There is no reasonable and realistic ground for expecting the spread of strong and effective unions to encompass the bulk of workers, regrettable as that is, without serious alteration of the system of labor relations itself. Even the establishment of weak co-determination schemes, as in Germany, would be a far stronger impetus to worker organization than is continued reliance on traditional union organizing drives alone. Most workers are not organized and most unions themselves are struggling parts of what Sidney Lens has labeled "little labor." Just as supportive government legislation was essential to the spread of trade unionism in the 1930s, so government action will be required again to assure organized protection for all workers; the European example, whether of the moderate capitalist type or of the more radical socialist variety, suggests that the most likely form of such government action would be the required establishment of worker participation bodies in all sizable firms. For unions, this change in the system of labor relations could provide a realistic opportunity for the spread of independent unionism to most workers. For government, it would promise more peaceful labor relations, a factor now becoming acute in relation to state workers as well as those in leading industries.

4. Collective bargaining involves serious problems of organizational control from the union and worker points of view.

The American collective bargaining contract is a relatively unique document among Western industrial nations, legally binding for a specified period and often incredibly detailed in content. These characteristics give certain advantages, of course, but the limits involved again raise the question of whether additional channels of worker organization are not also desirable. It is difficult, for example, to use a contract to specify general rules once every three years that can adequately meet the constantly changing work situation of modern industry. In the absence of a continuing works council with any power, the union's shop steward is reduced to reliance on relatively informal powers to meet changing needs and may often find himself restricted by an inflexible contract. It is this situation which underlies the increase in "wildcat" strikes that has disturbed union, management, and government leaders in recent years: workers, boxed in by the legal framework of the bargaining system, turn to illegal walkouts in the absence of any decision-making labor body capable of acting between contract expiration periods.

An equally serious problem of organizational control inherent in the bargaining system, from the union and worker points of view, is the necessity for reliance on management to implement contract provisions. It is an elementary principle of administration that it is an organizational defect to place program implementation in the hands of unsympathetic managers and bureaucrats. A union frequently finds that the provisions it thought it won at the bargaining table are administered away in practice, the theoretic legal enforceability of the contract notwithstanding. One of the causes of the Boston teachers' strike of 1970, for instance, was the failure of public management to implement a provision in the previous contract specifying a maximum class size, and this example is not exceptional. Only the development of an alternative labor body with managerial functions will assure that contracts will be sympathetically and effectively enforced.

5. Collective bargaining is excessively bureaucratic.

Even apart from the tendencies against participation in bargaining itself, discussed above, the grievance procedures meant to allow for adjustment of particular problems on a day-to-day basis are becoming unnecessarily top-heavy. Because such grievances, if not settled informally by the shop steward, must be sent up the union and management hierarchies rather than being adjudicated through decentralized self-management bodies, it is commonplace to find that bureaucratic delay often renders an original grievance irrelevant by the time it can be settled. Needless to say, this characteristic of the bargaining system works to the systematic disadvantage of the worker: the bureaucratic organization of work is far more in the interests of management than of labor. A prominent arbitrator, David Cole, has detailed the deterioration of the grievance function in large American companies in his book, *The Quest for Industrial Peace,* concluding that traditional grievance procedures "have been surrounded with so many safeguards that they have become almost self-defeating . . . they tend to enlarge rather than resolve problems." For this reason companies such as International Harvester have made token moves toward decentralized joint management in the form of floating union-management grievance teams with power.

6. Collective bargaining reinforces a regressive expectation system.

Related to the problems of participation mentioned earlier, the present labor relations system entails low expectations about the shop-level worker: neither the union nor the management expect him to feel responsible for work process or to concern himself with raising productivity or coordinating his work with that of other departments—these are managerial responsibilities. Given the collective bargaining system this is a virtually universal phenomenon, wishful management rhetoric to the contrary, because 1) the ideological underpinnings of the hierarchic organization of work demand low leadership expectations about worker capacity for self-management; 2) the absence of self-management bodies denies the worker a structure through which to exercise his responsibilities, and also denies him 3) the power to assure himself that the benefits of his innovation or exercise of responsibility will actually accrue to him and his peers; and 4) bargaining tends to involve conflict over division of the economic surplus and only rarely cooperation over its expansion. Yet if social psychologists have discovered anything it is that negative expectations tend to become self-fulfilling. In contrast, the relatively recent Scanlon Plans in dozens of American firms have shown that surprising productivity increases can be gained by a system of higher expectations and incentives to match, workers in some Scanlon plants being routinely placed in charge of introduction of the innovations they propose—another successful, if token, step toward self-management.

7. Collective bargaining has even failed to secure for workers control over the essential information needed for negotiations, let alone self-management.

The demand for "opening of the books" is an ancient and honorable—and unrealized—one, in spite of the great difficulty of workers' representatives to act effectively for their members and responsibility for the public without access to "managerial" information about profits, costs, inventories, price policies, and the like. This is true even of strong unions like the United Auto Workers, who find that the books are "opened" only when it is to the advantage of management to do so. This failure of management is, of course, rooted in the conflict model of the collective bargaining system, and has led to additional token steps toward self-management: 1) larger unions' research departments have tended, in effect, to duplicate managerial recordkeeping, replete with accountants and economists; 2) even smaller unions, as the United Electrical Workers in Lynn, Massachusetts, have recently found it desirable to duplicate management information systems for health claims. These steps are directly related to the problem cited earlier of the unreliability of unsympathetic management from the labor point of view, and may be the beginning recognition of the need to transform the bargaining system itself.

8. The collective bargaining structure is inappropriate for relating labor interests to those of the larger democratic community.

Under the present labor relations system even if a union's resources are not consumed by the bargaining process itself, the most to be expected is that the union will become one more interest group affiliated with some progressive coalition for change. When this is done on a conscious and systematic basis, as in the Community Action Programs of the United Auto Workers, governmentlike bodies are created within the union dealing with health, education, etc., potential parts of a future self-management system. While under the present system, for example, a union may join with parents to help elect a new school board, an institutionalized system of community participation in which labor played a major role as a matter of course would require teachers' councils (already extant in some unionized areas) meeting jointly with community representatives (from parents' groups, community school paraprofessionals, etc.) to determine local variations of general school policy. Unionism plus some form of self-management makes possible a far firmer basis for labor-related community participation than does unionism alone. (In fact, without a self-management structure union conflict with community participation-oriented forces is likely.) Similarly, with regard to comprehensive city planning, only a strong self-management structure can enable a rational, highly progressive local taxation and employment policy without the blackmail of entrepreneurial emigration. Without such a structure, unions and workers will always be manipulated as pawns in the conflict between the interests of management and the public interest.

Beyond Collective Bargaining

This is far from constituting a comprehensive list of the restrictive tendencies of the prevailing labor system, yet it suggests the reasons for the growing movement to reconsider the American bargaining system. This reappraisal is further motivated by growing antagonism toward national strikes, which constitute the one real power on which collective negotiations are based. The acceptance of the American labor system is part and parcel of acceptance of more intense and protracted labor conflict than prevails where even token steps have been taken toward self-management, conflict as restrictive in form on workers as it is costly to management and government.

Self-management is based on the principle that organizational health can be achieved only if those who actually do the work are given due weight in decision making. As the General Secretary-elect of Great Britain's one-and-a-quarter-million-member Transport and General Workers' Union recently stated, "those who invest their lives in a business have a bigger right to a say than those who merely invest their cash." Thus the question of self-management is at once a question of morality, of administration, and of labor strategy.

This is not to say that self-management is not without its own problems. Indeed, in a system dominated only by workers' councils, an equally strong argument could be made for the necessity of trade unionism as a coordinate form of worker organization. In such a system there would be several forces encouraging the self-management councils to adopt unionlike forms, just as American unions have reason to move toward self-management. First, unions are better able than councils alone to represent those interests of workers which are antagonistic to management (even self-management) interest in maximizing the economic surplus generated by the firm. In a free society, even the democratic organization of work would not justify suppression of the right of organized opposition to collectively determined interests. Second, the organization of production under monopolistic and oligopolistic management, private or public, requires the union of workers on an industry basis. While it is possible to envision an alliance of worker councils performing this function, the more centralized and professional structure of unions seems more appropriate. Third, unions would be needed to assure the independence of the self-management councils themselves. While independent councils have existed apart from strong unions, this existence has derived from sympathy of management or government, unreliable in the American context.

Thus, the crisis of collective bargaining need not suggest the demise of unions or even of bargaining, but it does lay the basis for a reevaluation in which the role of workers' self-management councils may emerge as central.

The Subversion of Collective Bargaining

Daniel Bell

Can the labor system as presently structured reasonably be expected to continue to protect the interests of those who work, or have the diminishing returns of bargaining made reappraisal necessary? One of the early and most influential articles in the movement to reappraise the current labor system was that by Daniel Bell, a professor of sociology at Columbia University, entitled "The Subversion of Collective Bargaining." When this article appeared in *Commentary* in March 1960, the country had just emerged from the Kefauver Committee revelations about "price administration" in industry, which showed how management exploited collective bargaining for its own profit. This lesson was reinforced by the then-recent steel strike, a prelude to a three-sided labor-industry-government conflict throughout the 1960s. Bell documents the argument that, although "the unions have been remarkably successful in achieving most of their goals," there is no longer reason to be optimistic about future gains unless the labor movement sees the necessity "to begin reorienting itself and to think of collective bargaining in a new and different light." Although his conclusions, which rightly urge the need for union political action and the demand for an annual wage, fall short of consideration of any fundamental alterations of the collective bargaining system, the criticism set in motion by Bell has been gathering momentum ever since.

Unhappy is a society that has run out of words to describe what is going on. So Thurman Arnold observed in connection with the language of private property—the myths and folklore of capitalism—which even thirty years ago was hopelessly out of date. How to find real words to describe the recent strike in the steel industry, or the consequences of the wage-price negotiations of the past decade? Two parties are locked in struggle, each seeking to articulate its claims over the other, while from the sidelines arise the moralistic alarms of spectators worrying about damage to the innocent public. But the desiccated language of collective bargaining is a trap; its syntax too constricting, its images too mechanical. The complex fact? The combat is a mimetic one, painfully real in the sense that emotions are aroused, but unreal because no economic loss can occur; in fact, each party, knowing in advance the price it will have to pay, pretty much gets what it sets out to get, and both end up with a profit—the corporation, usually, the greater gainer.

I am not suggesting that all this, like wrestling, is "fixed." Far from it. The antagonism between the contenders is quite genuine. But a highly intricate mechanism is at work in the game, and by now each side knows the unwritten rules. Sociologists have a phrase, "the unanticipated consequences of purposive actions," to suggest that things don't always work out as planned; and this is often the way of the world. As far as the corporations are concerned, the pattern of collective bargaining in this country follows an opposite principle which can be called "the utilized consequences of nonpurposive action," meaning that even if you didn't plan it that way, you can turn it to your advantage.

Over the past decade, the corporations have precisely learned how to turn the collective bargaining process—and the strikes —to their advantage. The powerful unions gain impressive wage increases; the powerful corporations gain an excuse for impressive price increases—which, in the case of steel and auto, have in almost every instance been more than proportional to the jump in wages. Who loses? Unorganized workers (e.g., textiles), workers in marginal industries, *rentiers,* pensioners, and the like. Is this just? It is hard to define an equitable standard. A deflationary situation would benefit the *rentiers* and pensioners. But why should this group gain rather than another? The present situation reflects existing market power, which in turn shapes the rules of the game. The first thing to be determined is not who wins and who loses, but the nature of the game itself, and whether it ought to be revised. The following, therefore, tries to sketch some basic characteristics of the current wage-price situation, to puncture some myths, to delineate some consequences, and to present some alternatives.

The single most important fact about contemporary corporate capitalism is that expansion comes about through "self-financing," through retained earnings derived from high, protected prices. In formal theory—the mythical language of private property—a firm went to the capital market for financing. It floated stock, people "risked" their money and got a share of the enterprise as their equity. Later, corporations went in for institutional borrowing; insurance companies or banks would lend large sums of money to a firm, taking debentures or perferred stock in return. In either case, some outside control theoretically existed; a legal equity was always exchanged for the money raised. The actual situation is vastly different. Few firms today, except for utilities, go to the capital market for funds. Tax laws make it costly to distribute all retained earnings as dividends and then "recoup" the capital, by the investors' fiat, through new stock. The managerial decision to utilize retained earnings for expansion allows the managers to reinforce their social power and gives them independence from outside control; their ideas become the decisive factor in determining the social use of capital surplus.

But it is equally important to understand that when expansion is financed through high protected prices, it is the *consumer* who does the financing, and he neither receives equity in the firm (not even the promise of future price reductions) nor has any say about how his money should be used. In effect, the whole process depends upon what I shall call a "hidden tax mechanism" through which corporations can raise huge sums of money without giving away anything in return. Public taxation is openly and hotly debated in Congress and in the legislatures; bills involving the raising or spending of money are subject to all kinds of pressure and become the cause of great political divisions. Yet under the banner of "free enterprise," a corporation can, through a protected price policy, "tax" consumers for its own purposes and do whatever it wishes with the money. In consequence of the recent expansion of steel capacity, for example, the industry—*at present demand under protected prices*—can supply all the steel the country uses in nine months rather than twelve. This means that the industry can "take" a three-month strike almost without reducing the average profit it would have made had no strike been provoked. In short, the strike is—that is to say, *was*—financed by the consumers.

The key term in the above argument, of course, is the concept of "protected price." A firm is interested primarily in its profit margins. If sales fall, the firm cuts production—and employment—rather than price. Firms with some degree of market control can do this. The chief complaint of the farmers is that, being unorganized—other than through government crop reduction programs—they cannot adjust production to demand, but have to let prices fall.

To anyone who has read with care the Kefauver Committee reports of 1958 on "administered prices" in the steel and auto industries, it will be clear that these industries exercise an extraordinary degree of market control and thus have been able to place themselves in a protected position. We can best understand how such control is exercised by looking at the "standard volume" system for setting prices used by the auto industry. This system, which was developed by Donaldson Brown for General Motors in 1924, is based on an equation of three variables—price, estimated average rate of plant operation calculated in terms of a percentage of total annual capacity, and net return on investment. The price set for a single car is thus a function of the other two variables. But how are these variables determined? Net return on investment is simple: General Motors has decided that it must get roughly twenty percent after taxes every year. "Estimated average rate of plant operation" is more complicated, however. The company figures in its best year on reaching only eighty percent of its theoretical maximum operating capacity because of seasonal and other fluctuations in sales; in an *average* year, it figures on reaching eighty percent of the production that can be achieved in its best year: thus it figures, theoretically, on using sixty-four percent of its capacity in any normal year. But in actual practice, the "standard volume" has generally been calculated on a fifty-five percent capacity. That is, General Motors so sets its prices as to plan for a return of about twenty percent after taxes on the assumption that its plants will operate through the year for a total of only 180 days, or thirty-six weeks. (General Motors could "take" a four-month strike and still come out at its predetermined margin by operating for the rest of the year at full capacity.)

The long-range target of "standard volume" is to make it possible for General Motors to recoup its net investment in five years, but this goal has been surpassed by a phenomenal margin. In 1955, for example, net earnings (after interest and income taxes) were sufficient for the company to recoup its *entire* net plant investment in only two years. The American Institute of Management, which made this calculation, pointed out that such a record was not exceptional for General Motors, but was, "in fact, a continuing characteristic of the enterprise being equaled or bettered in twelve of the preceding twenty years."

From 1950 to 1957, for every year except the last, General Motors' actual sales were, on the average, about thirty percent higher than the "standard volume" on which the company set its prices.[1] When asked whether some of these gains from the large volume should not have been passed along to consumers through lower prices, Harlow Curtice, then head of General Motors, told the Kefauver Committee: "[Our prices] are as low as they can be and still produce the indicated return on the net worth at the standard volume." Even, it would seem, when actual output was fifty percent greater than the "standard volume." As the Kefauver Committee said rather stodgily in its

[1] Thus, in 1950, General Motors estimated its "standard volume" at 2,250,000 units, in order to give it a twenty percent net return, and sold 3,812,000 units, or a sixty-nine percent margin of safety. In 1955, "standard volume" was 3,000,000 units, and factory sales were 4,386,000 or fifty-four percent above target. In 1957, when "standard volume" was estimated at 3,470,000, sales were a shade under (3,418,000)—the only year of the eight in which the target was not exceeded.

report: "It is clear that the use of standard volume as the basis of pro-rating expected costs and the desired aggregate profit in order to establish prices adds a considerable element of rigidity to these prices."

What this has meant in terms of the price power of General Motors can be grasped by tracing the company's net worth. In 1947, General Motors had a net worth of $1,428,000,000—on which it made a return, before taxes, of 38.8 percent. A decade later, General Motors' net worth was $4,582,000,000—on which it made a return of 35.6 percent before taxes. Of this increase in net worth of more than three billion dollars (or 221 percent), all but $395 million came from profits which were plowed back into the company. In short, the increase came from consumers who were making an "involuntary investment" in General Motors.

One important clue to the efficiency of a company and its ability to reduce prices is "the break-even point"—a measure that is based on the relationship between costs (divided into fixed and variable) and sales—and that gives us the figure at which the company begins turning a profit. Computations by Mr. Fred Gardner, a prominent management consultant, indicated that, including a high allowance for depreciation, General Motors' "break-even point" in 1956 was 48.8 percent of sales. Sales, of course, do not represent full capacity; if one took full capacity into account, General Motors' "break-even point" would probably come to somewhere between forty and forty-five percent of capacity.

These figures become even more significant in the light of the fact that Ford's "break-even point" in 1956 was 64.7 percent and Chrysler's 87.4. Clearly General Motors has little to fear in the way of real price competition from the other automobile companies. In a serious price war, General Motors, with its superior efficiency, could probably run Ford and Chrysler into the ground. It doesn't do so, first, because a position as a single auto monopolist would simply invite public regulation, and second, because Chrysler and Ford, as the marginal firms, hold up a neat "price umbrella" for General Motors.

Since the products of the steel industry are more diversified than those of the auto companies, the steel companies do not use any such simple measure as "standard volume" for setting prices. In general, the industry figures on making a fifteen percent net return on investment when operating at 100 percent of capacity. U.S. Steel argues that every dollar's worth of increase in employment costs will lead to an increase of more than $2 in total costs of production, and sets its prices accordingly. How does this claim square with U.S. Steel's "break-even point?"

In its presentation to a government commission investigating monopoly in 1937 (the Temporary National Economic Commission), U.S. Steel estimated that its "break-even point" then was 63.3 percent of sales. In 1956, an analysis by management consultant Gardner for the Kefauver Committee showed the "break-even point" to be 44.3 percent of sales. After the price increases in 1957—which had followed a large union wage increase—the "break-even point" went *down* to 38.6 percent of sales, or (since sales are lower than capacity) about thirty-two percent of capacity. In other words, by working less than two full days a week, U.S. Steel could move out of the "red" and make money.

How low should a "break-even point" be? The average "break-even point" of all U.S. industry is roughly fifty percent of capacity. A "break-even point" between fifty and sixty percent of capacity is considered "sound" since it gives most companies a margin wide enough to cover their fixed costs if sales fall sharply. In twenty-five years of computing "break-even points" for 1500 companies, Mr. Gardner testified, the lowest he ever encountered was that of U.S. Steel. The corporation, he said, could cut its prices by ten percent, and still end up with a "break-even point" of fifty percent of capacity.

The nub of the analysis, as applied specifically to the wage-price situation of 1957 (the last major wage-price increase in steel), is that when wages went up, prices—and profits—went up *even higher*. After the new contract with the union had been put into practice, a correlational technique showed a higher rate of profit at a lower rate of operating costs than in the previous year, and a decline in the "break-even point" as well. In brief, it was quite clear that the steel companies had used the negotiations as an excuse for boosting prices, in order to jack up their profit margins. As the Kefauver Committee concluded, "U.S.

Steel [can] cover its costs at an operating rate below forty percent of capacity and make very satisfactory profits while a substantial part of its capacity lies idle."

The point of all this (to return to the role of collective bargaining) is that the net effect of union pressure—apart from the gains which have been won for the small group of highly organized workers—has been to help install a mechanism whereby the large corporation is able to strengthen its price position in the market. In the past, price protection was achieved by "basing point" systems (now outlawed), price umbrellas (in which U.S. Steel set the lead), or informal collusion. Today the union serves as the vehicle. (According to Walter Reuther, for *every* dollar of increased labor costs since 1947, General Motors by 1956 imposed about $3.75 in cumulative price increases on the American car buyer. In effect, the United Auto Workers, taking a small share of the increased profits, has become, albeit unwillingly, the "junior partner" of General Motors.) The companies can truthfully say that they do not like the union negotiations, since other than wage demands are often involved (work rules, fringe benefits, etc.). And the companies are usually inclined to resist the union's demands strenuously. But it invariably turns out that the union negotiation offers a lovely opportunity to increase prices—and, with exquisite irony, to blame the union for inflation.

Are the unions responsible for inflation? Industry's argument is that they are, because, by raising costs, they set off a wage-price spiral. But simple economic logic exposes the patent falsity of this charge. To determine the true effect of union wage pressure, one has first to make a distinction between the *structure of wages* (i.e., the relative spread between industries—say, steel and textiles), and the *level of wages,* which is the total wage bill in relation to other economic factors. What union pressure may do is to affect the *structure* of wages: that is, it can increase the gap between one group of workers (who have a strong union) and another (which does not). It is quite possible that wage and subsequent price increases in one area of the economy *may* have a linked effect on others—though with all the propaganda about the wage-price spiral, the actual spread of this effect has *never* been traced, and even so eminent a conservative economist as Milton Friedman of the University of Chicago doubts that it can go very far.[2]

For actually the degree of impact of a wage increase in one area on the rest of the economy depends, simply, upon the stock of money in circulation. If this stock were held constant, then an increase in wages and prices in one sector could only cause a shift in the share of money to that particular sector—provided it were strong enough to impose its increases (i.e., provided that people needed the products of that sector more than they needed other products; or, in technical terms, the demand was relatively inelastic). Thus, there would be a change in the *structure,* but no effect upon the general *level* of wages and prices.

In practice, however, money supply is not held constant, but goes up (theoretically about four percent a year, or slightly ahead of the growth pace of the economy). This increase in the supply of money, which is the result of political decisions by the monetary controllers, has a far greater effect on the general price level than wage pressure could ever possibly have. The current inflationary situation is due in large measure to the $13 billion budgetary deficit that the government ran in meeting the 1957–8 recession. Although the administration refused to use direct government spending to counter the recession, it achieved the same effect by indirect methods (accelerated spending on committed programs, lower tax receipts, and the like). If any single factor can be held responsible for the inflation-deflation seesaw of recent years, it is the erratic timing of the Federal Reserve Board, which has either stepped a little too hard on the gas or jerked the brake a little too abruptly (as it is doing now). While the business community contradicts the basic precepts of economic theory in ascribing inflation to union wage pressure, conservative economists who know better have kept shamefully quiet.

But there is another argument which holds that union wage

---

[2] The steel companies themselves were in a wonderfully quixotic position. On the one hand, they claimed that steel wages, by rising faster than productivity, were inflationary; on the other hand, they protested vehemently that the effect of the increase of steel prices—which should reflect the steel wage inflationary pressure—was "negligible" on the cost of living.

pressure can put a particular firm or a particular industry in a difficult competitive position vis-à-vis other firms or products—it can "price them out of the market." This argument is plausible in theory, except that, if it were true, production would fall and unemployment would mount—which does not seem to be the case in the relevant sectors of the economy. Actually, the one element in the whole wage-price picture which has been almost completely ignored—the emergence of a large class of non–production workers within the manufacturing firms, and the consequent rise in salary costs—is a more likely candidate, if any single one is to be cast, for the role of "villain" than the unions.

By now it is commonplace that in the last decade the white-collar force has been expanding rapidly while the blue-collar force has remained virtually stable. This increase in white-collar force, however, has taken place not only in the so-called "tertiary" area (insurance, banks, real estate, services, education, recreation, and the like), but—through the proliferation of administrative services (personnel, marketing, merchandising, etc.), of research, and of automation—within the area of manufacturing itself. From 1947 to 1957, the number of non–production workers in manufacturing increased by sixty percent (from 2,400,000 to 3,900,000) while the blue-collar force remained almost stationary (a little under 13,000,000). In 1947, salaries (the mode of payment to white-collar workers) were one fourth of the labor costs in manufacturing; by 1957 they had gone up to one third.

There are two important consequences to this change in the composition of the workforce. One relates to productivity, the other to unit labor costs. In all their propaganda on the effect of wage increases, the corporations have talked of the rise in *employment* costs—but this is never broken down into unit *wage* costs (usually the unionized sector) and unit *salary* costs. Given the nature of industrial organization, direct production costs (wage costs) are more immediately subject to control than white-collar costs (salary costs). In other words, if productivity is broken down on a man-hour per production worker basis, and on a man-hour per salaried worker basis, the corporation can recoup its costs more easily in the first sector, where it can achieve economies and technological savings by substituting machines or tightening production schedules. The rise in the proportion of the salaried worker has acted as a drag on productivity, and on unit costs.

In sum, the argument I am making is that a significant share of the rise in manufacturing costs in the last decade has been due not to direct wage costs, but to an extraordinarily large increase in salary costs, which usually become an added fixed cost.

The Federal Reserve data available before the recession of 1957–8 show this shift in cost burdens quite clearly. Between 1947 and 1957, *unit* payroll costs (total wages and salaries) rose twenty-six percent, while unit *wage* costs increased by only sixteen percent.[3] Much of the payroll rise was a consequence of the rise in unit *salary* costs which in 1957 were almost *thirty percent* higher than in 1953.

This burden becomes even greater during a recession, for when production falls the large corporations cut down their blue-collar force while the white-collar force is maintained whole.

The picture within the steel industry is instructive. Table I shows the steadily rising slope of salary employment and the fluctuating course of blue-collar employment.[4]

But even more instructive when we consider the effect on costs of this new balance between production and non–production workers is a comparison of what happens to each class during a recession (Table II).

Two other items from the Kefauver data round out the picture. When the steel workers (or other such unions) win wage increases, the companies usually give "tandem" increases to the unorganized nonunion workers. When U.S. Steel submitted cost data to the Kefauver Committee on the effects of the 1957 negotiations, it indicated that its employment costs had gone up 21 cents an hour, against a union claim that wage

[3] In the period from 1953 to 1957, when the greatest increase in non-production workers took place, salary payments rose by thirty-seven percent while wage payments to the blue-collar force rose by only seven percent.

[4] Source: Background statistics bearing on the steel dispute, Tables 3a and 3b, U.S. Department of Labor.

TABLE I: STEEL EMPLOYMENT (in thousands)

	Production Workers	Administrative, Professional & Clerical
1950	532.9	78.1
1951	560.2	83.3
1952	486.5	84.2
1953	559.6	93.7
1954	492.5	88.3
1955	544.6	90.7
1956	532.6	97.6
1957	537.0	105.7

TABLE II: STEEL EMPLOYMENT

	Mid-1956	Autumn 1958	Drop
Semiskilled workers	250,000	200,000	20%
Skilled workers and foremen	175,000	155,000	11%
Laborers, helpers, misc.	120,000	90,000	25%
Clerical and sales	75,000	75,000	None
Professional and technical	30,000	30,000	None
Administrative	10,000	10,000	None

costs had only increased 16.4 cents. "Supplementary information provided by the corporation disclosed that the 21-cent figure is a weighted average of benefits extended to 161,500 members of the United Steelworkers, estimated at 19.4 cents per hour, *and simultaneous increases granted to 47,600 other* employees, estimated at 26.6 cents per hour." The union in its data had estimated that nonunion employees (principally white-collar) would receive the same cents-per-hour adjustment as union members. *Instead, nonmembers received increases which on the average were thirty-seven percent higher than the increase called for in the union contract.* As the Kefauver Committee said primly: "This may be excellent personnel policy, but there is some question as to the propriety of charging the cost of such a policy to the union agreement." . . .

But surely more is involved than the question of price increases. What is really at stake is the question of the "legitimacy of power" of the managerial groups. Who gives the manager his mandate? The traditional theory of private property has little legal or social validity in the age of the large corporation. A more plausible justification of managerial power is the argument that it allows for multiple, decentralized decision-centers to counter the dangers of arbitrary bureaucratic planning. But what checks exist on the enormous market power of the large corporation itself? Certainly not the market. As I have already tried to show, the corporations have been able to create a "hidden tax mechanism" which allows them to manipulate the market and to raise large sums of money for private expansion. Is such a thing socially desirable? For the situation amounts to this: in response to their own drives for status and power, the large automobile and oil companies have created a huge productive capacity, which in turn forces them to wage large coercive campaigns in order to stimulate consumption of their products—not only through advertising, but through political lobbying as well. One consequence is that Congress can pass a twelve-billion-dollar road-building program more easily than it can appropriate a billion dollars for schools. And we have the ludicrous spectacle, in New York and Los Angeles, of fantastic sums being levied for expressways—with houses torn down, views blocked, and open spaces cluttered—while public transport, which is faster and more economical, goes hang. Except for a few books by people like A. A. Berle, there has been little critical study in recent years of the social power of the corporations, and the questions of limits to that power.

As for collective bargaining, the other term in the general situation, we can say with some degree of truth that it has almost reached the end of its long career as an instrumentality for economic and social justice. The fact that in the major industries the big corporations have been able to subvert negotiations with unions by utilizing them as a device for masking a protected price policy calls the social utility of collective bargaining into deep question.

Collective bargaining has always been regarded as the chief means of achieving the traditional goals of unionism. These goals can be listed as follows:

1) to raise substandard wages;

2) to eliminate wages as a lever for comparative advantage between firms;

3) to eliminate discrimination and favoritism in the treatment of workers and to establish the worker's conception of equitable standards: e.g., the principle of seniority in layoffs and promotions;

4) to provide a juridical mechanism for grievances outside the arbitrary decisions of management;

5) to provide basic security and welfare for the individual worker through "fringe" benefits like medical care, pensions, and supplementary unemployment benefits;

6) to obtain a "fair share" of the profits of a firm;

7) to redistribute income in favor of the lower class groups;

8) to maintain consumer purchasing power, particularly during recessions.

Considering that the modern American trade union movement is only twenty-five years old, the unions have been remarkably successful in achieving most of their goals. But where does the labor movement go from here? The answer depends upon one's conception of the social role of the trade union. If a union's aim is simply to get a higher wage for its own members—the attitude of the building trades union, par excellence —it can then only become a partner in a collusive enterprise which strong-arms the rest of the community. This is what has happened—albeit unwillingly—to the auto and steel unions. But if the union has a wider view of its role in society—and seeks to enlist liberal and intellectual support for its claims— then it may have to begin reorienting itself and to think of collective bargaining in a new and different light.

Of the eight objectives outlined above, the unions have been able to achieve the first four, and most of the fifth. But the three strictly economic aims, which form the heart of present-day collective bargaining, have gone by the board. There has been little redistribution of shares between profits and wages, either as proportion of the national income or within firms. Nor has collective bargaining been the agency for maintaining purchasing power. The chief result of bargaining has been to favor strong unions at the expense of weak ones, to strengthen the monopoly positions of highly organized industries, and in consequence, to affect the *structure* of wages, but not the level (i.e., comparative shares). And the added fact that wage increases now run close to the ceiling levels of increases in productivity sets strong outer limits on the ability of unions to have *any* salutary effect on the economy through bargaining.

A simpler mechanism than collective bargaining for raising the standard of living of low income groups, or maintaining purchasing power during recessions, or creating relative equity between different groups of wage workers, is government fiscal policy. The unions could use their influence to win a tax reduction for the lower income classes of the country; this would be more equitable than pressing for the advantage of a particular group of workers, for it would be "across the board." Another thing the unions might do is exert pressure on the corporations to reduce prices, which would provide for a more equitable distribution of savings in productivity. Admittedly this is difficult. A union, its leaders say, exists to serve its own members; and the best way to do this is to fight for wage increases. As for other workers, let them go and do the same. But if union leaders adopt such a completely parochial view, they then forfeit the claims unionism has to the sympathies and allegiances of the liberal middle class and intellectuals. To help other workers— especially during recessions—it may be necessary to forgo direct wage increases and rely on government tax policy as the economic gyroscope. To engage in such action, however, the labor movement would have to become more political and begin thinking in broader social terms than it has grown accustomed to doing.

But is there no further innovating role for collective bargaining? I think that there is, that one last historic step remains to be taken—a true annual wage. Sociologically, this is the most revolutionary step the unions can take, but they will have to take it if they wish to consummate their long effort to give workers a legitimate place in society.

Historically, the worker has been treated as a commodity, to be paid by the piece or by the hour for his labor. However much one may declare (formally, as in the Clayton Act, or piously in Labor Day addresses) that labor is not a commodity, the existing system of wage payment shows that that is exactly how the worker is regarded. General Motors still pays its blue-collar force on the basis of every tenth of an hour worked, and despite some union-imposed restrictions, such as "call-in" pay (which guarantees a man at least four hours pay if he is called to work that day), wages are still determined by time or piece, as with any other commodity. The most bitter complaint of auto workers is that they have no way of knowing, from one week to the next, how many hours they will work in any given week; through the year, a man may get as many as twenty "short work weeks."

All this emphasizes the distinction between the production worker (who is regarded simply as "labor") and the salaried worker who is paid by the week, month, or the year. Salaried workers (usually of the white-collar class) are laid off less often (they are carried as part of standby, or fixed, costs), they are entitled to sick leave, excused for jury duty, and given a whole host of amenities often denied to the production worker. Why? Such practices are in part a carryover from the old notion of the production worker as an "interchangeable hand," and in part simply a status distinction enforced by traditional cultural attitudes toward manual labor. But is there any reason of an economic, sociological, or moral character for this "double standard" to continue? Increased costs, says management. Yet what of the gain in status that would accrue to the worker—the gain in psychological as well as economic security—if the double standard were abolished.[5]

In March 1958, the International Business Machines Corporation made the unprecedented move of placing its 20,000 regular production workers on a weekly salary basis—a move which, surprisingly, received little public attention. Like most blue-collar workers, the IBM production men had been paid on an hourly rate. As salaried employees they became entitled to

[5] Increased costs has been the cry of employers against every innovating device from shorter hours to pensions. Fifty years ago, corporations resisted workmen's compensation for accidents and the installation of safety devices on the grounds of increased costs. Yet today, in the changed climate of public opinion, what corporation would object to installing safety devices on the grounds of cost? On the grounds of mental health, one can justify the increased costs of reducing the pace of work, or the extreme division of labor. On the grounds of justice, one can argue for the elimination of the treatment of labor as a commodity.

full pay during absences due to illness or accident, as well as to paid time off for authorized personal reasons (jury duty, death in the family, etc.). IBM is not, of course, in a "seasonal" industry, and has therefore been able to take this step with comparative ease; but few industries in the United States today are seasonal—even auto is not wholly so—and those who are can use counterseasonal pricing devices to even out demand.

It is unlikely that American industry will eliminate piecework and hourly rates voluntarily; union pressure is needed through collective bargaining. But it is also unlikely that the unions, psychologically dispirited or with aging fat cat leaders, will launch the necessary campaign in the near future. Nevertheless, such a move would be the most important means the unions could find for reducing the "status barrier" between blue-collar and white-collar work—the very barrier in the way of organizing the white-collar workers. And without organizing the white-collar worker, American unionism, in the long run, cannot survive.

Collective Bargaining and Industrial Democracy

Chris Trower

A decade after Daniel Bell's article on the erosion of collective bargaining, the Canadian Labour Congress passed a resolution which recognized in industrial democracy the future of the present system of labor relations. Among the leaders of the reform movement behind this policy statement was Chris

Trower, a young union official whose views on collective bargaining are presented in the following article. This article, unlike the academic perspective of Bell, reflects the practical burden that the bargaining system places on the trade unionist and suggests the reasons why the militance urged by Bell may take the form of demands and political action around issues of industrial democracy.

Most of us take some pride in the fact that we live in a democracy; that we are free men and women rather than slaves; and that the freedoms we enjoy were bought with the currency of organized struggle and personal sacrifice. In the labor movement, we feel that our organizations are the direct descendants of that struggle; that it is our people who made those sacrifices, that we led and still lead the continuing fight toward a fully democratic and truly free society.

The fight is far from over. At the moment we have the forms of political democracy without the substance of social democracy, and the principal freedom we enjoy is the freedom to continue the fight. We have the right to elect the representatives who govern us and to this extent we enjoy political democracy. We have the right to negotiate terms and conditions of employment through our union and to this extent we have industrial democracy. But political democracy is a hollow sham so long as the mice (to borrow Tommy Douglas's analogy) continue to choose as governors either black cats or white cats; while industrial democracy can have meaning only to the extent that we control the government of industry. Social democracy depends upon the ultimate extension and use of both political and industrial democracy. But so long as men and women are subject to the control of others, so long as we are forced to spend most of our lives following orders, obeying rules, observing regulations, carrying out instructions, while someone else determines our destiny, we shall not know freedom. Freedom must be the ultimate goal of the labor movement.

In pursuing this goal we must recognize that support for the New Democratic Party will not, by itself, bring about an extension of political democracy, and that the periodic renegotiation of collective agreements does not constitute industrial democracy. If freedom is our goal, then industry will be democratic only when it is governed by those who work in it and governed for the benefit of the whole community. Once this ideal concept is accepted, we can move step by step toward its attainment both on the political front and across the bargaining table.

Winning acceptance for this concept presents some difficulties. It is not hard to find supporters for it when we consider it in abstract terms as an ideal. But it is even easier to find opponents whose opposition is based on the very fact that it is an ideal and therefore utopian, unattainable, and not worthy of discussion. In answer to that argument one should consider the fact that no progress can be meaningful unless it is toward an ideal. Without a point on the horizon toward which we keep moving, we have no way to measure progress. Without an ideal we may exchange one set of circumstances for an equal or lesser set and call it progress without even realizing we have taken a backward step. Other opponents have argued that it is an old concept from which the labor movement has steadily retreated. In answer to that argument, we should briefly review the history of that retreat, but, for the moment, it should be noted that the pendulum has begun to swing back toward this concept restated in the light of current experience. Finally, there are those who oppose the concept on the grounds that we already have attained all the industrial democracy that is necessary, that our task is simply to safeguard our role as a permanent opposition to management, that our function is to keep pressing for the same proportionate share of the wealth we produce because technological progress will provide us with prosperity. The answer to this argument brings us full circle because if we are concerned about freedom, we will want to determine our own destiny. If we care about democracy, we will not be content to have our prosperity determined by technological decisions in which we have no say, and if we are to have progress it must be progress according to our own measure, conforming to our own ideals. Our measure, our ideals, our goal is freedom. That is the concept for which we must win acceptance no matter what the difficulties.

Do We Already Have Industrial Democracy?

Let us consider these arguments in some detail. Taking them in reverse order, there is first the proposition that we already have industrial democracy. Any industrial worker is free to join a union and if the majority of the workers in a given bargaining unit join the same union, it can be certified as the sole bargaining agent for all the employees in that unit. While there are some differences in detail and method, and while certain types of workers are excluded from this procedure, it generally holds true throughout North America. Since the bargaining agent chosen in this way is free to negotiate a collective agreement covering all the terms of employment which the union wishes to bring under the scope of that agreement, and since the final terms will, on the one hand, be as favorable to the union as its bargaining power allows, and on the other hand, be accepted by a majority vote of the members it affects, it can be fairly said that this is democracy. Moreover, once that contract is in force, the union has the right to measure each act of management against the terms of the contract and if it believes there has been a violation it can force management to arbitration to settle the matter. Here is not only democracy but justice. Then, when the term runs out, the union can renegotiate the provisions of the contract and if it is powerful enough, force management to meet its terms. And so, the argument goes, all the elements of industrial democracy are there. We can control the acts of management, force them to accept our decisions, and generally advance the interests of our members in accordance with their wishes. There are, of course, excellent reasons for an employee to join and support his union. But we are talking about democracy in industry; the right to control the decisions that affect our working lives, not just at contract time or when we have a grievance, but hour by hour and day by day.

Anyone who has ever been a worker in any mine, mill, or factory in Canada, no matter how good his contract, no matter how powerful his union, will be quick to testify that there is no democracy in industry. By virtue of the fact that he is an employee, he must obey the orders of others in return for a wage. Whether he agrees with the orders or not, whether the orders make sense or not, so long as he is not asked to perform an unsafe or criminal act, he must obey or be guilty of insubordination. Insubordination, according to most arbitrators and all managements, is the most heinous of industrial crimes and punishable by instant dismissal.

Is this industrial democracy? By comparison to what we know as democracy, the average workplace is an unrelenting dictatorship.

Is Freedom Practical?

The question of personal freedom is at the very heart of the matter. The right to decide on one's own or as part of a group rather than the obligation to obey—that is the true test of freedom and the final measure of democracy. Any system that fails this test is neither free nor democratic, it is dictatorship.

Dictatorship in the form of management rights, it will be argued, is an essential function of our industrial system. Who would bother to work if no one had the right to issue orders and administer punishment? How could we produce and distribute the goods upon which our economy is based? Who would create the wealth that underpins our society? There is no ready answer to these questions. And it is unquestionably true that our civilization could crumble if it now depended solely upon a general willingness to cooperate in performing all necessary repetitive, boring, or distasteful work. The people we must depend upon have been conditioned not to cooperate but to obey orders in return for a wage and to compete for the right to do so.

Yet if we believe in democracy we must believe that people can learn to cooperate not just in the things they enjoy doing or that bring them an immediate, personal return, but also in the difficult and unrewarding jobs that must be done for the good of all. Cooperation is not unknown in our society; it occurs in any number of voluntary clubs, groups, and associations as well as in organizations like unions and political parties which depend for their effectiveness upon volunteer, cooperative work. If we trained people to be cooperative instead of competitive, if we measured success in terms of personal achievement instead of material possessions, we could begin to build a free society. It is an attitude of freedom we must develop; a desire for freedom we must encourage.

Human Rights or Management Rights?

But free choice is not the only point at issue. If we concede a necessity for some form of management control in industry in the present state of our society, we still cannot rely on collective bargaining to democratize that control.

The best contract can still be side-stepped by the simple expedient of automating the plant, closing it, moving it, changing the nature of the process or the product, or by any number of other methods that are available to a free management but beyond the scope of effective collective bargaining. It is true that these matters may be made the subject of collective bargaining and it has been suggested that unions be given the right to strike during the term of an agreement over this kind of dispute. But even this improvement would still leave the union in the position of trying to undo a decision already made, of trying to make the best of a situation that has already passed the point of control. It is a defensive position and all the retraining schemes, reallocation allowances, severance pay arrangements, short hours, long vacations, and supplemental unemployment benefits can never quite patch over the holes left by an automated, relocated, or closed plant.

And we are talking about things as they are now, not as they might be with a few key improvements in our present system. Our members have, at the very least, suffered the loss of years of seniority when plants like American Standard (Dufferin Plant) closed down. And in Sidney, our members faced the loss not only of their jobs but of their whole way of life when Dosco closed its steel mill. Only the intervention of the government and pressure on the part of the union brought a temporary solution to their problem, and that solution was at the expense of the public purse, not the company. It is this kind of management decision, made behind closed doors, without regard to any interests except those determined by an irresponsible management that cannot be condoned. Until the right to make such decisions is wrested from the hands of management and placed under democratic control there can be no industrial democracy.

The Problem of Shrinking Money

Finally, for those who think collective bargaining is the answer as it stands, without revision, there is the question of money. Much has been said about inflation that need not be repeated here. But for the average worker, inflation means that whenever he gets a wage increase, part of it brings his purchasing power back up to what it was when he last received an increase while the remainder shrinks almost daily in relation to the rising prices of the purchases he makes. If he is an employee of the International Nickel Company, a twenty-five percent increase in the price of nickel has little direct affect on him. He knows that it is the company's way of paying for his own wage increase plus a nice margin for added profits, but he is not likely to be a large purchaser of nickel so he is not affected directly. But indirectly the permutations of that increase as it takes effect product-by-product across the economy will return to him in the form of increased prices on almost every item he buys, thus reducing the amount of his wage increase. Economists like to refer to this effect as the "wage-price spiral," but for the worker and his union it is not a spiral but a treadmill. Until we have our hands firmly on the levers that control that treadmill we will have no industrial democracy.

To summarize the argument—not against collective bargaining itself, for it is indispensable, but against those who would have us believe that it constitutes industrial democracy—there are three key points:

1. Collective bargaining cannot secure for us freedom in our day to day working lives because it still leaves us subject to the orders of others.

2. Collective bargaining cannot protect us from the loss of our livelihood because this can result from a management

decision taken outside the scope of collective bargaining and in ways for which there can be neither adequate protection nor sufficient compensation.

3. Collective bargaining for wages without control over prices puts us on a treadmill, always catching up and having to run several quick steps in order to make a net gain of one.

But these are comments about areas which lie beyond the scope of collective bargaining as it is practiced now. It should be noted that for determining most of the subjects it now covers, including the level of wages, and regardless of any other change that might be made in industrial relations, no better system than collective bargaining has ever been devised. Moreover, it will be by means of collective bargaining that most of the essential steps toward industrial democracy will be taken.

Reevaluation

The remaining readings in this section draw upon the themes developed by Bell and Trower to indicate the emerging reevaluation of collective bargaining that has appeared in virtually every industrialized Western country. In 1969 a report of the Trade Union Seminar of the Common Market organization was written by Charles Levinson, General Secretary of the International Federation of Chemical and General Workers Unions, stated: "History will record, I believe, that 1968 was the year that industrial democracy advanced to the center of the industrial relations stage."[1] Levinson cited developments in

[1] Charles Levinson, "Background Report—Emergent Sectors of Industrial Relations," *Trade Union Seminar on New Perspectives in Collective Bargaining*, November 4–7, 1969, Paris: OECD, Social Affairs Division.

Yugoslavia, Hungary, Rumania, Czechoslovakia, Israel, West Germany, Austria, Switzerland, Holland, France, Italy, Scandinavia, England, Ireland, Japan, Australia, and Argentina.

The first reading is a vivid illustration of this development, an excerpt from the 1971 Workers' Control Program of the General Federation of Labor of Belgium. This article highlights the historical perspective of the FGTB on workers' control and places it in the context of a critique of the wage bargaining system.

A second article by Paul Blumberg, author of the recent and widely circulated book, *Industrial Democracy: The Sociology of Participation,* indicates how these union concerns have grown out of the failures of liberal reforms of the past. Included among these failures he discusses not only collective bargaining, but also the public corporation, advisory councils, and producers' cooperatives.

Last, a brief article by Ed Finn discusses recent bargaining demands of the Canadian Union of Public Employees, pointing up the relevance of the growing debate on workers' self-management to North America.

A Trade Union Strategy in the Common Market

Development Since 1945

After the last war, the working class in Belgium reached a new stage. Unions acquired a new status in society. They were officially recognized as the only representatives of the workers.

At the national level, through equal representation on national consultative bodies and by union representation in a large number of organs and commissions.

At the level of sectors of industry, by the spread of equal representation commissions and the possibility given to them of making their decisions obligatory by royal decree.

At the factory level, by the introduction of a statute concerning union delegations and by the creation of Factory Councils and Committees of Health and Safety. Only union organizations are empowered to present candidates at the elections to these bodies.

Social security was made obligatory, socializing a part of wages and thus assuring workers a minimum income in case of unemployment, illness, or injury. In addition, the link between wages and social security allocations—which are related to the changes in retail prices—aims at maintaining the purchasing power of workers and the socially insured. This kind of social legislation has been extended each year, with the object of consolidating on a legal basis gains of all kinds obtained by workers at the factory level or in one sector of industry.

The unions are continually extending their sphere of activity. At the factory and industrial sector level unions are continually widening their influence, from agreements regarding funds for social security to end-of-year bonuses or prosperity bonuses, to the rules governing hiring and firing of staff. Most of these agreements tend to limit the power of the head of the business—for example, by forcing him to recompense workers when he takes decisions which are unfavorable to them, such as shorter hours. Legislation relating to the closing of a business has the same objective.

After the liberation there were great hopes for democratization of the economy. The greatest effort at that time was directed toward the "organization" of the economy, a term used in fact to describe what should have been a *democratic* organization. The atmosphere of the resistance and the immediate postwar period had created a lot of hope, some of which was expressed in the law of September 20, 1948, which set up the Central Economic Council, business councils and Factory Health and Safety Councils:

The parallel development of democracy and capitalism carries with it the germs of an obvious contradiction. Whilst the progressive extension of the right of suffrage moved in the direction of bringing wider and wider sections of the nation to the exercise of political power, economic power remained the exclusive prerogative of the owners of capital.

Signatories to this law declared that they were aiming to bring about a first stage of economic democracy. They acknowledged that workers had an undeniable right to participate both in general planning and in business planning, not only in the details of social government but also in the direction of the economy. They therefore hoped to resolve the contradiction which had arisen between political democracy and economic power by formulating, under the banner of true democracy, laws dealing with both political and economic matters. These hopes were largely disappointed.

In fact, the experience of the past twenty years has shown that the law of September 1948 was not adequate to bring about economic democracy; it was, however, able to blaze a trail in that direction. In 1954 and 1956 reports presented to the FGTB congresses posed the problem of economic democracy and the structural reforms necessary for its realization. The 1956 report, "Holdings and Economic Democracy," illustrated in particular the stranglehold held by the oligarchs on our economy and underlined the need for flexible planning to place the economy at the service of the community. This report also dealt with the problem of the participation of union representatives in the management of social security bodies.

Present State of the Problem

The trade union movement, wherever it is strong, negotiates wages and the conditions under which these wages are earned. As a union gains strength, it will strive to obtain control over the conditions governing remuneration. For example, if one part of wages is derived from a productivity bonus, the union might demand the right to be informed about the development of productivity, and to receive information on production figures, hours of work, etc.

As far as the balance of power allows, the union will dispute those management decisions which may have adverse effects on this bonus—for example, when it turns out that a slowdown of production is directly due to errors on the part of management. It is only a short step from this to proposing certain modifications regarding production and equipment, either to insure that production figures (and therefore the bonus) should be improved, or in order to avoid unemployment. At the sector, regional, and national level, the very idea of democratic planning of the economy demands a universal challenge to management authority.

The union movement has gradually become aware of the interdependence of problems and of the need to approach them as much on the level of the enterprise as at trade sector or intertrade level, at regional level or with the whole community. With this in mind, the FGTB has demanded and obtained the right to sit on a number of bodies. It is essential that the various representatives be coordinated and included within a framework of a comprehensive policy that can enable us to act on behalf of the workers on various levels, public as well as private.

Today, the need for workers' control has become much more clear under pressure from two factors: the problems of employment and the alienation of wage-workers. Most often it is in relation to the problems of employment that the union is led to contest management decisions at the factory level, or at the regional or industrial sector level. During the course of the past few years, threats to employment have brought about awareness in the union movement of the need for preventative action which is one of the present reasons for the demand for workers' control.

The problem of employment implicitly raises all the other problems of life: that of future income, of careers, of the destiny of town and regions. Solutions to these problems will not take into account the aspirations of the working class unless the union movement opens up a new stage in the fight for limitation of management authority, to multiply the centers of democratic decision making.

Workers have become aware that this will not be attained only through nationalization of the banks and some important businesses. It demands an increase in the number of centers of democratic decision making at local, regional, and national levels. For the FGTB, the first stage in this direction seems to be workers' control at all levels in order to give real information to the workers in good time, so that they can direct their activities in full knowledge of the facts.

The improvement in the standard of living has not put an end to the problems of the workingman, that is to say, the problems he meets at his place of work, whether he is an industrial or white-collar worker or a civil servant. Modern technology restricts and often tends to abolish all personal independence in wage labor. The workers resent the present form of organization in the enterprise, tied as it always is to the social hierarchy, as if this were the immutable order of things.

Capitalism would like to see workers resigned to their fate in a society where the needs of the consumers would be made to measure, dictated by advertising. Thus resigned to his condition of wage earner, without any power over the daily reality of his work, capitalism's dream worker would expect little more of life than an increase in the amount of consumer goods and a hope of some chance happening, such as individual promotion, to get him out of his position and allow him to climb to some other work, which might give him a certain amount of freedom.

Georges Friedmann has very rightly pointed out that capitalism strives to maintain a barrier between the enterprise and the workers in it:

> Traditional capitalism exercises from this point of view a permanent and harmful influence on the wage-earners within the framework of their work place, by maintaining between the one and the other an unbridgeable psychological gap, and by constantly checking their deep need for participation by preventing them from using their moral and professional abilities fully in their work.

> This is one of the fundamental faults of this economic system, one which makes it essential to change it by the action of the working masses, in order to cater for the spiritual needs of man in a civilisation which fully exploits technical progress.

The result is a deep dissatisfaction which is not always expressed in a conscious manner:

Dissatisfaction, in fact, remains unexpressed at various levels of consciousness. First of all, in our competitive and conformist society, where an individual who is apparently jovial and satisfied is considered "well-adapted," "a successful type," and where, on the other hand, anyone who shows dissatisfaction in his work is regarded as a kind of failure, many people who feel dissatisfied hesitate under the pressure of their social environment even to admit the fact to themselves, let alone to others around them.

As Andre Gorz has emphasized, this dissatisfaction in the world of work often finds its expression in wage claims that do not provide a solution to the basic problem which motivates them, because the workers cannot resign themselves to being robots:

> They are more frequently motivated by a revolt against the condition of worker itself than by a revolt against the degree of economic exploitation at work. They translate these feelings into the desire to be paid as much as possible for time lost, for life wasted, for freedom alienated by working in such conditions; of being paid the largest possible sum, not because wages are placed above anything else in importance but because at the present stage of union action, one can dispute with the boss over the price of labor, but not over the control of conditions and nature of the work.

There will be no end to the basic dissatisfaction engendered by alienation at work by increasing wages or by decreasing the number of working hours. Work, like leisure or consumption, should be subject to the workers' choice. The part of their lives which wage earners devote to work cannot be left to the arbitrary decisions of management or to the inhuman "logic" of economic "laws." Only self-management of the enterprises exercised within the framework of a political democracy will give workers maximum control over their labor, as a stage toward mastery over their lives.

Workers' control appears, in the present relation of forces, as an obligatory stage which must be achieved in order to train workers in the tasks and responsibilities which they will have to assume in the world of the future.

On the Relevance and Future of Workers' Management

Paul Blumberg

In many respects, the issue of workers' management seems peculiarly irrelevant to the world of our own day, dominated by such overriding issues as war and peace, capitalism and Communism, the emergence of new independent nations, the crisis of economic development, the population explosion, the advent and consequences of automation, the quest for racial equality, and so on. The idea of "workers' control" seems curiously antiquated today, merely a quaint slogan of historical interest, based on political movements now defunct or impotent, on issues long forgotten, on premises which were perhaps even initially unsound, and on conditions which no longer exist. In short, history seems to have bypassed the issue of workers' management entirely.

My own view is that this historical judgment may be premature, and that workers' management may well become an increasingly important issue as we move into the final quarter of our century. This view is based upon certain signs and trends of our time, some overt but misunderstood, others more obscure and unrecognized. In this article, I shall summarize briefly what might be considered the major forces pushing in the direction of a renewal of the issue of workers' management.

The alienating character of much industrial labor, discussed so often since the days of Marx and still of prime importance in our world, seems to be substantially *mitigated* by the introduction of various forms of direct workers' participation. An impressive panoply of research findings demonstrates consistently that satisfaction in work is significantly enhanced by increasing workers' decision-making powers on the job. Under a great variety of work situations and among workers of vastly different levels of skill, work satisfaction has been shown to increase even though the technical process of production and the workers' tasks themselves remain unchanged. The cumulative weight of this research is slowly beginning to change the sociologists' image of the worker; to a growing number of writers, the modern worker is perhaps best understood as being oriented and responsive to participation.

Meanwhile, other "solutions" to the work alienation problem—such as a turn toward leisure, automation, anti-industrialism, and job enlargement—have all proved wanting, for one reason or another.

It must be noted, however, that although this research constitutes a major argument for a reconsideration of the issue of workers' management, scientific findings of this nature do not usually generate social or political movements and, in themselves, may have negligible impact on the course of history. At the same time, however, scientific evidence occasionally may be incorporated into ongoing social or political movements; witness, for example, the role of sociological findings in the movement to abolish racial segregation in American schools.

The growth and significance of public ownership *outside* the Communist world, both in the industrialized West and in the developing regions,[1] has been accompanied by a search for

---

[1] Public ownership in such "capitalist" countries as France, for example, is extensive: coal mining, electricity, gas, many banks, numerous insurance companies, railroads, aircraft, the Renault automobile works, radio and television networks, and much more. The public sector accounts for about twenty-five percent of the national gross fixed investment. For other Western countries, the percentages are as follows: Britain, 32;

appropriate administrative forms. The manifest failure of the public corporation to arouse the British workers' enthusiasm on the job stands as apt testimony that any kind of administration of the public sector that does not involve the worker directly in management, but only via remote representatives at the top, cannot hope to affect significantly the workers' attitudes toward their work or their company. This fact has been demonstrated on a wide scale: in West Germany (co-determination), in France (tripartite—government, employees, and the public administration of nationalized enterprises), and in Israel (the Histadrut or trade union-owned sector). The basic failure of all these schemes to change the meaning of work for the worker can best be understood by an observation G. D. H. Cole made years ago, comparing the psychology of *political* democracy with the psychology of *industrial* democracy. In politics, it is the events at the highest (national or international) level that matter most to the citizen, and about which he is most likely to be informed and interested. In industry, on the other hand, it is what occurs at the lowest level, on the factory floor, that matters most to the worker. A simple change in the locus of ownership at the highest level, from private to public, with no democratization of the workers' immediate situation in the shop and with no rights of direct participation, is likely to have a minimal impact on traditional problems of work alienation. This, more than anything, explains why these diverse forms of "industrial democracy at the top" have been failures from the point of view of the worker.

Nevertheless, workers' indifference cannot be overcome simply by involving them directly. And here we must take note of the record of joint consultation bodies, miscellaneous plant committees, and other advisory councils in England, France, Belgium, Sweden, India, Israel, and elsewhere. While these have involved workers directly or through representatives close to

---

Italy, 27; West Germany, 15–20; Sweden, 15; Norway, 14; Netherlands, 13; Belgium, 10. [Cited in Perry Anderson, "Problems of Socialist Strategy," in Anderson and Robin Blackburn (eds.), *Towards Socialism* (Cornell University Press, N.Y., 1966), p. 232]. In many areas of the developing world, especially in Africa and Asia, public ownership is even more extensive.

home, they have generally proved very disappointing and have failed to arouse workers' sustained interest. Perhaps because they are form without much content and have sharply circumscribed power and jurisdiction, workers often regard them simply as a waste of time. In Britain, France, Israel, and India, these bodies have achieved the most meager results, at best, and discussions of these forms sound like nothing so much as funeral orations.

Finally, producers' cooperatives, which do involve workers significantly in management, have repeatedly been proved both economically and socially an inappropriate vehicle for workers' management. Economically, they have always been plagued with chronic shortages of capital, stemming from their inadequate initial resources, and the hostile milieu in which they operate makes borrowing from the private capital market quite difficult. In the Western world, they are economically inconsequential, especially when compared to the flourishing consumers' cooperative movement.

Socially, producers' cooperatives have a tendency to "degenerate," as the Webbs and others observed long ago, due in part to the lack of outside public control of their activities. This "degeneration" takes some of the following forms: transforming the cooperative into a simple profit-making, profit-seeking business, indistinguishable from a private enterprise; exploiting a monopoly situation, often to public disadvantage (as has happened in Israel); closing off of cooperative membership; raising the cost of membership to a prohibitively high level; and resorting to the anticooperative device of taking on hired labor.

One cooperative form which has been successful, economically and socially, but which has been almost totally ignored by Western writers, is kibbutz *industry* in Israel. These factories in the fields account for an ever-increasing share of kibbutz employment and income, and they are generally organized according to kibbutz principles of democratic election of managers and rotation of offices. Although much attention has been given to the organization of kibbutz agriculture and communal life, research on the fascinating social organization of the kibbutz factory, which might have relevance to the industrial and the industrializing world, is almost nonexistent. With the exception of this unique form, however, the experience with producers' cooperatives has been largely a disappointing one.

The lessons of all the foregoing disappointments seem to be as follows: the failure of the public corporation suggests that direct involvement of workers is essential if the meaning of work is to be changed; the failure of advisory councils suggests that direct involvement of workers must take place within institutions that have significant powers; and the failure of producers' cooperatives suggests that the interests of the public must be safeguarded within the framework of any system of workers' participation.

As a consequence of these failures, there has been noticeable discontent with present systems of administering public property. For decades this discontent has expressed itself in a recurring quest, in the labor and Socialist movements, for new forms and new ideas. The issue, to what extent should workers participate in the management of the enterprises in which they are employed, runs like a thread through twentieth-century European politics; it disappears only to reappear again, for it has never really been resolved satisfactorily. It is clearly part of Socialism's unfinished business. And in this continuing discontent and failure to resolve the issue fully and finally lies the dynamic for further change and experiment with various forms of workers' management.

Industrial Democracy and Recent Union Demands

Ed Finn

The idea of janitors, maids, and other nonacademic staff having a voice in the administration of a university—proposed recently by the Canadian Union of Public Employees—has been made the butt of much editorial derision. The *Toronto Star* was the only newspaper to congratulate CUPE on its suggestion. Most other papers greeted it with gibes about "janitor power" and "beyond the pail." Very funny.

But is CUPE's proposal all that outlandish? Is it really absurd to ask that the employees of a university—or any other institution, for that matter—be allowed some say in the shaping of policies that affect their lives and livelihood?

At the nub of CUPE's approach to this question is the concept of industrial democracy. The history of organized labor can be viewed as one long struggle to push back the boundaries of managerial rights. These were once virtually absolute. But, little by little, employers have been forced by their unionized workers to negotiate matters relating to wages and certain working conditions. To this limited extent, at least, decision making has become bilateral and industrial life more democratic.

The scope of industrial democracy in Canada, however, is still narrowly confined. The union's restricted bargaining rights are exercisable only for a brief time at the termination of a contract. During the contract period, because of the widely held "residual rights theory," the employer is free to do anything not expressly prohibited by the terms of the contract, while the union can only do what the contract expressly permits. Consequently, the "government" of most business firms remains much more authoritarian than democratic. Management claims as an article of the private enterprise creed that efficient operation would otherwise be impossible.

The unions have never accepted any such limit on their right to joint determination. In recent months several of them, including CUPE, have begun to probe into areas that management has always roped off as its own exclusive preserves. The UAW, for example, has declared its intention to make car pricing policies a subject for negotiations in its next bargaining session with the Big Three auto companies. The Pulp, Sulphite, and Paper Mill Workers are bent on bringing to the bargaining table the paper companies' waste-dumping activities. The union's Canadian chief, Henry Lorrain, explained it this way: "Our members are the men who pull the switches to send effluent from the mills into Canada's waterways. We and our families live in the towns whose waterways are being polluted by this industrial waste. We can no longer sit idly by and watch the destruction of our precious natural resources."

More and more, unionists are taking the view that there are no "nonnegotiable" issues and that the relationship between an employer and his organized workers should be one of equals. They are able to quote several eminent labor relations experts to support that stand:

"The immediate source of authority in an enterprise," says Abbé Gerard Dion of Laval University, "comes from the consent of the various agents of production."

"Both parties approach the bargaining table without fetters and as equals," says Judge Bora Laskin. "There is no such thing as a residual right in either party."

"The unions have always had the legal right to participate in decision making," says Professor Stanley Young. "All they need is the economic power to exercise it."

Despite Professor Young's assurance, labor leaders would prefer to have this broader interpretation of their bargaining rights recognized. A program calling for a new legislative framework for industrial democracy, drafted in consultation with top union officials, will be submitted to the NDP convention in Winnipeg later this month. The NDP program would recognize the right of unions to bargain on matters traditionally held to be management prerogatives, such as production, manpower, investments, and research. But the attainment of a comanagement status is, for the time being, more idyllic than feasible. If it is ever to be achieved at all, it will only be in slow, painful stages, and most union leaders now are more concerned with reaching the first stage, that is, to obtain some control over the introduction of technological change, so that its adverse effects on workers can be alleviated. This means all material work changes have to be made subject to negotiations—something employers have so far fiercely opposed.

Next on the priority list will probably be a strong union push for complete access to companies' books, and for a full partnership role in the administration of jointly financed pension and welfare funds. Perhaps, in the years ahead, the main conflict between labor and management will be fought on this question of management's rights. The point at issue is whether corporations should continue to be run as "authoritarian private baronies" (to use David Bazelon's description), or whether they should—or could—be governed democratically.

III

Contemporary Models of Worker Participation and Self-Management

Introduction
to Section III

Co-determination in the Federal Republic of Germany, economic democracy in Sweden, and workers' self-management in Yugoslavia all illustrate the problems and the potential of various stages of industrial democracy. While rank-and-file pressure has been a factor in whatever advances have been made in this direction, the fact remains that the implementation of aspects of industrial democracy, in most countries, has come about through bargaining and agreements between industry and unions, through government legislation or by decision of a political party. The results achieved so far might seem impressive to an outsider, but to the workers and employees themselves they are far from satisfactory, as the current upsurge in direct action and demands for workers' control indicate. For the experiences described in this section, with the exception of the Israeli kibbutzim, "socialism from below" remains an ideal yet to be achieved.

"I work, and working I transform the world." The rank-and-file worker in the industrialized part of the world has not yet transformed the world but he is aware of his potential collective power and more and more frequently he attempts to break the chains imposed upon him by corporate management and the state. From Sweden in the north to Italy in the south, an increasing number of workers express their alienation and anger by demanding direct democratic control over the entire work process.

"What we want . . . is everything."[1] This demand of the unskilled Fiat workers in Italy during the summer of 1969 expresses brilliantly the political consciousness of a growing segment of Europe's working class. By demanding "everything" Fiat's 185,000 workers won a new fifteen-month collective agreement in June 1971. The agreement grants the workers a greater voice in changing the working environment, setting piecework rates and job classifications and standards, and in planning production.

In France, Italy, Czechoslovakia, and to a lesser extent other European countries, students have been in the forefront of the discussion and action for workers' control and self-management. In a recent interview, the national secretary of the Federation of Italian Metal Mechanics (FIM) gave full credit to the Italian student movement. Many students, he said, are now active in the plants and the union, pressing for workers' control.[2]

The pressure from below is clearly mounting. The following articles attempt to describe the current level of "industrial democracy" achieved in Sweden, the Federal Republic of Germany, Israel, and Yugoslavia, analyze their potential and the shortcomings, and illustrate the response of industry, governments, and unions to the growing militancy of rank-and-file workers. One lesson would seem to emerge from the experience in these and other countries. The struggle to reduce alienation and the attempt to establish social democracy cannot succeed until the principle of self-management and self-government is exercised at the level of the overall system as well as at the level of the smallest participating unit. None of the countries covered in this section has achieved this end.

[1] Quoted by Andre Gorz, "Workers' Control," *Socialist Revolution,* Vol. I, No. 6 (1970), p. 29.

[2] Abraham Rotstein, "The Strike at Fiat," *The Canadian Forum,* June 1971, p. 3.

Sweden

Sweden is considered by many American and Canadian liberals and social democrats to have an almost perfect system of economic democracy. Decades of uninterrupted social democratic government, a tax system which has narrowed the range of incomes and a vast network of public services have combined to produce a high standard of living and a system of industrial relations which is the envy of many reformers in Canada and the United States. The two contributors to this section bring a much needed measure of reality to this subject.

The extraordinary close cooperation between the Swedish Employers' Confederation (SAF) and the major trade union federations can only be understood against the background of decades of social democratic rule and the high degree of centralized organization of almost every segment of Swedish society. The specific Swedish pattern of employer-union-government collaboration has brought about a system which one Swedish economist has called *functional socialism,* where instead of widespread nationalization of industry there has taken place a process of socialization and regulation of certain functions which were previously regulated and controlled by the capitalists themselves. The extent of labor-management cooperation, the high level of centralized organization of employers and workers, and the role of the Swedish Government in labor-management relations are summarized by Wilfred List, the labor reporter of the *Globe and Mail* (Toronto).

The peaceful course of Sweden's industrial relations was recently shattered by massive wildcat strikes. Lars Erik Karlsson shows why rank-and-file pressure for workers' management has become a factor to be reckoned with by unions and management. The challenge has been well understood by government, employers, and the unions. Experiments in industrial democracy are carried out by all three. At the same time, Prime Minister Palme is continuing his step by step reform program in an attempt to meet the demands of militant workers and the left wing of his own party without arousing the all-out opposition of Sweden's business community. In December 1970, the government passed a law forcing banks to open their boards to representatives of the public in order to give added weight to social considerations in decisions dealing with investment.

The Confederation of Swedish Trade Unions (LO) in particular seems to have sensed the importance of the growing restlessness among Swedish workers. It has started a nationwide series of conferences on the working environment geared specifically to young workers who are the backbone of the emerging militancy. The record number of motions from unions and their local branches for the Eighteenth Congress of the LO included many dealing with industrial democracy. Many of these motions demanded immediate restrictive action on prerogatives to hire and fire workers and to manage and distribute work within enterprises.

The Eighteenth Congress of the LO, held in September 1971, may prove to have been a turning point in the history of Sweden's trade union movement. The program of action adopted by the delegates deals essentially with four related issues: working environment, industrial democracy, wage policy, and economic policy. The demands for a better working environment and for increased worker participation and control within enterprises would seem to have emerged as the two key demands of the LO. To attain a greater degree of industrial democracy, a series of new laws and collective agreements will be required. The Swedish Trade Union Confederation now insists that the right of the employer "to manage and distribute work at will" be abolished. Individual workers will have to be granted a wider scope of freedom and independence at the workplace which had hitherto been dominated largely by economic and technical considerations. Workers are to gain an influence in the selection of supervisors whose commanding position will have to be replaced by a system of cooperation between employees and supervisors. As Karlsson points out, the period leading up to the election campaign of 1973 will be of critical importance.

In Sweden the Byword Is Cooperation

Wilfred List

Sweden, a country that has experienced only three strikes of major significance in the past twenty-three years, is the signpost for industrial peace in the Western world.

The peaceful course of Sweden's industrial relations is all the more remarkable considering the country has a workforce of more than 3.5 million out of a population of about 7.9 million and that ninety percent of industrial workers and seventy percent of white-collar workers are union members.

For more than two decades students of labor relations have flocked to Sweden to study its system of industrial relations and to search for the answers to the stability in the country's labor-management relations. But neither royal commissions nor government task forces have been able to bring away with them a magic formula for easing conflict in their own countries. Is it all a mirage, or does Sweden have a secret prescription for avoiding industrial warfare?

The Elements of Peace

Industrial peace in Sweden is composed of a variety of elements that is difficult to separate and apply singly as the solution to labor-management problems elsewhere. But, the experience in Sweden offers a guide for labor-management harmony in other countries.

Sweden is an industrialized country with a high degree of specialization. Its standard of living is comparable to Canada's, and the normal income of an industrial worker is about the equivalent of $4,000 in United States dollars. But the big difference between Sweden and North America is that, in the Scandinavian country, compromise is preferred by labor and management to conflict, and reason to emotion. Unions are fully accepted as equal partners in the Swedish economy and labor has responded by a display of responsibility unmatched in North America. In Sweden, the byword is cooperation.

Labor violence is unknown, picketing is a rarity, wildcat strikes are almost nonexistent and both unions and management have a respect for each other seldom found in Canada. It is almost the idyllic state in terms of industrial relations. Sweden is one of the world's most highly developed industrial countries, yet the stability of its labor relations sets it apart from other developed lands.

The Swedish experience must be viewed against the background of its history and development. The rapid course of economic expansion in Sweden helped to smooth the path of social and labor developments. The homogeneity of the country's population, both in religion and in race, has been an important factor in averting disruptive social forces. But perhaps the key to the peaceful path of industrial relations is the high degree of organization in Swedish society. Sweden is characterized by its strongly centralized organizations which have developed over the past sixty-five years. Almost every element in the society is organized.

Employers in private industry are strongly organized into the Swedish Employers' Confederation, known as SAF, and the greater part of the industrial workers are members of the Confederation of Swedish Trade Unions (LO). White-collar workers are also unionized and belong to the Central Organization of Salaried Employees (TCO). To complete the picture, professional employees with degrees are banded together in the Swedish Professional Associations (SACO).

The Pattern for Bargaining

SAF, the dominant employer organization, has about 25,000 members employing more than 1.2 million persons. LO, with 1.6 million members, is the authoritative voice of the country's industrial workers; while TCO is the central body for about fifty percent of the salaried workers.

This high degree of union and employer organization has created a balance of power in Swedish labor relations that has served as a deterrent to conflict and has helped to promote the mutual interest of employers and workers. Although the big employer confederation and the Confederation of Swedish Unions set the pattern in bargaining, employers in banking, insurance, commerce, shipping, agriculture, forestry, and service trades have their own organizations and bargain directly with their union counterparts.

In recent years, the pattern for wage increases has been set in top level bargaining between negotiators for SAF and for LO. This is in direct contrast to the situation in Canada, where the Canadian Labour Congress plays no role in bargaining and no employer federation has wide bargaining powers.

This highly centralized form of bargaining precludes the development of many isolated strikes in which small units of workers are pitted against employers, such as we have witnessed in Ontario at the Tilco Plastics and Proctor-Silex companies. And, because of the virtually 100 percent organization among industrial workers, strikebreaking and strikebreakers are terms that have no meaning for Swedish employers or unions.

The employer and union organizations in Sweden have a tight power structure. The employers' confederation (SAF) sets its broad policies at a general assembly of 394 delegates, which usually meets once a year. These policies are refined by a general council of eighty-nine members, chosen by affiliated associations, and the application of the council's decisions is carried out by a board of twenty-seven members. But the detailed, day to day activities of SAF are directed by the managing director and his staff.

There is a similar structure within LO. A congress, comparable to conventions of the Canadian Labour Congress, meets every fifth year to discuss the general direction of LO policies. A general council of 140 delegates meets twice a year for a closer look at LO positions. But the real power is in the hands of a thirteen-member executive board elected by the congress, and headed by the president of LO. TCO, representing the white-collar workers, has a structure similar to LO.

The Swedish system precludes individual action. Employers must be prepared to subordinate their authority to that of SAF in collective bargaining. Every labor contract must have SAF's approval and affiliated members are liable to penalties if they ignore this rule or break the employer front in an open conflict by making a separate agreement contrary to the SAF line. Unions affiliated with LO also have a limitation on their freedom to take an independent course.

LO does not wield as much power over its affiliates as SAF. But any affiliate that calls a strike involving more than three percent of its membership must have the prior approval of LO; otherwise it forfeits its right to financial assistance from the central organization. As in Canada, union members in Sweden are often more militant than their leaders and the general policy of LO in relating its wage proposals to the economic realities of the country sometimes brings rumblings of dissent from sections of the union membership. But LO policy is invariably supported.

There are also strains and tension inherent in the collaboration at the plant level between the union officials and the employers. The union officer has to strive for an extension of the rights of workers for a voice in plant decisions and at the same time defend concessions made to the employer. But despite the problems of attempting to reconcile the interests of the members with that of the employer, the unions in Sweden appear to have more deep-rooted membership support than is the case in Canada. Perhaps this is because industrial peace in Sweden and collaboration between employers and unions have produced a standard of living in the country trailing only the United States and Canada, and one far above the standard prevailing in the rest of Europe.

How It Happened

The major foundation of Sweden's current industrial peace is a series of agreements called the Saltsjobaden Agreement, named after a resort which has become a traditional meeting ground for the top representatives from labor and management. These agreements, initiated in the late thirties, were designed to draw up ground rules for the parties and keep government out of the labor relations picture. As a first step, they formed a Labour Market Committee made up of seven representatives from each side. The committee has since become a permanent institution for the discussion of common problems. The basic agreement reached in 1938 is the underpinning for labor-management relations in Sweden today. It sets out the procedure for the negotiation of labor-management disputes and rules governing dismissals and layoffs, as well as adopting a system of dealing with labor conflicts which threaten essential public services.

The question of whether workers in essential services in Canada should have the right to strike is the subject of intense debate in this country. But in Sweden, the right to strike extends not only to civil servants, but to police and fire departments, and utility and hospital workers. However, it is questionable whether the right to strike would ever be exercised in a vital service area. Under the Basic Agreement, any conflict that threatens essential public services may be referred to a body known as the Labor Market Council which is composed of three representatives from labor and three from management. The findings of the council are not binding but, because the body is representative of both major power blocks, it is not likely that the parties to a dispute would risk moral censure by rejecting council recommendations.

For fifteen years the Council's strength was never put to test. In that period, from 1938 to 1953, there were no conflicts in the public sector. But in 1953 the country faced the threat of a strike in the electrical generating industry. Positions of labor and management were hardening when the issue was referred to the Labor Market Council. All were aware that failure would bring a renewal of demands for government regulation in public interest cases. The crisis was averted through a unanimous recommendation by the Council which was accepted by the conflicting parties.

Legislation in Sweden covering collective bargaining is not unlike the key provisions of the law in Canadian jurisdictions: it makes collective agreements enforceable and compels arbitration of disputes over their interpretation; it makes the intervention of a government mediator obligatory if the parties cannot reach agreement on a new contract; and it requires one week's notice of strikes or lockouts if mediation fails.

A problem in the central negotiations has been to achieve a balance between the wage issue and the requirements of the individual unions. Central negotiations and trade negotiations usually take place concurrently. But increasingly, the practice has been to bring highly specialized union problems into central bargaining because of the unwillingness of employers to make concessions to the unions involved until they are aware of the cost to be incurred in the central negotiations.

It is one of the characteristics of bargaining in Sweden that the mainspring of debate and agreement is a good knowledge of economic facts that are used not only to justify demands but also to test them in terms of what they mean to the industry and to the country as a whole. Labor in Sweden recognizes that workers can advance economically only through increased production and a healthy economy.

LO and SAF have a joint research bureau preparing wage statistics. In addition, economic data is available from the National Institute of Economic Research and the National Labor Market Board. The parties are free to interpret the statistics to bolster their own positions, but at least there is no argument over the validity of the statistics themselves. Bargaining is often conducted with the assistance of an impartial chairman, usually a skilled mediator who has served in that capacity before. If negotiations break down, eight district mediators are ready to step in to help solve the dispute in their respective regions—a process not unlike Ontario's conciliation services. In critical situations, the government appoints a special mediator or a three-man mediation commission. Marathon sessions, familiar to conciliators in Ontario, are carried on around the clock, and usually bring agreement.

The LO-SAF agreements provide for a minimum wage increase, with variations for different regions. But it is up to the individual unions and employer federations to decide how the increase will be applied in an industry or plant.

Unlike the situation in Canada, unions in Sweden do not normally take the agreements back to their membership for ratification. Many unions empower their negotiators to sign the agreement at the bargaining table.

The Right To Strike

Although strikes are rare, they have not yet disappeared from the Swedish labor scene. But there are massive deterrents arising out of the very strength of employer and union organizations. The balance of power means that the strike is used with great discretion and works strongly against any show of force. But the system is not infallible. The record is marred by a five-month strike in the metal industry in 1945, by a nationwide dispute in the food products industry in the spring of 1953 that ran for five weeks, and by a teachers' strike in 1966. But when strikes do take place, there are no outward signs. Law and order are maintained. Strikebreaking is shunned and employers simply close down.

A major test of Sweden's ability to maintain the peaceful course in industrial relations came in 1966 when the parties faced the toughest and most complicated wage negotiations they had ever experienced. The deterrent factor inherent in the existence of two major power blocks was vividly demonstrated in those negotiations. Despite the efforts of a commission appointed to mediate the dispute, negotiations broke down and

LO served notice of a ban on overtime. SAF retaliated by giving notice of a lockout for about 570,000 members of LO.

Under these crisis conditions, the commission renewed its efforts and eventually brought about an agreement that reduced the 45-hour work week to a maximum of 42½ hours and provided for a wage increase that incorporated a special allowance for workers with low incomes. Manfred Nilsson, chief of LO's Information Department, told me at the time: "Both unions and employers are so important in Sweden's highly organized economy that they feel an immense sense of responsibility."

The bargaining between SAF and LO that results in an agreement affecting the entire country is concentrated at the end in the hands of two persons: the chairman of LO, Arne Geijer, and the managing director of SAF, Bertil Kugelberg.

Wage-rates

Sweden's wage system is based primarily on piecework rates. Both employers and workers have accepted the need for new methods and techniques to improve productivity. While there is a difference between unions and employers on how to divide the fruits of higher productivity, the unions know that only by improving labor output can they increase wages without impairing the economy.

Piece rates account, in part, for the so-called wage drift in industry—a process under which earnings in some industries rise far higher than the negotiated rates. This later leads to demands for general increases of a size to allow workers in the low wage sector to catch up. Swedish workers are sold on piece rates—a system that is generally opposed by unions in Canada. Much of the in-plant bargaining relates to the piece rates.

Inge Carlsson, plant chairman at a modern shipyard in Goetenberg, told me that the union prefers piecework because it results in higher wages. "There are some people who say you have to work harder under this system. But it is a matter of working more efficiently." Piecework is also the basis for computing earnings in the construction industry. New agreements are negotiated for each project. About two-thirds of all hours worked by manual laborers is at piece rates.

The Labor Court

The matter of Sweden's Labor Court has been raised during discussion of the report of Ontario's Royal Commission on Labour Disputes. The court, which consists of seven members, including two representatives from labor and two from the employer group, has not had much work in recent years. Its prime task is to deal with grievances arising out of disputes over the interpretation of collective agreements, but the parties have been so successful in resolving their own differences that in 1966 only twenty-eight cases reached the Labor Court. The court also deals with claims for damages for breach of collective agreements.

In contrast to the recommendations of Ivan C. Rand, who proposed heavy penalties for unions and employees participating in illegal strikes, the Labor Court in Sweden is limited to awarding damages against employees and unions for losses incurred as a result of illegal action. The liability of an employee is limited to about $45. The union can exculpate itself if it can show that it made every effort to dissuade the members from their course. The award of the Court is final. But there is seldom any quarrel with a decision by the Court, because it has won the confidence of all parties by its balanced judgments.

One of the issues that does not intrude into the bargaining scene is union security. Compulsory union membership clauses are forbidden by SAF for any agreements held by its members. But since unions are fully accepted and have such a high degree of organization, the lack of union security clauses does not pose any problem for the unions.

Sweden can point the way for labor in Canada in the matter of structure. In contrast to the more than 110 unions in this country, Sweden has only thirty-seven within the LO group, and this number is to be reduced to thirty-two. By adopting the principle that all workers within one industry, whatever their trade, should belong to the same union, LO has been able to eliminate jurisdictional fights within and between unions. But centralization also has its critics. An SAF official explained that concentration of decision making within SAF means that it is not always possible for the employer federation to carry out the wishes of individual employers. But this must be weighed against the need for maintaining a united front of employers to preserve a bargaining system that prevents union whip-sawing tactics—by playing one employer off against another.

SAF believes that without industrywide bargaining in periods of labor scarcity, wages would spiral and many firms would find themselves at a serious disadvantage. The unions see in industrywide bargaining an opportunity for achieving their goal of gaining equal pay for equal work for all employees.

Although the bargaining has been at the central level, local unions, or clubs as they are called in Sweden, have not withered. They have been busy with local piece rate negotiations, works council activities, handling of grievances, and educational and recreational programs. The works councils underline the spirit of cooperation between labor and management in Sweden. Also indicative of their relationship is the fact that both SAF and LO have jointly published booklets outlining some areas of their cooperation—a sharp contrast to the separate compartments in which the two parties function in Canada.

Cooperation between unions and employers is carried into every phase of industry, from industrial safety to vocational training. The works councils have had ambitious goals, but as in Canada their achievement has not always matched their aspirations. But they have played an important role in improving productivity.

Cooperation is also carried into the difficult and often controversial area of work study, important in Sweden because of the role piecework plays in determining the income of workers. The joint enterprises also extend to the white-collar sphere under arrangements between SAF and TCO and its affiliated federations.

The areas of dispute between unions and management in Sweden are narrower than they are in Canada because many of the fringe benefits incorporated in Canadian collective agreements, often after bitter conflict, are written into that country's social legislation. All workers are entitled by law to one month's vacation with pay if they have worked a full year; a national pension is augmented by a supplementary pension financed by the employers, with contributions based on a percentage of earnings, as required by the National Insurance Act; health benefits are covered under Sweden's national medical services plan.

The question of protecting employees from the impact of technological change is one that commands the attention of unions, management, and the state. Recently, legislation was adopted giving employees of sixty or over who are laid off a monthly salary of about $160 when unemployment insurance expires and until the worker becomes eligible for a pension at age sixty-seven.

Labor Market Board

The problem of dealing with the impact of technological change and rationalization of industry is as acute in Sweden as it is in Canada. But there appears to be a broader-based, better-organized program in Sweden that is carried out within the framework of the country's Labor Market Board. The Board has many of the functions of Canada's Manpower Department, but despite the fact that it is not a department of government, resources at its command are far greater, and so is its authority. The governing body of the Board consists of labor and management representatives and two members of the Board. Its functions cover every phase of manpower and employment policies, all directed toward the goal of full employment. It has the power to initiate and terminate public works projects consistent with employment conditions; it initiates mobility programs that include provision for the purchase of houses owned by workers who are forced to seek employment elsewhere; it undertakes retraining schemes and makes recommendations for the release of tax-free profits that industry is permitted to place into a reserve fund for future use at a time when the Swedish economy or a region needs to be stimulated.

Labor Market Board policy has been effective if it is to be

judged by the country's unemployment rate. The rate last February was 2.7. In June it was 1.6. The Board also runs the country's employment service, one of the most efficient in the Western world.

The entire arsenal of labor market measures are applied, according to the need, if there is a shortage of employment opportunities. Public employment is expanded, vocational training is intensified, and the pace of public building and construction is accelerated.

One of the most valuable features of the cooperation among all groups in the labor market is the Swedish employers' practice of reporting in advance to the National Labor Market Board any anticipated layoffs and planned curtailment or discontinuance of production, as well as any plans to recruit labor. The Board is also the supervising authority for the Swedish system of voluntary state-supported unemployment insurance. The funds are set up by trade union organizations and are open to nonunion members. It is also possible for domestic workers and self-employed persons to join the funds.

Swedish employers and unions have also cooperated to form a joint insurance company to provide special group life insurance. The company, called the Labor Market Insurance Company, was formed in 1962 and has become Sweden's largest life insurance company with more than 100,000 employers and more than 1,100,000 workers as policyholders.

Job Training

Both SAF and LO place great emphasis on education. SAF operates a Supervisory Training Institute, which provides training in nontechnical subjects for about 1,500 supervisors a year at its up-to-date boarding school, Skogshem, just outside Stockholm. SAF also runs an institute for the promotion of industrial efficiency and has even arranged courses in time and motion studies for LO officials. LO has several schools which offer courses from a week to three months in a wide range of subjects, including political economy, safety practices, trade union problems, and social psychology. TCO has similar educational projects for white-collar workers.

There is growing stress in Sweden on the need to understand the individual and to help him cope with his problems. Although Sweden is a highly organized society, the welfare of the individual is receiving high priority.

Sweden offers many lessons for Canada. The Swedish system cannot be applied to Canada in its entirety as a pattern for labor relations in this country; but something of the spirit that prevails in Sweden could offer Canadian labor and management hope for improvement in their relations. Perhaps it's time now not only for a closer look at how labor and management get along in Sweden, but for an effort by the two parties in this country to apply the lessons of Sweden in their own relationships.

Industrial Democracy in Sweden*

Lars Erik Karlsson

Industrial democracy has now been under discussion in Sweden for close to fifty years. For long periods only the trade union press had space for it; but from time to time it has been taken up by the big dailies and television and given new topicality. During 1969–70 the debate was marked by a new intensity. So-called "progressive" politicians suddenly found it expedient to pay lip service to the importance of workers' participation. Norwegian sociologists held "salvation rallies" for employers,

* Translated by Frank Ward.

seeking to convert them to the straight and narrow path of industrial democracy. LO (the Swedish Confederation of Trade Unions) has been pressing for the setting up of experimental activities in private companies. Every political party in Sweden has made a progressive-sounding pronouncement on the question in its program. The Social Democratic and Liberal parties have special teams studying the matter. The only group so far not to have declared themselves in favor of industrial democracy are the employers, who, through spokesmen, have let it be known that "experiments with various forms of participation are perfectly acceptable provided no attempt is made to limit the decision making rights of executives." Industrial democracy is, in other words, fine, provided it is restricted to management!

Rarely has so important a social problem been debated so much with so little outcome. The joint industrial councils are good so far as they go, but one would have to have a very poor regard for democracy to think them enough in themselves. The growing demand for industrial democracy is interpreted in some quarters as the result of "increasing democracy" in our society as a whole. This is to be doubted. In spite of some noteworthy experiments with school and university democracy and intense discussion of municipal and industrial democracy, the signs in fact point to Sweden progressing more and more toward management by elite, centralization, and bureaucracy. Within local government, management, political organizations, trade unions, and—last but by no means least—within the economy as a whole, there is a relentless but silent movement toward concentration of power. Rationalization, promotion of efficiency, and specialization usually result in the number of decision makers actually becoming smaller and the individual deciding less and less.

The debate partly functions as a safety valve, which, paradoxically, serves to increase the trend toward concentration. But in the long run it can help to create a climate of opinion favorable to reforms which could set developments moving in a democratic direction. Before this can happen, though, the debate must be purged of the glib and euphemistic terminology developed by apologists of the status quo. Empty talk about cooperation must be shown up for the hot air it is and the true situation must be formulated as clearly as possible, so that a realistic plan of action can be drawn up.

In order to grasp why so little has been done about this question, in spite of Sweden having had a Social Democratic Labor government for nearly forty years, we must scrutinize the basic power structure of the country. Industrial democracy is radically different from other reforms. It cannot be brought about through the creation of more bureaucrats or by allocations from the treasury. It requires a drastic reform of those sectors—industry, commerce, trade, etc.—which together form the very backbone of the national economy. The true value of industrial democracy can only partly be formulated in conventional liberal economic terms, since it effects qualitative changes in people's lives rather than quantitative, material ones.

Since political democracy was achieved in Sweden some fifty years ago, a great number of important reforms have been carried through: national basic pension; ATP (the National Supplementary Pension Scheme)[1]; health insurance; and increased social welfare. Major reforms have been made in the educational system and the government has adopted a labor market policy. These measures have resulted in a great improvement in the lot of ordinary people. But in the long run they have also done much to further the interests of big business.

Many years have passed since the Swedish labor movement last increased its power in relation to that of the capitalists and employers. In spite of the "democratic breakthrough," most of

[1] Following a bitter political struggle at the end of the 1950s, the Social Democrats succeeded in introducing a major reform in the pension system. This meant that all employees would receive a pension which would, in real terms, correspond to two thirds of their income during their ten best-paid years of working life. Employers pay contributions to a central fund which at present stands at around Kr. 30,000 million; or about one fifth of the GNP in 1970. This is somewhat less than the total stock exchange value of Sweden's 100 biggest companies. In the course of the coming decade the Fund is expected to rise to Kr. 80,000 million.

society's institutions still retain their basically authoritarian character. The class society is characterized by strict division between the rulers and the ruled, and by big differences in income, status, influence, working conditions, and human dignity.

The judicial and educational systems, the press, the armed forces, management, and companies continue to be run according to bourgeois concepts. Economic policies are still determined by class-biased economic theories. The goal of maximum production, irrespective of what is to be produced or under what kind of working conditions, has provided the basis for a tacit understanding between social democracy and the business world.

On their way up the ladder, labor movement officials are compelled to modify their views somewhat. Big business must secure the cooperation of the workers' representatives, who have accordingly been absorbed into the power structure of bourgeois society. By allowing democratically elected officials to look after part of society's administration, the capitalists can proceed, undisturbed, to expand and strengthen their industrial empire. The Swedish labor movement has gained a certain degree of control over society's development through its party (the Social Democrats) being in power and through the strength of the trade unions. But this control is exercised in a capitalist society where the rules of the game have been decided by capitalists. This is why no truly serious attempt has been made to introduce reforms which might circumscribe the capitalists' power and lead to the official goal of socialism. It is permissible to administer, carry out minor reforms, patch up holes, and set right the blunders of capitalists, and generally support the latter in the quest for ever bigger profits. But we cannot, or will not, introduce reforms which are inimical to capitalism. It is for this reason that the question of industrial democracy has been held in abeyance for nearly fifty years.

The possibility of transforming the labor movement's passive attitude to capitalism into a determination to carry through fundamental reforms, thereby making genuine inroads into the capitalists' positions, depends very largely upon the movement's will and capacity to make a truly Socialist analysis of the dominant elements in our economic life and upon a much better standard of ideological training. White- and blue-collar workers alike must be shown that it is both desirable and possible fundamentally to change the companies in which they spend a major part of their lives, and in so doing transform the entire capitalist system of production. This calls for an effective critique of bourgeois ideology and organization; a clearly formulated alternative to these; and a long-term strategy for the transformation of society.

As long ago as 1923, a proposal was made by the Wigforss Committee on the setting up of joint councils in companies. Through these bodies workers' representatives would be able to protect the interests of the workers vis-à-vis the employers. The Swedish Confederation of Trade Unions and SAF (The Swedish Employers' Confederation) could not, however, reach agreement on the matter and both parties finally rejected the proposal. During the 1930s, a change occurred in the negotiating climate as a result of the "cooperative spirit" of the Saltsjobaden Basic Agreements (on negotiating procedure) and the question of representative bodies for workers once again came under review. But it was not until 1946 that the first agreement on industrial councils was signed. Under this agreement a council would be set up in companies with at least twenty-five employees (this was later raised to fifty) as soon as either of the parties concerned desired it. The councils would function only as advisory bodies and should meet at least four times a year.

The way in which the new councils functioned proved to be unsatisfactory and new negotiations were initiated. These resulted in the 1966 agreements between SAF and LO and SAF and TCO (The Swedish Central Organization of Salaried Employees), under which the councils were to function as bodies for both consultation and the issuance of information.

The possibilities the agreement opened up have so far, some four years later, been exploited only to a limited extent. It is hard to know why the councils have not been accorded any decision-making rights. It is my belief that this is principally due to the agreement having been based upon an entirely false conception of how a company functions. The agreement on co-operation shows that it is based upon "human relations" philosophy, which holds that conflict arising between management and employees is usually the result of misunderstanding, and that problem can be ironed out if only the parties concerned will call a meeting of the council and discuss the problem thoroughly. The unions presented a long list of demands at the negotiations (they asked, for example, that the councils be given certain decision-making powers, including the right to appoint foremen), but these were rejected by the employers. Since the agreement was in the form of a cooperation agreement, offensive action was out of the question. The result was a compromise. The agreement is at present so constituted that management, should it have a negative attitude to an industrial council's work, can effectively prevent it from taking decisions. Against this development, the council is dependent upon the efforts of the trade unions.

Freedom and the full realization of the self constitute two of the most important aims of democratic socialism. They are not merely compatible with the other socialistic aims such as equalization of wealth and incomes; they can actually help to bring about a society which is both democratic and Socialist. It is almost universally accepted that the creation of such a society involves the takeover by the state of a country's productive apparatus, either through violent revolution or by means of gradual reform.

Revolution is a proven means of achieving socialism's initial goals. But the price has always been high in terms of human suffering and destruction. In the established Communist countries, the goal of freedom from force and oppression appears, with few exceptions, to be as distant as it is in Western Europe and the United States. The injustices of capitalism have merely been replaced by bureaucratic injustices. The social democratic method of gradual reform has been beset by serious difficulties and has in no instance led to the attainment of a Socialist society. There are many who maintain that this is because such a society can never be brought about by peaceful means. But that such an approach has never yet succeeded does not prove that it is impossible. The true reason may be that the social democrats have simply used the wrong methods and have based their policies on a bourgeois liberal analysis of society, including market theories of economics.

Virtually every reform aimed at creating a more just and egalitarian society has either served to help capitalism to run more smoothly—through, for example, taking over responsibility for education, public health, telecommunications, the road and railway systems, etc.—or has been neutralized by adaptive measures on the part of companies and big business. Increased company taxation and inheritance tax have, for example, led to such devices as tax free funds and gifts of shares and money to the children of capitalists.

At the same time, Socialistic fervor within the Social Democratic party has dwindled and the dream of a Socialist society has given way to a welfare state ideology. With few exceptions, Swedish citizens now enjoy a certain minimum level of security and material well-being. But the equalization of living standards, which made great headway during the early decades of this century, largely came to a stop about twenty years ago. The process began as a result of the shift of power in favor of the workers, which was achieved through the political and trade union debut of the Swedish labor movement. Between 1947 and 1970, the variety of Socialism professed by the Social Democratic party has undergone a process of dilution. Though the clause calling for the takeover of society's productive apparatus has been allowed to remain in the party's program, the leadership shows little inclination to translate this aim into political action. In the light of the Communist system's failure they have instead chosen, as a substitute for socialization, to patch up some of capitalism's worst features.

A series of social reforms—general health insurance, ATP, improved social welfare and health service, etc.—has, as we have seen, provided the Swedish working class with a certain minimum level of material security. And through the trade unions, the workers have been able to secure for themselves a certain fixed share of what is produced.

But the older generation of social democratic politicians has a tendency to be complacent about what has already been achieved. They are reluctant to see remaining injustices, which include a profound lack of equality in incomes, status, power, etc. The private sector, which still controls some ninety percent of production, is stronger than ever today. Structural changes have led to economic power becoming concentrated into even fewer hands. Entire regions of the country are allowed to become destitute, the government's actions in this sphere being almost invariably inadequate. Due to a growing concentration of power, large segments of the economy are being run as monopolies. This results in competition dwindling and consumption being directed by intensive advertising. Within large companies there is a growing tendency toward specialization, which results in workers feeling less satisfaction in their work and a sense of alienation. "Free enterprise" consolidates its power at the expense of employees, consumers, and society as a whole. The result is the gradual deterioration of the human environment: destruction of nature, neglect to provide the northern regions of the country with adequate housing and public services, concentration of production within polluted urban centers, and—worst of all—increased social and economic divisions.

The class of capitalists and business executives responsible for the above is, from the democratic point of view, an unimportant one, comprising at the most a mere few thousand people. But the power this tiny group wields is immense. It was achieved by means of a gradual concentration of wealth. Big and financially strong companies squeeze out small and financially weak ones, while the private banks' investment trusts spread out their capital so that they can control a major part of Swedish industry by means of minority holdings. This concentration of power is partly the result of the unequal distribution of wealth on the one hand, and partly of the privileges which traditionally accompany formal ownership on the other. It is the owners of capital—or the dominant group within this class—who appoint executives and decide a company's location, production policy, investment planning, capacity utilization.

But the power of the capitalists extends far beyond the limits of companies and banks. Through buying up technologists, economists, and scientists at high cost they compel both central and local authorities to preserve inequities of wages and benefits. They enjoy great influence within the bourgeois opposition parties, to which they make large financial contributions; their voice also carries great weight in higher education and in research—due to the tax free funds they make available and to their practice of appointing professors to company boards. They have great influence over the press, both directly and through advertising. And they have immense political influence. The government is trapped between the Social Democratic party's radical wing on the one hand and "economic reality" on the other. This "reality" consists in the adaptive strategy of the capitalists in the fact of the state's intervention in the economy. By means of "investment strikes," dismissal of workers, closure of companies, and the movement of capital abroad, the capitalists can sabotage the government's attempts to implement Socialist policies. The government's reluctance to introduce capital levies, to nationalize strategic sectors of the economy and land, and directly to intervene in matters relating to company policy, shows they are afraid of retaliatory action on the part of big business. Every attempt to follow through economic policies which are wholly rational from the point of view of the majority but inimical to the interests of the capitalists is invariably greeted with a howl of indignation from the bourgeois press: "State interference!" they cry, and "Abuse of power!"

The social democrats' poor showing in the 1966 local elections resulted in a welcome new vitality in the ideological debate within the party and, in close cooperation with the trade union movement, it was possible to insure that the party retained power following the 1968 general election. The new radical spirit probably owed its origin—over and above the fear of losing the election—to the international current of ideas, which was characterized by a more profoundly critical attitude to the capitalist system. Another contributory factor was the growing realization that the much vaunted postwar social reforms had not after all really led to increased overall equality. The election campaign, in which special emphasis was placed upon the issue of equality, created a new mood which—unlike the welfare state ideology—was basically hostile to the structure and function of the capitalist system. Political developments during 1969–70, however, were a great disappointment to the left wing of the party and served to confirm the necessity for an intensification of the struggle for internal democracy within the party. Officials who turn a deaf ear to the demand for increased equality expressed by large sections of the people are enthusiastically applauded by the Conservative party and by *Veckans Affarer* (an influential Swedish business weekly). Such people must be made to resign or, through increased pressure from below, to change their political outlook.

The changes that can be made within the context of a capitalist system—as regards equality between owners and employees, men and women, and one region and another—cannot in the very nature of things be of a very far-reaching kind. In the short term, the lot of the low income earner can be eased through changes in taxation. Certain economic, localization, and labor market measures can help to level out inequities between different areas and sectors of industry. And trade union solidarity over wages can help to bring about equalization of income for different groups of workers. But all of these traditional measures—which are, needless to say, better than no measures at all—have shown themselves in practice over fully twenty years to be incapable of doing anything more than preventing a move toward increased inequality. Market mechanisms, mainly the actions of the companies, restore inequitable variations in wages and help to strengthen the concentration of industry in the big cities, often with the active support of social democratic municipal politicians. It is very unlikely that traditional tax measures will, to any appreciable extent, be able to bring about increased equality. Higher income earners, employers, and senior officials can—through price increases and concerted action, through professional associations—neutralize the effects of more sharply progressive income tax. After a few turns of the inflationary spiral we are faced with a virtually unchanged distribution of income.

This is scarcely surprising, since the basic distribution of power in Swedish society between employers and consumers, owners and employees, state and big business, is in no way changed as a result of marginal adjustments being made in the tax and social benefits systems. For this reason other methods of achieving increased equality must be found, which can insure that power relationships within society take on a much more democratic character. Influence enjoyed by capitalists must be reduced from above, through the state obtaining control over such vital economic decisions as localization, major investments, and closures; from the side, through state-owned companies increasing their share of the economy; and from below, through workers participating in the management of companies.

Representation on boards of directors through the acquisition of shares or new legislation can give the government effective control over all decisions which are of vital importance. The state-owned sector could expand rapidly if borrowings were made from the mammoth ATP Fund and by means of a rational reorganization of the companies. As far as the question of equality is concerned, these measures can only help to equalize certain regional and trade disparities. A decisive factor in the possibility of increased state influence leading to increased equality is the kind of policy which is followed within companies. If a more egalitarian way of running things is to be brought about within state-owned companies, a fundamental change must be brought about in wages, status, and distribution of power.

The factor which more than any other determines whether an employee is to be a high or low income earner is education. But education alone does not automatically insure higher productivity or a bigger salary. It is decisive, however, in regard to the employee's position in the company's hierarchy. Only those with a college education or the equivalent can in practice enjoy access to the better paid positions. The huge differences in incomes are dictated by the company's hierarchical structure, which requires that the dirtiest, most boring, and most dangerous working conditions be reserved for the less educationally qualified. Society does, of course, include certain groups outside the hierarchy—car dealers, lawyers, dentists, accountants, pop stars, for example. What all of these have in common, though, is that they have achieved their high incomes by being in a monopoly situation which frequently is maintained through restrictive practices. Similarly significant are those capitalists who, through astute speculation in land, works of art, or bonds, reap large unearned incomes.

The company's hierarchical structure is modeled on the *military* system. And the martial atmosphere is heightened by the triumph of Taylorism, time and motion studies, extreme division of labor, rate fixing, and—more recently—systematic job evaluation. The latter, together with merit rating and grading according to responsibility, education, and physical and mental effort, serves to create permanent disparities in wages and conditions. Such "systematic" codification, or merit evaluation, allegedly justifies inequities.

Investigations into the connection between power on the one hand and income and privilege on the other clearly show that those groups that are in power within an organization are able to appropriate a lion's share of incomes. Large companies with several layers in their scheme of organization and uneven distribution of power have a more inequitable distribution of incomes than a small company. In spite of all the talk of "qualified labor" there exists no truly objective way of measuring the value of work contributions. Job evaluation cannot tell us whether the engineer at his drawing board or the engineering worker at his machine is performing the more vital function. The fact is, of course, that the company utilizes the services of both and could not function if one or the other ceased to work. They are both units in the same system of production, in which distribution of incomes serves as a subjective way of evaluating a given group's bargaining position—or, to put it another way, power. Such evaluation is determined largely by the type of organizational system that has been adopted by the owners. The managerial classes, with incomes of Sw. Kr. 100,000 (about Can. $17,000) and over would find it hard to justify their high earnings were it not for the system of graduated incomes under which earnings descend in steps. Without this system it would be difficult for them to obtain the cooperation of their immediate subordinates, which is essential if the company is to function effectively. If promoted staff are to be willing to exercise authority they must receive higher salaries than the workers they are appointed to lead. The owners purchase the loyalty of the small wage earners in order to achieve control over the largest groups at the base of the company pyramid. Unable to defend this unjust wage system with logic, they talk instead of "market powers." These allegedly immutable and eternal powers are in fact usually the actions of the monopolized and minority-owned companies themselves. In order to defend their own privileges they refer to the activities of their own group. Talk of market powers constituting a hindrance to institutional reforms is a perfect example of doubletalk. It is wrong to reject demands for reforms within companies on the grounds of market conditions, which are determined by prevailing institutional conditions. If a semiskilled worker has a lower market value than an engineer, this is principally because he has been allotted a narrow and underdeveloped role and is easier to replace.

Another factor which helps to create inequality is the trend within the economy toward increased concentration in industry. Highly effective management frequently requires that production be carried out at a few large units. So long as ownership remains in the hands of a privileged minority, so long as the rights which accompany ownership continue to be exercised, and so long as growth occurs mainly through the self-financing of companies, then economic growth within the country as a whole will lead to increasingly big differences in income. The claim that wages and other incomes should be adjusted to the current market situation must be rejected and we must demand instead that incomes in our society be distributed according to political evaluation. The old Socialist maxim, "From each according to his ability, to each according to his need," must be our guiding principle in the setting of wage rates.

Because of the passivity of the Social Democrats, who show signs of becoming bourgeois, the capitalists were able to strengthen their grip on the Swedish economy during the 1960s. Intensification of production, close supervision, and discipline, have been the consequences of this development for workers and lower grades of office employees. A fast-growing corps of technologists and economists, under orders from the capitalists, is carrying out increasingly inhumane work studies. The volume of work submitted to such treatment has trebled over the last decade. The wage system has been made more complex and, as a result, more difficult for workers to check on. This in turn has worked against efforts to have demands made at local negotiations met. Local strikes are forbidden by law, and fully fifteen years have passed since the Swedish Federation of Trade Unions has called an official strike. The introduction of a technically advanced production system has resulted in the subordination of safety considerations to the demands of the profit motive, and unsanitary and demoralizing jobs are becoming increasingly common. Over eighty percent of the Federation's members believe that their jobs involve health risks. In addition, many older workers will face the threat of redundancy in the 1970s because they are no longer regarded as "profitable propositions."

The capacity of welfare state reformism to further the interests or working people—whether economically, socially, or culturally—appears to be exhausted. This is a consequence of the structural changes which have been taking place in international capitalism. International pooling of capital, coupled with an ever growing volume of exports (which now represent some fifty percent of total industrial production) threatens to bind the economy of Sweden—and her policies—even more closely to the imperialist nations.

The near impotence of welfare state reformism in a capitalist economy means that there is a growing disparity between what should be done on the workers' behalf and what in fact can be done within the status quo. The Social Democratic party and the trade union movement, which have always been intimately associated, are becoming increasingly centralized and bureaucratic. The movement's leadership functions more and more as mediator between the working class and big business.

In early 1970 the entire Swedish establishment was severely shaken by a series of "wildcat" strikes. It all began with 5,000 miners at the iron ore mines in northern Sweden going on strike for over two months. The fact that these mines are state owned effectively demonstrated the corporative connections between labor officials and capital. The whole collective bargaining machinery was in jeopardy. Prime Minister Palme was compelled to declare: "The interests of society as a whole demand respect for the law." So much for his professions of Socialism. Growing pressure from below, with as much as seventy percent of the public in sympathy with the strikers, in addition to hundreds of shorter strikes throughout the country, has led to revitalization within the trade union movement. More and more officials are realizing that their days in office are numbered unless they can satisfy demands for a decent working environment, security of employment, participation, and the systematic reorganization of the economy. In my own capacity as member of a Swedish government commission which is experimenting with different types of workers' participation in nationalized companies, I have encountered in many of these enterprises a strong militancy on the part of the local unions. A new consciousness, especially among the young, has begun to appear. The local unions in several companies are getting ready to form a workers' management. The biggest obstacle to the attainment of this is collusion between the government and private capital. The latter regards the prospect of the democratization of state-owned companies (which constitute only five percent of the industrial sector) as a dangerous menace. If Socialist methods of organization prove to be practicable within state-owned industries, then the objections of big business will be proved wrong. At the same time, a climate of opinion in favor of a wide range of Socialist reforms will have been created.

Those belonging to the left wing of the Social Democratic party are determined eventually to replace the existing "mixed economy" with a combination of overall planning by the government on the one hand, and workers' management on the other. This opinion is gaining ground and is likely, in the course of the 1970s, to gain a majority of adherents both within the party and the Federation of Trade Unions. With the bitter memory of a lost election in the 1940s still in mind—the result of hasty socialization—the labor movement is likely to concentrate more on industrial democracy than on nationalization. Few reforms result simultaneously in bettering the conditions of the workers and undermining the power of the capitalists as does the old Socialist demand for workers' power in companies.

The Federation of Trade Unions has created a commission to look into the question of industrial democracy and will be presenting a series of proposed reforms to its annual congress in September 1971. The commission is examining four principle aspects: representation on boards, staff policy, security of employment, and organizations of shop floor operations.

There is a strong demand for workers to receive initially half of all the places on the company's board; for the joint councils to be accorded decision-making powers in regard to personnel matters and for the employer's right to hire and fire at will, as well as to organize and direct production being restricted considerably. These demands, no doubt, will never be achieved as a result of negotiation; it must fall to a Social Democratic government to pass suitable legislation. If this proves to be the case a fierce battle is likely to shape up during the 1973 election campaign, with big business and the bourgeois opposition parties (Center, Liberal, and Conservative) on the one side, and the trade union movement, the Social Democratic party, and the Communist party (which has seventeen seats in Parliament) on the other. The outcome of this battle will depend on many different factors. Success is conditional upon the mobilization of active cadres within both sectors of the labor movement—some few hundred thousands of people; it will also depend upon the countermeasures of the capitalists being anticipated and rendered ineffective. The big private banks and export companies must therefore be nationalized.

The old Marxist tenet that the state apparatus is a weapon in the hands of the economically dominant class holds true only to a limited extent in the case of Sweden. It is scarcely likely that, in the event of a war between the capitalists and a Socialist majority party, the former would be able to mobilize the police and army on its side. Decades of Social Democratic rule have resulted in numerous vital posts in public administration being held by confirmed Socialists. And while the propaganda media wielded by the forces of reaction here are daunting enough, they are by no means as awe-inspiring as their counterparts in any other capitalist country. The most serious obstacle to the Swedish labor movement beginning fundamentally to transform the country into a Socialist society is presented by international trade ties. The risk of trade embargos, exclusion from monetary cooperation, and even outright military pressure, is very great.

If Sweden, in isolation from such monopoly-capitalist countries as the United States, England, France, and Germany, were to develop in a truly socialistic direction, then certain material sacrifices would almost certainly have to be made. But the alternative is unacceptable: an increasingly centralized, bureaucratic, and dehumanized consumer society characterized by huge social and economic inequities. The inescapable result of such a development would be class terror on the part of the capitalists, the rapid growth of a revolutionary Left, and the degeneration of the reformist labor movement. Within three years we shall most likely see which road is to be followed.

Federal Republic of Germany

The idea of worker participation in management dates back to the pre–World War I period when the modern labor movement had its beginning in Germany. While the original legal framework was in no small part the result of pressures from radicals within and outside the trade union movement, the final outcome was at best a compromise which bore the stamp of strong management and trade union opposition to the demand of the radicals to place management's executive power in the hands of the works councils. The modern version of co-determination arose in the years following World War II and the passing of the Co-determination Act covering the iron, steel, and mining industries. Co-determination in these industries offers somewhat wider opportunities for union–worker participation than the more limited Federal Works Constitution Act.

While West Germany's system of co-determination differs in many important respects from the Swedish model, there are a number of striking similarities. Neither system has given the rank-and-file workers much control and neither system has dealt successfully with the growing alienation of workers and employees. Both systems have placed substantial power in the hands of the trade unions. One observer of co-determination has stated that: "Co-determination has created elite positions for the trade unions concerned and this has fostered oligarchic tendencies within the trade union movement."[1]

There are a number of important political and strategic considerations which should be borne in mind by anyone attempting to judge the revolutionary potential of co-determination. The German Trade Union Federation (DGB), despite its occasional radical rhetoric, is very clear on one point which is well put by the DGB executive board in the article that follows: ". . . it is by no means the intention of co-determination to destroy the authority of the management. Nor is it intended that workers, acting through their delegates, should take over management." Co-determination "presupposes a system of free enterprise based on the principle of a free market economy." While different in content and structure, co-determination fulfills the function which collective bargaining fulfills in Canada and the United States.

The DGB article illustrates how co-determination has come about, how it functions, and why the trade union movement continues to press for the extension of these rights to all sectors of West German industry. To anyone who has viewed co-determination as a potentially revolutionary instrument in bringing about fundamental social and economic change in the Federal Republic of Germany, Helmut Schauer's critique will come as a shock. Schauer illustrates—convincingly, we think—that co-determination has failed to deal with the most serious problems of West German workers and employees. It is today pursued by the trade unions as a conscious policy to rationalize the existing capitalist social relationships.

[1] Friedrich Fürstenberg, "Workers' Participation in Management in the Federal Republic of Germany," *Bulletin No. 6,* International Institute for Labour Studies, Geneva: 1969, p. 129.

Co-Determination in the Federal Republic of Germany*

Co-determination is not a measure that can be implemented in individual establishments and enterprises independently of the social environment in which it operates. The desire for self-determination, therefore, must always be seen within the framework of the possibilities and needs of community life. Society must be so organized that it accords to every individual maximum opportunity for the free development of his personality, while the individual must always exercise his individual freedom within the consciousness of his social responsibility. Freedom and responsibility are as inseparable as the two sides of a coin.

It is not easy to assert the freedom of the individual in the modern mass and industrial society, and less easy to expand it. In the political sphere, laws and regulations are increasingly making their impact on the rights of the individual. In industry and in the economy as a whole bureaucracies and administrative apparatuses are continually expanding. In addition to all these matters is the inherent dynamic of economic development; where it brings greater prosperity, it is only at the expense of ever growing concentration and the increasing power of great enterprises. Under the influence of these developments man becomes more and more a mere "cog in the wheel."

* This article represents a collective effort on the part of the executive board of the West German Trade Union Federation (DGB).

New forms of dependence and constraint threaten the individual's rights of freedom, even in the affluent society. And for this reason workers and their delegates and representatives must exercise eternal vigilance in order to insure that the form of society emerging in the political, economic, and social spheres is so ordered that it provides adequate guarantees for self-determination and joint responsibility. This can be guaranteed only if the society in which we live and the exercise of authority in it have the sanction and approval of all those affected. In other words: a free and democratic order of society can be assured only if those who live in it jointly acknowledge and accept it as such. This can come about in a legal and orderly manner only if those in power at any given time (always with the right of reelection) are elected by those governed, and if the latter are able to control the authorities in the exercise of their power, and to dismiss them from office if they no longer enjoy their trust and confidence. The natural exercise of authority, and subjection to authority, is not abrogated under such a system; it is merely subject to its continued acceptance by those affected. The principle of the exercise of authority is thus contained within the limits of the institutionally guaranteed obligation that it shall be exercised only for the benefit of the governed, and that it shall be confined to its objectively essential bounds. In other words: power is tied to responsibility; anyone exercising power must at all times be conscious of the fact that he can continue to exercise such power only so long as he respects the freedom of those subordinate to him.

Such a system presupposes that every individual has a claim to accurate and adequate information on all questions affecting his freedom and his social responsibility. Further, it is essential that all grades of society should be in a position to form a free and independent judgment on all important developments in the society in which they live. Moreover, every individual must be in a position, in free association with others of his own persuasion, to insure adequate consideration for his own ideas within the play of forces in a pluralist society. If these conditions are fulfilled, then the free development of the individual is quite possible, even within the framework of a modern mass and industrial society, with its manifold forms of political and economic dependence.

In the political sphere the principles of a free social order have long been operative. By means of a division of power in the state, by the formation of political parties, by virtue of general, equal, and secret franchise, and protection against arbitrary action, the influence of the citizen on political decisions affecting his civic freedom and obligations is secured.

And so we have a position in which certain basic democratic rights are acknowledged in the political sphere, but not within the social and economic systems. In the economic sphere in particular, essential changes must be made. A truly free society can endure in the long run only if freedom and a sense of responsibility can be freely developed in all spheres of life. This is by no means to assert that the principles of a free and democratic system within the economy could be accomplished in the same forms and with the same methods as in the state. The forms to be implemented here must be such that, on the one hand, they limit the freedom of the individual to the least possible extent, but that, on the other hand, they do not unnecessarily restrict the autonomy of the enterprises operating in a free market economy. Those persons who live in and are affected by the economy should be enabled to exercise influence, in the sense of the free development of the overall market economy system, on decisions taken in the administration of the enterprises, and on the implementation of these decisions at plant and enterprise level. Co-determination and co-responsibility at these various levels must be in accord not only with the general principle of the personal freedom of the individual, but also with the functioning of the economy.

A general conception of co-determination of this type presupposes a system of free enterprise based on the principle of free market economy. In all those instances in which the economy is subjected to a central administration, there can be no genuine form of workers' cooperation or co-determination at the various levels of the productive process. All really important decisions affecting the volume and type of production as well as the forms of administration within the economic system are made by the central authorities and the ministries, with the result that there is little or no room left for co-determination and joint responsibility at enterprise and workshop level. Any form of co-determination to be exercised inside the enterprises by those affected by the process of the economy and particularly by the workers, is practically ruled out.

Genuine co-determination, therefore, demands at least in certain sectors of the economy autonomous undertakings operating within the framework of a free market economy system. The principles governing a free order of society can still be implemented in vastly different ways in different branches of the economy.

The Principles Underlying Co-Determination

In the Federal Republic, the question of co-determination at plant and enterprise level remains in the foreground. The reason for this is that, after the Second World War, the trade unions succeeded in obtaining extensive concessions for the workers in these sectors. Co-determination at levels above plant and enterprise level in all questions affecting economic policy was, and continues to be, a trade union demand, but so far no institutions have been established to give effect to this demand. If the general principles discussed in this article are to be made operative in enterprises and individual establishments, it is necessary to show how they can guarantee as far as possible the development of individual responsibility and individual initiative without hampering the fulfillment of the objects of the establishment or enterprises within the economic system. In every case the aim must be to insure that the economy not be operated and developed solely with the object of achieving maximum material results; it is equally important to insure its development along humane lines. And this is the object of co-determination: experience has shown that an economic system which takes full account of man as a human being is, in the long run, also materially the most successful.

Safeguarding Personal Basic Rights

Any form of co-determination would be purposeless if it did not, in the final analysis, serve the needs of every individual employed in working life. Failing direct and indirect beneficial effects on the position of the workers, no justification can be adduced for it. In correspondence with the basic values of free society it must be shaped so that all those who jointly form an enterprise and are subject to its authority both provide the legitimation for such authority and control it. This is to say that it is by no means the intention of co-determination to destroy the authority of the management. Nor is it intended that the workers, acting through their delegates, should take over management. It is rather the intention that management should be placed institutionally under an obligation to exercise its authority in the sense of a trusteeship, not to abuse its authority, and to act at all times responsibly.

Decisions taken within an enterprise affect the owners who have placed their capital in the form of the means of production at the disposal of the enterprise in the fulfillment of its declared objectives, but they also affect primarily the workers who work with these means of production. Irrespective of the conflict of interests between the two groups, the object of the enterprise, the production of goods and services, can be accomplished only by cooperation between them. Co-determination, therefore, means primarily that the fate of an undertaking cannot be determined by the owners alone.

This demand has long encountered strenuous resistance: only the representatives of the owners, it was asserted, could conduct an enterprise profitably and productively. Behind this view was the concept that an enterprise is simply an economic structure in which the production factors, labor, capital, and land, are combined.

This view, however, is false. An enterprise is not merely a combination of production factors under a single management. An enterprise is not merely an economic, but also a social structure; it is a cooperation of human beings. It is not possible to reduce human beings in an enterprise—in contrast to the capital invested—to the status of a mere "factor." Man in the course of his daily labor is not only a factor and a means of production; he is called upon to devote his whole person to his task. And for this reason he is entitled to demand that the basic values of a free order of society should retain their validity in the world of labor, that he be respected as a person, and that he bear his share of responsibility. All this amounts to the right to co-determination.

Co-determination places no restrictions on the legitimate rights of the owners of the means of production. But rights of property justify at best a control over things, never a control over men. It is unworthy of a free order of society that some men, merely because they own the means of production, should exercise mastery over other men.

That is not to say, of course, that within an enterprise everybody is entitled to have a say over everything. The representatives of the workers and the representatives of the employers must work together as equal partners. And in this connection the well-being of the enterprise must be secured and promoted within the framework of the free market economy. On the other hand, within the framework of the policy of the enterprise the social problems of the workers must be dealt with as matters of equal importance with the business problems of the employer. The system of authority and subordination at enterprise and workshop level cannot, of course, be abolished. But the operation of co-determination must guarantee that the individual is called upon to obey only technically essential instructions and is not subjected to any form of arbitrary treatment. Workers have a legal right to the fulfillment of these demands, and work rules must take full account of them.

In the institutionalization of workers' demands, full account must be taken of the actual needs of the enterprise and the workshop. In the course of the operation of co-determination in the coal and steel industries arrangements have been worked out which take full account of the interests of the workers, but which have also proved advantageous to the employers.

In this fashion co-determination represents an institutional measure, by virtue of which the position of the worker in an enterprise or workshop is shaped in accordance with the basic values of a free and democratic society. There are, of course, limits to the regulations that can be institutionalized. Co-determination cannot solve every problem of the workers, insofar as it has its basis only in the administrative organs of the enterprises. But co-determination does make it possible, by influencing the selection of the persons who make the decisions as to what happens in the workshop or enterprise, the nature of the decisions reached, and the implementation and completion of managerial planning, that matters affecting the workers receive equal consideration with economic problems.

Man in the Structural Order of Society

It was first demonstrated that co-determination rights can derive from personnel rights. The justification for co-determination can also be supported on quite different grounds. A free and democratic society can be assured only if binding norms for the guarantee of freedom in every sector are assured. The safeguarding of the maximum attainable scope for the freedom and responsibility of the individual is, however, jeopardized in all Western industrial societies. The growth of the great enterprises leads to the establishment of vast bureaucratic apparatuses, which exercise their power not only "externally" on the market, but "internally" on the lives of the thousands and tens of thousands of persons employed in these enterprises. Over and above this effect they can influence the prosperity and well being of whole cities and districts by virtue of their size and economic power. In contrast to the political order, in which the individual is protected by a multiplicity of legal rights, within the vast enterprises he is in constant danger of being a mere "cog in the wheel"; he finds himself engaged, transferred, dismissed, for reasons beyond his comprehension. He feels himself to be the helpless victim of an anonymous system. The managements of the great enterprises are so powerful that they can, and do, even influence political decisions.

A comprehensive free and democratic system, however, demands that no undue influence should be brought to bear on political decisions by the economic sector, and further, that free and democratic principles should operate within the economy. Co-determination can make an essential contribution to this end. Through the operation of co-determination, management of the great concerns is subject to a permanent form of control by those groups directly affected by their decisions. This control will be exercised not by the state, but directly within the organs of management, by those affected. By virtue of this private form of control, which is the implementation of the "principle of self-administration," the need for state intervention in economic processes is considerably reduced. Since the rights of the workers within the enterprises are institutionally guaranteed, and their activities and initiatives are thus personally engaged, clearly discernible spheres of influence emerge within which their freedom can develop.

At this point another question arises, that of whether the scope for freedom of action in economic life cannot be secured by other means than the German system of co-determination. In this connection the following should be noted: rapid and continual growth necessarily entails structural crises in individual branches of industry, and constant changes and reorganization in nearly all enterprises. In such situations, economic and social problems cannot always be solved by global economic-political measures. Particularly in regard to the workers, it is not always possible, within a dynamic and changing system, to safeguard their status by measures taken after the event. In order to insure real security for the worker, without at the same time placing obstacles in the way of essential technical progress, it is necessary that representatives of the workers, from their trade unions and from the plant itself, should sit in consultation with management at the planning stage of all important new projects in order to take due account of the economic and social consequences involved. Such consultation, which is all the more necessary in view of the rapid pace of changing conditions, becomes a matter of course if a structure already exists in which it can take place.

Further reasons which make it plain why co-determination was introduced in Germany are to be found in historical developments following the First and Second World Wars, and in the basic policy and organizational structure of the German trade unions. The following sections will illustrate these points in greater detail.

Institutions of Co-determination at Workshop and Enterprise Level

Corresponding with the complicated structure of office and workshop, as well as enterprise organization, it is necessary to operate co-determination at varying levels and in varying forms.

At office and workshop level the works council (*Betriebsrat*) is operative. It is the independent representative of all workers in a given establishment. The employer is not represented in the works council. Even though, according to law, the members of a works council need not be trade union members or sympathizers, it is found in practice that more than eighty percent of all works councilors do in fact belong to trade unions, and regard themselves as delegates of their unions. The rights of the works councils are laid down in detail in the works constitution law (*Betriebsverfassungsgesetz*). In principle they do not apply to any matters regulated by collective agreements. The rights of co-determination apply mainly to social matters, and to internal work regulations. In personnel matters the works council has rights of consultation on engagements, regrouping, and transfers and discharges. In economic questions it is empowered to exercise influence on managerial decisions in cases where the direct security of employment is patently jeopardized.

In all other cases, the workers in an establishment have the right only to demand information on important managerial decisions concerning production processes and the financial status of the enterprise. This information is supplied in the Economic Committee *Wirtschaftsausschuss*—joint works committee—in which staff and management have equal representation. The works council is authorized to conclude work agreements with management, except on basic terms and conditions, reserved exclusively to collective agreements with the trade unions; that is, in Germany, the rights and obligations of the workers are regulated not only by collective agreements based on the relevant law, but also on work agreements. Since the trade unions cannot be expected to dispense with properly organized and independent representatives of their own—despite the customarily close and friendly cooperation with the works councils—they arrange in most places for the election of their own direct representatives, the *Vertrauensleute*—shop stewards—who work in close cooperation with the works councils, but above all with the trade unions in order to promote specific trade union aims and policy.

The powers of the works councils and the shop stewards are, however, inadequate to fully safeguard the rights of individual workers and staffs as a whole, in a completely satisfactory manner. The reason for this is that particularly important decisions are made at top managerial level. In order to influence these decisions in the interests of the workers, and at the right time, other institutions are necessary. These institutions cannot be, and are not intended to be, a substitute for the works councils and the shop stewards; they work in close conjunction with them at those levels where the internal co-determination arrangements are inadequate for the exercise of effective influence at top managerial level. At this level, decisions are made on extensive new investments, on the closure or partial closure of a plant, on the introduction of new automatic processes, and on other matters involving far-reaching social consequences for the staff.

But not only in questions of major policy is it important that influence should be exercised in behalf of the workers. They are affected by the normal methods of conducting the business of an enterprise, and by the spirit and the attitude in which managerial decisions are made and implemented. And for these reasons, the workers and their trade unions demand a share in the permanent control of management, and influence on the selection of the persons who exercise actual power within the enterprises. These concepts have been realized in differing measures not always to the satisfaction of the trade unions.

In order to illustrate this point it is necessary to give some indication of the structure of company organization in Germany. For this purpose we will take as typical and most important the form of the joint stock company (*Aktiengesellschaft*). This is a three-tier organization: the supreme governing body is the annual general shareholders' meeting (*Hauptversammlung*), a control and supervisory organ; the other two bodies are the Board of Supervision (*Aufsichtsrat*) and the management (the Board of Management or *Vorstand*). The supreme body meets annually and makes basic decisions affecting the enterprise, such as the raising of new capital, election of the board of supervision, the articles of association, methods of raising new capital, closing down the enterprise. The Board of Supervision in its capacity as a control and supervisory body meets three or four times a year. It appoints the Board of Management, advises, supervises, and controls its conduct of business and exercises influence on important decisions. The Board of Management (*Vorstand*) has its independent functions; its rights and obligations are defined in company law. It conducts the business of the enterprise on its own responsibility.

The workers have no representation at the annual general meeting. In the Board of Supervision (with the exception of enterprises in coal and steel) the workers hold one third of the seats as specified by the works constitution law (*Betriebsverfassungsgesetz*). Pursuant to the law on Co-determination (*Mitbestimmungsgesetz*) and the amending law (*Mitbestimmungsergänzungsgesetz*), the Boards of Supervision in coal and steel enterprises have equal numbers of representatives of shareholders and workers, with equal rights and obligations. The boards of management under these two laws must also have a Labor Director, who cannot be elected against the votes of the workers' representatives on the board of supervision.

The most effective form of representation of the interests of the workers is therefore insured in the coal and steel industries by the presence of equal numbers of their representatives in the boards of supervision and the labor director on the board of management. It is true that, in addition to safeguarding the interests of the shareholders, the function of the board of management is also to pay heed to the interests of the staff and the public, but its main concern is the interests of the shareholders. And for this reason the trade unions have been particularly concerned to insure that, on the one hand, a position was created that in the case of all managerial decisions the interests of the workers are adequately considered, and that, on the other hand, the persons selected to fill responsible positions should be fully aware of the human responsibilities entailed in the exercise of their office and not prepared to subordinate human considerations to unilateral financial interests. The presence and authority of the labor director guarantees that in planning of managerial decisions the interests of the staff will be adequately considered.

By virtue of their equal representation on the boards of supervision, the workers' representatives can exercise effective influence on the long term policy of an enterprise and on management's day to day conduct of business.

Since the workers' groups on the boards of supervision include representatives of the trade unions, the works councils, and qualified persons selected from public life, it is always guaranteed that the interests of the workers will be safeguarded. In the boards of supervision of enterprises governed by the works constitution law, the workers, as previously indicated, hold only one third of the seats. The result has been that, in practice, they are scarcely able to exercise any effective influence. In these cases joint responsibility for policy is not matched by a corresponding possibility of exercising effective influence.

Empirical inquiries have shown that the operation of the institutions of co-determination at the various levels (work council and economic committee), in the boards of management (labor director) and the boards of supervision (equal representation), can and does give optimal consideration to the interests of the staff, without in any way adversely affecting the competitiveness of the enterprise.

It is necessary to stress one point: an indispensable condition for the success of the form of co-determination here described is the continuous training of workers' representatives in economic and industrial problems, as well as the expert advice of their trade unions. The introduction of a system of co-determination offers only the opportunity to exercise effective influence. The extent to which this opportunity is exploited depends on the energy, the expertise, and the natural aptitudes of the workers' representatives.

The Trade Unions and Co-Determination

In the course of their varied history the trade unions have never regarded themselves solely as the representatives of the interests of the workers. It has been a part of their policy at all times to pay heed to the interests of the community as a whole, within the limits open to them. This they did during the period of terror and repression under the National Socialist regime, as well as immediately after the Second World War. In those days no one was prepared to dispute their right, as one of the groups bearing no share in the guilt for preceding events, to speak for the whole people. When at that time they raised the demand for co-determination, they had the support of leading politicians of all parties. The program on which co-determination was based had already been formulated in a more or less rudimentary form after the First World War. A reintroduction of the system was a part of the program drawn up during the war by the German resistance movement associated with Oberbürgermeister Goerdeler, as well as by the German exile trade unionists abroad.

Following the total political and economic collapse of Germany, the demand for workers' co-determination became a decisive element in the trade union concept of a new order of society. In the basic principles laid down at the Foundation Congress of the German Trade Union Federation it was stated that formal democracy—that is, the franchise in itself—was not sufficient to guarantee a truly democratic economic system. It was, therefore, essential to complement the democratization of political life by a democratization of the economy. It was no longer believed that socialization and a planned economy could of themselves guarantee the achievement of this aim.

The particular character assumed by German co-determination and its institutions is attributable to certain characteristic factors. For instance, the German trade unions do not normally conclude collective agreements with individual enterprises, as do, for example, workers' organizations in the United States. As a general rule collective agreements are concluded on a regional basis. Such agreements cannot naturally take account of every individual problem arising in every individual establishment. They do, however, contain overall provisions on conditions of employment, the application of which can be defined in work agreements negotiated between the works council and management. The aim of the German trade unions must be to insure the establishment of duly authorized special institutions capable of dealing with the specific problems of the workers in individual establishments and enterprises, such as are provided for under the system of co-determination. Fruitful cooperation at enterprise level is consequently possible, since, as already stated, the trade unions have always regarded themselves as co-responsible for the interests of the community as a whole, and have safeguarded the interests of the workers in the consciousness of their overall responsibility.

The trade unions have not so far succeeded in implementing their conception of co-determination at plant and enterprise level, and at higher levels, as a single entity. Their representatives have been able to safeguard the interests of the workers at higher economic levels, but have not been able, through the medium of such statutory institutions as a federal economic or social council to exercise effective influence on economic and social policy as a whole. It is true that the trade unions have various ways and means at their disposal, through personalities sharing their views, to make their influence felt in the parliamentary, the preparliamentary, and related spheres.

The main weight of trade union influence must, however, continue to be applied in the establishments and enterprises in which the trade unions, by virtue of the co-determination laws, have established varying rights of control within the managements and administrative organs. The individual institutions of co-determination work in close cooperation with the trade unions, though they are by no means completely controlled by them. For example, the works council is elected by all members of the staff of an enterprise (even though in practice most of them are trade unionists). The workers' representatives on the boards of supervision, which control the operations of management, must, according to the provisions of the Works Constitution Law, normally be elected from among persons actually employed in the establishment. It is only on the boards of supervisions elected according to the Co-determination Law of 1951 that persons from outside the establishment itself may be elected, in addition to those from within the establishment. Finally, the labor director, who as a full member of the Board of Management is a specialist for labor problems, is expected to show special understanding of the needs and wishes of those employed in the establishment. He is elected by the whole of the board of supervision, in exactly the same way as other members of the Board of Management. It is true that by the operation of this system the trade unions are in a position to exercise a certain influence on their representatives in the organs of co-determination, but it is entirely fallacious to believe that such influence is adequate to insure the frequently alleged "centralized control" of industry.

The presence of trade union representatives in the organs of co-determination is based not least on highly practical considerations; the representatives from the enterprise itself are best qualified to understand the specific problems of the enterprise, whereas those appointed by the trade unions have a wider comprehension of the situation of the branch of industry and the economic situation as a whole, and, in many instances, a specialized knowledge of certain sectors of entrepreneur policy and intentions. In this fashion, and by virtue of the cooperation of all co-determination representatives, an optimal representation of the workers' interests is achieved.

There is also an important political reason for the presence of official trade union representatives in the institutions of co-determination, and that is that there must be a guarantee that all institutions of co-determination work in close cooperation with the trade unions, since only in this way can it be assured that, by the exercise of trade union power and influence, the entrepreneur accord to co-determination the respect that it is due, and that the workers' representatives in the enterprises may rely on advice, help, and protection in the difficult situations that can arise. In addition, mutual understanding between the workers' representatives and their organizations is essential. It has been proved that the trade unions, as the recognized representatives of the workers' interests, cannot, and may not, be excluded from the operation of co-determination. And for this

reason, all institutions of co-determination in all German enterprises do in fact work closely with the trade unions. In the
course of the never-ending discussion on co-determination, and
in connection with the economic questions affecting management, it is often thought that the Labor Director might find
himself subjected to a conflict of loyalties. It is argued that it
must often be impossible for him to pay heed equally to the
interests of the enterprise and the interests of the staff. In the
background of such arguments is always the implied reproach
that the Labor Director is only the "extended arm" of the trade
union movement within management. There can be no question
of any such problem. The Labor Director must, it is true, enjoy
the confidence of the trade unions, but he cannot, in his role as
an equal and fully responsible member of the Board of Management, be a trade union representative. In practice it has been
clearly shown that the Labor Director is not subject to more
internal conflicts than other people. In the modern industrial
society every individual has to contend with conflicts of loyalty,
as, for instance, when a member of a party accepts ministerial
office; when a Protestant Minister of Culture becomes responsible for Catholic sectors of the population; when a member of
the Board of Management of an enterprise feels constrained to
consider the interests of the community when reaching decisions
affecting the enterprise. Actual experience with the operation of
co-determination has shown quite clearly that the trade unions,
acting through their representatives in the organs of co-determination, have been able to safeguard the interests of the workers
without detriment to their function as partners in collective bargaining, or to their own independence.

Recognition of these facts led to the particular emphasis
placed on co-determination in the basic program of the DGB
adopted in 1963. According to this program, co-determination
is defined not merely as an aim, or an instrument, but as one of
the bases of a progressive and social order of society. The economic and political discussion of co-determination has played
an extraordinarily important role in the trade union sphere. The
outcome of these considerations is the demand for a comprehensive legislative reorganization of the right of economic co-
determination within the framework of a fundamental reform of

company law. Our demand is that the system of "qualified co-determination" valid in coal and steel shall be extended into other fields. Further, knowledge and understanding on the part of the general mass of trade union membership of the meaning and importance of co-determination is to be considerably increased, and the training and qualifications of those actually entrusted with its functioning are to be considerably improved.

A further aspect is that the problem of insuring co-determination at levels above that of plant and enterprise is to be more vigorously pursued, in order that proposals may be made for a realistic and effective representation of the workers in the sphere of overall economic policy.

The German workers and their trade unions are fully conscious of the fact that, while the current legislative provisions governing co-determination represent an important step along the road to the democratization of the economy, they are still far removed from the principles required by a truly free and democratic order of society.

Critique of Co-Determination

Helmut Schauer

The aim of Co-determination (Mitbestimmung) *of the German Trade Union Federation* (Deutscher Gewerkschaftsbund— DGB) *is not elimination of capitalist power and the self-determination of the toiling masses, but rationalization of the existing social relationships.*

Out of the demolished arsenal of postwar unionist views about the "new organization of economy and society," only co-determination has remained on the program of the DGB. Obviously the trade unions mean more by co-determination than the appointment of labor directors (*Arbeitsdirektor*) and a parity in the boards of supervision (*Aufsichtsrat*), the model of which the DGB wants to have introduced into all large corporations. German trade unions link almost all their activity to co-determination: wage negotiations, concerted action with the government on economic policy, works councils (*Betriebsräte*), self-management in insurance companies, participation in institutions dealing with labor law, etc. Co-determination has become so much the key word of trade union functionaries that there is even talk about political co-determination.

These ideas of co-determination, however, correspond as little to the idea of popular sovereignty, which once fathered bourgeois democracy, as they do to the idea of Socialist democracy. In this sense, "democratization of economy and society," which supposedly should come about through co-determination, has nothing at all to do with democracy.

The parallel which the trade unions often draw between political democracy and economic co-determination is absolutely justified; but only in the sense of parliamentary democracy, which has become the instrument of manipulation of the large mass of dependent citizens by a tiny social and political power elite. This is also known in the DGB, since it has been repeated again and again for many years by political scientists. The parallel between political democracy and co-determination therefore indicates that the trade unions themselves do not take the democratic element in co-determination as seriously as their rhetoric would indicate.

The unions' justification of co-determination means, for instance, that their ideology of co-determination does not include the destruction of the existing structure of authority in society. The DGB instead advances the concept of the "functionally necessary gradation of decision-making authority in enterprises." Managerial authority in industry is presented as natural and essential. Hence it is not only accepted, but protected. If authority, together with the social conditions and principles on which it is based, is natural and necessary, it is no longer legitimate to question it. The subject is withdrawn from the discussion. The profit-oriented power of the entrepreneurs and their agents appears therefore as naturally related to effort and achievement, as a "functionally determined power structure," which stands beyond moral judgment.

How far this kind of functional thinking is already fixed in the minds of the trade union bureaucrats is shown in the reasoning of the DGB which justifies the appointment of bankers to the boards of supervision in industry, with the argument that these gentlemen will, because of their knowledge and information, represent the common interest of society: "What is good for the *Deutsche Bank* is good for the German people." The DGB has managed to join the profit motive with the general welfare of society.

The DGB argues that co-determination improves the decision-making process in enterprises by forcing management to seek the approval of those directly affected by the decisions. Even a brief look at the organizational realities shows, however, that this arrangement can lead to a more efficient as well as a more flexible power structure. Even in those enterprises in which workers and employees have the right to elect representatives to the board of supervision, the election is more like a game than a serious decision: there is no way of making decisions on alternatives to the policies of management through the choice of representatives. The factory assembly is more a propaganda forum for the workers' councils and management than an organ that would permit workers and employees to form independent and competent judgments determined by their needs.

Neither the directly elected representatives on the Board of Supervision, nor those delegated by the unions are in any serious way accountable and controllable. Co-determination merely creates the illusion of popular control of elected representatives. In reality, they are largely independent and easily integrated into the existing functions of management. Even the trade unions have never made a serious attempt to make their representatives account for their action on the Board of Supervision. The DGB is, in fact, proud that within the system of co-determination in the coal mining and iron and steel producing industries, they have never exerted their influence on their own representatives. This failure to exercise democratic accountability must be contrasted to the DGB's servitude vis-à-vis management.

The DGB welcomes the existing authoritarian relationship between elected representatives and their constituency when it declares: "Within large and complex social structures, the individual can only express his will indirectly, through mediation by his elected and trusted representatives." In this sentence only one phrase is true: indirectly, through mediation. As, in feudalism, the autonomous towns and provinces, which were subordinated only to the emperor, were made "dependent"—that is to say, lost their autonomy—by being subordinated to an additional power, the regional authorities, so the workers are made additionally dependent through their so-called representatives. In cases of conflict they are dependent on their representatives, without being able to check reliably their interpretations and integrity and to develop their own ideas and actions.

Not only is the system of representation authoritarian but in addition the works council is supposed to serve two masters. It is supposed to represent the interests of the workers and employees as well as look after the interests of the enterprise. The unions as well as many works councils fought for a long time against this impossible situation but have now largely accepted it. Even those representatives who honestly desire to serve the interests of their constituents are prisoners of these authoritarian structures and regulations. The structures and dynamics of co-determination cut them off from their base. Their isolation begins with their difficulty in obtaining adequate and continuous information. While the delegates of the Board of Supervision as well as the members of the Joint Production Committee (*Wirtschaftsausschuss*) have far-reaching rights to information, they are pledged to silence if the competitive position of their enterprise could be adversely affected by the dissemination of such information. In practice, relevant and important information is thus not available to the workers and employees. The result of this secrecy is that workers are not able to evaluate such information and are thus unable to react to and develop their own alternative actions.

The trade unions frequently demand an improvement in the information system. They are, however, unwilling to make the "opening of the books" a central demand of their campaign against the authoritarian corporate structure of enterprises.

Their purpose, in practice, is to legitimize the existing authoritarian conditions and their demands for an improved information system are empty window dressing for the benefit of their members. This contradictory position of the trade unions is especially well expressed in an appeal for co-determination in the planning of manpower by the expert on automation of the metal trade union (IG Metall), Dr. Günther Friedrichs, when he says:

> The managements of the enterprises often refer to two arguments when they deny the workers prior information and participation on manpower planning. First, they want to avoid unrest within the plant or postpone it as long as possible. Second, they fear that the competition could become alerted and take advantage of this information. Neither argument is valid. Competition generally is better informed about technical planning of the enterprise than the workers employed in it. Besides, not all workers are supposed to participate in manpower planning, but only a few elected representatives, who are pledged to silence. Unrest inside the factory is not avoided but rather encouraged by secrecy. Today, many people participate in the process of planning and there will always be some leaks. Rumors create much greater unrest than open information and negotiations. Intelligent works councils will furthermore support rumors and even exaggerate them at certain times, if they see in this a possibility to gain access to information and enforce early negotiations.

Friedrichs thus seems to favor even subversive propaganda, but not in order to set into motion an education in democratic decision making and not in order to strengthen the power of the workers, who are only to be manipulated by information in order to support the independent interests of the representatives in their negotiations. When this exclusive information system is assured, the pledge to silence will be accepted; otherwise, the employers may come to understand that an open information system does not create unrest and is compatible with an orderly function of an enterprise.

Those examples, which can be multiplied *ad infinitum* show that, according to the DGB, co-determination should be based on an authoritarian structure. At best, it can contribute to the formalization and refinement through manipulation of existing power relationships. The increasing application of the scientific method in production only strengthens this tendency. It demands greater efforts to break open this institutionally perfected and rationalized dictatorship inside the enterprise.

Co-determination does not signify representation of the interests of the workers but an organizational form of social compromise.

Co-determination is supposed to extend the influence of the workers to general issues on investments, market planning, decisions about output, and so forth. This increased influence, however, should always take into special account the social consequences of those decisions. The representatives of the workers are expected to take direct responsibility for capitalist production. They participate in determining a system of production and distribution which consciously produces inferior products, which forces the workers to participate in unnecessary and useless work which only serves the continuation of this irrational system and which makes them into helpless robots of production and consumption. Co-determination blocks the objective interest of the worker in the abolition and substitution of this system by a rational economy. Co-determination is not a step toward the overthrow of capitalism. It is a form of sociopolitical regulation and adjustment of interests which corresponds to neocapitalist conditions of production. The central meaning of the ideology of co-determination for the trade unions goes back to a general change in the purpose and politics of the trade union movement.

The classical workers' movement, solidarity of the trade unions in defense of the workers' interests, and the use of the strike as their ultimate weapon, is dead. The reformist workers' movement was no match for the carrot and stick approach of the new capitalism, which, aided by state intervention, rearmament, planned obsolescence, the oppressive use of technology in relation to its limited social possibilities, imperialist expansion and finally, by the widespread introduction of social welfare, has been able temporarily to avert its impending crisis with relatively full employment and controlled growth. What is left of the old trade union movement is a system of structures reduced to insurance agencies which offer the workers a slice of the pie of capitalist "social progress." They can no longer represent the workers' interests independently determined, using the class methods of demonstrations and strikes. The workers are bound tighter and tighter to the social, economic, and income policy of the state by a network of institutional links, and reduced to a passive wage-relationship with autonomous trade union bureaucracies. The new consciousness and leisure creating industries have manipulated the masses into a state of political adaptation to the status quo.

To the extent that trade union struggles under those conditions still take place, they resemble maneuvers staged by some high command whose result is fixed at an office desk rather than democratic resistance movements; and often enough they only act as a release of accumulated dissatisfaction.

The trade union bureaucracy tries now more and more to build up its participation in capitalist institutions and to get the most out of them for its clientele. The trade unions have become an institutionalized power inside capitalism, but they are no longer an independent force to develop opinions, let alone actions for meaningful work, in which dependence and alienation would be overcome. The most they wish for the dependent worker is always within the framework of the necessities of capitalist production. And where these necessities demand it, this "best" will include a worsening of the workers' social rights. The "representatives of the workers" cooperate in those compromises, accept them, explain them to the workers, and defend them against criticism. As "insurance associations" they owe answers to their clients, who are socially affected by such decisions. Those decisions may be materially negative, but they must give the impression that the trade unions did their best, even though the solutions found may be hurting the workers.

In practice, the role of the unions as interest groups turns them into mediators and disciplined organs for the publication and dissemination of the sociopolitical decisions of the ruling system. They participate in reaching sociopolitical compromises favorable to the capitalist and always within the limits set by the capitalist system. The trade unions, as institutionalized interest groups, operate within this narrowly defined margin. They have no opportunity to change these limits or to break out of them. Their policy, therefore, anticipates these compromises. The unions can maintain their role as interest groups only because it has become evident that the interests of the workers cannot go beyond the limits set by the capitalist system.

Wherever the representatives of the workers in the enterprise have become professionalized and the works councils have become bureaucratized, they have become isolated and removed from the collective will of the workers. Individual workers and employees are forced to bargain with their own "representatives" much as they would with a commercial trade agency, for the sale of their labor power at the best possible price. Wherever representatives of labor have reached this stage, their power rests solely on existing law which limits them as mediators of an interest group. The power to mold the works council is now in the hands of management, which can allow its demands or, should it refuse to be obedient, refuse the demands and thus undermine its position. The vast majority of works council members have finally accepted this role as self-evident.

Now they are fully dependent on finding forces inside the management of their plant, which are willing to cooperate in regulation of day to day social problems. In the co-determination of the coal mining and iron and steel producing industries, the introduction of the labor director led generally to the consolidation of the social management inside the plant in close cooperation with the works councils. Personnel and manpower policies, and frequently the organizational decision-making processes, have been rationalized. In the recent period of growth, it has also been possible to improve the level of compensation.

Those are the preconditions, and the balance sheet of success, upon which the trade unions want to extend co-determination. They start from the assumption that social problems which arise from growing automation should be taken into account at the level of investment planning, which is not assured by the existing institutions. This, however, presupposes that the consequences of automation can be corrected through continued economic growth under conditions of increased international competition. If this assumption proves to be false, co-determination fails completely. Contrary to the official success story of the trade unions, the recent crisis in the mining industry has raised serious questions about the above assumption. The head of the mining workers' union, Walter Arendt, was forced to admit at a recent trade union congress that co-determination has not prevented closures in the past and will not prevent them in the future. As long as the owner has the right to dispose of his property, decisions in our society will be taken in the interest of the capitalist.

We have to add here that the miners' union (IG Bergbau) revealed its true character during the crisis in the Ruhr area. Instead of fighting for a broad regional plan, defined by the needs of the miners and their dependents which would have allowed for the inevitable changes in the economy of the area, it carried out a reactionary policy maintaining the current level of underground mining which would only lead to increased profits for the mine owners with few benefits to either the miners or the economically weakened region.

That, however, is the logical consequence of institutionalized trade union representation in co-determination, in whatever form and in whatever field. As soon as sharper signs of crisis appear and the margin for sociopolitical compromises tightens, the trade unions show their inability to develop autonomous and effective actions and alternatives. The clearer and more exposed the disciplinary function of the trade unions in response to the rebellious workers becomes, the more irrational and demagogic becomes the phony radical rhetoric they use in their attempt to confuse and smash any resistance from below.

The trade unions want to make a bargain with the ruling class: in return for permission to extend co-determination to all industry, they offer the consent of the workers to operate within the limits of capitalist class society.

Our remarks have not yet fully explained why the German

trade union movement, unlike the Anglo-Saxon and Latin unions, has put such stress on co-determination, nor do they cover the whole rationale put forward by the DGB. One could trace the origin of this rationale to the rather unique history of the German labor movement and German capitalism, particularly the period since the revolution of 1918 to 1919 when the ideology of co-determination and the institutional participation of unions was used as a defensive tactic against revolutionary movements. We must, however, ask ourselves how this tradition is actualized today.

The DGB declares that the trade unions

> start from the assumption that democratic order has to be stabilized and developed in all areas. In a country whose free part is directly confronted with another economic and social system, any other position would endanger the democratic order which is still struggling for stability. Such behavior is by no means self-evident. Anyone who wants—from whatever camp and for whatever reasons—to push the trade unions out of their present positions of responsibility, does not necessarily weaken the trade unions as interest organizations of the workers; he weakens the democratic order. He must be conscious of the consequences, which will come about, if co-determination and responsibility are denied to the largest organized alliance of people in this state. Without integration of the worker a living democratic order is unthinkable.

Remarks which point in the same direction could be added at leisure. So, for instance, Werner Hansen from the DGB executive declared a short while ago, one should not be surprised by demands for socialism if one is against co-determination. Newspaper advertisements of the DGB present co-determination as a bulwark against radicalization.

Here indeed lies the essence of the whole problem of co-determination. Because in the disputes between trade unions and employers as well as in those between adversaries and supporters of co-determination, the subject is no longer primarily about material goods and participation. Of course, the different bureaucracies fight for positions. The political content of these negotiations, however, is the question of how the workers could be most effectively organized to assure their dependence and integration.

The trade unions want to bargain with the trust of their followers, which is at their disposal, for positions of extended co-determination. For that they offer the dependent and integrated worker-citizen, for whom dependence has become self-evident and who approves of it. According to the DGB, co-determination would play an important sociopolitical role in making the dependent status of the worker *appear* to be as tolerable as possible, and to further his independence to the extent possible within the accepted limits. The DGB wants "to 'personalize' as far as possible the worker in the framework of the existing order, that is, to let him have influence in the formation of his own conditions of work." Thus the dependent workers should consider themselves subjects and approve and if necessary defend, in this context, their actual role as objects controlled from outside by capitalist production. The output principle and the profit motive of capitalist production should become their own criterion. The victims of capitalism are supposed to appear as its agents.

This concept presupposes, of course, that up until now the dependent workers have not yet been fully integrated into the capitalist system. And here the propaganda of the employers comes in with the proud slogan, "Men who have come of age don't need a guardian," starting from the assumption that the workers already had the illusion of being emancipated. In fact, the concept of the DGB is contradictory in this point. It bases itself actually on the remains of the traditional workers' movement which still preserves factors of reformist tendencies, which, however, are much too weak to force the employers into concessions. On the other hand, the whole praxis of the trade union movement acts as a brake to any radical trends, which leads the employers to accept the extension of co-determination.

Nevertheless, the strategists of the DGB can base themselves on a far-reaching need. They start from the assumption "that the majority of workers have reached a new level of individual and social consciousness. A section of organized labor is no longer willing to accept without questioning the existing relations of power in the workplace as natural" . . . "The intention of the workers is not only, as is frequently supposed, to achieve an organizationally effective system of responsibility and decision-making within the enterprise. Essentially, their goal is participation in the general development of the enterprise."

As we know through many social science research findings, there actually exists among the workers the need for universal self-determination of work. Thus co-determination is frequently understood as actual democratization of work. The trade unions want to exploit and transform this need.

The DGB campaign for co-determination does not extend the possibilities of democratic resistance; it furthers the transition to the authoritarian state.

We know from the history of capitalism of various forms of fighting crises and of maintaining power. They all signify, however, the exclusion of the masses from political and social decision making and their mobilization for the respective goals of the capitalist ruling class. The forms of organization of class dictatorship coincide in every era with the special historical conditions, political or economic. Today it is not National Socialism (Nazism) which is the object of debate. After its defeat, German capitalism has developed new forms of power structure.

Social dictatorship in neocapitalism does not need in each case to coincide with terrorism and formal destruction of the workers' movements or with suppression of every special interest representation of the workers. It need only insure that the latter submit their economic and sociopolitical behavior to the needs of capitalist production, and that they respect this predetermined framework.

This submission of the German trade unions came about in the beginning of the fifties. The form of this integration, however, changed with the transition to global state control and the politics of economic growth of the great coalition (of the Social

Democratic Party (SPD) and the Christian Democratic Union (CDU) and its concerted action on economic policy. It is only in this context that the political significance of the DGB campaign for co-determination becomes fully comprehensible.

The change of position inside the trade unions, which now is accomplished, began during the late fifties and the early sixties with the dispute between the reformists around Georg Leber and the traditionalists with their hero, Otto Brenner. Leber, at that time, demanded a recognition of the trade unions as a force for law and order to be accomplished through joint commissions of employers and unions as social partners, and through some kind of obligatory union membership. It is unnecessary to examine in detail at this time why he essentially failed in his concrete proposals. His general social concept had in any case as a goal the integration of the trade unions as permanent corporations tightly limited to professional interests. The demand to acknowledge the role of the state could only mean the submission of the trade unions to the respective economic policy of the state and its obvious and unquestionable acceptance, since the trade unions had long ago accepted parliamentary democracy. The recognition and co-responsibility of the trade unions of and for capitalist productions with special consideration of the labor force, which is today incorporated in the trade unions' program for co-determination, is in essence—if not in all details—the program proposed by Leber. With the acceptance, by the trade unions, of co-determination as their leading ideology, Leber's corporatism had basically succeeded.

Different from Leber's earlier anticipation, the corporate role of labor has today also become a fact on the level of state economic policy. Brenner and the traditional reformists in the trade union leadership had certainly already at that time accepted the capitalist state as a given fact. In cooperation with the Social Democratic Party (SPD) they continued, somewhat more militantly, their opposition to the neoliberal government and its hostility to national planning. This limited socialist critique of capitalism, in accordance with Keynes' theory of active state intervention in manpower policies and economic growth, was upheld by union activists in the technically and organizationally advanced chemical and metal industries against the neoliberalism of Chancellor Erhard. They could not afford to give up this policy as long as the foundation for a sociopolitical compromise, i.e., full employment and controlled economic growth, was not fully guaranteed through active state economic policy and global control. The Social Democrat and Keynesian Günther Schiller (Minister of Economy) seems to offer this guarantee with his policy of "concerted action." One could say: Brenner could give up his opposition only after Leber joined the Government. But with the reconciliation within the trade unions and between government and trade unions, which was thus created, the latter had to give their stamp of approval to corporatism, that is to say, institutionalized submission to the demands of state economic policy. It must be remembered that industrial planning of fluctuation and growth starts with planning of total income which is then distributed in favor of the owners of capital. The trade unions are forced to participate in this policy of "concerted action" and thus legitimize it, unless they are willing to turn to a general opposition against all parties, including the Social Democratic party which is now in power. As a result of past policies, this option has long ago vanished.

This development of the trade unions toward corporatism is no longer revocable. It has found its culmination in co-determination. This is also true for the DGB's latest campaign for co-determination. It signified a practical step, a dress rehearsal, for the further integration of the trade union movement into corporate capitalism. It helped to bring about a conciliation with those pockets of traditional trade unionism whose actions and engagement still contribute significantly to the life of the trade union movement. The optimism, which was spread by the pseudo-offensive for co-determination, played a part in creating the climate in which the submission of the unions to the policy of "concerted action" could take place without great difficulties. By supporting the pseudo-offensive for co-determination, the Social Democratic party was able to divert the dissatisfaction of trade unionists about the enactment of the emergency laws. During the 1950s, criticism within the trade union movement of co-determination in the coal mining and iron and steel producing industries was gradually replaced by absolute acceptance of these policies. The remaining pockets of militant trade unionists have seen the DGB campaign for co-determination as an "accomplishment" of integration and repression by which the disintegrating workers' movement in the Federal Republic of Germany was made aware of its defeats and its loss of Socialist policies.

With some of the traditionally oriented trade unionists this then leads to a rather distorted relation to reality which pushes them again and again to grotesque displays of distorted rhetoric. Part of this phony rhetoric is the occasional attempt by Otto Brenner (Metal Workers Union) and his supporters to present co-determination as a step in the emancipation of labor and the overthrow of capitalism, and even to raise the possibility of a strike for co-determination. Such rhetoric is in complete contradiction to actual trade union policy, including that of the Metal Workers Union. Its purpose is to protect the strengthening of corporatism from the criticism of the Left.

Corporatism is a form of the regulation of class relations which corresponds to the authoritarian character of the neocapitalist state. In essence, it means not only the loss of an independent Socialist vision, but also the disappearance of the possibility of formulating independent political alternatives. Social and political relations in their entirety are in fact guaranteed and defended by the trade union hierarchy without any attempt of serious criticism. The trade union hierarchy has neither the ideas nor the strength to offer resistance and to act as guarantors of political democracy beyond the defined framework of the authoritarian system. Despite its rhetoric it is thus unable to activate the forces for freedom and democracy.

Instead they take part in enforcing and strengthening the authoritarian power of the state because they accept and respect the class state as arbiter over social conflicts. They cement the political apathy of the workers with their own indoctrination which presents the social and political relations of power as natural. They treat social conflicts as unpolitical and thus limit the range of experiences and actions to unpolitical professional interests. Co-determination, which after 1945 began as a bastion against the fascist past, has itself become part and parcel of the new authoritarian state.

Israel

Studies on workers' participation in management frequently include the experience of the Histadrut (Israel's General Federation of Labor) while the kibbutz development is usually left out in the literature dealing with labor–management relations. This is unfortunate, since workers' and community self-management in the kibbutz represents the only large scale and ongoing example of direct democracy that is open to observation and analysis.

While the Histadrut illustrates a series of attempts, largely unsuccessful, to institutionalize joint management in its industrial sector, the kibbutz experience represents a micro-example of self-government combining all members of the collective in a direct decision-making mechanism which integrates economic and sociopsychological factors without an unwieldy authoritarian hierarchy. The kibbutz experience is thus of special importance to anyone concerned with the democratic values of self-government and their application in practice.

Worker Participation in Israel

Keitha Sapsin Fine

Since the Second World War, both highly industrialized nations with advanced levels of technology and thoroughly bureaucratized organizational structures and the newer developing countries which equate modernization with rapid industrialization have evinced interest in introducing worker participation plans into industrial decision making as a means to improve morale and increase production. But in addition to comprising a managerial strategy, the concept of workers' participation is linked historically to three sets of theories about the nature of man, work, and society: 1) the Marxian, which posits that man's labor under a Communist order could be a humanizing and self-actualizing experience rather than the self and product alienating one it is under capitalism; 2) an amalgam of utopian, non-Marxian Socialist and contemporary sociological notions, which hold that alienation arises from the specific kinds of human relationships generated by industry and that, therefore, it is these relationships which must be changed in order to combat alienation; and 3) the human relations tradition which, using the rhetoric of social science, accepted the etiology of worker alienation in the processes of industry but then developed an elaborate rationale for increasing worker, and thereby industrial, performance under the guise of improving management–worker relations in the plant.

Today, the man-centered solutions of the first two schools to the alienating effects of capitalistic development have largely been subordinated to production criteria. The humanistic ethical belief that all men have an inherent right to participate in and intimately control democratically the major decisions which affect their lives is usually obscured. But there are exceptions which reveal the human and industrial potentialities of worker self-government, for example in Yugoslavia and in the authority relationships in Israeli kibbutz industry. A considerably less persuasive but perhaps even more important case for understanding organizational impediments to participation is seen in the attempts of the Histadrut, Israel's General Federation of Labor, to institutionalize joint management in its industrial sector.

The unique development of Israel's so-called labor economy in large part along cooperative lines, her rapid industrialization, and the present conflicts among the mix of ideological and economic patterns which govern her political and social life combine to make the country a veritable laboratory in which to study theories and applications of worker participation. This article will review worker participation in some Histadrut and kibbutz industries against the continuing importance of the special and intricate historical and ideological tapestry from which each pattern has emerged.[1] On the basis of the available

[1] In addition to Histadrut and kibbutz industries, a third type of socially owned industrial enterprise common to other countries also exists in Israel, urban producers' cooperatives. Our discussion will not encompass workers' control in this worldwide movement, both because it is not unique to Israel and because there, as elsewhere, producer cooperatives founded on an unstable combination of individual and Socialist beliefs in the possibility of industrializing without creating a working class have been subject to rapid turnover and decline. This often has been due to: their transformation into profit oriented capitalist-like structures employing hired labor, competing in the marketplace, and with peculiar credit problems. Although there are still approximately 200 small producers' cooperatives in Israel in diverse light industries and services, the movement is of decreasing importance, and its staying power can be related to financial and other links to the Histadrut. Accessible but scanty information about this particular form of cooperative in Israel can be found in Walter Preuss, *The Labor Movement in Israel* (Jerusalem: Rubin Mass, 1965), pp. 199–202; and Ferdynand Zweig, *The Israeli Worker* (New York: Herzel Press and Sharon Books, 1959), pp. 232–7. A useful sum-

data, I shall discuss the success of the various plans for alleviating or preventing worker alienation, improving industrial performance, and maintaining or introducing changes in human relationships within an enterprise; success, it will be seen, is not necessarily related to the degree of industrialization in the society, the size or technological complexity of an industry, the material incentives which accompany the plan, its symbolic (perceived) value, or its geographical location (urban or rural). Rather, it seems to be related to the pervasiveness of a belief (value) system in a community or its subunit (i.e., a plant) in which democratic notions about human equality are operationalized in direct decision making by producers who integrate psychosocial with economic factors.[2] The organizational result must be deliberately antibureaucratic with the mechanisms or workers' control providing cohesion supportive to both individual and socioeconomic needs.

National and Social Ideologies in Israel

Cooperative ideologies have always played a large role in Israeli life. In an historical perspective, they result from a peculiar convergence of objective conditions and ideologies containing both national and social elements.[3]

Two major ideologies contributed to the development of the labor economy: the official (or General) Zionist ideology with

mary of other available literature is contained in Paul Blumberg, "Producers' Cooperatives as a Form of Workers' Management: The Case of Israel," *Workers' Management in Comparative Analysis* (unpublished Ph.D. dissertation, University of California at Berkeley, 1966), ch. 7.

[2] Another way of looking at this is to define the situation in terms of an absence of the managerial mode of decision making which can be characterized as institutionalizing 1) a bifurcation between decision makers (managers) and producers and 2) hierarchical authority relationships. Under the prevailing conditions of the "new industrial state" another managerial objective is to widen the economic arena controlled by the enterprise.

[3] Eleizer Rosenstein, "Histadrut's Search for a Participation Program," *Industrial Relations* (February 1970), p. 172. A brief interesting discussion of Israeli Socialism can also be found in Zweig, *op. cit.*, pp. 273–93.

its strong nationalist character, and Labor Zionism, a fusion of individualism, Marxism, and non-Marxian Socialism. Both originated from the dissatisfactions of the middle class and intellectual Jews of East Europe and Russia in the nineteenth century. The General Zionists focused on a critique of the unbalanced concentration of Jewish economic life in nonessential and non-manual occupations. Their goal was to found a national home in order to build a balanced working class of both manual and white-collar workers and in the process to reestablish contact with the land. In their commitment to nationhood as salvation, General Zionists cared little whether a labor economy developed under capitalist or Socialist auspices, and in fact many of them both saw themselves as, and became members of, a land-owning class. The fact that the overall movement first took Socialist directions was related to the absence of enough private capital to send it in another direction and to Labor Zionism, but the original ambivalence also helped prepare the way toward the later shift in the direction of capitalism.

In both Marxist and non-Marxist forms Labor Zionism was brought to Palestine about 1905 by young people who entered in the second large wave of immigration (*aliyah*). Marxist Zionists attempted to fuse Marxism and Zionist nationalism into a theoretical justification for a Socialist labor economy in Palestine. They argued that Jews must concentrate geographically in Palestine where they could enter primary occupations and organize as a prerequisite for waging the class struggle. This point of view provided the platform for the Palestine *Poalei Zion* party, founded in 1906. Non-Marxian Labor Zionism maintained that a united Zionist struggle was a greater goal for a Jewish proletariat than the class struggle. But its advocates also believed that the ideal Jewish state had to be Socialist, that is, embrace the ideal of human equality and reject capitalist structures and competition. They argued that capitalism would actually prevent economic development in Palestine by driving away Jewish labor, which looked to work opportunities in Palestine to provide them with a European standard of living.

Finally, an individualistic yet quasi-Socialist variant of labor Zionism indigenous to Palestine was developed by A. D. Gordon, who immigrated there late in life to live as an agricultural worker. Gordon preached what was in effect a "religion of labor," in which personal and national salvation were to be achieved through dedication to manual, and especially agricultural, labor. While he strongly rejected Marxian notions of the class struggle and thought Socialists would contribute more to and derive more from a national society by individual commitments to work than by theorizing about the arrangement of social institutions, Gordon was also unalterably opposed to "parasites" who lived by others' labor. Therefore, like the Socialists, he embraced national ownership of land and the means of production, although his primary orientation remained to nationalism and the liberating force of labor. Gordon's thought formed the basis of *Hapoel Hatzair,* the Young Worker party.

The common thread in all these ideologies was their "pioneering spirit" and commitment to establishing a healthy new national community based on egalitarian and collective living patterns. The immigrants believed that such a community would clearly enable Jews to develop a working class, nationalize their occupational structure, and therefore live normal social lives.[4] During the first quarter of the century the ideological differences among the immigrant groups began to give way to immediate practical needs, and a number of highly politicized organizations emerged to meet them. The most important of these were: the two parties *Poalei Zion* and *Hapoel Hatzair* which initially undertook social welfare and cultural activities, and later also provided jobs for newcomers, for example by negotiating road construction contracts with the British; the nascent agricultural and urban trade unions which also served as labor exchanges, markets, and provided health services and financial aid; and the kibbutzim which were simultaneously committed to their own communal autonomy and to building Israel.

As the two political parties grew stronger and assumed more of the burdens of developing and providing social services for the new land, rivalry increased and duplication of institutions

---

[4] Eleizer Rosenstein, *Ideology and Practice of Workers' Participation in Management: Experiences in Israel, Yugoslavia and England,* pp. 311–2, unpublished Ph.D. dissertation, University of California at Berkeley, 1969.

and services became common. In 1920 they finally agreed voluntarily to transfer their service branches to a new organization, the Histadrut, which would assume responsibility for all matters regarding economic and cultural activities and settlement. Membership in the Histadrut was to be open to all workers. Between its founding and statehood in 1948, the Histadrut in effect fulfilled many of the functions of a government: it negotiated immigration policies with the British; it helped socialize and settle immigrants in towns and the countryside; it undertook work contracts with the Mandatory Power; it organized and coordinated trade unions to fight for better working conditions; it established formal schools, training programs and health plans; it published literature and sponsored other cultural programs; it engaged in defense; and it provided financial aid. In 1923 the Histadrut also formed a cooperative association, *Hevrat Haovdim* with a mandate to undertake economic development activities; by the 1930s *Hevrat Haovdim* began to purchase and operate private industries that were in difficulty in order to prevent a decline in the economic base and the job opportunities upon which British immigration policies were calculated.

It is important to understand that throughout the early colonizing years the absence of private capital, dependence on outside help, and the constant state of emergency all acted to mitigate against the development of an open class struggle, and incidentally, against a lot of pure trade union organizing as well. During this period, the majority of funds garnered by the Histadrut were raised, administered, and distributed cooperatively with one purpose in mind: to build a strong national home. Because this purpose had materialized on the foundation of cooperative ideologies, for a long time workers and organizations alike identified their self-interest with the national interest.[5] The cohesiveness among all parts of the developing society also helped to popularize the notion that a national "community of workers" had truly been achieved.[6] Not until the 1940s

[5] *Ibid.*, p. 321.

[6] The overlap is perhaps best illustrated by the fact that since 1930, when *Poalei Zion* and *Hapoel Hatzair* finally merged to form *Mapai*, it

when Histadrut had grown into a complicated and somewhat centralized organizational structure with multitudinous and often fairly autonomous departments, industries, and organizations attached to its two major wings—the organizational branch which included the trade unions, and the economic branch—and not until waves of Middle Eastern immigrants changed the character of the Israeli population and in so doing further diluted the European flavor of Israeli Socialism, did the myth of harmony explode.[7]

Today the purest version of the collective ideals contained in the national and social ideologies under which Palestine was colonized are the kibbutzim. Affiliated with the Histadrut through marketing and purchasing cooperatives, but largely self-sustaining units, their special attributes—"openness toward relations with the general society and the flexibility of their normative structure"—allowed them to insulate themselves from its bureaucratic storms and yet maintain their original goals of nation building, developing a working class, and communitarian life.[8] While they have been subject to many corroding pressures, to a remarkable extent they have been able both to meet the needs of the greater economy for more agricultural goods, and also to industrialize to meet their own changing needs without sacrificing either their values or principles of workers' control by direct democracy. In many ways the kibbutzim are the conscience of Israel. They provide the model of participatory democracy which, in combination with modern managerial ideologies, Histadrut has tried to introduce into its industrial labor economy.

---

has been the leading party of both the government and the Histadrut. The leadership in both at all levels is nominated by party list and elected by proportional representation. The left wing of *Poalei Zion* became the Israeli Communist party.

[7] I am indebted to Rosenstein, *op. cit.,* pp. 354–84, for a cogent discussion of the shift in Histadrut ideology, and the gap between the theory and the practice.

[8] Menachem Rozner, "Communitarian Movements, Self-Management, and the Kibbutz Experience" (1969), unpublished paper, courtesy of the author.

The Industrial Setting[9]

The Israeli economy is today a diverse mixture of private, government, labor union, and cooperative ownership, often in combination, in both urban and rural settings. Although industrial value output doubled between 1950 and the early sixties, it is still plagued by a balance of payments problem, an industrial workforce of about 160,000, many of whom are unskilled laborers from the diverse Jewish cultures of the Middle East, and enormous social welfare and educational problems. Most industrial establishments are still small: 95 percent employ less than 50 persons although the greatest number of employees (48.3 percent) work in plants with over 50 employees, and 18.8 percent work in the 45 largest plants with over 300 workers apiece. Ninety-five percent of the enterprises are owned by private individuals and fall under managerial hierarchical control patterns, although this statistic discounts the fact that the public and labor economies together provide well over half the job opportunities in the country. The government owns and runs a number of the largest industries, particularly those supplying raw materials and related to the defense industry, and also often provides capital for private and labor owned enterprises. The General Federation of Labor (the Histadrut) owns only a small percentage of Israel's factories, but these are among the largest. Together, all the Histadrut's diverse economic activities account for 24 percent of the national employment, 23 percent of the national product, and 19 percent of the country's exports. Cooperatives and the predominantly agricultural collectives account for about 2.8 percent with 7.9 percent of the employees.

A special word about the Histadrut is in order. The Histadrut is still a combination trade union, economic entrepreneur, social

[9] Data Sources: *Statistical Abstract of Israel,* 1967; Rosenstein, *op. cit.,* p. 171; Milton Derber, "Plant Labor Relations in Israel," *Industrial and Labor Relations Review* (October 1965), pp. 39–40.

security agency, and educational institution. In these functions it represents about half the Israeli population, that is, four out of five, or nearly a million, Israeli adults (including wives of members and non-Jews). It is thus actually a powerful mass organization whose membership is direct, personal, and open to every worker eighteen years old and over. Clerical and service workers make up the largest group of members (40.1 percent) followed by workers in industry and construction (30.4 percent), agriculture (16.6 percent), and others (12.9 percent), including public works, students, and pensioners.[10] Over the years, the volume and diverse nature of the membership, as well as the practice of electing the leadership by party lists in proportional representation, and making administrative appointments the same way, has encouraged a concentration of power at the different leadership levels which reflects the power of the government and thus of the ruling Mapai party. There is, of course, personnel overlap between its trade union and economic branches, although the latter has its own managing board and secretariat. Centralization is considerable, but is counteracted in two ways: first, by the entrenched power of old, well-established local labor councils, and second, by the autonomy of the management in the Hevrat Haovdim enterprises.

The economic branch, Hevrat Haovdim (of which every member of the Histadrut is also a member) entails eight economic activities: agriculture, the largest, with 41.2 percent of Histadrut employment; industry, 18.2 percent; building, 11.2 percent; trade, 3.9 percent; banking and finance, 2.5 percent; transportation, 8.3 percent; public services, 13.7 percent; and personal services, 1.0 percent.[11] These can be grouped into three main divisions by the extent to which Hevrat Haovdim controls them:[12] (1) the "Administrative economy," which includes the construction trades, banks, insurance companies, and about seventy industries collectively owned and managed under four major enterprises: (a) *Solel Boneh* for construction,

[10] Histadrut Annual, 1966, p. 89, cited in Rosenstein, *op. cit.*, p. 325.

[11] *Meshek Haovdim (The Labor Economy) 1960–1965,* publication of the Institute for Economic and Social Research of the Histadrut (Tel Aviv, 1967), p. 10, cited in Rosenstein, *op. cit.*, p. 344.

[12] Rosenstein, *op. cit.*, p. 345.

(b) *Koor,* for industrial acquisitions, (c) *Hamashbir Letaassia,* for consumption products, and (d) *Teus* for small businesses; (2) the cooperative unions; (3) the kibbutzim, moshavim, and the producers' and service cooperatives, the largest group in terms of employment (60 percent) and net product (51.8 percent). In the early fifties many of the kibbutzim deliberately began to introduce light industry into their economy. Of the 230 kibbutzim, 170 now operate industrial units of 20 to 250 persons, employing 47 percent of all industrial workers in the Histadrut economic sector.[13]

The trade union branch of the Histadrut now claims to represent 90 percent of Israeli employees. Membership in an appropriate national union is by assignment upon joining the Histadrut. All dues are paid directly to the parent organization, thus insuring dependency by individual unions. Unions are organized on the basis of craft, profession, industry, or where large size is a factor, by employer. The trade union department of the Histadrut is headed by a member of its Executive Committee; it applies union policies determined by the Conference and Council. National and local union structures replicate those of the Histadrut. Day to day affairs are the province of the secretaries of the local unions who are also members of the local labor council in a geographical area. In turn, they work with the elected workers' committees in the various enterprises. Daily paid (manual), monthly paid (technical/professional), and sometimes clerical workers each elect a committee by majority vote from what are in effect informal party lists. Each has one fulltime Secretary; office space is usually provided by the employer who sometimes also contributes a salary equivalent to that earned at the Secretary's previous job. The main functions of the workers' committees are to enforce the collective bargaining agreements at the plant level, resolve intraworker conflicts, provide educational and cultural activities, and administer the Histadrut's many social welfare programs.

---

[13] Seymour Melman, "Industrial Efficiency Under Managerial Versus Cooperative Decision Making: A Comparative Study of Manufacturing Enterprises in Israel," *The Review of Radical Political Economics,* Vol. II, No. 1 (Spring 1970), p. 11.

Centralization of this branch is reflected in several ways: by the extent of national level bargaining; by the power of the local labor council rather than a local union to call strikes, etc.; by the practice, contrary to theory, of appointing national and regional secretaries from above rather than using the electoral procedures provided; by the fact that the workers' committees are subject to scrutiny by both its local union and the local labor council which legally controls its very existence.

Because of the long-standing close relationship between government policy and economic needs—aptly illustrated by the fact that the General Secretary of the Histadrut participates in top level government decisions—the entire range of industrial relations, including the wage structure, is considered a national issue. Thus it is not surprising that private sector agreements concerning wages, conditions of employment, such as hours and fringe benefits are negotiated industrywide under collective bargaining between the trade union branch of the Histadrut and a manufacturers' association which has almost universal membership.[14] The government, however, has considerable influence over hiring through the national employment office (run by the Histadrut until 1959); because of the political overlap, managers in government industries also wield much autonomous power. In turn, the unions in effect control dismissals and

[14] The local labor council handles negotiations with employers who are not members of the manufacturer's association. The special nature of the Israeli wage structure is worth a note. The underlying policy goal is to provide everyone with a European standard of living. The wage is divided into the flat wage, cost of living, family and seniority allowances, incentive bonus, the employer's contribution, and overtime. Through the middle 1950s the cost of living allowance often amounted to half the total wage, particularly in the lower skill levels. Combined with the family allowance and high social benefits the adjustment contributed to the egalitarian nature of the Israeli wage structure, but they also had an inflationary and distorting effect on the economy out of proportion to productivity. In addition, the small wage differentials, tied to inadequate job scaling, and the increasing differential nature of the workforce, led to considerable unrest—disputes and even strikes. As a result, since the late fifties, there has been a more realistic revamping of salaries in relationship to costs and productivity, but, at the same time, while wage differentials are still small, they have become tied to educational levels and other class characteristics.

promotions—numbers (negotiated) and decisions on the individuals involved—through the local plant committees. The terms in Histadrut industries whose employees are represented in a separate union within the Histadrut, the National Organization of Workers in Histadrut Enterprises, have in the main followed the guidelines set in the private sector, with the exception of greater fringe benefits. In all cases, labor relations at the plant level, which includes a provision for binding arbitration, have primarily reflected a bargaining approach. Grievances are worked out between the plant manager, the plant personnel department (if one exists), and the secretaries of the local workers' committees, rather than at the departmental or shop level. This is in part due to the weak position of the foreman who is a union member but is appointed by the management, and consequently, because he is often caught in the middle (especially in Histadrut industries), tends to pass on personal relations problems to others. The plantwide election of representatives to two and sometimes three workers' committees also helps skew authority upward.

Worker Participation in Histadrut Industries[15]*

After statehood, industrial growth, and more complex technologies and tasks stimulated increasingly sharp divisions of labor between workers and managers. In the ensuing years, the

---

* For reasons of space this discussion has been omitted. The major findings are summarized.—ED.

[15] The paucity of recent empirical research on workers' participation plans is a problem everywhere, and no less so in Israel. This discussion utilized—and the reader is referred to—the following works in English: Milton Derber, "Plant Labor Relations in Israel," *Industrial and Labor Relations Review* (October 1965); and "Worker Participation in Israeli Management," *Industrial Relations* (October 1963); Rosenstein, *op. cit.;* Irving Sobel, "Israel," in Walter Galenson, *Labor in Developing Economies* (Berkeley: University of California Press, 1962); G. Stoddard, *The Histadrut Plan for Workers' Participation in Management* (Brooklyn College, 1960—unpublished report cited in Rosenstein); J. Y. Tabb and A. Goldfarb, *Workers Participation in Management: Expectations and Experience* (Israeli Institute of Technology, 1970).

Histadrut leadership made three largely unsuccessful attempts to institutionalize worker participation in its industrial sector. The first, the Joint Production Committee Plan, formalized in 1945, primarily served as a mechanism for some communications and consultations between management and workers and was instrumental in introducing a system of production norms and premium payments, first into Histadrut and then later into all industry. But managerial resistance to sharing power, worker reluctance to vary well-established norms without drastic technological changes in evidence, and worker apathy toward activities other than those related to setting norms and premiums combined to stagnate the program.

Ignoring the persistence of these problems, a second effort, the Joint Council Plan, which theoretically was to provide in-plant control over all business except wages and benefits, was instituted in 1956. It immediately bogged down in a power struggle among the trade union department, the political leadership, managers, and workers, and was dead by 1960–1. In 1960 a self-evaluation by the Histadrut showed that: 1) workers' representatives blamed the Histadrut executive, the *Koor* central management, plant managers and worker apathy for the failure; and 2) managers blamed the original plan, imposition from above, lack of central management leadership, and no real clarity as to their duties and responsibilities for the failure even prior to the plan.

Despite these two abortive attempts, top Histadrut officials refused to abandon the projected second stage of the Plant Council program, Joint Management. In the midst of rampant internal controversy several pilot attempts at joint management were made during the sixties, although it was not until 1968 that a uniform set of rules and regulations was agreed upon. Moreover, these provided for only the weakest kind of worker participation—consultation—rather than for the workers' control supposedly envisioned in the official rhetoric. The Joint Boards had virtually no control over wages, benefits, or hiring and firing; managers were generally uncooperative at both central and plant management levels; workers wanted to tie profit-sharing to participation regardless of productivity, and in any case remain a numerical minority, insuring a bargaining atmosphere at the meetings. All local industry decisions were subject to review by the central management. Furthermore, a 1967 followup study confirmed a high positive relationship between experience with previous plans and negativism and mistrust toward the method of activity of the Histadrut.

Several factors seem evident as a result of the three attempts. First, the goals which were embodied in the traditional ideology and which were so important to the economic development of Palestine are no longer relevant to the attitudes and aspirations of either Histadrut managers or workers. There is no longer any valid reason for assuming that Histadrut and worker ownership of the means of production are coextensive. The Histadrut leadership is clearly opposed to decentralized workers' control and is ambivalent toward participation. Political interlocking between the government and the Histadrut has helped to substitute policies that enhance economic development (and *Mapai* interests) for those that favor social goals. The new ideology is thus revealed as an unsuccessful wedding of human relations theory to General and Labor Zionism.

Yet participation plans are still turned to repeatedly. One reason is undoubtedly the extent to which residues of the traditional ideology are yet a part of Israel's political mythology. It also appears that the social elements from the founding ideology are used by the Histadrut leadership to help preserve as much power and position for themselves and the organization as possible in the face of what is now a highly competitive pluralistic society in which neither membership in nor the Histadrut itself is a primary requisite for public authority.

Second, in the internal struggle between democracy and bureaucracy the management strata has clearly emerged on top, having thoroughly internalized that part of the official ideology which stressed efficiency and production, and dismissed the ideals of service to the workers and the nation.

Third, both workers' attitudes and the top leadership's rhetoric toward participation reveal a lack of real concern with the sources of work motivation, a stance not easily modifiable in light of the new ideological inputs and objective societal conditions.

Fourth, genuine worker self-determination in the Histadrut

industries is now also constrained by several other institutional factors: 1) the existence of a bureaucracy which in itself inhibits the development of truly collective worker organs; 2) the national collective bargaining agreements whose format determines the relegation of qualitative issues to the sidelines; 3) the structural relationship between the Histadrut and the unions which prevents worker control over work processes; and 4) the diversity of Histadrut interests and membership which often results in an intraorganizational schizophrenia.

Finally, we cannot avoid noting that Israeli workers have themselves failed to organize outside the Histadrut.

Industrialization of the Kibbutzim

SOCIAL ORGANIZATION OF THE KIBBUTZIM

It is common knowledge that collective agricultural settlements pioneered the colonization and development of Palestine.[16] Today 240 kibbutzim with approximately 90,000 members in units averaging 250–300 persons are scattered over Israel. They produce about 33 percent of the agricultural and 8 percent of the industrial products of the country, and have supplied many of the outstanding leaders of the modern state.

Members of the original movement, fleeing hostile European countries and stimulated by the challenge of settlement, carried the seeds of Socialism and Zionism to Palestine prior to the First World War. There, they established many settlements, similar in socioeconomic organization and values, although often differing in religious and political affiliations. During the 1920s the various kibbutzim cohered into several federations for purposes of religious and political unity, to undertake activities more effectively performed at a central level (for example, allocation of new manpower), and in order to present a common front in bargaining for needed financing with the Jewish

[16] Technically, there are three types of agricultural cooperatives in Israel: the wholly collective kibbutzim; the moshavim, or cooperative small landholders' settlements; and the moshav shitufi, a combination of the other two.

National Fund, from which settlements still lease some land, the Jewish Agency and the Histadrut. The federations still perform similar functions today, and in addition, individual kibbutzim now also belong to giant purchasing and marketing cooperatives.

The principles of direct democracy which underlie the social organization and administration of the kibbutzim are their outstanding characteristics and strength. These principles—voluntarism, cooperativism, and egalitarianism—aim at the "complete identification of the individual with the society."[17] Individuals internalize the collective goals embodied in the principles and feel no conflict between private desires and the needs of society.[18] This process is facilitated by the psychology of "total inclusion" induced by the framework of the kibbutz, by overlapping among institutional areas, and by the "functional interdependence" (i.e., "the overlapping of the ecological unit with the social unit and the economic productive unit") created by the close linkages between kibbutz institutions and life patterns.[19] Integration is also the aim of the educational process and all decision-making mechanisms. The most important mechanism for social control is nonformalized public opinion—which replaces hierarchy elsewhere.

Practically, identification is actualized in a process of direct decision making in the weekly meetings of the general assembly of the kibbutz. These meetings are the central forum for communications among all members—they serve to integrate and balance the various interests of the social groups and departments in the kibbutz. Free discussion takes place with no time limit; votes are rarely formal. The unitary ideal is reflected in the absence of a separation between executive, legislative, and

---

[17] Menachem Rozner, "Principal Types and Problems of Direct Democracy in the Kibbutz," monograph published by the Social Research Center on the Kibbutz at Givat Haviva, 1965, p. 1. The most recent, but largely unpublished to date, research on kibbutz industrialization and its effects is ongoing by the Social Research Center in conjunction with the Institute for Social Relations at the University of Michigan. Sources cited were made available by the author.

[18] Rozner, *op. cit.*, p. 10.

[19] *Ibid.*, p. 27.

judicial powers. In its executive functions, the general assembly takes decisions by majority vote in the case of disagreements, and ratifies departmental proposals. As a legislature it makes policy decisions on aspects of kibbutz life, discusses and votes on budgets, and sets precedents on problems. As a judiciary it makes final decisions on individual cases, and interprets previous decisions and codes.

The general assembly annually elects a secretariat of eight to ten members who are heads of the committees which deal with various aspects of kibbutz life; these include the economic secretary, the treasurer, the works manager, and the heads of the social, education, and cultural committees. The secretariat is chaired by a general secretary whose duty is to coordinate all the activities. It meets in advance of the general meeting to work out any conflicts beforehand and synthesize interests. It has the power of decision on some questions of administration, but never on matters of principle, on which it can only prepare proposals. The secretariat also initially appoints and works with the branch managers for each sector of the economy.

The social conditions which support all these mechanisms are the relatively small scale of the unit (that is, size commensurate with direct access to decision making); a high degree of social awareness on the part of the membership; absolute equality among members—which carries the assumptions of no individual economic rewards or privileges and the responsibility of the kibbutz for satisfying the needs of its members; a number of persons able to carry out multitudinous functions within the society; and, of course, a wholly voluntary commitment to and participation in the society. A major goal of kibbutz life has always been to satisfy the needs of members for self-realization, and thus the creative expansion of job opportunities, based on an assumption of the positive relationship between work and satisfaction, is a continual problem. A major means of dealing with this has been by way of job rotation, primarily used for disagreeable work or where the potential for self-actualizing activity is low, and in managerial roles to prevent the solidification of a Weberian type bureaucracy.[20]

---

[20] *Ibid.*, pp. 14–5. Since the forties there have not been enough professionals to permit job rotation in these roles. The rotation of office hold-

It is generally agreed that in the past these conditions for direct democracy were met by the social and economical organizational structures of the kibbutz. They in turn were made possible by the very strong network of cooperatives surrounding the kibbutz, which acted as a "buffer zone" between the kibbutz and the greater society, allowing it to preserve its autonomy, yet also easing adaptation to the requirements of modernization by permitting a continuous process of change to occur in an absence of open conflict between the kibbutzim and the larger society. The problem currently is to understand if and how recent changes—heterogeneity of population, the emergence of several generations, growth, complexity, technology, and industrialization—have affected the ideals and organization of the kibbutzim. Specifically, one must ask key questions at two levels: first, whether the requirements of modernization—such as technological specialization—are antithetical to the preservation of kibbutz values and to decision making by direct democracy; and second, whether the development of the entire society has so altered conditions externally supportive to a kibbutz way of life that efforts by the kibbutzim to change their organizational structures to meet new social conditions, yet preserve their basic values, will founder on causes outside their control.

It has been suggested that features of both the social system of the kibbutz and its members are supportive of a transfer of work from agriculture to industry within the framework of collectivism.[21] Some such aspects of the value system of the kibbutz are its ideological flexibility which encourages a response to changes in objective circumstances by reinterpretation of norms; its future planning orientation which provides for constant change; and the continued emphasis on production and productive work as a service to the kibbutz with a concomitant opposition to specialization and professionalization. Important

---

ers in kibbutz social organizations is one to two years; two to three years in economic organizations and three to five years in public service jobs outside the kibbutz. In addition, in any one year nearly fifty percent of the membership serve on kibbutz committees.

[21] Menachem Rozner, "Social Aspects of Industrialization in the Kibbutz" (Givat Haviva; Social Research Center on the Kibbutz, 1969), p. 285. Available from: Givat Haviva Educational Foundation, 150 Fifth Avenue, New York, New York 10011.

characteristics of the social and economic structures are the absence of rewards attached to a work position, the general network of social relationships, few role distinctions, and the norm of rotation in managerial functions. Attributes of individuals which encourage a belief in modernization without a loss of collectivism include their previous experience in transforming themselves from urban immigrants to a new class of agricultural laborers; the generally high level of technology, efficiency, and planning they introduced into agriculture; their own high educational levels and the desire for more training; the dispersion of managerial ability because of the democratic principles on which the kibbutz is organized; individual initiative; and achievement need as a reward in the absence of other kinds of incentives.

The General Economy of the Kibbutz

The chief economic strength of the kibbutzim has remained agricultural. In the early 1960s kibbutzim provided 18.7 percent of Israel's agricultural labor force, and cultivated one third the arable land and one third of its irrigated area.[22] They lead in the cultivation of noncitrus fruits and farm 18 percent of the fruit plantations. They produce 26.8 percent of the eggs, 40.6 percent of the poultry meat, and about 30 percent of the beef in the country. Although they also cultivate 40 percent of the nation's field crops and 12 percent of the vegetables, there has been a decided shift toward the moshavim in these sectors. Overall, by 1964 kibbutz agricultural production had increased to seven times its 1949 level compared to six times for the country as a whole, leveling off at about 31 percent between 1960 and 1964. Kibbutz agricultural productivity is almost uniformly higher than that of the general economy or the moshavim; between 1949 and 1960 it increased at an average annual rate of about 10 percent. By the same token, available

[22] Eliyahu Kanovsky, *The Economy of the Israeli Kibbutz* (Cambridge: Harvard University Press, 1965), p. 129. Altogether the labor economy works seventy percent of the 1,200,000 acres under cultivation. Statistics that follow are from this source.

data on agricultural worker output also indicates a higher degree of efficiency and rapid growth in labor productivity—not unexpectedly, since the kibbutzim have always strived to become self-supporting units, when possible voluntary savings are high and have always been reinvested.

Despite their almost uniformly higher rates of productivity, however, the kibbutz economies ran at a pronounced deficit until the late thirties, and again between 1954 and 1960; only since 1961 have small surpluses been recorded. This situation can be explained by a combination of factors external and internal to the kibbutz that affect its profitability. These include: higher production costs induced by early overdiversification, remote locations, poor soil, drought, and higher labor costs because the institutional setup requires a higher number of labor days per member than, for example, in the moshav; periods of adverse agricultural prices, the chronic manpower shortage; high interest rates in the absence of large savings; high educational expenses; and the steep annual rise (5 percent to 6.5 percent) in the standard of living between 1955 and 1964.[23] In addition, ideological beliefs concerning the concept

___

[23] *Ibid.*, pp. 87–125. The chronic manpower shortage is one of the most severe problems faced by kibbutzim today. The decline of the kibbutz movement as a whole has been largely due to the fact that a majority of immigrants since 1948 came from Middle Eastern cultures with strong traditions in support of a patriarchal family as the center of religious, social, and economic life. This life style was incompatible with the ideology of the kibbutzim. Therefore, new immigrants who chose an agricultural way of life gravitated to the noncollective moshavim, which have outstripped the kibbutzim in growth. In addition, the advent of statehood exacerbated defections. In the Hakibbutz Ha'artzi Federation (the strongest), defections averaged 5.6 percent yearly between 1949 and 1959, versus a preindependence rate of 2 percent to 2.5 percent which was more than replaced by immigration (*ibid.,* p. 137). In addition, about 10 percent of the kibbutz membership has always worked outside the kibbutzim in "public duties," mainly in the Federations, the Histadrut, the government or other services. Boris Stern, *The Kibbutz That Was* (Washington, D.C., Public Affairs Press, 1965), p. 105. Finally, the rural to urban population shift common to all developing countries and a "generation gap" took their toll on growth, as did rampant ideological controversies throughout the movement in the early 1950s. Since 1960 the total kibbutz population seems to have stabilized around 80,000 or 3.6 percent of the Jewish population. Perhaps eventual

of leisure, the refusal to "weed out" less profitable units which would be obliterated by competition in a capitalist system, and opposition to the use of hired labor have compelled the kibbutzim to become capital- rather than labor-intensive economies.[24] The reversal toward small surpluses in the early sixties was the result of financial and planning help from the government, more sophisticated—if more profit oriented—economic analyses by the kibbutzim, a stabilized population, returns from earlier conversions to fruit and cattle, and perhaps most important for our purposes, the benefits from and continued development of generally profitable nonagricultural enterprises.

As we examine the development and organization of kibbutz industry below, we should keep in mind that the gap noted between rates of productivity and profitability in agriculture on the basis of efficiency/effectiveness (cost/benefit) criteria does not hold in the research available on kibbutz industries, particularly when they are compared with their counterparts in the private sector.[25] This suggests that explanations which rely on the institutional setup (the organization) or on the ideology of the kibbutzim to explain adverse profitability are at best incomplete and at worst erroneous. As we shall see it is also misleading to analyze the shift since the thirties from a labor to capital-intensive economy as a negative one on the grounds that the reluctance to employ hired labor has been a financial drain on the kibbutzim.

Industrialization

Unlike the ideological foundation underpinning an agricultural way of life, industrialization of the kibbutzim was primarily stimulated by the pragmatic needs of communities some dis-

---

settlement of new lands retained as a result of the 1967 acquisitions will present the opportunity for a rebirth of the movement, although this does seem both unlikely and politically undesirable.

[24] Opposition to the use of hired labor has clearly also curtailed development and obviated the chance for economies of scale. Its use, particularly as kibbutzim have industrialized, has been extremely controversial and is an issue to which we shall return.

[25] Melman, *op. cit.*

tance from urban and service centers. During the thirties land and water shortages, fluctuations in labor needs due to the seasonal nature of agriculture, and the necessity for kibbutz members to seek outside employment in order to supplement the community's income acted as a further inducement to industrialize.[26] But for the most part, the early endeavors were considered adjuncts to the agricultural way of life, not substitutes for it. It was really not until World War II, when British needs provided the major impetus toward industrialization, that the kibbutzim seriously began to look toward manufacturing as a labor activity worthy of development. After independence the government's deliberate emphasis on agriculture depressed the trend until after the mid-fifties when farm products came into surplus and the entire society began a large scale industrial push.[27]

Both economic and noneconomic reasons underlie the rapid industrialization of the kibbutzim from this time on: the desire for a stable source of income and a better standard of living (nothing in kibbutz ideology ever dictated a life of eternal poverty and hardship); a generalized commitment to diversify, partly in order to provide new kinds of jobs for and thus retain younger members; an aging population no longer able to undertake heavy agricultural work; an increasingly efficient and mechanized agricultural sector which required less labor; the need to help absorb the new influx of immigrants; and because by producing goods needed by the collective a kibbutz could reduce its dependence on the market economy.

Those kibbutzim that have industrialized are generally the older and best established. The hundred or so founded since statehood are generally the smallest and weakest communities

[26] Industrialization was clearly more related to the wish to reduce kibbutzim dependence on the Jewish Agency and later on the overall society than to the desire to reduce the number of members working in public sector jobs.

[27] Between 1958 and 1964 national income from agriculture declined from 13.6 percent to 9.9 percent while income from manufacturing rose to 25.4 percent (Kanovsky, *op. cit.*, pp. 39–4). Stern also notes that in the same period, a comparison of the growth of manufacturing in twenty veteran kibbutzim—with that in the whole economy showed that the latter increased by 21 percent and the kibbutz activity, including handwork and workshop operations, increased 79 percent.

and are heavily subsidized. Ideologically, it is interesting that the most industrialized kibbutzim are affiliated with the Left but non-Communist Hakibbutz Ha'artzi Federation (the strongest), which controls the Socialist and second most important Israeli party, Mapam; and with Hakibbutz Hameuhad, a militant Socialist group which controls the Ahdut Ha'avodah party, rather than with the Ihud which is connected to the ruling Mapai party.

Since the mid-fifties, the numbers of kibbutz industries, those employed in them, and production as a proportion of their annual income (now one fourth to one third) and the national figures have all increased steadily.[28] In 1956 kibbutz plants represented 1.5 percent of the total number and employed 2.4 percent of the industrial labor force; in 1964 the numbers of plants had fallen to 1.2 percent of the national total but the percentage of the national workforce they employed had risen to 3.4 percent. In 1963 approximately 150 separate industries represented 5 percent of the total Israeli gross industrial production, or about £I 200 million. Most plants today employ about 40 workers; nine employ between 100 and 500. Although the largest number of enterprises remain small, these figures indicate their size is increasing.

Organization of the Kibbutz Factory

Kibbutz industries are broadly organized in two ways. Some have been established regionally, in which case an industry is owned jointly by several kibbutzim, sometimes in conjunction with other sectors of the economy, or run by a kibbutz federation. This form has been an increasingly popular way to expand industrialization while avoiding the ideological and social implications attendant to an individual kibbutz employing hired labor. The majority of plants, however, are relatively small enterprises whose budgets are an integral part of the economy of a single kibbutz. These industries are thus subject to the priorities and policy decisions of the general assembly of the

[28] The following data are based on Kanovsky, *op. cit.*, pp. 60–4.

kibbutz. In general, with modifications for the peculiarities of an industry, their organization has followed that in the agricultural sectors. In some cases, size and particular requirements have led to modifications in the arrangement whereby the plant and the general institutions of the kibbutz are not so highly integrated, in which case the industry usually has more financial independence. Other differences have been observed in the division of authority between the worker assemblies and the management boards, and the degree of rotation of managerial duties. In both forms of kibbutz industry hired workers are represented by their own workers' committee, like those in private and Histadrut firms.

The organizational structure of the factory itself is designed to preserve feelings of independence among hitherto agricultural workers in an industrial setting, and to facilitate cooperative decision making in the plant.[29] A general meeting of workers is convened monthly to receive information from the plant management team and discuss and decide the factory issues within its authority (which depends on the degree of integration of the plant into the kibbutz). It is chaired by a worker elected for one year who is also an *ex officio* member of the management board of the factory. The management board meets weekly to discuss and decide current issues. It is composed of: the two or three key management officials in the plant; the top office holders of the kibbutz—its chief manager, treasurer, and secretary; two rank-and-file workers elected for two years by the workers' general meeting, one of whom is its chairman; and an elected representative of the "younger generation" to insure direct communication with youth if they are heavily represented in the workforce. In addition, a management team for the factory is elected for a minimum of three and maximum of four years from among the most important office holders of the kibbutz. Each year the general assembly nominates a special committee to draw up a slate of candidates. Its recommendations are then discussed by both the factory board and the workers' general

[29] For this discussion, I have relied on the format for the organizational structure of the kibbutz factory decided on by the Central Committee of Kibbutz Ha-artzi Federation, reprinted in full in Rozner, *op. cit.*, pp. 12–4.

meeting, after which their conclusions go before the kibbutz general assembly for discussion and confirmation. It is recommended that members of the management team be on the board for a year as preparation for team membership.

Authority is distributed between the workers' general meeting and the management board on major issues as follows:

1) On yearly production plans:
   a) The board discusses and recommends the plan;
   b) The plan is discussed in the workers' general meeting;
   c) The plan, incorporating any changes, is then discussed and decided on by the kibbutz management committee;
   d) The plan must finally be confirmed by the annual kibbutz general assembly in the context of the overall economic plan for the kibbutz.

2) On development and investment plans: these undergo the same ratification process as the yearly production plans.

3) Concerning decisions on technological matters:
   a) The technological committee, including professionals and one member of the factory management team, discusses technological issues and recommends solutions.
   b) These recommendations are discussed and decided upon by the factory board.
   c) The recommendations of both are then referred to the monthly general workers' meeting.

4) On work norms: Within the framework of work norms accepted by the entire kibbutz, modifications are made to meet specific needs of a factory, such as shifts, breaks, meals, etc.
   a) The factory board recommends changes to the workers' general meeting.
   b) The workers' general meeting discusses the issues and has the power to accept, reject, or modify the board's recommendations.

5) In regard to training: The board and the workers' general meeting annually jointly discuss a training program both within and outside the factory; the program must include a long range professional training program, and must be

accepted by the kibbutz and integrated with its other training programs.

6) Concerning rotation: The nominating committee also recommends the rotation procedure for the management team of the factory. This is planned several years in advance to assure adequate training periods. Implementation is gradual to insure continuity among the management. Rotation applies to:

a) The management team;

b) Staff and line offices: It is recommended that two persons be trained for each staff role in order to prevent anyone's being "locked in" by professionalism, and thus to realize interdependency between staff and line. Departmental managers and superiors are elected by the workers' general meeting upon recommendations from the factory board.

c) Rank-and-file jobs.

7) On grievances: Complaints against the management, workers' disagreements, etc., all go to the workers' general meeting for settlement.

It can be seen that some central features of cooperative decision making are actualized by this structure. First, the decision-making process is democratic and as direct as possible, taking into consideration both in-plant issues and the resource allocation, production, and consumption priorities of the entire kibbutz. Second, authority is diffused throughout the entire community and among workers in the plant. The system of rotation assures that decision making is neither hierarchical nor a function of occupation. Third, personal and work relations are primary and overlapping, facilitating communications at all levels within the plant and community. Fourth, worker motivation and interest in plant operations is a function of voluntary commitment to and responsibility for the entire kibbutz, the participatory decision-making process, and the incentives built into the rotation system, rather than dependent on material rewards. The incentives in the system—status and importance to the overall kibbutz—are interlocked with identification with the wider community, and confer no special decision-making power. Fifth, since the ideological purpose behind kibbutz industry is the provision of new and useful work for members and increased output for the benefit of the community, rather than an expansion of managerial control or profit maximization *per se* at the expense of the psychological and social needs of workers, no worker is ever "let go" because his skill is no longer needed. Admittedly, the labor shortage—partly offset by technological intensity—helps provide full employment, but this is a different point than the underlying reservoir of mutuality on which the cooperative organization rests. Finally, it seems only fair to point out that the kibbutz factions are run democratically as part of the operational democracy of the entire community. But they are still governed under, in effect, a tripartite system in which factory workers do not alone control or even veto the major policy decisions.

Efficiency and Profitability in Kibbutz Industry

Research on the specifics of industrialization in the kibbutzim is still nascent, but against all the assertions of managerial ideologies, that available shows a positive correlation between non-authoritative patterns of decision making and efficiency and profitability when compared with matched enterprises in other sectors of the Israeli economy. A recent study of data from a stratified then paired sample of twelve industries demonstrated, within the limitations of the data, that cooperative organization of industry can be as or more efficient a means of production than, and provide a viable alternative to, the ideals and practices of managerial organization.[30]

Each enterprise examined was matched with respect to industry and product (tools, instruments, die casting, plastics, machine shop, canning) and had the same raw materials, technologies, manufacturing processes, and marketing needs; no operating techniques were known. Data was obtained from ordinary unpublished records and was reclassified where necessary to assure consistency. The median investment was £I 847 for managerial firms and £I 1,861 for kibbutz factories. Both

[30] Melman, *op. cit.* See also note 2.

kinds of enterprises obtained capital from essentially the same sources in the private market, and although they paid comparable interest rates, the fact that the kibbutz factory was backed by its community may have given it a better credit rating. Industrial efficiency was measured in terms of capital productivity; labor productivity; profit per production worker, i.e., maximizing outputs in relation to inputs; and administrative costs, i.e., outlays for necessary decision making.

The comparative productivity of labor in the managerial and cooperative factories was calculated (by equal weighting) contrasting output (net sales) to inputs (man-hours). The cooperative decision-making plants' median sales per production worker man hour were 26 percent higher. The comparative productivity of capital was measured by 1) output (profit) as a percentage of input (capital invested) and 2) output (sales) as a percent of input (fixed assets). Cooperative enterprises had a median profit of 12.9 percent of capital, and median sales of 3.6 times fixed assets, as against 7.7 percent and 2.7 times for managerially controlled plants. Cooperative plants thus bested managerial ones by 67 percent greater profit/investment and 33 percent greater sales/fixed assets. Median profit per production worker was 115 percent greater in the cooperative plants. Administrative costs, measured in terms of the number of administrative employees per hundred workers revealed a median value of 17.3 in the cooperative enterprises versus 19.9 in the managerial ones, or 13 percent lower costs in the former. When the position of each firm was ranked in regard to the above criteria, performance in the two kinds of enterprises showed: 8 almost equal performances, 15 where cooperative plants performed better, and 7 where managerial plants led. By industry type, only tool plants clearly led in more than two criteria.

Another recent study of ten paired plants also confirms these results.[31] It demonstrated that 1) for the proportion between output and capital invested, the coefficient was 3.6 for kibbutz industry and 2.6 for private enterprise; 2) the proportion be-

[31] Reported on in Rozner, "Social Aspects of Industrialization in the Kibbutz," *op. cit.*, p. 7.

tween output and labor input showed a coefficient of 12.3 for kibbutz and 10.3 for private firms; and 3) in regard to managerial versus direct production labor, the coefficient was 17.8 for kibbutz industry and 18.9 for private enterprises.

These findings of efficiency and profitability are an important demonstration that industrial effectiveness need not be a function of managerial methods of supervision and decision making. The organizational structure of kibbutz industries clearly results in the kind of cooperation supportive of stability and hence maximal operation of the production system.[32] Rural location was also found unimportant. Cooperation is obviously made possible by a combination of ideological, moral, and structural elements in the greater community. It is significant that these features seem to initiate precisely the conditions of efficiency and profitability that modern managerial ideologies look for from the syndrome of participation—satisfaction—increased production which they try to implement by a series of worker participation plans imposed from above. In sum, then, functional effectiveness comes not only from the structure of decision making, but also from the relations between the specific organization and its wider society.

Social Aspects of Kibbutz Industrialization

Lest it be assumed that the industrialization of the kibbutz has proceeded smoothly with no ramifications on its social organization, we must hasten to correct the impression. Several companion effects—not all positive—to the industrialization process have been noted, and it is important to examine these as much to point out the kibbutzim's creative search for solutions as to underline lessons for others.

The first set of problems originated in the personalities of kibbutz members and in some peculiarities of the social system.[33] Preconceptions about the alienating effects of industrial

[32] Melman, *op. cit.*, p. 27.
[33] Rozner, "Social Aspects of Industrialization in the Kibbutz," *op. cit.*, pp. 5–6.

work led workers accustomed to traditional agricultural labor to doubt their ability to adapt or to achieve work satisfaction. The ideological premise that only agricultural work is nonalienating was hard to overcome.

Then, too, the inherent limitation of the kibbutz size (averaging 250 to 300 members) raised a question as to whether the kibbutz would be relegated to backward low-technology industries. This was a complex problem because it involved several issues: the use of hired labor; whether converting to capital intensive high-technology industries would be economically feasible; the implications of technological reliance as well as participation in the industrial marketplace for the ideological basis of the society. To a certain extent the size problem is a deceptive one that does not necessarily interfere with the principle of cooperative decision making so long as "workable decision-making subunits" and techniques for integrating them can be maintained.[34] Here technological innovations, like information processing by computers, can be helpful, for they carry no intrinsic value orientation but rather acquire value attachments from the use to which they are put. The size limitation actually encouraged the manpower-poor kibbutzim to innovate labor-saving devices through a high per worker rate of capital investment in technology and training. Kibbutzim have also solved the problem of a possible conflict between large size industries and their values, by setting an optimal plant size and then starting a second industry, thus better integrating industrial work into the requirements of kibbutz life.

On the other hand, the use of hired labor has been a real problem. We have noted that as kibbutzim diversified into industrial activities, the number of members employed elsewhere has diminished. Concomitantly, agricultural production rose but, thanks to the new agricultural technologies, required less manpower. The wish to industrialize, as well as recognition of its potentially greater profitability, led to decisions by industrialized kibbutzim to cut back on their numbers of agricultural branches and to shift members into industrial work. This was part of an overall trend among kibbutzim, but the change to

[34] Melman, *op. cit.,* pp. 31–2.

highly technological and capital intensive labor activities did not wholly relieve the endemic manpower shortage. Nearly all kibbutzim historically employed some hired labor to help in special agricultural chores such as harvesting, but the industrial push—especially pressures to expand rapidly and the necessity of selling industrial products in a competitive capitalist market—ballooned their numbers until in 1963 two thirds of the 6,000 industrial workers were hired labor. However, it is important neither to confuse the use of hired labor with the industrialization process itself nor with any consequences—for example, the use of the same kinds of investment principles that characterize the private and Histadrut sectors—to the kibbutz economies which have resulted from the trend toward a capital versus labor intensive economy. More labor alone would simply not have solved the economic problems of the kibbutzim, particularly in light of the changes in the nature of the Israeli population, and the priorities, development policies and loan procedures introduced following independence. The turn toward new technologies filled a social need for new forms of useful work as well as an economic one. It did require capital intensive manuevers, but the finances were available not because the kibbutzim had abandoned cooperative work principles for the marketplace but because the overall economy was now more stable and able to reallocate monies that had been committed unnecessarily to agriculture. This is not to say that the change-over to a capital-intensive and industrial economy has not met with resistance nor been fraught with ideological conflicts— especially, as we mentioned, over the separation of work from the land—but it is to be argued that if we understand all the reasons for it, in the long run the shift can be regarded as a progressive response to an old dilemma and to changes in objective circumstances. In addition, it may allow the kibbutz to survive and prosper as a viable economic and social unit in Israeli society.

The use of hired labor *per se* is today loudly and rightfully condemned as an abuse of traditional kibbutz ideology and mores. Employing workers both directly contradicts the settlers' original commitment to build a Jewish labor economy based on the conquest of work and a primary relationship to the land,

and it violates the Marxist exhortation against the exploitation of labor by capital. The use of hired labor is thus a conspicuous exception to an otherwise moneyless society based on the principle "From each according to his ability; to each according to his needs." It clearly ties a kibbutz and the general economy closer together than is desirable. It is also argued that the use of hired labor undermines the interest and willingness of members to do unpleasant work for which they are not remunerated.[35] In addition, the presence of salaried workers is said to destroy the basis for real human equality by introducing into the kibbutz a body of workers who labor under the supervision of members *cum* "managers." Further, because the values and life styles of hired workers are so obviously different tensions arise, setting a bad example for kibbutz children who are less able to distinguish their society from other forms of economic organization. Obviously too, the presence of a mixed labor force makes job rotation more difficult. The tremendous guilt attendant to employing workers has contributed to an ironic situation: although such workers are unionized under the Histadrut, their job security is ultimately subject to the ability of the employing kibbutz to replace them with its own members. Outbursts of antagonism have occurred which have even resulted in occasional strike action against employing kibbutzim.

There is little question that failure to resolve this problem has partially curtailed the expansion of kibbutz industries and has forced them to forgo such economies of scale as might exist in a country of mostly small- and medium-size industries, but the crucial issue is the debilitating effects of the conflict, and the ambivalence whch it engenders, in the social structures of the kibbutzim. Apart from eliminating hired labor entirely, several solutions have been tried.[36] These include: the payment of

[35] Stern, *op. cit.*, p. 109.

[36] See *ibid.*, pp. 110–4, and Kanovsky, *op. cit.*, pp. 65–7. The regional enterprises jointly owned by several kibbutzim, or in combination with other sectors, try to exempt themselves from the dilemma by using a convenient ideological fiction; i.e., that they are not really part of the inclusive economic and social structure of the kibbutz. It is true that these industries are financially independent of the budget of one kibbutz and are often incorporated, yet a participating kibbutz receives the wages of any members employed in a regional business.

higher wages and larger fringe benefits; profit sharing; workers' participation in management; the conversion of industries into cooperatives with special financing and training for the workers in the hope that kibbutz supervision will become unnecessary (one kibbutz has done this); the transfer of all plants from individual kibbutz to corporations jointly owned by a federation or to public ones owned together with the Histadrut, the Jewish Agency, and the government so that all workers, including participating kibbutz members, would be employees of a public corporation; farming out some traditional work to cooperatives in order to free members for industrial labor; and the allocation to a special fund for the benefit of hired labor the difference between what they are paid under union rates and the equivalent of the wage labor of kibbutz members.

It is obvious that none of these solutions gets at the heart of the problem, which is in the last analysis related to the survival of kibbutz Socialism. The depth of the feeling against the use of hired labor and yet the irrevocable commitment of the kibbutzim to industrialization were sharply outlined by two events in 1963. In the summer, the three major kibbutz federations submitted to the executive council of the Histadrut a detailed draft of recommendations designed to eliminate hired labor within three years from all existing agricultural and industrial operations directly operated by kibbutzim either by reorganizing them into cooperatives or by turning them and any joint projects using hired labor over to an administrative agency chosen by the respective federation which would involve workers in management and profit sharing. Kibbutzim would not be allowed to start new industries for which they could not supply labor from their membership, and all kibbutzim were urged to develop ways to cooperate with each other to fill manpower shortages. In February of that year, however, the kibbutz movement as a whole had also set up a new organization clearly intended to spur industrialization. It provided for the coordination of and planning for new industrial projects; it was to serve as a forum to discuss common problems; and it intended to supply experts to consult on technical and economic problems.

Since 1963 the need for industrial expansion on the sound basis of social needs and economic criteria has not abated, but neither has the commitment to "avoid, limit, or ameliorate the ideological and social implications of these developments. . . ."[37] Some hope is offered that it is economically feasible to solve this issue by a recent finding that small enterprises utilizing higher technology are superior to large ones employing some hired workers both in terms of efficiency and profitability.[38] This again seems to support our contention that industrial effectiveness can result from operationalizing cooperative labor principles on a foundation of common ideology and values.

Another obvious problem for the kibbutzim has been to organize the structures of the enterprises uniformly. This has not always been possible, and differences in management patterns and in the actual authority of the workers' meeting have been noticed.[39] In some, the workers' general meeting does make the authoritative decisions concerning production and investment planning, the work conditions, and the schedule, and acts as a grievance board. In others it has become a transmission belt for *a priori* decisions of management; and rotation principles are less religiously applied. Research reveals these differences to relate to the degree of integration of the industry into the kibbutz. The remedy has been redoubled efforts to apply the uniform standards outlined above. But on the whole, while cross-national research with Italy and Yugoslavia has exposed the influence that managerial arrangements have on worker consciousness, it has also demonstrated that differences of opinions and positions among levels in kibbutz industry are small compared with comparable enterprises elsewhere.[40] In the kibbutz both feelings of participation in decision making and actual involvement by workers are recorded to be higher.

Then, too, it would indeed be naïve to ignore what are real observable differences between agricultural and industrial work. The technological structure and the interdependence of tasks

---

[37] Kanovsky, *op. cit.*, p. 67.

[38] Rozner, "Social Aspects of Industrialization in the Kibbutz," *op. cit.*, p. 7.

[39] *Ibid.*, p. 8.

[40] *Ibid.*, p. 11. The cross-national research is part of the larger project of the Institute for Social Relations at the University of Michigan of which the Rozner papers are the first releases on the Israeli part.

both conditions the autonomy of the work task and also interferes with the commitment to advanced study which had accompanied agricultural work.[41] Efforts to remedy this are directed toward developing new technical and professional skill levels suitable to industry in order to provide a solid basis for future job enlargement and rotation, especially into managerial functions; and toward finding the kinds of technology and enterprises best suited to kibbutz values, its way of life and worker needs for self-realization, as well as to economic requirements.

Where a dichotomy between the more professional and highly skilled workers and the semiskilled or nonskilled workers has been observed, attempts are made to reinforce the authority of the workers' general meeting and to deliberately inhibit the emergence of class distinctions and power tied to occupations. Thus, the rotation system exempts purely professional jobs for which specialists are required and concentrates on managerial positions which involve authoritative decisions. And where, despite kibbutz mores, some hint of a tendency toward generalized impersonal regulations disintegrative of social cohesion in the work group has emerged, the kibbutzim have tried to cut back on the numbers of hired workers and have either more firmly integrated an enterprise into the kibbutz economy or removed it to the regional level.

Finally, in order to help assess the future of worker self-management in kibbutz industries, we must ask whether the patterns of direct democracy crucial to the kibbutz movement have been drastically altered by the new developments we have discussed. The increasing internal differentiation—between age groups, in motivation and education, between new and old members, between agricultural and industrial work groups, and in the kinds of work activities—would suggest that it would now be more difficult to maintain internal cohesion by means of public opinion, the traditional control system. One would also suspect that specialization, and thus more departmentalization, would undermine the overall awareness of kibbutz members, leading to an increase of apathy, and therefore result in a need for more explicit rules to regulate social behavior.

[41] *Ibid.*, pp. 9, 11.

Research on these hypotheses has been done by analyzing changes in function of the general meeting, the organizational structure of the kibbutz, and types of participation by members in kibbutz activities in different size kibbutzim.[42] It has been found that although there does seem to be a decrease in participation (measured by attendance) at general meetings as the membership of a kibbutz increases, this does not seem to be mainly related to the size of the kibbutz, but rather to specific conditions, such as a decline of awareness due to specialization. Members criticized the general meeting for not fulfilling its executive functions, especially in economic matters. As a result, suggestions were made that proposals brought for ratification should be more detailed with clearer alternatives, a better information system devised prior to the meetings, and that departmental meetings be open to all members. In addition, kibbutzim have tried to create a "criss-cross structure" of clubs and groups to serve as integrating channels between the individual and the society. These deliberate attempts to increase interactions in order to inhibit a decline in awareness inimical to democracy reveals a commitment to preserve the general meeting as a forum for problem solving. Moreover, while there has obviously been a proliferation of organizations and undeniable tendencies toward institutionalization, formalization of roles, and codification of norms, it is argued that the principles underlying kibbutz organization and the methods by which they are applied are basically not conducive to the emergence of bureaucratic organization. It is maintained that the diffused overlapping personal relations found in kibbutz life inhibit centralization, the emergence of rewards affixed to the job, hierarchy, and formal immutable job qualifications, and thus actually contribute to the efficiency of the organization. Of course, the absence of economic differentiation is crucial.

The problem of whether functional differentiation itself leads to apathy and the emergence of class differences is more difficult. Current findings do not ignore this possibility—despite the fact that the kinds of participatory activities in both large and small kibbutzim are the same—nor the impact of personality

[42] Reported on in Rozner, "Principal Types and Problems of Direct Democracy in the Kibbutz," *op. cit.,* pp. 10–20. The author surveyed 24 kibbutzim in 1961.

differences, but stress that a balance of positive and negative rewards (for example, community status but no power for doing a difficult job) in each job acts to preserve an analogous "change-over" rate in office holding at all levels, whatever size the kibbutz is. It seems clear that this kind of rotation system certainly helps to mitigate against debilitating apathy. Finally, higher education among younger members and the expansion of training programs is also thought to sustain a commitment to participation and equal rewards in order to prevent class stratification.

Critique

In sum, then, rapid industrialization has certainly resulted in some marked socioeconomic changes in kibbutz society. But overall, the flexibility of the kibbutz way of life seems to have thus far prevented a profound disintegration of the principles and structures of cooperative democracy which are its hallmark. This can in part be attributed to the network of cooperative relations and institutions uniting kibbutzim that provide a buffer zone between kibbutz values and those of Israeli society, but it must also be credited to the special kibbutz values and ideology. In turn, these support complete identification between the goals of the industrial labor unit and those of kibbutz society, facilitating a viable model of community—if not precisely worker control.

The Future of Workers' Participation in Israel

At the beginning of this study we posited that the success of workers' participation is dependent on a broad foundation of ideological and social support for, and an operationalized commitment to, cooperative and direct decision making which utilizes psychological as well as socioeconomic criteria. Where these conditions are fulfilled a nonalienating work situation and a chance for accomplishing major changes in human relationships can coexist along with effective industrial performance. Where either ideology or practice is ambivalent or works against professed ends, where worker participation plans are imposed from above without a clear understanding of their need or purpose on the part of any one group of participants, or where demands on the workforce for participation exceed perceivable benefits thereby often necessitating a material adjustment, feelings of involvement and satisfaction will not be realized even when industrial production may be rising due to other factors.

The failure of the various attempts to introduce worker participation plans into Histadrut industry is symptomatic of vast changes in the ideology and practice of Israeli social, political, and economic life, especially the shift toward capitalist development policies and changes in the composition and motivation of the workforce. The extension of both public and private ownership and a redefinition of these sectors following independence were also inimical to workers' control.

Moreover, the loss of the traditional social and national goals represented by Zionist Socialism meant the disappearance of a prime bulwark against the rise of economic and managerial elites. The labor movement, which once epitomized the ideology of workers' management, rapidly bureaucratized in almost a classic Weberian sense, thereby opening itself to the incursions of managerial ideologies and competitive ethics. Opposition on the part of Histadrut leadership toward decentralized workers' control and ambivalence toward participation, hostility on the part of managers, and a wage-benefit orientation and deepening distrust toward their union-employer by workers combined to insure the failure of the participation plans that were tried. Yet the old ideology continues to exert a strong pull and it remains mandatory to embrace participatory solutions for problems of alienation and productivity in the industrial sector of the Histadrut economy.

On the contrary, because of the almost complete congruence between the economic, social, and political values in the kibbutzim, these communities have been able to industrialize without yet suffering any profound disruption of their social structures from changes in the nature of the work or the effects of technology. Determination to preserve their democratic ideology facilitated a transfer of cooperative principles and procedures from the rest of kibbutz life to kibbutz industries, even where industrialization was initially opposed by a minority of the membership. Further, participation by individual kibbutzim in federations—designed primarily for mutual aid and strength— helps to insulate the social system from the pressures of dramatic change in the society at large and provides both the necessary psychological and actual distance for a mutually advantageous relationship with the greater society. Strict adherence to economic equality, the absence of material rewards attached to an office or occupation and the immediacy of decision making have helped to actualize the self-control of kibbutz industries. Thus, it should be evident that the future of workers' control in Israel is tied to the ability of the kibbutzim to resist the most insidious kinds of class distinctions. This means, for example, that they must solve the problem of hired workers in such a way as to leave Socialist principles and their practice intact.

Finally, if we were to enumerate lessons from the Israeli experience, they seem to be the following: first, it is possible to industrialize an economy without introducing a major disconnection between ownership and workers provided social values and structures are inclusive enough to withstand the major dislocations that accompany a change from an agricultural to a technologically based economy; second, where bureaucratization or a division of authority between workers and managers has already begun, and is accompanied by a fundamental shift in social priorities, it will be increasingly difficult if not impossible to reassert nonauthoritative human relations; third, although its worker control is rooted in the culture of the kibbutz and its institutions are highly interdependent, it should be possible to apply some of the specific mechanisms, such as the procedures for direct democracy, elsewhere, provided a fierce commitment exists to make them work; finally, since it is unlikely that other units of production will have the inner coherence which characterizes the kibbutzim, they must not only be able and willing to restructure themselves internally but also to act as positive forces for change on their societies, for only in this way does it seem they can avoid inertia and debilitating incursions from without.

Yugoslavia

The Yugoslav experiment in workers' self-management is important for a number of reasons:

It is more far-reaching than experiments elsewhere, and it is taking place within a unique Socialist context, with the distant vision of Communism its final goal. This precise framework allows for detailed analyses of the constantly changing socio-economic relationships and processes from the early days of the break with Soviet command economy and the introduction of workers' self-management in 1950, through the current transitional phase. Against this historical, political, and cultural background it is easy to see the formidable barriers that stand in the way of proclaimed policies of workers' self-management and social self-government. The dynamic element in Yugoslav society has attracted the attention of many observers, since nowhere in the capitalist world is it possible to observe such a widespread and intense discussion about, and experimentation with, fundamental sociopolitical issues.

There is another quite different element that attracts observers to the Yugoslav experience. If we disregard for the moment the dynamic character of Yugoslav society and instead focus on the present political and economic system in that country, we can see the emergence of an alternative to the traditional models of Western capitalism and Soviet command economy—a model based on a labor-managed market economy or, to put it differently, a participatory economy.[1]

The political experience in Yugoslavia over the past twenty

[1] See Jaroslav Vanek, *The General Theory of Labor-Managed Market Economies* and *The Participatory Economy: An Evolutionary Hypothesis and a Strategy for Development,* Cornell University Press, Ithaca, 1970 and 1971.

years provides us also with a growing body of theoretical insights about the potential of new forms of democracy. Socialist democracy, as conceived by the Yugoslavs, presupposes the full participation of all citizens in the political process. A representative body which does not derive directly from basic productive and other socioeconomic relations (i.e., from citizens united functionally in a workplace or other communities of interest) will be ineffective in representing the interests of the working people. Coupled with the principles of functional representation is the principle of rotation of elected government and political functionaries. The system of functional democracy, and of rotation of elected delegates, is further strengthened by the power of the electors to recall their elected delegates. The Yugoslavs have thus built up a strong system of checks against the emergence of informal power groups and political professionalism.

The representative parliamentary form of democracy as practiced in Western capitalist countries is seen by the Yugoslavs to be unable to provide for the full participation of its citizens in the political process. A representative body which derives from the unorganized "general citizen" cannot be effective in representing the working people. By its very nature, it becomes a protagonist of the "general interest" and thus an easy target for manipulation by informal political and economic forces.

The article that follows describes the context within which workers' self-management operates, discusses structural and political innovations with particular emphasis on those taking place at the level of the workplace and the community, and raises some of the problems and contradictions facing Yugoslavs today.

While we are aware that we cannot compare Yugoslav society with that of the United States and Canada, one problem in particular is of critical importance to those of us here who advocate and struggle for "power to the people" in the community and in the workplace. In Yugoslavia, what direct democracy exists at the grassroots level has come about in one of two ways: either by spontaneous action or by legislation. (Libertarian Socialists will have little difficulty praising the former and criticizing the latter.) Many innovations in direct Socialist democracy on the local level have come about only by means of the pressure exerted by workers in their workplaces and by citizens in their local communities. It is equally true, however, that when political restrictions have been removed from above —as has been the case with the controversial Constitutional Amendment XV—the results have not been uniform and on many occasions have led to the reintroduction of authoritarian patterns of decision making.

Amendment XV, in essence, removed the previously detailed regulations governing the number, nature, composition, and power of the various organs of self-management within enterprises and placed the power to determine these matters directly in the hands of the working people. Officially this move was hailed as an effort to "stimulate workers to exert greater influence on the further development of workers' self-management."[2]

Two things have happened since the passage of Amendment XV. In some enterprises workers' rights have been strengthened and the scope of direct decision making has been enlarged. In many enterprises, however, the pressures of competition within Yugoslavia's labor-managed economy have led to the reintroduction of authoritarian patterns of decision making.

It is difficult to draw any final conclusions from the Yugoslav experience, largely because of the dynamic character of the system. The one lesson that would seem to emerge at present is this: the struggle to reduce alienation and to establish Socialist democracy cannot succeed until the principle of self-management and self-government is exercised at the upper levels of the system as well as within its smallest units. Decisions of national importance are still made by the Communist leadership, and it is by no means clear that the removal of all controls would benefit the majority of Yugoslavs. The current upsurge of cultural and economic nationalism in Croatia has increased the power of the "centralizers" within the League. The role of the League of Communists remains, for the time being, the crucial factor in future developments.

[2] Ivan Paj, "The Orientation of Self-Management in Enterprises," *Yugoslav Survey,* Vol. XII, No. 1 (1971), p. 33.

Workers' Self-Management in Yugoslavia

Gerry Hunnius

The Social Context

The Yugoslav system of Socialism must be evaluated in terms of the region's history, which continues to have a powerful impact on the political situation.[1] The dominant features in the history of the Yugoslav people have been the conflict between nationalities and resistance to foreign domination. The Communist Party of Yugoslavia (CPY), founded in 1919, was the first truly *Yugoslav* party in the history of that country, insofar as it united within its ranks the many nationalities and minority groups. The national liberation struggle during World War II acted as a strong unifying factor in the birth of the Socialist Federal Republic of Yugoslavia.[2]

Yugoslavia is a multinational state of over twenty million inhabitants. The Slav peoples, who constitute a great majority of the population, belong to five main ethnic groups: Serbs, Croats, Slovenes, Macedonians, and Montenegrins. Each of these groups has its territorial center in one of five autonomous

[1] A good if somewhat dated introduction to the Yugoslav system is Hoffman and Neal, *Yugoslavia and the New Communism*, New York, Twentieth Century Fund, 1962.

[2] The most recent study of the nationality question in Yugoslavia is Paul Shoup, *Communism and the Yugoslav National Question*, New York, Columbia University Press, 1968.

republics. A sixth republic, Bosnia-Herzegovina, has a population consisting of Serbs, Croats, and Yugoslav Moslems. In addition to the six republics, two autonomous provinces have been created within Serbia. Kosovo-Methohija (Kosmet) has an Albanian majority, and Vojvodina in northern Serbia has a mixed population including a large number of Hungarians. Minorities in Yugoslavia make up about ten percent of the total population. Equality under the law is guaranteed to all citizens in Article XXXIII of the Constitution. Incitement to national, racial, or religious hatred is unconstitutional and as a rule this law is rigorously enforced.

When the nation of Yugoslavia was created at the end of World War II, it was a country devastated by war. According to Yugoslav sources, over thirty-six percent of the country's industry was destroyed and some 1,700,000 people had lost their lives. Added to this was the extremely low technological and economic base of the country. Industrial development in most of Yugoslavia up to that period was concentrated in extractive industries which were largely in the hands of foreigners. Only in Slovenia and Croatia did a native industry exist. All these factors made the task of nation-building extremely difficult.

In addition, many social and economic factors must be kept in mind in any serious attempt to evaluate the Yugoslav experiment in self-management:

The low level of education and industrial experience of a great part of the working force, including sections of the managerial personnel. The steady stream of peasants deserting rural areas for the cities has vastly increased the number of unskilled and semiskilled workers. While the government has done much to combat illiteracy and provide vocational training, the problem is still a serious one with direct implications for the development of self-management.

The division between the more industrialized northern regions and the less developed southern parts of the country.[3] While regional equalization is the official policy of government

[3] The rich/poor division of the country is directly related to the nationality question. Slovenia and Croatia in the north and parts of Serbia have the highest standard of living. The rest of Yugoslavia is relatively undeveloped.

and party, progress in this respect has not been up to expectations. The introduction of workers' self-management in 1950 and the economic reforms of 1965 have reduced the resources and the role of the federal government in aiding the development of poorer regions and have shifted part of the burden on enterprises and banks. The battle between the developed and underdeveloped republics is a part of every aspect of Yugoslav politics, and resentment is directed against the federal government by the rich as well as the poor republics.

The Political Framework

Yugoslavia has undergone a series of revolutionary political changes during the past thirty years. The rapidity of recent institutional changes can perhaps best be understood by viewing them as an attempt to move from a preindustrial into an industrial era while simultaneously fostering the values of postindustrial society. In addition to the cataclysmic changes involved in pursuing a policy of industrialization and decentralization, Yugoslavia is also experiencing a sociopolitical revolution in attempting to unite hitherto hostile nationalities and minority groups within a constantly changing political system.

The Yugoslav political system in the immediate postwar years was modeled on that of the Soviet Union. This first period came to an end in the late 1940s with the break with the Soviet Union. Since 1950, Yugoslavia has been moving toward increased decentralization of the economy; lately this has also begun to be extended to the political/administrative structures. The elevation of the Commune to the "basic sociopolitical community"[4] was accompanied by a number of significant innovations. Election of deputies to the Federal Assembly (and the power to recall them) was granted to commune assemblies. In the early 1950s, a constitutional provision delegated responsibility over all activities not expressly reserved to the districts,[5] the republics, and the Federation, to the local communes. A year later, a provision was passed stipulating that local ad-

[4] The term sociopolitical community refers to communes, provinces, republics, and the Federation. Sociopolitical organizations include the League of Communists, the Socialist Alliance, the trade unions, etc.

[5] Districts have now been abolished.

ministrative agencies were responsible only to their own local
assemblies and councils and no longer to republican and federal
governmental agencies.

The 1963 constitution and subsequent amendments initiated
a number of far-reaching structural changes in the parliamentary system intended to give the self-managing organizations of
associated labor more direct influence in representative bodies
on the communal, republican, and federal levels. The federal
assembly now has five councils (chambers), three of which
represent the functional interests of self-managing working organizations from the basic areas of the economy, education and
culture, welfare and public health. Every parliamentary act
must be passed by two chambers, that is, the Chamber of
Nationalities acting in conjunction with one of the other four.
Recent changes in the election of these functional chambers of
the federal and republican assemblies have retained the principle of indirect voting,[6] but the composition of the electoral
body now consists of members of the communal assemblies
and delegates of work communities in the commune (enterprises and institutions), while formerly it was the communal
assemblies alone which elected deputies to the functional chambers of republican assemblies and the federal assembly. This
has increased the influence of local work communities in policy
making on the republican and federal level. Of particular
interest is the fact that university and high school students have
obtained the right to be elected to the Chamber for Education
and Culture.[7]

The fourth council (the sociopolitical council) is elected
directly by citizens in the communes. Finally, the Council of
Nationalities, elected by the assemblies of the republics and
provinces on a basis of parity, insures the equal participation of
the various nationalities and minorities in the policy making of
the federal government.

The entire process is geared to replace the "professional
politician" by delegates who, as a rule, retain their professional

[6] The official designation of these functional chambers is "Chambers
of Work Communities." In Croatia, direct voting by the citizens has been
introduced in the election of the functional chambers.

[7] "An Assessment of the Elections," in *Socialist Thought and Practice*,
No. 34 (April–June 1939), p. 59.

connection with the self-managing structures that delegated authority to them. The delegates are responsible to their voters and may be recalled. The assemblies are not only legislative bodies but also function to an increasing extent as territorial self-management bodies, coordinating and integrating the mechanisms of the many self-managing enterprises, institutions, and organizations in their territory.

Bureaucracy, statism, and opposition to self-management are considered to be the official enemies of the regime. Elaborate provisions have been built into the political process to prevent these tendencies from gaining the upper hand. Rotation of elected representatives is meant to preclude the formation of power groups and to check political professionalism. No one can be elected to the same post twice (or three times in certain cases) in succession.[8] This does not, however, prevent a deputy of the federal assembly being elected to a republican assembly and then reentering the federal assembly. The principle of rotation suffers in practice from certain defects and at times may appear to be a game of musical chairs with functionaries moving from one sociopolitical organization to the next (from the League of Communists to the trade unions, etc.) and back again. Occasionally someone is retired to make room for a newcomer.[9]

The Sociopolitical Organizations

For a long time after the war the Communist Party, later renamed the League of Communists of Yugoslavia (LCY), functioned as the originator of all important legislation, including the decision, in 1950, to introduce self-management. Even

[8] Direct Socialist democracy is fundamentally at odds with traditional parliamentary democracy. The latter is seen to be dominated by the struggle for power among competing parties with the victor holding a monopoly of decision-making power. Accountability of deputies to their political party is, in a system of direct democracy, replaced by direct and continuous accountability of elected deputies to their constituents. Rotation and recall of elected deputies and the retention of their jobs in their respective places of work are seen as integral parts of a system of direct Socialist democracy.

[9] There is an element of humanity in "retiring" unwanted functionaries (on pension), particularly if we compare this practice with the less humanitarian practices used in the immediate postwar years.

today, decisions of national importance usually originate with the leadership of the League. On the local level, the League is supposed to provide guidance and leadership without exercising direct control. The problem of transforming itself from an organ of power and control to an ideological and political vanguard is one of the most complex issues facing the LCY. Increasingly, at least on the local level, the League is expected to define problems, elaborate goals and make its influence felt through example and discussion. Individual members of the League are expected to take an active part in the self-management bodies.[10]

The actual influence of the League on self-management bodies within enterprises varies from case to case.[11]

Present trends in League membership are somewhat disturbing in terms of the future of self-management. Studies indicate that the number of highly skilled blue-collar workers who are members of the League has steadily increased during the past eight years, while at the same time the number of blue-collar workers on the whole has increased less rapidly than the number of white-collar workers. Horvat argues that the mentality of the white-collar worker in Yugoslavia is closer to the bureaucratic mentality than that of the blue-collar worker.[12] The continuation of this trend within the LCY may pose a future threat to the system of self-management.

Criticism of the LCY is on the increase among prominent communists. Mijalko Todorovic, secretary of the League's Executive Committee, commented at the Ninth Session of the Central Committee: "The League's principal weakness today springs primarily from its still over-great amalgamation with power, the slow process of democratization of relations within it, its unsuitable structure, and the ideological heterogeneity among its ranks."[13]

[10] In 1968, the membership of the LCY was 1,146,084.

[11] Albert Meister, *Socialisme et autogestion: l'experience yugoslave.* (Paris: Editions du Seuil, 1964), p. 84; and Hoffman and Neal, *op. cit.,* pp. 244–5.

[12] For further details see: Branko Horvat, *An Essay on Yugoslav Society,* White Plains, N.Y.: International Arts and Sciences Press, 1969.

[13] Mijalko Todorovic, "A Revolutionary Vanguard—The Abiding Need of our Self-Managing Community," in *Socialist Thought and Practice,* No. 31 (July–September 1968), p. 17.

The use of other sociopolitical organizations as transmission belts for the party ideology and policies is no longer acceptable. In practice, organizations such as the trade unions and the Socialist Alliance[14] are going through a period of adjustment and change. These organizations are meant to provide channels for political expression. They are also supposed to perform the difficult task of coordinating, linking, selecting, and modifying the numerous initiatives, pressures and proposals of individuals and self-managing bodies. The fact that the clash of contradictory demands at times leads these organizations to resort to the use of power is an illustration of the extreme complexity of their position during the present transitional phase.

Some Comments on the Economy

"The Yugoslav system of social ownership and workers' self-management can be viewed as one in which labor employs capital, instead of a system in which capital employs labor, as is the case under capitalism."[15] Theoretically all citizens possess ownership rights and delegate authority to manage property to autonomous enterprises and institutions which in turn are *managed by the workers* directly or through their elected organs of self-management. Three key economic components are at work in the Yugoslav economy:

1. *Workers' self-management* of the publicly owned enterprises.

2. *Social planning,* which consists of an intricate network of enterprise plans, commune plans, and indicative planning by republican and federal agencies.

3. *The market mechanism.*

Integration of the plans and activities of individual enter-

---

[14] The Socialist Alliance is a mass organization of over eight million members. It grew out of the People's Front which began before World War II and which played an important part in the Liberation struggle (1941–5). While the Socialist Alliance attracts Communists and non-Communists alike, it accepts the basic assumptions of the Yugoslav system and its leadership is made up largely of members of the League of Communists.

[15] This formulation is borrowed from Joel E. Dirlan, "Yugoslav Pricing and the Public Interest" (mimeographed, 1968), p. 10.

prises is now increasingly being transferred to autonomous associations of producers, economic chambers, and other groups. The flow of command has been partly reversed[16] and the individual enterprise is increasingly becoming the focal point and originator of important decisions relating to planning, production, and investment (the latter in cooperation with the banks). This transfer of government functions to autonomous associations of producers is one step toward the final goal of the "withering away of the state."

The process of decentralization, economic decision making, and the increase in reliance on the market mechanism culminated in the reforms of 1965 which transferred to the enterprises and banks the bulk of the remaining investment resources still in the hands of the sociopolitical communities.[17] The market forces were further strengthened by a relaxation of price regulation and the reduction of barriers to imports. The convertibility of currency, one of the declared aims of the government, is meant to facilitate Yugoslavia's participation in the world market.

Thus the use of markets to allocate resources at the microlevel coexists with social ownership and the use of social planning to achieve macroeconomic objectives.[18] The debate

[16] After World War II, the flow of command in the economy originated with the control agencies of federal government and proceeded, via the economic ministries and the directorates (one directorate for a specified number of enterprises) to the individual enterprise. With the introduction of the new system in the 1950s, the administrative ties were cut to give more freedom to the periphery. Gradually, the flow was reversed. Initiatives now originate increasingly in the periphery.

[17] The League of Communists in one of the Resolutions passed at its Ninth Congress, demanded that, "the entire process of reproduction should be under the control of the working collectives which earned, accumulated and pooled their resources. The producer must wield a greater and more direct influence on the policies of the banks and on their business activities, and the banks must together with them shoulder economic responsibility for the results and development policies of the self-managing organizations." Resolution on "Socialist Development in Yugoslavia on the Basis of Self-Management and the Tasks of the League of Communists," Ninth Congress of the LCY, in *Socialist Thought and Practice,* No. 38 (January–March, 1969), p. 33.

[18] Howard M. Wachtel, *Workers' Management and Wage Differentials in Yugoslavia,* Ph.D. dissertation, University of Michigan, 1968 (mimeographed), p. 1.

between the organizational principles of centralization and decentralization has been under way for a long time in Yugoslavia and continues today.[19]

While enterprises are autonomous and exercise entrepreneurial functions, they are not *fully* autonomous. In cases of decisions which involve damage to other enterprises or to the wider community, restrictions can be imposed[20] from the outside.

Structure and Function of Workers' Self-Management

Yugoslav legislation defines an economic organization as a work organization

—that is founded according to the law;

—that performs a given type of economic activity (in commodity production, trade, services or finance);

—that performs its activity autonomously in conformity with its statute and other provisions;

—that manages a share of social property directly or through its elected organs of self-management;[21]

Yugoslav economic legislation and practice are based on the concept of self-managing enterprise as a "Socialist commodity producer."

[19] Since I will not deal in this article with the theory of labor-managed economy, I refer the reader to the studies of J. Vanek: "Decentralization Under Workers' Management: A Theoretical Appraisal," in *American Economic Review*, Vol. LIX, No. 5 (1969), pp. 1003–14. And J. Vanek, *The General Theory of Labor-Managed Market Economics*, Cornell University Press, 1970. Vanek considers the labor-managed system to be superior by far to any other system in existence. He bases his judgment on strictly economic criteria. The advantages of such a system, he argues, become even stronger if we consider broader human values. Readers may also find it useful to consult Branko Horvat, *Towards a Theory of Planned Economy*, White Plains, N.Y.: International Arts and Sciences Press, 1964.

[20] As a case in point, enterprises as a rule cannot decide, themselves, on their own termination.

[21] *Workers' Management in Yugoslavia (1950–1970)*, Belgrade: Medunarodna Politika, 1970, p. 36.

The workers employed in an enterprise organize work and management according to the following objectives:

1. Optimum utilization of the socially owned means of production and constant increase of productivity.

2. Promotion of the direct interest of the workers in their work and their most effective participation in the management of all productive and other activities.[22]

The internal organization of the enterprise is regulated by its statute. Since the passing of Amendment XV, the only structural legal requirement is the establishment of a workers' council. Other and additional self-management bodies are to be regulated by the statutes of each enterprise.

In contrast to the vertically (hierarchically) structured industrial organizations where status, prestige, rewards, and power increase as we ascend the pyramid, and administrative and legislative power is united in management, the Yugoslav model is horizontally (democratically) structured with the following features:

1. Decision-making power is divided by distinguishing between administrative and legislative power.

2. The veto power is in the hands of the general membership or its elected representative bodies instead of being in the hands of the director or general manager.

3. Tenure, admission, and dismissal of all personnel is decided by the general membership or its representatives. Administrators are elected and recalled, depending on how successful they are in the view of the general membership and its elected organs.[23]

The division between administrative and legislative power implies two hierarchies. One, concerned with self-management, includes the working units, the workers' council, the managing board and the director. The second hierarchy approximates the conventional chain of command with workers on one end,

---

[22] *Ibid.* See also Article X, paragraph 2, of the 1963 Constitution of the S.F.R.Y.

[23] Ichak Adizes, *Industrial Democracy: Yugoslav Style—The Effect of Decentralization on Organizational Behavior,* New York: The Free Press, 1971, pp. 4–5.

followed by supervisors and heads of working units, and managers at the other end.[24]

Another way of looking at the functioning of the self-management system within an enterprise is to see it in terms of two levels of authority—the professional, dominated by skilled, highly skilled, and lower managerial personnel, and a second level which bases its judgments on the social and political values of the wider community.[25] The protagonists of this second level are the sociopolitical organizations represented within the enterprise. This is again a typically Yugoslav solution insofar as a function of the central government has been replaced by nongovernmental organizations which base their influence largely on persuasion.

The Organizational Framework in Enterprises

Yugoslav enterprises operate within a framework of workers' self-management. The supreme authority within each enterprise is the workers' collective which consists of all members of the enterprise. In all but the smallest enterprises, the workers elect a workers' council which meets approximately once a month and is charged with making decisions on all major functions of the enterprise (prices on its products whenever these are not controlled, production and financial plans, governing of the enterprise, allocation of net income, budget, etc.). The workers' council elects a management board, in practice largely from its own ranks, which acts as executive agent. At least three quarters of the members of the management board must be production workers.[26] The board meets more frequently than the workers' council and works in close cooperation with the director, who is an *ex officio* member. The workers' council is elected for a period of two years, half of its members elected every year. Its composition is supposed to approximate the ratio

[24] B. Kavcic, V. Rus, E. E. Tannebaum, *Control, Participation, and Effectiveness in Four Yugoslav Industrial Organizations,* (mimeographed), Llubjana (March 1969), p. 1.

[25] This view has been supported by Dr. Branko Horvat at a seminar given at the American University, Washington, D.C., November 25, 1968.

[26] This provision is, in practice, frequently violated.

between production workers and employees. Meetings of the workers' council are usually open and every member of the working collective is entitled to attend. Decisions are made by majority vote and the members of the council, individually or as a group, can be recalled by the electors. No one can be elected twice in succession to the workers' council, and more than twice in succession to the management board.[27] The management board is elected for a period of one year and is answerable for its work to the workers' council, which may recall individual members or the whole board at any time. Service on management boards and workers' councils is honorary and members do not receive payment. The director is the actual administrative manager of the enterprise. He is responsible for the day-to-day operations and he represents the enterprise in any external negotiations. In theory, but only infrequently in practice, he can be removed by the workers' council, which also determines his term of office.

The most recent innovation in the organizational structure of the enterprise is the emergence of the working (or economic) unit.[28] The working unit may represent a department, or in

[27] It is not clear what effect Amendment XV has had on these provisions. In general, all decisions as to tenure and election are now to be made by the workers' council of each enterprise.

[28] For a part of a working organization to be able to become a working unit, the following prerequisites are necessary:

—That there exists an integrated technological and operational process on a specified area, plus the necessary means of production;

—That tasks can be determined, within the plan of the working organization as a whole, for such a narrower framework of a working organization within the latter's plan as a whole;

—That it is practicable to observe the execution of the planned tasks for such a narrower organizational part of a working organization as well as to ascertain separately its economic results, viz., as a quantity demarcated from the working and operating results of the rest of the working organization;

—That a material base can be established for such a narrower organizational part of a working organization, to provide the foundation for the transfer of a series of self-management functions from the central indirect bodies of the working community to a narrower organizational part; and

—That it is economically justified to establish a working unit.

Vojislav Vlajic, *The Working Units,* Belgrade: The Central Council of The Confederation Trade Unions of Yugoslavia, pp. 20–1.

large enterprises, an entire plant. The establishment of the
working units introduces significant additional elements of direct industrial democracy into the system of self-management.
The current controversy about their role centers largely on their
degree of authority in relation to the distribution of the income
of the enterprise as well as the distribution of personal income
to the members of the working units. Increasingly, entire enterprises are being divided into working units, including the managerial staff, the accounting service, and the production departments.[29] Relations between these units are conducted on the
basis of contracts and payments for services rendered. Disputes
arising between working units are dealt with by an arbitration
commission appointed by the central workers' council.[30]

Small working units are managed directly by the entire
membership. Decisions are made at meetings, usually called
"the conference of the working unit." The introduction of direct
decision making is the main feature distinguishing the smaller
working units from the enterprise as a whole. In the latter,
direct decision making is largely limited to occasional referenda
and voters' meetings prior to election.[31] In larger working units
the conference elects a council which it can recall at any time.
The conference also appoints a manager (foreman) after announcing an open competition for his post.[32]

One of the democratic features operative in the Yugoslav

[29] The Confederation of Trade Unions of Yugoslavia (C.T.U.Y.) has
been the most consistent advocate for the extension of decision-making
authority on the part of working units.

[30] There is really no adequate treatment in the English language on
this important innovation. The best available source on the working
unit is: *Stellung und Aufgaben der ökonomischen Einheiten in den jugo-
slawischen Unternehmungen,* by Gudrun Leman, Berlin: Verlag Duncker
& Humbolt, 1967.

[31] The holding of a referendum is compulsory for certain important
questions such as the decision to merge with another enterprise. The results of a referendum are binding on the workers' council. If an issue
is defeated in a referendum, it cannot be raised again for six months.

[32] The appointment of the foreman requires a two thirds majority of
all members of the working unit, as well as the approval of the management board of the enterprise. His removal takes place by the same
procedure, and his term of office prior to the passing of Amendment XV
was four years.

system is the recall. Figures on the frequency of recalls are not easy to come by, but information available for 1956 shows the following: 999 members of workers' councils (0.8 percent) and 476 members of boards of management (1.2 percent) were recalled in enterprises with thirty or more workers. Of this total 1,474 recalls, 254 were initiated by a government department or agency, 181 by the director of the enterprise, 542 by an organ of self-management, 372 by the entire collective of the enterprise and 124 by socoipolitical organizations. No data is available on the frequency of recalls of elected communal deputies, but it appears to happen only infrequently. Responsibility on the part of elected deputies to the voters has not yet reached the level hoped for and voters, as a rule, do not yet constitute an organized political force permitting the effectual use of the recall. We should note that in 1956, the system of self-management in industry was only just beginning to be put into practice.[33]

The authority of the foreman is usually limited to the implementation of decisions made by the self-management bodies. He alone cannot discipline a worker, or register complaints. The final verdict in a disciplinary case will be given by the disciplinary committee of the working unit.[34] The foreman's basic responsibility, in addition to the implementation of decisions already made, lies in the area of training and coordination (with other economic units as well as with the central workers' council).

To describe the legislative and administrative functions within an enterprise would go beyond the scope of this article. Very briefly, they may be summarized as follows:

1. Legislative Functions and Organs

Referenda: As indicated before, mergers, relocation of plants, disagreements between working units and the central workers' council are among the decisions made by referendum. The referendum is one of the key elements of direct democracy within enterprises. Preparations for referenda are extensive and

[33] *Workers' Management in Yugoslavia,* Geneva: International Labour Office, p. 91.

[34] Adizes, *op. cit.,* p. 46.

the sociopolitical organizations operating within the plant are involved in organizing discussions on the purpose of the referendum.

Zbors (*Conventions*): Zbors elect and recall the governing bodies and pass amendments on the enterprise statutes. They are consulted on all key decisions such as manpower policies, modernization, and wages.[35]

Working (*Economic*) *Units:* Working units and their councils, the central workers' council, and the managing board have been discussed above.

2. Administrative Functions and Organs

The administrative branch of an enterprise is made up of the director of the enterprise, director of plants and departments, and the foremen of the working units.

The Director: The role of the director is of particular importance and continues to be surrounded by controversy. Prior to the passing of Amendment XV, his term of office was four years. Today, his term is decided upon by the workers' council, which also appoints him and dismisses him.

During the administrative period, prior to 1950, the director functioned as an agent of the state. While he had almost complete power within the enterprise, his responsibilities were limited since all decisions on the operation of his enterprise came from Belgrade. The typical director during this period was a person whose main qualification was his political reliability. With the introduction of workers' self-management and the increased autonomy of the enterprise, the role of the director has become somewhat more ambiguous. As the chief executive officer of the enterprise he is directly responsible to the central workers' council; at the same time he is supposed to act on behalf of the wider community. He retains a veto power over decisions of the workers' council which in his view violate the law; the commune, however, as representative of the wider community, retains some influence in his appointment and dismissal. His skill and educational background are now of far greater importance than his political loyalty. Increasingly, relations between the director and the workers' self-management bodies have

[35] *Ibid.*, p. 37.

come to play an important part in the development of the enterprise.

Pressures put on the director to maintain economic efficiency and at the same time adhere to national guidelines, combined with his responsibility to the self-management bodies have made it increasingly more difficult to attract qualified people to the position.

The legal duties of the director are mainly administrative ones. In theory, he has virtually no right to make decisions, since these are reserved exclusively to the general membership and their elected representatives. In practice, however, we shall see later, the director has extensive influence[36] and the ambiguity of his position is very real. The director has great influence but little legal authority, and hence, little clear-cut responsibility, while the workers' council has legal authority but lacks influence.

Another reason for the confusion surrounding the role of the director is the fact that, until recently, his role was circumscribed by a vast profusion of legal statutes, beyond those found in the statute of the enterprise. Changes in federal law have been so frequent that it has been virtually impossible for anyone to be fully aware of them.[37]

As of 1969 (after passage of Amendment XV) enterprises were given the right to define for themselves the role of individual as well as collective executive bodies. In many enterprises this has meant a strengthening of the managerial bodies including that of the director. New executive bodies, such as directors' boards and business boards, have been created, thus legitimizing to some extent the actual influence of the director and the managerial groups. Opposition to this trend, and particularly to the effects of Amendment XV, has come from sections of the League and from the trade unions.[38]

---

[36] By influence we mean actual as opposed to merely potential power. Influence derives from formal and informal positions.

[37] Jovo Brekic, "Model of the Function of a Director Under the Conditions of Development of Self-Management," *Ekonomiski Pregled* (Zagreb), No. 1–2 (1968), pp. 53–75 (JPRS: 45,794, p. 76). Note: *The Constitution* refers only in a general way to the rights of the director.

[38] The last large-scale appointment (by the workers' councils) of directors prior to the enactment of Amendment XV took place in 1963. At

The Collegium and the Extended Collegium: The Collegium is composed of the top administrators, including the heads of departments, and is presided over by the director. Its purpose is to aid the director in carrying out the policies of the enterprise entrusted to him. The Collegium has no decision-making power and performs, in essence, the function of a staff meeting.

The Extended Collegium includes foremen and experts in addition to the top administration. It discusses matters submitted to it by the Collegium.

The Politikal Aktive: The Politikal Aktive, another nonelective body which, like the preceding two, exists in almost every enterprise, comprises all sections of the self-managed enterprise. In addition to top management, the heads of *all* governing bodies are represented as are the secretaries of the plant committee of the League, the trade union, and the Youth Brigade. The existence of these three groups is not stipulated by law or in enterprise statutes. According to Adizes, "their existence and functioning seems to be dictated by organizational necessities; a central, unifying group is needed as a centripetal force when the organization's authority and power are highly segmented. . . ."[39]

Informal Groups: Informal groups within enterprises include the many clubs established by the local trade union branch and the Youth Brigade, and the Majstors (masters) composed of skilled workers who repair the machines.[40]

---

this time, 2,727 directors were renominated. 421 were not renominated and were replaced by new appointments. It is interesting to note that about two percent of directors (in enterprises) are women. Their percentage increases to over thirteen percent in Social Service Institutions (*Statisticki Godisnjak Jugoslavije 1969,* Belgrade: Federal Institute for Statistics, pp. 69 and 71).

[39] Adizes, *op. cit.,* p. 47.

[40] According to Adizes, the Majstors are a highly cohesive group and very influential. (*Ibid.,* p. 47.)

Integration, Supervision and Protection

Internal Supervision

In a very real sense, the various self-management bodies within an enterprise are supervisory bodies. The internal affairs of an enterprise are publicized widely, both within and outside the enterprise, and the sociopolitical organizations in the commune as well as the communal assembly are expected to act on any illegal or antisocial activities within the enterprise. Each enterprise is plugged into a network of internal and external organs, agencies and institutions which bind it to the wider community.

Important function of the internal supervisory mechanism of an enterprise is performed by the uniform national accounting system which permits comparative analyses on all levels by the commune, the banks, and the various inspectorates. The chief accountant of the enterprise plays a key role here. He is relatively independent of the self-management bodies and his appointment and dismissal must be approved by the commune. Financial reports are usually submitted to the workers' management bodies by the chief accountant in person.[41]

Administrative Supervision

A number of specific supervisory bodies within the wider community have the right to check on the legality of the operation of the enterprise and the accuracy of its reports to the communal, republican, and federal authorities.

Yugoslav enterprises are public institutions. While direct administrative interference in the work of the self-managing bodies of an enterprise is not permitted, it nevertheless cannot close its doors to the authorities. The financial inspection

[41] *Workers' Management in Yugoslavia,* Geneva: International Labour Office, 1962, pp. 233–4. This description applies to the period prior to the passing of Amendment XV.

service warrants special attention. Since 1960, the financial inspection service has been part of the "social accounting service," and as such, is attached to the National Bank. The social accounting service is an autonomous institution which keeps track of the use made of all social property. It maintains accounts for each enterprise and makes regular reports to government agencies, including the local commune. Its reports are also submitted to the relevant workers' council, thus initiating a cooperative relationship between the financial inspection service and the self-management bodies within the enterprise. The inspection service relies to a considerable extent on the cooperation of the chief accountant of the enterprise. The social accounting service can, on its own authority, hold up any irregular or unlawful transaction by the enterprise and it can block the accounts involved as a precautionary measure. At the same time, enterprises have been given the authority to appeal financial and administrative actions on the part of the social accounting service to the economic courts which have the power to annul the decision.[42]

Social Control and Integration

The gradual reduction of administrative controls throughout the Yugoslav socioeconomic system is placing added responsibility on the sociopolitical organizations. The League of Communists, and the trade unions in particular, are expected to act as integrative forces in relation to the self-management bodies in enterprises and institutions. The local commune performs a similar service with regard to the enterprises located within its boundaries.

The administrative controls discussed in the preceding section are intended to provide local authorities and other organizations concerned with a continuous flow of information which will enable them to determine their own economic and social policies in relation to that of the enterprise.

The entire system of social control is highly complex, not

[42] The economic courts can also reverse decisions taken by the administrative departments of the local commune, which have certain supervisory authorities in relation to the enterprises.

only because of the large number of organizations involved, but also because their relation to the enterprise is frequently undefined and is based on persuasion rather than legal authority. On the local level, there is substantial overlapping of personnel between the political organizations, the commune assembly, and the self-management bodies within the enterprise. Members of self-management bodies are frequently also members of the "council of working communities" of the local commune.[43] The communal branches of the sociopolitical organizations inevitably include prominent workers from various enterprises. In theory, the integrative functions of these bodies are based on the principle of cooperation. Social control has thus been transformed into "mutual social control."

A further paradox of this arrangement arises from the dual function of the sociopolitical organizations. On the one hand they operate as representatives of the wider community and can be said to perform an integrative role vis-à-vis the enterprise, while on the other hand they are frequently called upon to perform a protective role in support of the self-management bodies.[44] The description of the trade unions as "transmission belts" of directives from the center was an adequate assessment of their political role prior to the introduction of self-management in the 1950s, but this is no longer entirely accurate. While the top leadership of the Confederation of Trade Unions of Yugoslavia continues to be almost indistinguishable in its politics from that of the League of Communists, many of the local branches are beginning to function autonomously. The existence of increasingly popular and powerful workers' councils and economic units within enterprises has brought about a change in the composition and the politics of many local trade union branches which is beginning to make itself felt at the national level. The same process is at work, to a lesser extent, within the League of Communists.

[43] As a rule, the communal assembly consists of two chambers: the communal council, elected directly by all the voters in the commune and the council of working communities, or economic council, elected by the workers and employees of working organizations.

[44] One such example is the support given by the trade unions to the economic units, frequently against pressures from banks and other centralist forces in the commune, republic, or federal government.

A quick review of the specific functions of the most important organizations and institutions of social control will illustrate the complexity of this aspect of their work.

The most important element of social control is the commune. The dividing line between the autonomy of the enterprise and the commune's power of social control continues to be a subject of controversy. It is only very recently that the courts have begun to pass judgments on disputes between communes and enterprises. Until a sufficient number of precedents has been accumulated, we can expect this controversy to continue.

In a number of fields, the commune has the legal right to intervene in the affairs of the enterprise, while in other areas its powers are limited to making recommendations which constitute the moral and political pressure of the wider community on the activities of the enterprise. The problem of combining the autonomy of the self-managed enterprise with the interests of the wider community is one of the main concerns of Yugoslavs. The solution to this problem is essential for the realization of Socialist democracy.

The driving force behind the system of workers' management is the distribution of net income of the enterprise. It is also one of the issues which frequently brings about conflict between the interests of the workers and those of the wider community, and it has apparently been one reason for the introduction of the referendum within the enterprise. According to one study, most of the referenda held in Yugoslav enterprises between 1953 and 1960 have dealt with the distribution of net income.[45] This is a particularly serious problem for those communes whose budgetary resources are inadequate. In such instances, the commune is forced to rely on the cooperation of the enterprises within its jurisdiction.

Yugoslav observers are continually discussing the problem

---

[45] *Workers' Management in Yugoslavia,* p. 240. There have been instances when managing organs of enterprises have held views different from those of the working collective. The introduction of the referendum was to guarantee the implementation of the will of the working collective, regardless of the views held by the managing organs. The use of the referendum does not, however, necessarily solve a clash of interest between the working collective of an enterprise and the wider community.

posed by the existence of two forms of self-management within the commune. This unresolved problem can be stated in the following questions: to what extent is there a basic contradiction between self-management in the enterprise and in the commune? To what extent do these two units of self-management overlap in their decision-making authority? Insofar as there exists a basic contradiction, to what degree is it organizational and structural, and to what extent is it based on real economic and political differences in the stated goals of enterprises and communes? To what extent does commune "localism" lead to "communal ownership" and to what extent does the same phenomenon in an enterprise lead to an attitude of "corporate ownership" as opposed to the declared aim of social ownership.[46]

Practice over the past few years supports the view that there are, at present, two separate forms of self-management in the commune, each with a distinct existence of its own. Both forces of self-management represent an element of direct democracy which is intended to lead to the gradual withering away of the state. The enterprise represents the clearest form of collective self-management. Direct decision making by the workers is becoming increasingly common, both through the use of referenda and the increasing importance of the economic units. The same trend is only slowly gaining momentum in the commune, where direct decision making is less frequent.

There seem to be two basic responses to the contradictions between group interest and general interest within the commune. A large number of observers view the conflict as a necessary and dynamic part of a growing Socialist society. Remedies are not to be found by replacing the system producing these conflicts but rather by adaptations and a continuous process of education and persuasion. The experience gained by hundreds of thousands of citizens who serve on the various self-management bodies in enterprises, communes, sociopolitical

---

[46] We are not referring to the legal definition of "corporate" and "communal" ownership, but rather to an attitude on the part of the self-managing organs of enterprises and communes, which translated into practice distorts the Socialist democracy envisaged by the Constitution.

organizations, and republican and federal assemblies is felt to be one of the best ways to create an attitude which will harmonize individual and group interest with that of the wider community.

Another view sees the solution in the formation of a uniform system of self-management within the commune which would respect the internal autonomy of the enterprise, but would subordinate it to the commune in all questions of communewide importance.

Today virtually all enterprises are grouped in voluntary associations according to the type of their economic activity. This form of economic cooperation was provided for by legislation passed in 1965, but it was not until four years later that the practice became widespread. According to Yugoslav sources, the most frequent motives for association in industry are: "Joint production and joint sales; adjustment of production programs and specialization with a view to ensuring a better utilization of productive facilities; joint purchase and use of licenses; joint purchase of primaries and other materials; imports and exports of goods; joint design, investment, assembly, overhaul, research and similar operations; and joint use of equipment and installations."[47]

Membership in the "economic chambers" is compulsory for all enterprises and other economic organizations. They are formed on a territorial basis within the federal economic chamber. According to the law, the economic chambers cannot limit the self-management and the independence of enterprises, and their resolutions take the form of recommendations. Their influence is, however, great. To a considerable extent they function as the extended arm of the central government. In 1958, representatives of the government became members of the governing bodies of the chambers along with the representatives of enterprises. According to Hoffman and Neal, this new composition of the economic chambers, which makes them representative of enterprises and of government, is a typically Yugoslav solution insofar as it delegates to a nongovernmental

[47] Joze Monavec (editor in chief), *Twenty Years of Yugoslav Economy* (Belgrade: Medunarodna Stampa-Interpress, 1967), pp. 27–8.

agency an activity which would otherwise be a function of the government.[48] One Yugoslav observer has recently complained that "the unique Chambers of Economy should really be self-governing organizations of the economy and not just 'transmission points' between the state and the economy."[49]

The Protective Functions of Courts, Sociopolitical Organizations, and the Federal Labor Inspectorate

In theory, all enterprises are expected to protect the workers in the exercise of their constitutional rights. A worker may take his grievances to the workers' council, the managing board, the director, the local trade union or League branch, or in certain specified instances, to the courts. Since the workers' councils are the most vital units on the enterprise level, most grievances seem to be handled by them.

Provisions for court action, however, do exist. The constitutional court may intervene at the request of individuals, the working collective or a section thereof, as well as by request of the assemblies of sociopolitical organizations, in cases of a violation of the self-managing rights of workers and in cases of violations of the law, or the statutes of an enterprise.[50] The constitutional court has annulled regulations adopted by enterprises, such as a decision stipulating a deduction from a worker's salary, this "being appraised as having the character of a fine."

In cases which do not deal with constitutional issues, a

[48] Hoffman and Neal, *op. cit.*, p. 244. The authors note that the chambers are increasingly occupied with the preparation and enforcement of government regulations, and that some of their decisions are legally binding on enterprises.

[49] "Chambers—A Form and Expression of the Self-Organization of the Economy" (unsigned), *Privredni Pregled* (Belgrade), December 9, 1967, p. 9, and December 12, 1967, p. 11 (JPRS: 44,007, p. 26).

[50] Nikola Balog, "Foreword," *Laws of Enterprises and Institutions,* Collection of Yugoslav Laws, Volume XIII, Belgrade: Institute of Comparative Law, 1966, p. 12. The largest number of requests to initiate proceedings were submitted by individuals (70 percent) followed by enterprises and other self-managing organizations and by assemblies of sociopolitical organizations. (*Yugoslav Survey* (Belgrade), August 1968, p. 8.)

worker who has exhausted the possibilities of protest open to him within the enterprise and has had the final decision of the workers' council go against him, may, if he considers that his rights have been violated, take the dispute to a court of general jurisdiction.[51]

Enterprises may refer mutual disputes to permanent courts of arbitration for settlement. These courts are formed at the level of the republican and federal economic chambers as well as in communes as specified by federal law.[52] A similar function is performed by economic courts which are situated in most large economic centers throughout Yugoslavia. The hierarchy of these courts extends from the local level to the constituent republics, to the supreme economic court in Belgrade.[53]

The federal labor inspectorate, and those of the republics, have at their disposal teams of labor inspectors who have the power to enter an enterprise at any time during working hours without prior notice.[54] Their main task is to check on the adherence to safety regulations and rules for the protection of labor. In cases of a violation of any safety regulation, the labor inspector has the power to order the elimination of the defect within a time limit specified by him.[55]

The Establishment of Personal Income

"Payment according to work done" is the governing principle of the present system in Yugoslavia. This is seen as a transitional principle during the present Socialist stage. At the same time it is regarded as an educational tool training each worker to make his own decisions based on a system of rewards and punish-

[51] "Rules on Mutual Employment Relationships in the '14 Oktobar' Industries," article 115, p. 107. Similar provisions are incorporated in the Rules of other enterprises.

[52] "Basic Law of Enterprises," articles 206 and 207, pp. 69–70.

[53] Vjekoslav Hraste, "Economic Courts," *Jugoslovenski Pregled,* No. 11 (Belgrade), November 1966, pp. 393–8. (JPRS: 40,435, p. 21.)

[54] "Decree to Promulgate a Basic Act Respecting the Protection of Labor" (article 104), *Sluzbeni List,* No. 15 (Belgrade), April 5, 1965. (International Labour Office, Legislative Series 1965—Yug. 3, p. 19.)

[55] *Ibid.,* Articles 104, 105, and 108, p. 19.

ments which encourage self-guidance.[56] Individual workers are rewarded for cooperating with their group (usually their working unit) and are rewarded according to the performance of the group. Personal income can be either a fixed salary or a variable salary dependent on the income of the working unit and that of the enterprise.

In practice the worker shares in the profit of his working unit and the profit of his enterprise. Basic salary is determined by job evaluation.[57] The crucial problem of establishing the value of labor, however, has not yet been solved. Earnings for the same kind of work differ greatly. According to one Yugoslav writer, these differences are frequently as much as 50 percent and sometimes even 100 percent.[58]

The Distribution of Income in the Enterprise

The basic economic categories in the system of income distribution are: gross income (total receipts), operating expenses, depreciation, total income, and legal and contractual obligations of the enterprise and personal income.

Total income is the amount that remains after deduction of operating expenses and depreciations from gross income.[59] After deduction (from the total income) of contractual obligations, a minimum sum for personal income (based on the minimum level established by law) and the part earmarked for the use of the wider community (taxes), the remainder is divided by the self-management bodies into the personal income fund

[56] Adizes, *op. cit.*, pp. 49–60.

[57] The struggle for and against egalitarianism is a constant feature of the Yugoslav scene. Wage differentiation in the economy fluctuates around 1 : 5. In the field of cultural activities they approximate 1 : 3. Most wages, however, revolve around the average. Comparing this to income differences in the Netherlands, Professor Tinbergen concludes that income distribution in Yugoslavia can be considered as *relatively egalitarian*. (Jan Tinbergen, "Does Self-Management Approach the Optimum Order?" *Yugoslav Workers' Self-Management*, p. 119.)

[58] Mitja Kamusic, "Economic Efficiency and Workers' Self-Management," *Yugoslav Workers' Self-Management*, p. 91.

[59] For a more detailed summary see, *Workers' Management in Yugoslavia* (Belgrade), Medunarodna Politika, 1970, pp. 41–3.

and the various enterprise funds (the business fund, the welfare fund, and reserve fund).

The distribution of income is complicated by the fact that the authority of the various self-management bodies (workers' council and working units) in the distribution process and the methods used in determining the income of working units and the personal income of workers are not regulated by law, but are instead outlined in the statute of enterprises or in contracts drawn up on the basis of the statute.[60] Thus we find widespread variations, both in the role of working units in income distribution and in the methods used to determine their income and that of individual workers. The subject of the distribution of income remains one of the most hotly debated issues in Yugoslavia.

The proportion of income at the disposal of the self-management bodies has increased from a low of twenty percent in 1959–60 to approximately sixty percent in 1968. Since then it has fallen slightly. The planned ratio of distribution is seventy percent to the working organization and thirty percent to the wider community (commune, republic, and the federal government).

The gradual reduction in the role of the federal budget can be illustrated by the following figures:

Changes in the institutional allocation of investment resources between 1961 and 1967 show the following: the percentage of investment resources at the disposal of banks has risen from 0.9 percent (1961) to 43.8 percent in 1967, while that of the government declined from 61.7 percent (1961) to 13.4 percent (1967). During the same period the percentage at the disposal of enterprises increased from 29.5 percent to 33.4 percent.[61]

While banks are supposed to function as autonomous entities governed by a board made up of their founders (usually enterprises and/or communes), in practice banks still operate to a significant degree as extended arms of federal authorities. The

[60] "The Basic Law on the Determination and Distribution of Earnings in Working Organizations," Article 2 (JPRS: 46,433, p. 198).

[61] *The OECD Observer,* No. 31 (December 1967), p. 43.

trade union movement recently demanded the establishment of complete equality between banks and enterprises by the end of 1970,[62] a goal which is not likely to be achieved that soon.

Influence Structure in Yugoslav Enterprises

A great deal of research has been done on the perception of influence among workers. Tannenbaum and Zupanov, in their study of fifty-six workers attending a two-year course at the Workers' University in Zagreb,[63] have analyzed the perceived and ideal (desired) control curves as seen by the respondents. The results refer to the two hierarchies within enterprises: one, including the workers as producers at one end, followed by supervisors, heads of economic units and the director at the other; the second including the workers' council at one end, followed by the managing board and the director at the other. The two curves are represented below.[64]

The authors of this study point out the large discrepancy between actual and ideal degree of control for the workers as a group. Since the workers' council is selected by the workers and is composed in large part of workers, this discrepancy seems to suggest that the workers' council does not give the workers a

[62] *Yugoslav Trade Unions* (Belgrade), January 1969, p. 5. *Note:* The Basic Law on the Assessment and Distribution of Income in Work Organizations, which came into force in January 1969, has given work organizations increased powers in the distribution of income within enterprises, as well as within groups of enterprises (autonomous compacts). (*Yugoslav Trade Unions,* July–August 1970, pp. 6–7.)

[63] These respondents comprise a very special group, which includes a relatively high proportion of formally educated, highly skilled, and highly aspiring workers. Approximately eighty-nine percent are members of the LCY (as compared to 10.6 percent of workers in the district of Zagreb). Thirty-nine percent are first line supervisors. The respondents spend part of their time at the university while working four hours a day in Zagreb industries.

[64] Josip Zupanov and Arnold S. Tannenbaum, "The Distribution of Control in Some Yugoslav Industrial Organizations as Perceived by Members," in Arnold Tannenbaum, *Control in Organizations,* New York: McGraw-Hill Book Co., 1958, pp. 98–99. (Chart used by permission.)

sufficient sense of control.[65] One partial explanation is indicated by the results of another study published in 1961, which found the workers' council oriented toward management and official views.[66] There is also evidence to the effect that man-

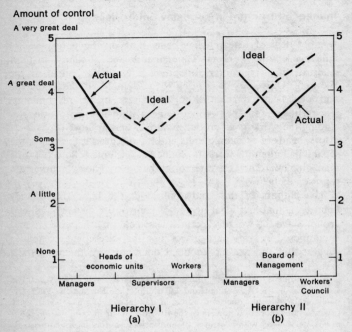

Figure 1.* Actual and Ideal Control Curves

agement, including the managerial staff, the director and frequently members of the management board, are the most active participants in meetings of the workers' council. The complexity of many of the issues under discussion and the control over

65 *Ibid.*, pp. 97–8.

66 David S. Ridell, "Social Self-Government: The Background of Theory and Practice in Yugoslav Socialism," in *British Journal of Sociology* (March 1968), p. 66.

relevant information in the hands of management, can give the latter a powerful advantage in having their proposals accepted by the workers' council.[67]

The establishment of economic units and the increasing delegation of authority to them has been one attempt to reduce the discrepancy between actual and desired control. This introduction of direct democracy is one of the more significant political innovations in recent years. Zupanov and Tannenbaum suggest that the discrepancy between the ideal and the actuality can also be attributed in part to the rather high ideals expressed by the respondents. They point out that discrepancies are smaller in American industrial organizations studied, "not because the actual curves are more positive, but because the ideals are more negative.[68]

The high ideals held by respondents in this sample and others which have in the main supported these findings, are one of the hopeful signs in the development of self-management in Yugoslavia.

The survey undertaken by Bogdan Kavcic and released in 1968 is similar in its conclusion to a number of other studies and can thus be viewed as presenting a more or less accurate picture.[69]

In summarizing the results of several studies, Veljko Rus points out:

1. Workers tend to favor an increase in the influence of all groups other than top management.

2. Workers' desires are consistent with the theory of workers' self-management (the workers' council should have the most influence).

3. These aspirations seem to have weakened somewhat by 1968. Latest studies show that workers' desires still place the workers' council at the top, but the desired influence of

---

[67] See, e.g., Jiri Kolaja, Workers' Councils: *The Yugoslav Experience,* New York: Frederick A. Praeger, 1966, pp. 19–20 and 26.

[68] Zupanov and Tannenbaum, *op. cit.,* p. 109.

[69] Reprinted by Veljko Rus, "Influence Structure in Yugoslav Enterprise," *Industrial Relations,* Vol. IX, No. 2 (1970), p. 150. *Note:* B. Kavcic is director of the Center for Public Opinion Research of the Republican Council of Trade Unions of Slovenia.

managers is now almost equal to that of the workers' council.[70]

The changing role of the trade unions, from transmitters of the directives of the central authorities to a position where they

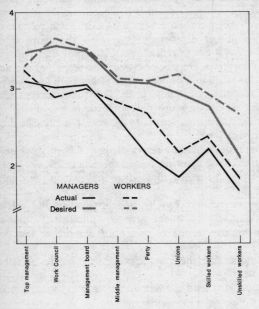

Figure 2.* Influence as Perceived and Desired by Managers and Workers, in 92 Industrial Organizations

Note: N = 1,489 workers and 501 managers.

Amount of influence: 4 = very great; 3 = great; 2 = little; 1 = none.

(This chart originally appeared in Yugoslavia in Bogdan Kavcic: "Distribucija vpliva v podjetjih industrije in rudarstva v Sloveniji," RS ZSS *Javno mnenje,* stev. 15, 1968.)

* Source: *Industrial Relations* (Vol. IX, No. 2), Institute of Industrial Relations, University of California, Berkeley. Reprinted by permission. Chart by Veljko Rus.

70 Veljko Rus, pp. 155–7. *Note:* This trend *could* be interpreted as resulting from a more sophisticated understanding of self-management on the part of the workers and a greater degree of satisfaction with the functioning of the workers' council vis-à-vis management.

begin to act more openly on behalf of the worker, is evident in the large gap between the actual and desired influence of the trade unions as perceived by workers.[71]

Composition of the Self-Management Bodies

It is important to remember that the workers' council is not a homogeneous group. It consists of semiskilled and skilled workers; white-collar employees and management personnel; Communists and non-Communists; trade union members and workers not connected with any sociopolitical organizations.

Certain small changes took place in the composition of the workers' councils and the management boards between 1964 and 1968. The number of females and youths decreased. In workers' councils, persons with a background of university education (or schools of higher learning) accounted for five percent in 1964 and eight percent in 1968, while the share of skilled and highly skilled workers remained constant. Changes in the composition of the management boards were more pronounced. The number of skilled and highly skilled workers dropped by thirteen percent in the same period, while that of persons with university or higher education increased by five percent.[72] Skilled and highly skilled workers, however, still constitute the largest single group within workers' councils and management boards. In 1966 they constituted approximately fifty percent.[73]

[71] The relatively weak influence of trade unions on the enterprise level should be seen in its historical context. Self-management was introduced from the top, that is, by decision of the Communist party and the government, and the traditional function (prior to 1950) of the trade unions was challenged overnight. It would seem reasonable to expect that if self-management came about through the pressure and action of trade unions, their role, function, and influence would not suffer the decline evidenced in Yugoslavia.

[72] *Jugoslavija Izmedu VII i IX Kongresa SKJ, 1964–1968* (Yugoslavia between the VII and IX Congess of the League of Communists of Yugoslavia), Belgrade: Savezni zarod za statistike, 1969, p. 19.

[73] Of a total of 150,339 members of workers' councils, 81,504 were highly skilled and skilled workers. Of a total of 50,422 members of the boards of management, skilled and highly skilled workers amounted to 25,100. *Statisticki Godisnjak Jugoslavije* (Statistical Yearbook of Yugoslavia), Savezni Zarod Za Statistiku, 1968, p. 65.

Dr. Kratina of the Institute of Social Sciences in Belgrade recently undertook a survey of workers' opinion. The research was carried out in the Crvena Zastava Automobile Works of Kragujevac in central Serbia. One of the questions related to the opinion of workers on the desired composition of their workers' council. The results are shown below.

The opinion of workers concerning the groups of producers which should have more representatives in the workers' council of the enterprise.

The "supremacy" of skilled and highly skilled workers is supported in Dr. Kratina's sample.[74]

There is a definite tendency today for people with higher educational qualifications to get elected to the *central* organs of self-management. No adequate figures are available about the composition of councils of working units, but it seems that these are dominated by highly skilled and skilled workers.

The present distribution of influence in Yugoslav enterprises undoubtedly arises partly from the predominantly peasant background of most workers. As their skill and educational level increase, we may expect to see changes.[75] It must also be remembered that in critical situations it is the workers' council that makes decisions, not the director.[76]

Workers' Self-Management and Attitudes Toward Work

The most interesting and complete study on the subject of the motivation of workers was done by Josip Obradovic. The study, which was conducted in 1965, covers 537 workers in twenty

[74] Husein Kratina, *Samoupravna i Druge Organizacije u Preduzecu*, (Self-Managing and Organizational Structure of Enterprises)', Belgrade: Institute of Social Sciences, 1968, Table 8, p. 53.

[75] We should recall here the tremendous educational potential of the self-management system which exposes close to a million citizens, on a rotating basis, to a unique learning process.

[76] See, e.g., Rudi Supek, "Discussion at the Symposium on Yugoslav Workers' Self-management" (Amsterdam, January 7–9, 1970), M. J. Broekmeyer, p. 256. Supek argues that in critical situations the workers' council *and* the party organization make the final decision.

Groups of Producers	All participants in the inquiry	Unskilled & semiskilled workers	Skilled & highly skilled workers	Workers with primary school education	Workers with secondary, schools of higher learning or university education
	%	%	%	%	%
1. Skilled workers	60	61	67	50	41
2. Highly skilled workers	51	35	69	38	48
3. Foremen	46	31	56	52	58
4. Engineers and technicians	34	28	31	24	55
5. Unskilled workers	29	49	17	29	11
6. Economic and financial experts	29	20	25	48	58
7. Semiskilled workers	26	45	18	24	3
8. Administrative and office staff	8	9	5	21	8
9. Leading officials in other than production units	5	8	2	2	6

enterprises.[77] Of the six different dimensions studied by the author, three are significant for our purposes: "General work satisfaction, work alienation,[78] and feeling of control over how the job is performed."

Some of Obradovic findings are, in brief:

1. Participation in workers' councils and/or management boards results in significantly greater general job satisfaction (except among automated workers).

2. *Participants* in automated and mechanized enterprises have a greater feeling of control over their jobs than do *nonparticipants*. There is no significant difference for handicraft workers.

3. The greatest surprise came in these findings on work alienation. For all three occupational groups, participants in self-management organs are *more* alienated than nonparticipants.

A few comments and explanations are in order at this point. This survey by Obradovic measured *formal* membership in the self-management bodies only. No attempt was made to ascertain to what extent these two self-management bodies and the individuals within them did, in fact, make use of their formal decision-making powers.[79] Considering our findings, discussed

[77] The purpose of this study was to compare the attitudes of members of workers' councils and management boards (participants) with workers of the same education and sex performing the same kind of work who were not members of any organ of self-management. The comparison was made across three different levels of technology: handicraft, mechanized, and automated. Obradovic defines handicraft as "the form of work organization which requires workers to perform a number of different jobs using a number of different kinds of tools." For details of the methodology used and survey of the findings, see Josip Obradovic, "Participation and Work Attitudes in Yugoslavia," *Industrial Relations,* Vol. IX, No. 2 (1970), pp. 161–9. The material of this section is based on the above cited sources and an interview with Obradovic on April 25, 1969 (in Zagreb).

[78] "Work alienation" is based on the Marxist concept of alienation and is derived from standard scores of two scales which measure 1) workers' inability to express their personality and their intellectual abilities through the act of production, and 2) inability to control work results.

[79] Obradovic is now conducting a study of twenty enterprises to determine the *actual* extent of participation and its effects on attitudes.

here in the section on influence structure, it is not unlikely that *participants* were so frustrated with their first experience in self-management that their alienation increased.[80]

Obradovic concludes that participation in self-management should not be overemphasized as a source of satisfaction. His study shows that workers list wages, working conditions, and possibilities for advancement highest in their list of desired job characteristics. Participation in self-management bodies came fifth for participants and sixth for nonparticipants.[81]

The Galenika Pharmaceutical Company: A Case Study in a Crisis Situation[82]

The Galenika Pharmaceutical Company had two thousand workers and a well functioning workers' council and managing board. As a result of the introduction in the early 1960s of a handling fee for filling prescriptions, the internal market for drugs was cut sharply and the pharmaceutical industry had to turn to exports in order to continue its growth. Galenika decided to merge with two Belgrade drug companies. In a subsequent evaluation of their combined operations, management found that the factory could manage with ten percent fewer employees and thus save ninety-five billion (old) dinars a year

[80] It can also be argued that the definition of alienation used in the above survey was too narrow to register some of the nonalienating attitudes of the workers. A case in point is the result of a recent attitude study which shows that a very high percentage of workers felt responsible for the success of their enterprise. (V. Rus and R. Agger (discussion), Ljubljana, Summer 1970.)

[81] Paradoxically, an investigation of the Institute of Social Research at the University of Zagreb (1968) shows that about twice as many workers (roughly 30 percent) believe that self-management is functioning better now than it did in the pre-reform (1965) period, and that the organs of self-management had a greater influence now (1968) than they did in the pre-reform period. Those who gave no answer or felt that there are no differences comprise together the largest group. (Mitja Kamusic, "Economic Efficiency and Workers' Self-Management," Broekmeyer, p. 84.)

[82] David Tornquist, *Look East, Look West: The Socialist Adventure in Yugoslavia,* New York: The Macmillan Company, 1966, pp. 174–80.

in salaries. The ensuing process of bargaining and decision making is a fascinating illustration of self-management in action.

The principal actors in this battle were management, the workers' council, the economic units, the League of Communists, and the local trade union branch. Management suggested firing one hundred and sixty employees. This was based entirely on economic considerations and did not go unchallenged. The sociopolitical organization, particularly the League of Communists, insisted that other criteria be considered before any workers were dismissed: marital status, other sources of income, political activity, participation in self-management, job evaluation, number of days missed due to illness, status as a veteran, and labor discipline. The League suggested that good workers should not be laid off but be shifted instead to other departments.

The most important decisions were made in the economic units on the basis of recommendations from management and the League of Communists. One economic unit with thirteen employees to be laid off made the following decision, which was typical of the decisions reached throughout the enterprise:

M.D. Superfluous but good clerk. We will find a place for her.

O.P. Messenger. Good discipline. Should be kept.

R.V. Charwoman. Has something to fall back on. Should be laid off.

J.M. Messenger. Allergic to drugs. Has chance of another job. Should be laid off.

D.B. Janitor. Has other income. Should be retired on his pension.

L.T., F.S., R.M., and A.O. Should go because they were only hired for three months.

T.V. Janitor. Vote on his case split. Should stay.

D.F. Janitor. Ailing, veteran, no one to take care of him. Should stay.

I.K. Watchman. Tends his farm and comes to work tired. But is wounded veteran with four children. Should be transferred to another unit.[83]

[83] Tornquist, *op. cit.*, p. 177. Another economic unit which had no surplus workers agreed to lay off six unsatisfactory workers to take up a surplus from other units.

The next stage in the decision-making process involved a review by the political organization, "to be sure that friendship and enmity played no part in the decisions."[84] The final decisions were made by a five-man commission of the central workers' council which gave notice to 97 of the 160 employees on the original list proposed by management. But the process did not end there. The 97 dismissed workers were given the right to appeal to the managing board. The delicate balance of power between self-governing workers, political organizations, and management resulted in the dismissal of 85 workers.

At this stage, the workers' council decided to grant twenty million dinars to the director to be used in helping the dismissed workers find other jobs. Negotiations between the director and the local employment security office, which had a small working unit manufacturing cardboard cartons, resulted in the hiring of thirty workers in return for a loan by Galenika for the purchase of new machinery. This left the number of jobless at 55. Positions for another 20 workers were found in a nearby distillery which wanted to lease one of the buildings Galenika had vacated at the time of the merger. The director offered to lease the building if the distillery would hire twenty of his laid-off workers. Other jobs were found for 17 workers so that, in the end, only 18 highly qualified office workers were left without jobs. While the job market in Belgrade was flooded, there were vacancies in other parts of the country. If these 18 workers were not able to find employment by the time their severance pay had run out, they were promised further help in finding employment.

It is difficult to know how representative this example is, but it appears that this kind of thing is fairly widespread. The League of Communists, in this particular case, acted as spokesman for the wider community, bringing pressure to bear on all the parties involved.

[84] *Ibid.,* p. 177.

Observations and Comments

One of the most important issues for the present and future of the Yugoslav economic system is the task of integrating the autonomous self-managed enterprises into a complete economic system of self-management. Self-management must transcend the limits of the enterprise to a much greater degree than has so far been the case. Economic integration was initiated a few years ago by the central authorities. Today, integration is beginning to take shape, however slowly, from below, fostered by enterprises, economic chambers, associations of enterprises, banks, and the sociopolitical organizations.[85]

The transfer of authority to autonomous groupings of associated labor, without loss of the integrative element necessary for a Socialist economy, is perhaps the most difficult task facing Yugoslavia. What is being attempted is a replacement of centralism from above by a democratically controlled centralism from below. Branko Horvat, one of Yugoslavia's leading economists, argues that the state apparatus faces an economically paradoxical situation insofar as it is responsible for the actions of subjects over which it has little control. "The paradox," he argues, "is specious because the impossibility of *administrative, bureaucratic* control does not signify the impossibility of control in *general*. But the problem is that nonadministrative control (although potentially effective) is enormously more complex, and that it requires not only much greater expertise but also a major psychological strain to make an *administrative* apparatus exert *nonadministrative* control."[86]

The entire process of switching from administrative (governmental) control to a mixture of democratic control and integration from below, coupled with persuasion, education, and

[85] We should recall that many of these integrating factors, especially the banks, the economic chambers, and the LCY, must still be looked upon as centralist organs although certain changes in the opposite direction are now taking place.

[86] Horvat, *op. cit.*, p. 118.

political leadership by the organs of self-management and the sociopolitical organizations in cooperation with a transformed administrative apparatus, is extraordinarily complex and difficult. Its realization would mean not only a completely new role for what is traditionally called the administrative apparatus; it would also realize the ambitious goals of the 1963 Constitution: a democratic Socialist democracy based on genuine self-government. The gap between theory and practice, however, is still very large.[87]

The goal of self-managing Socialism—to bring about the integration of man as a citizen and as a producer, and to do away with the "dualism between public and private existence" —has not yet been achieved.[88] Whatever advance there has been has been restricted to the micro-level. Direct democracy, which is an essential part of this integration, is a reality only in certain sectors at the base of society (enterprises, local communities and communes).

One of the strongest arguments for the immediate withdrawal of centralist influence over the economy comes from the technologists and their academic and political supporters. They base their arguments on economic efficiency *and* democratic liberalization. What is rarely admitted is the fact that workers have very mixed feelings about the laissez-faire Socialism advocated by some of the technocrats.

A recent study by Professor Josip Zupanov queried workers on some of the problems now confronting enterprises.[89] Interviews conducted in ten Croatian factories in 1966 (one year after the introduction of the reforms) showed that the majority of workers favored the continuation of price controls. Only in the managerial group did the survey find a majority in favor of

[87] See A. Meister, "Comment evolue l'autogestion yougoslav?" *Economie & Humanisme,* No. 191 (1970), p. 34.

[88] See Rudi Supek, "Power Structure of Statist and Self-Governing Socialism," Part II, Prepared for the Joint Conference of the Center of Comparative and European Studies and the Bureau of Applied Social Research, Yale, 1970, p. 15.

[89] Interview with Josip Zupanov, Zagreb, April 23, 1969. The results of this study have been published in *Ekonomist,* No. 3, 1967.

the elimination of price controls, and even in this group one third wanted controls to continue.[90]

In response to the question whether an unprofitable enterprise should be kept going with government support in an attempt to improve it, or closed down, the majority of workers opposed closing. White-collar employees and supervisors were approximately evenly divided in their opinion, while the majority of managers and staff were in favor of closing down unprofitable enterprises.[91] The income principle of remuneration according to work performed is supported by the government and all sociopolitical organizations in Yugoslavia, yet it has encountered opposition from workers as well as from intellectuals. The main problem as seen by the critics is the existence of unequal operating conditions. Personal income is thus dependent on a number of factors beyond the immediate control of individual workers and the enterprise as a whole. The size and technological nature of the means of production, the possible monopolistic position of an enterprise, and the availability of resources are just a few of the external factors which have a direct bearing on the net income of the enterprise and thus the personal income of the workers.[92]

Contradictions and Problems

"Anarchist tendencies" and "primitivism" are labels attached by the Yugoslavs to excessive reactions to the paternalism described above. Technical and administrative staff are seen as embodiments of bureaucracy. Attempts by workers' councils to limit their authority or to remove them from office, according to many Yugoslav observers, frequently has handicapped the normal operation of enterprises. According to one report, this has at times resulted in hostility toward technical improvements and scientific management.[93]

[90] In 1966, over seventy percent of prices were centrally controlled.

[91] Interview with J. Zupanov, Zagreb, April 23, 1969.

[92] Not infrequently, workers, who see their demands for a more egalitarian distribution of income blocked, resort to direct action in the form of wildcat strikes.

[93] *Workers' Management in Yugoslavia* (I.L.O.), p. 277.

"Particularism" at the enterprise level, and "localism" at the level of the commune, describes an attitude of excessive self-interest at the expense of the wider community. The multiplicity of organizations and institutions at the enterprise and commune level are expected to curb and correct such tendencies. The problem is nevertheless a serious one and could easily become more pronounced as additional authority is given to local units.[94]

Particularism at the enterprise level, strengthened by increased market competition, has been accompanied by instances of a certain "profiteer mentality" and greater concern on the part of individuals over monetary benefits.[95]

The tendency on the part of some enterprises to reduce self-financing of their production funds, coupled with demands for increased personal income, is seen by one Yugoslav economist as an example of "enterprise particularism."[96]

Conflicts in Yugoslavia's planned market economy appear most frequently between the *short term interests* of the worker (increased income) and his *long term interests* (investment, modernization, etc.). Another aspect to the operation of the market which is more difficult to measure, however, is its negative effect on the consciousness and behavior of citizens in a Socialist society. The fact that this phase is proclaimed to be transitional does not detract from the potential seriousness of the problem.

The self-managing system in its openness, in fact, permits and often encourages contradictions.[97] Development through contradiction is seen as being based on an authentic interpreta-

---

[94] On a different level, the problem also affects the relations between the republics.

[95] R. Supek, "Problems and Perspectives of Workers' Self-Management in Yugoslavia," Broekmeyer, p. 226.

[96] Ivan Maksimovic, "The Economic System and Workers' Self-Management in Yugoslavia," Broekmeyer, pp. 138–9. Such tendencies have manifested themselves before in other historical settings. Guerin talks about "parochial egoism" developing with the self-managed sector of Catalonia during the Spanish Civil War. (Daniel Guerin, *Anarchism,* New York: Monthly Review Press, 1970, p. 137.)

[97] We are excluding here conflicts which have their origin in external factors.

tion of Marxism.[98] To borrow the term used by an American radical, it leads to a system of "creative disorder."

The Commune and Self-Government

Local self-government in Yugoslavia has evolved from a network of National Liberation Committees formed during the War for Liberation (1941–5). This network of elected local organs was further consolidated in the Constitution of 1946 and in subsequent laws passed in 1949 and 1952, until in 1955, the "Law on the Organization of Communes and Districts" came into force.[99]

Workers' self-management was introduced prior to the establishment of the communal system. At this time it became increasingly clear that genuine self-management in the economy was not feasible unless it was accompanied by self-government in the political system. After extensive debate and experiments, the 1955 law establishing the communal system was passed. The communal system has undergone many changes since that date and must still be regarded as being in a process of change.

As the power and jurisdiction of the commune has increased, its size has increased as well. Today, there are 501 communes in Yugoslavia, with an average population of 40,000 and an average territory of 500 square kilometers. In practice, the tendency to increase the size of the communes has resulted in the merging of urban centers with surrounding rural areas in the expectation of creating economically viable entities.[100]

The most important political organ in the commune is the assembly. The individual citizen is perceived to have interests and requirements both as a citizen of the commune, and as a worker in his workplace. Since all these interests should be

[98] Rudi Supek, *Power Structure of Statist and Self-Governing Socialism,* p. 20.

[99] We will not discuss the period prior to 1955 when the local organs had relatively few independent powers and instead functioned largely as executors of republican and federal agencies.

[100] There are, however, rural communes with as few as 3,000 inhabitants and twenty urban communes have a population of over 100,000 each. The territory of the commune is determined by republican law.

represented in the policies of the communal assembly, a system of two chambers has been established: the communal chamber, elected by all adult citizens in the commune, and the chamber of working communities, elected by the working people in enterprises and institutions, who thus exercise a double vote. The latter chamber is representative of the working people in the basic areas of the economy, education and culture, social welfare and health services, and public services. One Yugoslav writer has noted that the chamber of working communities "in a sense constitutes a lengthened limb of the workers' councils and management boards of enterprises and institutions, for through the chamber of work communities, the position taken by these bodies of management is transmitted to the commune assembly and their influence is exercised on the policies of the commune."[101] The communal assembly is thus designed to represent citizens both as consumers and as producers. As a general rule, the two chambers pass laws in joint sessions. At present, there are 40,791 councilors in communal assemblies, about equally divided between the two chambers.[102] Some of the larger communes have begun to experiment with four functional chambers and we may expect this trend to accelerate in the future. Elements of direct democracy can be found in meetings of voters, referenda on important communal and local issues, and decision making by local communities of which there are 6,335 with 79,228 elected councilors.[103]

The communal assembly is autonomous in its decision-

[101] Dragoljub Milivojevic, *The Yugoslav Commune,* Belgrade: Medunarodna Politika, 1965, p. 14.

[102] *Statisticki Godisnjak Jugoslavije 1969,* Belgrade: Federal Institute of Statistics, 1969.

[103] *Statisticki Godisnjak Jugoslavije 1968,* Belgrade: Federal Institute of Statistics, 1968. Neighborhood or voters' meetings must be convened *at least* twice a year, either by the communal assembly, the neighborhood organization, the Socialist Alliance, or ten percent of the voters living in a given neighborhood. These meetings deal largely with parochial issues and function as public opinion forums. Through these meetings, ordinary citizens are able to block proposed actions of the communal assembly. (William Kornblum, "The Yugoslav Communal System: Decision-Making in Housing and Urban Development," *The New Atlantis,* No. 2 (1970), pp. 17–8.)

making power within the legal framework laid down by the constitution and subsequent federal acts.[104] The communal authorities are also obliged to enforce federal and republican laws, as there are, as a rule, no republican and federal bodies of authority within the territory of the commune. The communal bodies, however, are not subordinated to republican or federal authorities.

While in theory the communal assembly is the highest decision-making body in the commune, real power is frequently wielded by a combination of formal and informal decision makers. A recent survey of seventeen communes illustrates the distance between theory and practice.[105]

Referenda in local communities have increased in the last few years. They are usually connected with self-help efforts on the part of citizens. An example of this is the financing of schools and kindergartens for which funds are not available through regular channels.[106] The initiative for such referenda may come from the commune itself or from meetings of voters or

[104] The composition, organization, type, and number of communal organs, as well as their range and scope are determined independently by the communal statute. (Zivorad Kovacevic, "Yugoslavia," *Studies in Comparative Local Government,* Vol. IV, No. 1 (1970), p. 91.)

[105] The following data, unless indicated otherwise, is taken from Janez Jerovsek, *Structure of Influence in Selected Decisions,* Llubljana (mimeographed), April 1969. The paper is part of a larger study conducted by the "Institute for Urban Planning in the SR of Slovenia," the Institute of Sociology and Philosophy and the School of Sociology, Political Science and Journalism, all of Llubljana. Eighteen leaders were interviewed in each of the seventeen communes which were arranged into two groups; underdeveloped and developed. Research done elsewhere in Yugoslavia largely confirms the conclusions reached by Jerovsek. See also Janez Jerovsek, "The Structure of Influence in the Yugoslav Commune," *The New Atlantis,* No. 2 (1970), pp. 31–47.

[106] There is a potentially dangerous trend inherent in the "self-help" referendum. We should remember that self-help of citizens in poorer communities is a response to the present inability of the commune to meet its obligations. If this trend continues, "self-help" referenda in poorer communities could become a conservative alternative to equalization. At least one recent survey indicates clearly that the poor rural communes outpoint the rich communes in terms of voluntary popular initiatives. (Philip E. Jacob, "Values Measured by Local Leadership," *Wharton Quarterly,* Summer 1969 [reprint].)

Groups	Influence Exerted %	Influence They Should Exert %
1. Socialist Alliance of Working People	3.0	3.4
2. Voters' Meeting and Local Communities	2.3	14.8
3. Trade Unions, Veterans' Association	—	0.7
4. Mayor, Deputy Mayor, and Department Heads of Communal Administration	30.2	11.7
5. Administration of Communal Assembly, Professional Services	2.0	0.7
6. Communal Assembly, Councils of Communal Assembly*	37.0	56.0
7. League of Communists, Secretary of Communal Committee of LCY	4.7	4.0
8. Leaders of Political Organizations	3.0	1.0
9. Political Organizations	2.7	2.0
10. Working Organizations, General Manager of Working Organizations, and other leaders	12.1	4.7
N.A.	1.0	1.0

* The councils are the political executive organs of the communal assembly for particular fields of activity.

teachers. Proposals for voluntary self-help are almost always passed. The cost of administering referenda is so high that they are held only if a favorable response can be expected with some certainty.[107] In a recent survey undertaken in Slovenia, about

[107] Voluntary self-help may take the form of an agreed-upon additional tax for a specified purpose and over a specified period of time. It can usually also be honored by supplying materials or one's own working

one half of the top administrative personnel in communes favored an extension of the scope of referenda to include important political and economic issues that are presently decided by the commune assembly. About one half of the deputies of the republican assembly in Slovenia wanted to see referenda introduced on republic-wide issues.[108]

Yugoslav theoreticians consider the commune the nucleus of a future Socialist society. The commune implies a self-governing social and political structure that has been removed from centralized state control. It is argued by Yugoslavs that the constitution is unclear on the vital question of whether the commune and the enterprise are two different forms of self-management cooperating and coexisting with each other, or whether the commune is the basic sociopolitical collective which unites all other units within its territory. While the constitution speaks of the commune as "the basic sociopolitical community" through which the citizens shall "coordinate individual and common interests with the general interests" (Article XCVI), it treats separately the self-management of enterprises and that of the commune. Nowhere does it specifically treat the mutual relations of these two forms of self-government, nor does it stress their unity. Practice supports the view that there are two separate forms of self-government in the commune, each with a separate existence.

It is not clear which direction developments will take, but the odds over the *long term* seem to favor the formation of a uniform system of communal self-government which would respect the autonomy of enterprises and institutions as to their internal self-management but would subordinate them to the commune in all questions of commune-wide importance.[109] Such a

---

time in place of a financial contribution. As a rule, at least fifty percent of citizens polled must approve the proposed project before it can be put into practice.

[108] Interview with Dr. Drago Zajc, Center of Research in Public Opinion, Llubljana, April 21, 1968.

[109] There are also pressures in a direction contrary to the philosophy of communal self-government. It would seem at least possible that Yugoslavia's desire to enter the world economy as a full trading partner would result in a further pressure toward efficiency and larger industrial units which could move economic decision making upward and away from

merger of workers' control and community control based increasingly on direct decision making of the producer and citizen is seen by many Yugoslavs as the next step in creating their Socialist democracy. Rudi Supek has recently argued that modern technological development confirms that self-managing forms do not develop exclusively in production communities: "They spread to living communities, which are interlaced and mutually conditioned in their functions, with an outspoken tendency to favor living communities at the cost of production communities."[110]

The Nomination and Election Process

A few words should be said about the election process in Yugoslavia. The present system of nominating and electing representatives applies not only to communal, but also to provincial, republican, and federal elections. Because of the importance of the nominating process, and the cautious introduction of elements of direct democracy, we will attempt to outline this process in some detail.[111]

In the first stage, open meetings of voters (citizens) discuss candidates and make preliminary nominations. This stage is openly democratic and, as a rule, no attempts are made to obstruct the "free will of the people." Each commune has several such meetings with an average of 2000 to 3000 voters attending each one. The meetings of voters then send their *preliminary* nominations to the commune nominating conference, which is organized by the Socialist Alliance. The partici-

---

the commune. The tensions produced by Yugoslavia's desire to remain independent, enter the world economy *and* strengthen self-government have not been resolved. One asset of some importance is the fact that the problem is recognized.

110 Supek, *op. cit.,* p. 278. See also Rudi Supek, "The Fate of the Production Community," *Praxis* (International Edition), 1965, No. 2–3.

111 I am grateful to Muhamed Kesetovic, member of the Executive Council of the Federal Conference of the Socialist Alliance, for the factual information relating to the nominating process. Interview in Belgrade, April 16, 1969. The comments made in this connection are solely my responsibility.

pants in this conference are delegates from all the sociopolitical and other citizens' organizations registered in the commune.[112]

This second stage is more complex and consists of a mixture of direct and "organized" democracy. The Socialist Alliance, apart from organizing the nominating conference, fulfills two political functions.

It makes sure that those candidates favored by the Alliance are nominated (the practice today is to nominate at least two "approved" candidates), if they have not already been nominated at the voters' meetings.

In cooperation with delegates from other like-minded organizations, it attempts to filter out those candidates nominated at the voters' meetings who are considered to be undesirable.

The nominees selected by the nominating conference then go back to the voters' meetings for approval. At this third stage, deletions and additions are possible but in practice difficult to achieve. It takes either one third of the voters meeting in a given commune or at least ten percent of all voters of all the meetings to effect a change. Difficult as it is to reintroduce candidates deleted at the second stage, or to delete nominating conference selections, this did happen during the 1969 elections.[113]

The nominating process is thus of greater importance than the actual election. It is, in a sense, a typical example of direct democracy tempered at present by elements of "political guidance" on the part of the Socialist Alliance.

[112] Delegates from several commune nominating conferences create a federal nominating conference (one for each federal electoral unit). The same process applies essentially to the election of all those assembly chambers which are elected directly by citizens.

[113] There are, of course, other ways to persuade an "undesirable" candidate to withdraw. If he happens to be a member of the League of Communists, pressure can be put on him by the League. If he holds an elective position, such as mayor of a commune, it can be made clear to him that he would lose the support of the sociopolitical organizations in any future attempt to run for public office.

The Challenge

The future of Yugoslavia is still very much an open question. The continued, if diminishing, presence of the state is justified because it appears to be the only alternative to the chaos of private, capitalist production.[114] To the degree that a system of Socialist democracy, based on self-management in a planned market economy, emerges as a viable alternative, to that degree will the state (and the LCY) wither away. Horvat has pointed out that, "Control of production without the state as an intermediary means control by direct producers, which in turn means that the equality of proletarians is transformed into the equality of masters."[115]

It is difficult to escape the conclusion that unless a considerable degree of democratization takes place within the leadership of the League of Communists, a fundamental contradiction is likely to arise between a still limited but expanding system of direct democracy at the base and a political system based on a monopoly of power exercised by the top decision makers. Such a clash of interests is not likely to arise until self-management in enterprises and communes has reached its full potentialities within present limitations. It may never arise if current trends within the system continue in the direction of stated objectives of a Socialist democracy. The crucial point will be reached when democratization introduced from above has produced a sufficiently powerful and confident movement at the base to challenge the fundamentally undemocratic way in which the process of democratization is being introduced throughout the country.

Meanwhile, radicals in the West are becoming increasingly alarmed by certain tendencies that could, if allowed to prevail, undermine the Socialist basis of the Yugoslav economy. Foreign investment in Yugoslavia, a steady increase in private enterprise

114 Horvat, *op. cit.*, p. 8.
115 *Ibid.*, p. 8. In this connection it is relevant to note that there exists a tendency in Yugoslavia to replace the present governmental organs by a Congress of Self-Governing Communities as the only and supreme power (Supek, Broekmeyer, p. 259).

activity (particularly in the growing tourist trade), and increased dependence on trade with the West (particularly with Italy and West Germany) are some of the reasons for their alarm. In addition, the role of the banks and trading companies and the problem of development in the poorer regions present serious challenges to the Socialist economy.

Foreign Investment

The necessity of foreign investment for the development of the Yugoslav economy seems to have been decided, but the modifications needed to attract investors are still the subject of heated debate. Discussions within the League now center on two areas: the possibility of permitting foreign investors to take part of their profits out of the country immediately, and ways to accommodate the demands of potential investors for a share in the management of those enterprises in which their money is being invested.

The Role of the Banks and Trading Companies

Yugoslav society today appears to be highly atomized, functioning on the basis of contracts between autonomous, self-managed units. This is essentially a Proudhonist conception of society. What is alarming is the growing power of the "intermediaries," the banks and the trading companies, which monopolize and control foreign exchange and thus have great economic and political power. An important issue now is the question of how to control and decentralize these mediating agencies.

The problem is extremely complex and controversial. Until now, the League has not been too concerned about the atomization of society since it felt that it provided the necessary integrative element—control. To what extent "capitalist tendencies" mushroom in the near future will depend ultimately not so much on the legal foundations of the economic system as on the "social orientation of all decisions relating to economic processes. . . ."[116] This means, in effect, that the LCY will have to exercise its moral leadership. Today many Yugoslavs are questioning whether the League can meet this challenge. Given the determination not to reintroduce centralist administrative controls, and the likelihood of some form of decentralization of the assets and functions of the trading companies, the danger of further atomization and increase in capitalist tendencies is very real.

The Dilemma of the Less-Developed Areas

Federal control of funds for regional development has now been eliminated and the money turned over to the republics, with the exception of the fund to aid the underdeveloped republics. Controversy centers on the demand of poorer regions for more investment and the reluctance of the more industrialized parts of the country to provide funds for that purpose. At the moment there is no financial incentive for enterprises in Croatia and Slovenia to invest in the less developed republics since the income from such investment must remain at the place where it has been invested. In addition, branch operations can at any time declare their independence from the parent enterprise. Discussion taking place now centers around a possible compromise that would allow the parent enterprise to retain a percentage of the income of any new branch plant.

As the old guard of Communists is gradually replaced by new and younger elements who seem to be more concerned with material gains than with Socialist democracy, while capitalist methods and tendencies make inroads by means of foreign investment and the encouragement of material incentives and competitiveness, it might appear that Yugoslavia is on the way to becoming the first country to upset the law of economic development by changing from a Socialist society to a capitalist one. I believe, however, that we should withhold such a hasty

[116] Zoran Vidakovic, "The Function of the Trade Unions in the Process of Establishing the Structure of the Yugoslav Society on a Basis of Workers' Self-Management," Broekmeyer, p. 54.

judgment, despite the many indications that point in this direction. If we accept the possibility of a labor-managed market economy as a viable Socialist alternative to the capitalist mode of production, and if we take into consideration the roots of self-management which have gradually been strengthened over the past twenty years, we can avoid the temptation to pass judgment on a society still in a state of rapid change. It is generally assumed by outsiders as well as by many Yugoslavs that the new generation now assuming more responsible positions in government and the economy is uniformly devoted to material gains, if necessary at the expense of Socialist ideas of solidarity and equality. This is not entirely true. Parliament and party are committed to Socialism and absolutely opposed to the restoration of capitalism. The private sector is not important and has no political influence in the system. Alternatives are openly debated in the party, the trade unions, the Socialist Alliance, and other sociopolitical organizations. With the possible exception of Cuba (and perhaps China, of which we know too little), no other country encourages debate among the masses on fundamental issues relating to its future.

It is argued that exposure to the experience of self-management will result in increased demands to close the credibility gap between what is and what is desired, particularly since the latter enjoys at least the formal support of the political leadership and the constitution. Training for self-management involves a very large number of Yugoslavs on a rotating basis. In 1967–8 close to 700,000 people served on bodies of self-management in working organizations, institutions, and sociopolitical communities (commune and province, republic and Federal).[117]

Direct Socialist democracy or Socialist self-government must embrace all parts of society. Self-governing elements must grow into self-governing bodies leading to a complete self-governing society. Self-management is not just an extension of traditional, parliamentary democracy into the workplace, but a new form of democracy permeating the entire fabric of society.

[117] Interview with Momcilo Radosavljevic, Director of the Center for Self-Management, Belgrade, April 15, 1969. Not included in this number are the elected representatives of the sociopolitical organizations.

A member of the radical Yugoslav journal *Praxis* has issued the following challenge to political movements everywhere: "If a political movement fails to exhaust the real possibilities for the introduction of the system of workers' self-management (as the backbone of social self-government), it is not a *workers'* movement in the proper sense of the word. The criterion should be the fullest use of *every* possibility for this objective, not only after taking over power, but also while in opposition. . . ."[118]

[118] Svetozar Stojanovic, "Social Self-Government and Socialist Community," *Praxis* (International Edition), Vol. IV, No. 1–2, (1968), p. 104. (See also *Kritik und Zukunft des Sozialismus* by the same author, Munich, Carl Hanser Verlag, 1970, p. 74.)

IV

Workers' Control:
Strategies for Change

Introduction
to Section IV

Workers' control, at first glance, would appear to be a relatively simple proposition. Citizens elect their own leaders in the political sphere; let them do so in the economic sphere as well. Pass a law giving the employees of a corporation the rights and powers which the stockholders now enjoy—or, if we don't want to go that far, then let the workers share these powers with the present owners and managers. This is how it is in Sweden and West Germany: why not in the United States and Canada?

In fact, the concept of workers' control is much more complex and far-reaching—and it is precisely for this reason that we distinguish true workers' control from the joint consultation or co-determination schemes of Western European countries described in Section III. Workers' control, to us, means a fundamental restructuring of the economic order. In the plant, it does not mean simply replacing one set of anonymous electors with another; it means extending a democracy of participation to the shop floor through decentralized cooperative decision making. In the larger economy—and this is equally critical—it means appropriating control of fundamental economic decisions to the people as a whole, and deciding democratically on the allocation of resources. A corollary of this is that workers' control means taking this economic power away from the tiny elite which now owns and manages the huge corporations of North America's private economy.

It is a large order. Such changes do not come about easily, nor do they come simply by passing laws. Indeed, with workers' control at this point little more than a slogan in the United States and Canada, one may well wonder how we can even approach the ideal of a socially owned and democratically managed economy. What might be a strategy for building a movement capable of changing the present system?

The answers suggested by this section's essays are necessarily tentative, and in some cases contradictory. This is no accident, for the debate is just beginning, and the problems of strategy have no clear solutions. Disagreement is inevitable—and, we hope, a healthy sign. Building a movement for workers' control will require a fresh look at our society's institutions, and new ideas about how to change them. The essays which follow are one contribution to that movement.

Workers' Control Is More Than Just That

André Gorz

If workers' control is a strategy for broad social change and not simply another "industrial reform," we have to begin thinking about it as such. But what does it mean to see workers' control as part of the struggle for socialism? And what are the implications for workers' control struggles themselves? The following article, taken from a speech by the author to a 1970 Toronto conference on strategies for change, begins to answer these questions. André Gorz assesses the possibility that demands for workers' control can lead to more basic changes in the economic system and, drawing upon his long term familiarity with Western European labor movements, suggests some forms which successful workers' control movements might take.

When we speak about workers' control we usually have some very different things in mind. Some see workers' control as an end in itself, i.e., as something that can and must be won within the framework of the capitalist system, to improve the situation of the working class. Others look at workers' control as something that will never be won as long as capitalism exists, and that must be championed for precisely that reason. According to this second view, which I personally share, workers' control is not an end in itself. It is mainly a means or method, a means whose true significance can be understood only if we place it in a strategic perspective of social and political revolution.

A few factual examples may illustrate why and how the issue of workers' control has become so relevant in recent class conflicts all over Europe, and also to show why long drawn-out struggles for control have never and nowhere led to complete success.

There were times when the working class could act on the assumption that there were heaps of ready cash in the bosses' safes or the corporations' banks. Traditional union action rested on the hypothesis that the employer, if pressed hard enough, would eventually give in and grant higher wages and better working conditions. Traditional working class action assumed the corporations' finances and the system as a whole to be flexible. But this assumption no longer holds true. Flexibility has been organized away and replaced by rigid planning of all the factors on which production depends. Thus:

— the quickened pace of technological innovation calls for advance planning of the corporation's future investment;
— the greater weight of fixed capital compels long term financial planning of amortization, depreciation, reserves, and financial costs;
— increased international competition prevents unforeseen higher costs from being offset by higher prices;
— rigid financial planning also calls for rigid predetermination of labor costs.

This overall rigidity of modern management policies tends to jeopardize the traditional bargaining power of labor unions. Wages nowadays tend to be predetermined; and not only wages, but also the working process itself. Therefore, management tends to react very sharply to unforeseen wage demands that would jeopardize the corporation's financial planning. Unplanned wage demands tend to be considered as a direct attack on the logic and balance of the capitalist system. Both management and the state tend to fight such demands by accepting a trial of strength and meeting the working class in head-on clashes.

Of course, if we fight hard enough, we can force the corporations to give us a little more than they would like; we can temporarily throw the capitalist system out of balance and make small inroads into the plans and the profits of corporate capital. But experience has taught us that this kind of success can be only temporary. Within a relatively short time, one of two things will happen:

1) Capitalists may consider that the profits which the new wage rates leave are not attractive enough and that they, the capitalists, do not have sufficient power to take away from the working class what it has just won. In such a situation, the bourgeoisie will close down the plants, fire part of the workers, organize a recession; capital will go on strike and wait until the working class is sufficiently weakened to become submissive again.

2) The alternative to this extreme solution is more common: within a relatively short time, capitalists will restore what they consider to be attractive rates of profit by taking away at least part of the wage increases which we have won.

There are various ways of taking them away from us. For example:

—rising prices reduce our real wages;
—work is intensified and part of the workers laid off;
—those who remain have to work faster and harder;
—the work process is not only speeded up, it is "rationalized," which means: new equipment is installed, skilled work is replaced by unskilled work, the evaluation of jobs and skills is made according to new criteria.

In short, workers are made to pay dearly and heavily for their increased wages. Their subjection to so-called scientific organization of the work process becomes more and more rigid.

As you know, the new time and motion measuring systems break down the act of working into minute motions, and no longer allow for individual variations in work speed, nor for any kind of significant individual bonuses. Wage rates are negotiated when the system is introduced and are not open to revision. Management is intent on making long term deals with the union and on using the union as a kind of police force to see to it that the workers fulfill their part of the bargain. Wage increases are planned in advance as part of the deal, and shop floor rebellion against working conditions tends to be answered by lockouts.

Thus scientific management closes the trap on the workers. We are now learning that the laborer's subjection to the work process had something artisanlike in the past: work speeds and piece rates could be tampered with to a certain extent. But no longer. Management policy has become global, and so has the subjection of the workers. Working conditions are rigidly predetermined and can no longer be influenced by individual meddling.

Workers thus will remain at the complete mercy of despotic and arbitrary managerial decisions unless they win sufficient power on the factory floor to refuse new work rules, work speeds, new definitions of skills and of rates and so on—unless, in other words, they win direct power over the work process. That is what workers' control is mostly about, at first sight. We need control over the working process in order to prevent managements from taking away from us with one hand what they grant with the other hand. We need control for strictly economic reasons, so as to counteract the power of management to burden us with more and more exhausting work and with deteriorating working conditions in exchange for some meager wage raises. But if this is so, then it also must be quite clear to us that the struggle for control will be even fiercer, even more merciless, than the struggle for wages. The struggle for control, even more than the struggle for increased wages, aims at checking the profit which capital can make on our labor. Therefore, management will fight demands for control with all overt or covert means at its disposal. Just as management will grant us higher wages when it can't help doing so, only to try and take them away from us at a later stage, so management may grant us, at certain moments, powers of control—only to try and destroy these powers at a later stage, be it by force or by deception. Control is not something that can be won once and forever. It is something which, once we have won it at least partly, will have to be defended in ceaseless battles, or else we shall lose it again. Genuine workers' control is something quite intolerable to capitalist management, however enlightened it may pretend to be, because genuine workers' control attacks at its very source the domination and exploitation of labor by capital.

This you probably know from experience, although some may have had different experience in certain advanced factories which try to introduce so-called job enrichment. This is something which we will try to discuss later. In my view, the important point, for the moment, is that the struggle for workers' control is necessarily an extremely bitter struggle which cannot be won and which cannot even be *waged* within the traditional framework and ideology of the unions.

To make this point clear, I'd like to submit to you a few critical considerations about the history and the limitations of the union movement. Originally, the unions developed out of the workers' need for self-defense and self-organization. In their early stages, when they were still genuine organs of workers' self-organization, unions tended to be quite radical. We still witness this radicalism whenever a new union is built up from scratch through the initiative of rank-and-file militants who get together and try to do things as they see them and fight for demands they deeply feel, no holds barred. This is something which happened in recent years in Detroit, for example, with the League of Revolutionary Black Workers.

This type of revolutionary union movement, however, has become something exceptional. Overall, the big national unions are now *institutions* which see it as their task not to overthrow or even to question the capitalist system, but rather to defend the interests of the working class within the framework of that system. This change of attitude, of course, can be historically explained: for decades, there was no concrete prospect of a proletarian revolution in the West. The working class proved incapable of overthrowing the system. Top union leaders understandably felt that it was pointless to insist on revolutionary demands that could not be achieved in the absence of a revolutionary situation. Though some of them did not completely discard the hope that such a situation might arise again, they thought it was realistic in the meantime to fight for things that could be won right away, such as better wages and other improvements. The more intelligent capitalists openly or discreetly encouraged this realistic attitude: bargaining over demands is cheaper than fighting over them. Fundamentally, then, corporate capital was reconciled to the existence of labor unions and showed willingness to recognize them officially, but on two conditions:

1) Unions must voice only demands that are realistic, that do not call capitalism into question, that are *negotiable*.

2) Once an agreement has been bargained out, unions must stick to it and prevent the workers from breaking it.

Wherever these two conditions were accepted, labor unions turned into permanent institutions holding legal rights and responsibilities: they became permanently structured and therefore hierarchical and bureaucratic organizations; they held tremendous bargaining power, but they also held the power to discipline and to police reluctant workers. As institutions holding institutionalized power within the capitalist state, union bureaucracies of course showed less and less inclination to jeopardize their self-interest by stimulating demands and aspirations that were incompatible with the logic and the power structure of the capitalist system. Demands that could not be won by bargaining and by juridically defined forms of action were considered pointless. Demands that had no chance of being accepted by capitalist managers were thus eliminated from the outset. They were eliminated because top union leadership could not engage in risky and losing battles. Realism thus led union leaders to translate all demands that sprung up from the rank and file into propositions that would prove acceptable and negotiable to the representatives of capital. The objective function of labor unions has thus become a function of ideological and political mediation, and union leadership has become a conservative force.

Now, the question we must ask ourselves is: can this type of centralized and bureaucratic unionism wage an effective struggle for workers' control? The answer is an emphatic "No." Labor unions that feel responsible for discipline at work; labor unions that feel responsible to the capitalist managers for keeping the factories going; labor unions that commit themselves not to strike as part of the bargain they have entered; in a word, labor unions that behave as institutional mediators within the capitalist society are inherently incapable of leading an effective struggle for rank-and-file demands for control—except if control itself can be institutionalized and subordinated to regulations that will make it ineffective. This is a point which has been well documented in Western Europe as well as in the United States.

Of course, some people will object that labor unions' leadership has become conservative and timid only because the working class itself is apathetic. Union bureaucrats everywhere, particularly in my country, like to assert that the masses would not understand and accept a more aggressive and combative union policy. Facts prove these assertions to be false. The truth is that the bureaucratic machines of institutionalized labor unions are very much afraid of losing control over the working class, since the unions draw their institutional strength and bargaining power from their ability to keep the laboring masses under control. Most top union leaders are frightened of the wild and uncontrollable demands and outbursts that would explode from the rank and file if the workers were free at any moment to gather, discuss, and decide what their grudges are, what they wanted to do about them, and how. And this is precisely what would happen if genuine workers' control were fought for on the shop floor, i.e., if demands and actions could be decided permanently *from below* without control and mediation *from above*.

At present—and as long as the centralized and bureaucratic structure and organization of the big unions persists—it is practically impossible to know how the working class really feels about its condition in the factories, in the offices, and in society. The impressive number of wildcat strikes which has developed in recent years does, however, point to the fact that an untapped potential of combativeness and radicalism exists, a potential which the traditional structure of labor unions tends to repress. Let me give you a few examples of this.

In Great Britain, for example, more than eighty percent of all strike action in recent years was wildcat. These strikes were and are called by stop stewards, not by the unions themselves, on issues relating to wages and to workers' control. Some people of course will say that these issues are always specific and do not prove great radicalism and class consciousness. Quite true: after all, more than half of the British working class votes Conservative.

The question we must ask, however, is: what political and class consciousness would the working class have if their national organizations were as democratic and as aggressive as the elected and revocable militants on the shop floor? We have no idea about this, but there is an interesting story which I'd like to tell you about the dangers of taking so-called working class apathy at face value.

In the early sixties, a British professor of sociology by the name of Goldthorpe made an extensive investigation of the Vauxhall workers at Luton. He wanted to find out what class consciousness they had left, how they felt about their work, about wages, about life generally—and what chances there were that acute conflicts would break out in a well-managed and advanced big factory. Professor Goldthorpe had about eighty percent of the Vauxhall workers interviewed individually. His investigation lasted two years. His conclusions were optimistic: he found the Vauxhall workers to be completely integrated into the system. They had, so he said, no deeply felt grudges. They were rather satisfied with their wages. They neither liked nor disliked their work; they looked at it as a rather boring but inevitable part of their life. They didn't want to give it much thought. Their general attitude toward work, according to Professor Goldthorpe, was to perform it so as to get rid of it; they wanted to forget about it at the end of the working day, to go home, watch television, grow vegetables in their garden, fiddle around in their home. Their working life was rather marginal to them and what really mattered to them was their life at home, which was their real life. Therefore Professor Goldthorpe concluded that class consciousness was practically nonexistent at Vauxhall, that the workers were behaving according to middle class patterns, and that class struggle belonged to the past.

The Goldthorpe report was still at the printer's when a few militants got hold of a résumé of Professor Goldthorpe's conclusions. They had this résumé mimeographed, and handed out a few hundred copies. A week or so later, the *Daily Mail* printed a report on Vauxhall's profits. The net profit for that year amounted to about £ 900 per worker, and this net profit had been sent back to General Motors in the United States. This piece of news was also circulated among the workers. The next day, something happened which the *Times* reported as follows:

> Wild rioting has broken out at the Vauxhall car factories in Luton. Thousands of workers streamed out of the shops and gathered in the factory yard. They besieged the management offices, calling for the managers to come out, singing the "Red Flag" and shouting "string them up!" Groups attempted to storm the offices and battled the police which had been called to protect them.

The rioting lasted for two days.

Now this is what happened in an advanced factory where the union was strong and where eighty percent of the workers had been interviewed and been found to lack class consciousness. What does it all mean? Does it mean that Professor Goldthorpe was stupid? It certainly means that Goldthorpe made a major mistake: he interviewed each worker separately and found each worker to be individually *resigned to,* if not *reconciled with,* his condition. He concluded that all these thousands of individual resignations made for a collective apathy. And then something happened which he had not thought of: all these workers who had said individually "That's how life is, there is nothing much that can be done about it," all these workers started to discuss things among themselves. They started to discuss them because the conclusions of Mr. Goldthorpe were circulated in the factory. And as they discussed things, they found out that they all felt alike: they felt apathetic but frustrated; they *were* apathetic because, as individuals, in their individual isolation and loneliness, no one could do anything to change things. But when people start talking about their loneliness, their frustration, their powerlessness, they cease to be isolated and powerless. They start melting into a group which holds immeasurably greater power than the individual power of all those who compose it.

In other words, the very investigation of Mr. Goldthorpe about the lack of class consciousness helped tear down the barriers of silence and isolation that rendered the workers apathetic; the Goldthorpe investigation itself stimulated an explosion of class consciousness and combativeness.

This is by no means an isolated example. As a matter of fact, wherever extensive interviews and investigations have been made inside factories, they have been followed within a very short time by violent outbreaks and spontaneous strikes. What happened at the Vauxhall works in Luton also happened at the Firestone plant in Oslo, Norway. It also happened at the Ford plant near Cologne, Germany, where the head of the local union had complained for years that wages, working conditions, and labor relations were so good that there was nothing much that the union could do in the factory. In this case, it so happened that the head of the Ford union died and was replaced by an inquisitive young militant. The new man decided to have a more thorough look at things. He handed out questionnaires, inviting the workers to say freely how they felt about a variety of issues: about working conditions, about working speeds, about piecework, about the foremen, etc. The replies were devastating. The immense majority of workers complained bitterly about working speeds, monotony, nervous exhaustion, lack of breaks, despotic behavior of the foremen, and so on. A summary of the replies was circulated. And a week later, when management announced that the assembly lines would have to be speeded up provisionally, just for two days, the whole factory broke out into a strike for the first time in fifteen years.

The same kind of story could be told about the Alfa Romeo car factory at Milan, Italy, about the shipyards at Genoa, about the Pirelli tire factory at Turin, about the steelworkers at Dunkirk, France. What does it all mean? First of all, it shows that when workers are given a chance to discuss and decide among themselves—in open gatherings—the grudges and the claims which they want to voice, their demands and their methods always prove more radical than what top union leadership had expected. Free discussion and exchange within the rank and file about factory life almost inevitably lead to violent outbursts of protest and unforeseen strike action.

What lesson are we to draw from this? The lesson, I suggest, is that a potential of frustration and of revolt lies permanently dormant within the working class and that, in so-called *normal* periods, no one knows how deeply the working class feels oppressed, exploited, frustrated, and dominated. *No one* knows about it normally: neither the union leadership, nor the workers themselves. We do not know about it because there are no words to convey and to make clear how we feel. We have no words to speak about our oppression, our distress, our bitterness, and our revolt against the exhaustion, the stupidity, the monotony, the lack of meaning of our work and of our life; against the contempt in which our work is held; against the despotic hierarchy of the factory; against a society in which we remain the underdogs and in which goods and enjoyments that are considered normal by the other classes are denied to us and are parceled out to us only reluctantly, as though we were asking for a privilege. We have no words to say what it is and how it feels to be workers, to be held in subjection, to be ordered around by people who have more and who pretend to know more and who compel us to work according to rules *they* set and for purposes that are *theirs,* not ours. And we have no words to say all this because the ruling class has monopolized not only the power of decision making and of material wealth; they have also monopolized culture and language. They are not only taking away from us our strength, our health, our labor, and the meaning of work; they also take away from us the means to communicate, including the words, the language we speak. There is no language available to say how we feel because we are never given a chance to say things and be heard.

There are no papers, no movies, no books about factory work and life. The work and life in the factories—and also in the huge offices—is something this society doesn't want to hear about. For decades the ruling class has sentenced the working class to live in terrifying silence. They have sentenced the working class to be prisoners not only of rules and laws that cannot be discussed or questioned, but also to be prisoners of an estranged language, of a language which is pervaded with values and with an ideology in which there is no room for what we feel and want.

It is because the working class is silenced that explosions of discontent always come as a surprise and always are violent. It is because we have no words to say what we want and no means to make it come true that we have to resort to violence as a way of saying: enough is enough, we won't play by the rules any longer, we won't take any more of it. Violence is the first and necessary step by which the oppressed refuse their oppression. Violence expresses effectively a total and immediate refusal of the established order and its discourse. But sporadic violence remains a substitute for the effective destruction of this order. Last year, after days of violent strike action and street riots, the Fiat automobile workers at Turin invented a magnificent slogan. It said: "What do we want? Everything." All right: we want everything right away, we want to overthrow capitalism, abolish all inequality, build a society of equals; we want to change life. But how do we go about it? Outbursts of violence are but the first and indispensable step toward it. But they are not enough. They liberate us momentarily but they don't change things. Changing things requires effective and sustained action, and sustained action requires a method and an overall view of the ends and means of struggling.

So, then, we have to ask again: what are we really fighting for? What does workers' control really mean to us? I submit that it means much more than improving working conditions in this or that factory without changing anything else. To make this clear, let us assume that we work in plants and offices that produce napalm for the war in Vietnam, miniature radio transmitters for the C.I.A., canned food containing chemical additives that may damage people's health, pornographic magazines, and the like. Are we capable of saying something like: "I don't mind producing napalm and pornography as long as it pays and as long as the job is not too hard?" I suggest none of us is capable of *saying* such a thing, though many of us are actually engaged in doing such things. How can this be explained?

The explanation, I submit, lies with the division of labor. Labor is divided both socially and technically. It is divided socially insofar as there are those who have wealth, power, and higher education—and who make the decisions; there are those who have only a higher education and who loyally serve the powerful, thereby getting certain privileges; and then there is the mass of those who have no wealth and no education (or a technical and specialized training only), and who fulfill the sharply defined and rigidly predetermined tasks which they are given. There can be no question about not fulfilling the task: you have to take it or leave it. You are compelled to do it not because someone is ordering you to do so, but because the process of production has been organized in advance to give each laborer one precise and narrowly limited job to do, without any possibility of doing something different or of doing his job in an unprescribed way. This sharp limitation and narrow specialization of jobs does not mean that they hold no initiative and responsibility. They may call for inventiveness, hard thinking, and sustained concentration. But things are organized such that no one knows enough about the other aspects of the process of production to be able to wonder what the heck he is really doing; things are organized such that no one is capable of taking initiatives and making decisions on the job that would call the overall process of production into question. In other words, every job holder is a cog in the machine; every job holder is responsible only for the work that is assigned to him and not for the overall product that will grow out of it. Responsibility for the overall product lies with a handful of top managers only; and once they have made their decisions, they organize and divide the work process into thousands of fragmented and predetermined little tasks, forcing everyone to comply with their decisions without really knowing what they are all about.

In a word, the technical division of labor, i.e., the way in which the jobs are parceled out, is not only an organization of production: it is also a technique of domination, a device to keep workers ignorant and to keep them in subjection. This is ever more true nowadays than fifty or a hundred years ago. Nowadays, the tremendous increase in the productivity of labor and the potentialities of automation make virtually possible a total and radical transformation of the work process: repetitive jobs could be abolished in most places; where they cannot yet, they could be performed alternatively and only for short periods, by everyone; multilateral training and comprehensive education could be made accessible to all; the barriers between manual and intellectual work could be torn down; rotation of jobs, collective debate on and responsibility for the methods of production and the quality of products could be made the rule. Free time could be tremendously increased and become socially creative if waste, parasitism and militarism were eliminated. All over the advanced capitalist world, the working class as a whole and each worker individually have much more insight, skill, knowledge, know-how and creative capacities than they are allowed to show in their jobs. All over the advanced capitalist world, an unbearable discrepancy develops between the stupidity, fragmentation, and irresponsibility of jobs and the actual or potential creativity of job holders. It is an obvious fact that capitalist management cannot call upon the creativity of the working masses: this would be incompatible with the right of hiring and firing people, to which management clings. Why should the masses put their creative capacities at the service of bosses who will make the workers unemployed if they become more efficient and thus more productive? Why should reduced costs and increased efficiency be our concern if what we produce is wasted, if there aren't enough jobs for all, if our right to earn a living is made dependent on our willingness to make useless and destructive things like weapons, tailfins, and moon rockets? Why should we want to be creative in our work if it does not serve the needs of the people but only the needs of capital for growing profits?

Capitalist management dare not call upon the creativity of the masses for fear of having all these questions explode. To prevent them from exploding, the division of labor is organized to make people feel more ignorant and incompetent than they are, to keep them in subjection, and to divide them by arbitrary barriers and differentiation of status and salary. The difference between skilled and unskilled workers, between workers and technicians, between technicians and engineers, is arbitrarily created as a technique of domination and of fragmentation of the working class. Every one of us knows from experience that this hierarchic division is irrational and senseless, that there is no such thing as a hierarchy of competence, that the competence of the workers is not smaller but only different from the competence of a technician, that wage differentiation does not rest on merit, on performance, on efficiency, but on *social* criteria, and that education serves much less to increase a man's competence in production than it serves to breed *social attitudes* and conformity to the values and ideology of capitalist society.

So then, in my view, when we speak of workers' control, we speak of the capability of the workers to take control of the process of production and to organize the working process as *they* think best. To organize the work process in such a way as to stop it from being oppressive, mutilating, soul-destroying and health destroying; to organize it to allow for the maximum display of each worker's initiative, responsibility, creativity; to organize it to replace forced labor and authoritarian division of labor by free cooperation.

Ultimately, there is no difference between workers' control and workers' power. Workers' control is one step, a first and partial step toward seizing power within and over the process of production. The struggle for workers' control is a struggle for power and therefore it can be waged effectively only if it demonstrates in itself our capability of exercising power over the process of production. To demonstrate this capability, we need not wait for anyone's approval or agreement. We had some recent examples, in France and Italy, where workers started rotating and swapping jobs which they considered to be interchangeable, though fourteen different wage rates were applied to these jobs. And they demanded equal pay for all. We've had the famous example of the Pirelli tire factory at Turin where the 5000 workers of a huge complex plant established new work speeds without any technician's or engineer's help and had the whole factory run at varying speeds, just to prove that they were capable of making it function smoothly their own way and that piece rates were nonsense. And we also had the important "reverse strikes" in Western France and in Japan, where public transport workers went "on strike" by making public transport a free service.

In all these and many other instances, the workers did not demand control as something that can be granted to them by the bosses; they struggled for control by simply taking control of the factory or of the shop and by having it function their way. Indeed, control is not something we can ask for and be given: it is something we have to take and that will be given to us because we have taken it already and won't give it up. Therein lies the great superiority of struggles for control over traditional trade unionism. A strike for control is different from all other strikes because strike action in itself is already an exercise in workers' power. It is different from traditional strikes because the workers don't go home and wait until their spokesmen have made a bargain with management. In a strike for control, the masses themselves, i.e., the workers' assembly, decide what can and must be done here and now.

Such strikes are exercises in workers' democracy, in workers' self-government and self-determination. They produce their organs of self-government, workers' councils and workers' committees, committees that are responsible only to the general assembly of the workers, delegates that can be recalled at any moment. All forms of bureaucracy, of representative democracy, of delegation of power are liquidated in these moments of self-organization and of direct democracy. In such moments, repressed needs and aspirations explode; the working class experiences its capability of self-rule and of mastering and modifying the work process. It experiences the possibility of refusing domination by management and by the state, as well as by union or party bureaucracies. It undergoes, in a word, a revolutionary experience; and if action lasts long enough; if it is not stifled by bureaucratic control from above; if the workers who gather and debate freely in open assemblies have time to produce new leaders and vanguards, workers' councils will spring up, i.e., the specific organs of collective, revolutionary self-organization and of collective power.

But neither the workers' councils, nor the factory or shop committees, nor the workers' power they stand for can prevail unless the political power of capitalism is broken, unless the capitalist state itself is overthrown and the capitalist relations of production and division of labor are abolished. The struggle for workers' control must either develop an all-out attack against all forms of hierarchy, against all forms of monopolization of power and of knowledge, against all forms of domination and bureaucracy, including the so-called socialist state bureaucracy, or else whatever power the workers have won in action within the factories will be broken and rendered meaningless in a very short time.

The workers' councils and committees that spring up during mass action and wield effective power over the production process cannot become lasting organs of dual power within the present system. They cannot coexist for long with the power of capitalist management and of the capitalist state. They can coexist with them only antagonistically, in periods of acute struggle that must take the form of a trial of strength. If such a trial of strength is not rapidly won by the working class; if it is not carried forward by political vision and organization; if it does not transcend itself into a generalized all-out offensive for a completely new society, then the organs of workers' power or workers' control must inevitably degenerate.

As we have again seen recently in Italy, there can be no protracted draw, no uneasy truce between organs of workers' power and the power of capitalist management. There can be no coexistence between these two opposed and unreconcilable powers because their trial of strength, if it is not won all-out by the working class, must end up in bargaining and settlement. But a settlement will only be accepted by management if its terms fit into the logic of capitalism and allow management to win back undisputed power. Moreover, settlements are necessarily compromises, compromises must be negotiated and negotiations cannot be conducted by the workers themselves, but only by delegates speaking on their behalf. These delegates may win some improvements and some new rights for the workers. They may win *token* rights of control *on behalf* of the workers. But the right of workers' control *by the workers themselves* will never be won within the present system. It will never be won because, as I said above, the present division of labor splits up the workers of any factory, differentiates them hierarchically, isolates each group from all the others, prevents the free flow of communication, plunges each individual in harassed loneliness. All the capitalist firm may be willing to grant is control by appointed delegates on behalf of the workers. But *delegated* power of control is something totally different from *direct collective* power. Delegation gives rise to a new group of mediators who will tend to be offered privileges, bureaucratic and institutionalized status, to keep the workers *under their* control. This is exactly what happened in Sweden.

You may ask, then: what is the point of fighting for workers' control if we can't get it? Or if we could get it only in a different social system? The answer is twofold:

1) As Max Weber said, it is only by pursuing the impossible that we will make what is possible come true. It is only by fighting for genuine workers' power as *we* see it that we will corner management into granting us rights and conditions that would never have been granted if we kept asking for them politely and reasonably. Token rights of control are better than nothing if we are able to use them to keep the fight going for full and genuine rights. Improvements such as job enrichment are better than nothing if we are able to use them to keep questioning and fighting the division of labor everywhere. And they are better than nothing also because workers who are not intellectually, morally, and nervously destroyed by work will be ready for more advanced struggles involving our way of life inside or outside the factories.

2) And an even more important point: the results of the struggle for workers' power cannot be measured by its immediate outcome. The main result of this struggle is that it changes people, it changes ourselves. It is something like a self-educational process. Through it, we discover, or rather we invent, the

working class's capability of self-organization, of self-determination, of control over the production process. We discover that workers are by no means as incompetent as the division of labor wants to make them feel, that competence is, to a large extent, a myth maintained by those who rule us and by an educational system which is instrumental in differentiating people, not in educating them.

Every struggle for workers' power that involves large numbers of people; every struggle that results in the formation of workers' councils and committees, in open assemblies, in free debate, in the exercise of direct democracy and of collective power, every such struggle prepares the working class to become the ruling class and to abolish all extraneous forms of power from above.

Of course, the genuine organs of workers' power that spring up during struggles will not and must not outlast every struggle. They will wither away when the battle is over, when a compromise has been made. But they will spring up again more powerfully at the next opportunity. They will have formed new militants and new natural leaders. They will be indispensable organs of dual power during and after a Socialist revolution. They will be necessary if we want to build a Socialism in which the state withers away, in which political power is checked and balanced by the direct democracy of the councils.

All this, of course, leads us far beyond the question of workers' control proper. But I think we have to look beyond and put the struggle for control in a strategic perspective. Without such a perspective, without a political instrument that will link the struggle for control to the struggle for workers' power in and over society, this struggle cannot go beyond the stage which it has reached in Great Britain, for example, and in which it has been blocked for years: i.e., an uninterrupted chain of wildcat strikes which effectively paralyze production and effectively weaken British capitalism, but which do not succeed in changing the pattern of production and the class nature of society.

If we want to go beyond this stage, we need a political, strategic, and theoretical vision. And we need an instrument for producing it and for coordinating our struggles.

The Debate on Workers' Control*

Ernest Mandel

The following article, by the Belgian economist and editor Ernest Mandel, reports and argues the lessons of a particular experience: what the goals of workers' struggles have been in Belgium, what strategies and tactics have been (or might be) used, what the pitfalls and problems are. The essay deals with a specific situation, but its conclusions may be applicable elsewhere. At the least, it provides insight into the process by which workers' control might move from an idea to a reality; furthering that process, of course, is the purpose of this book.

The article also introduces a topic to which this section will return in subsequent essays, the role of unions in advancing workers' control. This issue in particular is a source of disagreement among our contributors and should prove to be a question of some importance in the development of a movement for workers' control.

What Is Workers' Control?

The demand for workers' control is the order of the day. The FGTB (Fédération Générale des Travailleurs de Belgique—General Workers Federation of Belgium) is calling a special

* This article was originally published in five consecutive issues of the Belgian weekly newspaper edited by Ernest Mandel, *La Gauche:* December 21, 1968, to January 18, 1969.

congress on this subject. Many British trade unions have adopted it. In France the most left-wing workers and students have made workers' control one of their main demands. And in numerous plants and factories in Italy the vanguard workers not only call for workers' control but do their utmost—as at Fiat— to put it into practice at the right times.

This is an old demand of the international working class. It arose in the course of the Russian revolution. The Communist International adopted it at its third congress. It played an important role in the revolutionary struggles in Germany in 1920–3. The Belgain unions raised this demand during the twenties. Trotsky incorporated it into the Transitional Program of the Fourth International. André Rénard (Belgian left-wing trade union leader) took it up again toward the end of the fifties.

But in the course of the past two decades, the demand for workers' control has fallen into disuse in the broader labor and trade-union movement. Two generations of workers have received no education on this subject. It is, therefore, an urgent matter to define the meaning and the implications of workers' control, to show its value in the struggle for socialism, and to distinguish it from its reformist variants—co-determination (mixed labor and management decision making in the plants) and "participation."

Workers' control is a transitional demand, an anticapitalist structural reform par excellence. This demand stems from the immediate needs of the broad masses and leads them to launch struggles that challenge the very existence of the capitalist system and the bourgeois state. Workers' control is the kind of demand that capitalism can neither absorb nor digest, as it could all the immediate demands of the past sixty years—from wage increases to the eight-hour day, from social welfare legislation to paid holidays.

At this point we can dismiss an objection raised by sectarian "purists": "Calling for anticapitalist structural reforms makes you a reformist," they tell us. "Doesn't your demand contain the word 'reform'?"

This objection is infantile. It is also dishonest—at least on the part of those who do not oppose fighting for reforms on principle. We might be able to understand the argument, difficult as it may be, if it came from certain anarchists who reject the fight for higher wages. These people are wrong, but at least they can be given credit for being logically consistent.

But what can be said of those who support all the struggles for increasing wages, for decreasing the workweek, for lowering the pension age, for double pay for vacations, for free medical care and free medicines, but who, at the same time, reject anticapitalist structural reforms?

They don't realize that they, too, are fighting for reforms; but the difference between them and us is that they fight only for those reforms that capitalism has time and again proved it is capable of giving, of incorporating into its system, *reforms which thus do not upset the system itself.*

On the other hand, the program of anticapitalist structural reform has these very special characteristics: it cannot be carried out in a normally functioning capitalist system; it rips this system apart; it creates a situation of dual power; and it rapidly leads to a revolutionary struggle for power. Wage increases—as important as they may be for raising the level of the workers' fighting spirit, as well as their cultural level—can do nothing of the sort.

Actually, the whole argument of our "purist" opponents is based on a childish confusion. Fighting for reforms doesn't necessarily make one a reformist. If that were the case, Lenin himself would be the number one reformist, for he never rejected the struggle to defend the immediate interest of the workers. The reformist is one who believes that the fight for reforms is *all that is needed* to overthrow capitalism, little by little, gradually, and without overthrowing the power of the bourgeoisie.

But we proponents of the program of anticapitalist structural reforms are not in any way victims of this illusion. We believe in neither the gradual advent of Socialism nor the conquest of power by the electoral parliamentary road. We are convinced that the overthrow of capitalism requires a total extraparliamentary confrontation between embattled workers and the bourgeois state. The program of anticapitalist structural reforms has precisely this aim—bringing the workers to start the struggles that lead to such a confrontation. Instead of this, our "purist" critics are generally satisfied with struggles for immediate demands, all the while talking in abstractions about making the revolution, without ever asking themselves, how will the revolution really be made? An eloquent example: May 1968 in France.

The general strike of May 1968, following the one in Belgium in December 1960–January 1961, offers us an excellent example of the key importance of this problem. Ten million workers were out on strike. They occupied their factories. If they were moved by the desire to do away with many of the social injustices heaped up by the Gaullist regime in the ten years of its existence, they were obviously aiming beyond simple wage scale demands. The way they rejected, en masse, the first "Grenelle agreements" (reached between the de Gaulle government and the union federations May 27), which would have given them an average wage increase of fourteen percent, clearly reflects this wish to go further.

But if the workers did not feel like being satisfied with immediate demands, they also did not have any exact idea of precisely what they did want. Had they been educated during the preceding years and months in the spirit of workers' control, they would have known what to do: elect a committee in every plant that would begin by opening the company books; calculate for themselves the various companies' real manufacturing costs and rates of profit; establish a right of veto on hiring and firing and on any changes in the organization of the work; replace the foremen and overseers chosen by the boss with elected fellow workers (or with members of the crew taking turns at being in charge).

Such a committee would naturally come into conflict with the employers' authority on every level. The workers would have rapidly had to move from workers' control to workers' management. But this interval would have been used for denouncing the employers' arbitrariness, injustice, trickery, and waste to the whole country and for organizing local, regional, and national congresses of the strike and workers' control committees. These, in turn, would have furnished the striking workers with the instruments of organization and self-defense indispensable for tackling the bourgeois state and the capitalist class as a whole.

The French experience of May 1968 shows one of the main reasons why the demand for workers' control holds a prime position in a socialist strategy aimed at overthrowing capitalism in industrialized countries.

In order for united struggles around immediate demands, culminating in the general strike with occupation of the factories, to lead to the struggle for power, workers cannot initiate the most advanced form as something abstract, artificially introduced into their battle by the propaganda of revolutionary groups. *It has to grow out of the very needs of their fight.* The demand for workers' control (which involves challenging the power of the bourgeoisie at all levels and which tends to give birth, first in the factory, later in the country at large, to an embryonic workers' power counterposed to bourgeois power) is the best bridge between the struggle for immediate demands and the struggle for power.

There are two other reasons why this demand is so important at the present stage of capitalism and of the workers' anticapitalist struggle.

Capitalist concentration, the growing fusion of the monopolies with the bourgeois state, the ever-increasing role played by the state as guarantor of monopoly profits in imperialist countries, the growing tendency toward organization and "programming" of the economy under neocapitalism—all these main characteristics of today's economy transfer the center of gravity of the class struggle more and more from the plant and from the industrial branch to the economy as a whole.

In the "managed" capitalist economy, everything is tightly interlocked. An increase in wages is annulled by a rise in prices and taxes, or by indirect fiscal manipulations (for example, increasing social security taxes or reducing workers' benefits). Regional employment levels are upset by capitalist rationalization or by moving investments to other areas. Every effort is made to impose an "incomes policy," tying wages to productivity, but at the same time denying workers the means of accurately determining productivity.

The trade union movement cannot make any serious headway if it limits itself to periodic fights for adjusting or increasing wages. All the logic of the national (and international) class struggle brings the unions to *challenge the relationship* between prices and wages, wages and money, wage increases and increases in productivity, which the employers—and the governments in their pay—seek to impose on them as "inevitable." But this challenge cannot be mounted effectively, that is, in an informed way, unless the books are opened, unless secrecy in banking is done away with, unless the workers drag out and expose all the secret mechanisms of profit and of capitalist exploitation.

It goes without saying that, in the same spirit, workers' control must be exercised by the elected delegates of the workers *in view of the entire working class and the nation as a whole,* and not by few trade union leaders meeting in secret with a few employers' leaders. We shall come back to this, because the distinction is extremely important.

We are living in a period of more and more rapid technological change—the third industrial revolution. In the course of these changes, various branches of industry, various occupations, various jobs, disappear in the space of a few years. The capitalists constantly strive to subordinate the work of men to the demands of more and more expensive and more and more complex machines.

At the same time that manual labor is little by little disappearing from the factories, the number of technicians directly involved in production is decreasing. The level of training and education of workers is rapidly rising. The tendency toward general academic education up to the age of seventeen or eighteen, which is becoming more common, is a very clear indication of this.

But the more education workers have, the more inclined they are to fight for their rights—and the less will they stand for the fact that those who run society, the directors and the executives, often know less about production and the functioning of machines than the workers themselves, yet tell the workers what they must produce and how they should produce it. The hierarchical structure of the enterprise will weigh all the more heavily on workers as the gap in technical knowledge between workers and employers dwindles and becomes maintained only by an artificial monopoly on the details of the functioning of the enterprise as a whole, which the employer jealously keeps to himself.

Statistics on the causes of strikes, in Great Britain as well as in Italy, reveal that industrial conflicts less and less concern questions of wages per se and more and more concern the organization of the work, the process of production itself. Belgium is a little backward in this connection, but it will catch up soon enough!

The demand for workers' control, by involving the immediate right of inspection and veto for workers in a whole series of aspects of the life of the enterprise—while declining all responsibility for its management, as long as private property and the capitalist state are still in existence—thus answers a need born out of social and economic life itself. The structure of the enterprise no longer corresponds to the needs of the economy nor to the aspirations of the workers.

In this sense, this demand is eminently anticapitalist, because capitalism is not definitively characterized by low salaries nor even by a large number of unemployed workers (although periodic recessions remain inevitable and important). It is characterized by the fact that capital, that capitalists, rule men and machines. Challenging this right to rule, and counterposing another kind of power to it, means taking concrete actions to overthrow the capitalist system.

Participation, No! Control, Yes!

Experience teaches workers that their immediate and future fate depends on the functioning of the economy *as a whole*. They more and more conclude from this that it would be useless to fight just to defend their purchasing power or to raise their wages without concerning themselves with prices, with the cost-of-living index, with fiscal problems, with investments, and with the capitalist "rationalization" of the enterprises.

In fact, the capitalist class too often manages to "recoup"

wage increases by way of price increases or increases in direct or indirect taxes which are saddled on the workers.

It cheats at the escalator-clause game by faking the index or by applying the notorious "index policy" (price increases that avoid or skirt around those products selected for calculating the index).

It nibbles away at the power of trade unions by systematically removing investments and enterprises from those areas, thus re-creating unemployment (the Liège metal workers know a thing or two about this!). It always assures itself a reserve supply of labor by arranging the coexistence of rapid growth areas with areas that are underdeveloped or on the decline.

In short, it pulls all the strings of economic life and economic policy to defend its class interest.

If from now on workers are content with demanding wage increases, they are sure to be fleeced. This does not mean that struggles for wages and immediate demands are no longer needed or useless—indeed, the contrary is true. But it means that we must not limit ourselves to demanding for labor a larger portion of the new value it alone has created. It means that labor must challenge the functioning of capitalist economy as a whole.

In the old days, employers were content to defend their divine right to be "captain of the ship"—the sacred right of property. Every trade union demand that required some sort of interference in the management of the enterprise (to say nothing of the management of the economy as a whole) was rejected with indignation as "usurpation," a first step toward "confiscation," "theft."

But today the capitalists' arguments have become more flexible. From the argument of the divine right of employers, the bosses have prudently retreated to the argument of "defending the enterprise." They admit implicitly (and sometimes explicitly) that workers should "have something to say" on what happens in their enterprise, their locality, indeed the economic life of the country as a whole. (Certain international treaties, such as the one creating the European Economic Community or the Common Market, even circumspectly mention the right of workers to be "associated" with solving the problems of the international economy.)

This evolution in the thinking of the owners of industry obviously corresponds to an evolution in the relationship of forces. When capital was all-powerful and labor feeble and divided, the employers were able to rule by brute force. When capital becomes weak, because its system has entered the stage of incurable structural crisis on a world scale, and labor organizes and becomes considerably strengthened, more subtle means of domination have to be invented; otherwise, the whole system of domination runs the risk of disintegrating.

Thus we pass almost imperceptibly from the cynical doctrine of the "sacred rights of property" (that is, "might makes right") to the sugarcoated and hypocritical doctrine of "human relations." Thus is born the mirage of the "plant community" in which capital and labor should be associated "in due regard for their legitimate interests."

But the evolution of industrial doctrine is not simply a passive reflection of the evolution of the relationship of forces between social classes. It also reflects a tactical aim of the capitalists. This tactic seeks to involve the trade union organizations, or even representatives elected by the workers, in a *daily practice of class collaboration*. It is supposed to defuse the explosive character of the social conflict and immerse the working class in a permanent climate of conciliation and bargaining—a climate that blunts all militancy and all attempts to counterpose the organized power of the workers to the financial power of the capitalists.

An analogy can be made between the change in the bourgeoisie's attitude beginning in 1914, first with respect to the social democracy, then the trade union leadership, and now this evolution toward a more flexible attitude concerning the "exclusive and sacred rights of private property."

In all three cases, the bourgeoisie sought to weaken its class adversary by seduction, after having vainly tried to smash it by violence, repression, or economic pressure. Thus social democratic ministers have been "integrated" into coalition governments. Union leaders have been "integrated" into labor–

management committees. Why not "integrate" workers' delegates into factory councils "associated with management"?

The experience with co-determination in West Germany is especially revealing on this subject. It has been a powerful means of sapping the strength of the trade unions and militancy of the workers.

The workers had the illusion of having acquired "rights" within the plants; the plants became, in their eyes, to a certain extent "their" plants. But when a turn in the economic situation took place, they lost not only their bonuses (accorded by the capitalists in the period of great labor shortage), but even a part of their "normal" income, if not their jobs.

The capitalist plants once again revealed their nature: that is, a domain where the employer is the reigning monarch, leaving to his beloved workers only the illusion of an "association"—a booby-trapped "association."

De Gaulle invented nothing new with his "participation." Having to sell their labor power to employers who are free to hire them when the "profitability of the enterprise" requires it, workers remain proletarians. Having free command over men and machines (very often acquired with the money of others, that is to say, the state's), employers remain what they were before—capitalists.

Naïve pundits, advocates of class collaboration, retort: "You, wicked Marxists that you are, you preach class warfare to the bitter end, while the sweet and reasonable capitalists are ready to make concessions and to put their class struggle under wraps." Obviously, the reality is nothing like this.

Seeking to ensnare the workers' organizations and the workers in the trap of class collaboration, the employers pursue, from their side, a relentless class struggle. They keep their weapons intact: financial riches, capitalist ownership of industry and banks, subordination of economic life to their profit needs.

But, at the same time, they paralyze or seek to destroy the sole weapon workers have at their command: their capacity to organize and to launch a common struggle for their class interests, that is, operating workers' organizations for the benefit of workers. In looking to subordinate these organizations to "the general interest," while the economy is more than ever dominated by capitalist profit, the capitalists have obtained a resounding victory in the class struggle against the wage workers.

This is why trade unions and workers must refuse to make the slightest concession to the "team spirit" the employers spread around. Workers must systematically refuse to take the slightest particle of responsibility for the management of capitalist enterprises and the capitalist economy. Inspection in order to challenge, yes; participation in, or sharing of, management, no. That is where the interests of the workers lie.

Two arguments are often counterposed to this traditional position of the working class movement, which André Rénard was still strongly defending in "Vers le Socialisme par l'Action" (Toward Socialism Through Action). First of all, it is claimed that the workers, despite everything, have a stake in the survival of the enterprises: doesn't the disappearance of a large plant mean the loss of thousands of jobs, an increase in unemployment? This argument overlooks the fact that in the capitalist system competition and capitalist concentration are inevitable. In "associating" the fate of the workers with that of the plants, one not only risks tying them to the losers in a fierce battle. One also carries capitalist competition into the ranks of the working class, when all experience has shown that it is only by their class organization and their class unity that the workers have any kind of chance of defending themselves against the capitalist system. The same argument has no more validity when applied to regions. "We don't want socialization of cemeteries; that's why we have to join the bosses to save our (!) industries," certain trade unionists say.

The sad thing about this is that these industries are not at all "ours" but the capitalists', even if nine-tenths of the capital does come from state subsidies. These industries are subject to the laws of capitalist competition. To drag the workers onto that path is to subject them to the dictates of profit making and profit. It is to acquiesce to "rationalization," to increased productivity, to the speedup, to intensified exploitation of the workers. It also means accepting reductions in the number of jobs. From that to accepting layoffs, even reductions in pay, it is only a step.

As soon as you take the first step on this path, the employers' blackmail becomes all-powerful. In order to smash it, it is necessary to reject collaboration from the very beginning and start to enforce maintenance of the level of employment by structural anticapitalist reforms.

"Workers' Control" and "Participation" Are Exact Opposites

And then there is a more subtle argument. "In order to control, you have to be informed. Why not participate with the sole aim of gleaning information?" The sophist adds that there is no absolute distinction between participation and control.

The answer is very simple: everything depends on the objective to be achieved by the action and on the practical course that is followed. Is it a question of "participating" but not accepting the slightest responsibility for the management of the enterprise? But what opportunity should we wait for then, before revealing to all the workers the much touted "gleaned information"? Such a course is out of the question; the capitalist would refuse to play this game; the cards are stacked against them! Right! But if we didn't reveal this information, if we accepted secrecy, "cooperation," and bits of "co-responsibility," wouldn't we be playing the capitalist's game? In appearance, the difference between "participation" and "confrontation" is hard to establish; but all we have to do to realize the difference is to record, in each instance, the reaction of the employers, even the most "liberal" employers.

"Then you just want agitation for the sake of agitation, demanding the impossible," reply the defenders of the bourgeois order. Not at all. We want to replace one system with another, the class power of capital with the class power of the workers.

To this end we want the workers to have a very clear understanding of the thousands of ways the bourgeoisie, in the present system, has of deceiving them, exploiting them, fleecing them. That's why we demand workers' control. And if a radical change in the relationship of forces makes this demand realizable—for a brief transitional period—we would want, in order to realize this demand, that workers organize in such a way as to create, within the plants and the economy as a whole, a counterpower that would rapidly become the nucleus of a new state power.

"Participation" means: associating the workers with capital; accepting secret arrangements with capital, permanent secret meetings, economic "coordinating" committees, and even "control committees" (such as those in gas and electricity), where the workers actually control nothing at all but become co-responsible, in the eyes of public opinion, for the exorbitant rates charged and for the fat profits of the monopolies.

"Workers' control" means: full and complete disclosure; discussion of all "secrets" of the enterprise and the economy in front of general assemblies of the workers; baring all the intricate machinery of the capitalist economy; "illegal" interference of the workers in all the prerogatives of property, management, and the state. This in itself signifies birth of a new kind of power, infinitely more democratic and more just than that of bourgeois "democracy," a power in which all the workers (eighty-five percent of the active population of this country) together would make the decisions that determine their destiny.

The CSC's Position: Participation, Yes, But . . .

On several occasions the CSC (Confederation des Syndicats Chrétiens—Confederation of Christian Unions) has tried to bend its efforts toward the problem of the nature of the plant. In 1964 it had already devoted a report to the problem. The report, "Responsible for the Future," presented at its twenty-fourth congress in October 1968, goes back to that subject at great length. The swan song of Gus Cool, as president of the CSC, was precisely the presentation of that report to the congress. A special resolution on "The Reform of the Plant" was presented to the same congress.

All these documents bear the seal of the same contradiction. The CSC holds a certain doctrine: class collaboration. Its rank-and-file activists, and especially its members, engage in a practice and are subjected to an experience which, whether one likes it or not, is called class struggle. What the leadership of the CSC is trying as hard as possible to do is to reconcile these two irreconcilable elements.

When the leaders of the CSC describe what the workers go through in the enterprise system—which they don't want to call by its proper name, the *capitalist* system, so that they have to resort to all kinds of meaningless and innocuous euphemisms, such as "today's enterprises," "present-day enterprises," "the modern system," etc.—they often put their finger on their members' sorest spots.

Plants are often closed. (Without sufficient grounds, adds the resolution of the twenty-fourth congress. But "insufficient grounds" from what point of view? From the point of view of the stockholder who wants to protect his interest?) There are mass layoffs. Even in good times, unemployment reappears because production, which has increased, is accomplished by a decreasing number of workers. This unemployment stands to increase still more, because of the "successive waves of automation, the continuous installation of computers, or very pronounced mechanization." The individuality of the man on the job is more and more threatened by "new techniques of organization, of production and management." The hopes of the younger generation are cruelly dashed by the way in which economic life is developing. And so forth.

Those are contentions which undoubtedly would meet with the approval of the majority of the 900,000 members of the CSC. They live through this, daily or periodically, and feel it in the marrow of their bones. It is not necessary to add any lengthy discourse to explain these elementary truths: in the factory, it is the capitalist who is in command. His profits come before the interests of the workers and of "human people."

What Cool, Keulers, Dereau, and Houthuys—the new president of the CSC—did not add, but which nonetheless is of very great importance, is that these wounds result neither from the bad will of the employers nor from lack of mutual understanding between employers and workers, but from the implacable logic of the capitalist system.

If the employer does not subordinate the operation of the

enterprise to the imperatives of profit making, he will realize less profit than his competitors; he will receive less credit; he will be able to accumulate less capital; he will not be able to keep up with the latest techniques. At the heightened tempo of today's competition between capitalists, nationally and internationally, he would soon be liquidated by his competitors.

It follows, therefore, that it is impossible to eliminate these sore spots and at the same time maintain the capitalist system. "Humanizing" production relationships while maintaining private property and the capitalist economy is like wanting the animals of the jungle to stop eating one another while maintaining the jungle itself, with all that it implies.

Listen to the worthy Mr. Cool as he sheds a tear on the altar of the "economy of service":

> We are really at the service of the worker, at the service of his real happiness, and doesn't our era prove that happiness consists in "being" as well as "seeing"? Happiness, that is to say, is not only thinking of one's self but also of others in the world who are hungry, who not only know poverty but who die of starvation . . . ? Don't we attach too much importance to money, to material well-being, even to the extent of sacrificing to them our freedom as producers and consumers, our freedom as human persons? Doesn't material well-being feed a growing selfishness, to the detriment of the solidarity that unites us, not only with the workers in our plants, in our community, in our country, but with all workers, with citizens throughout the world, especially those who are bent beneath the yoke of injustice?

A beautiful flight of eloquence—even if we find the reproach aimed at Belgian workers that they attach "too much importance to money" in rather bad taste, considering the average level of wages (especially for youths, women, and the less skilled, who are especially numerous in the ranks of the CSC).

But where does this "growing selfishness" come from, if not from the sacrosanct "free enterprise" system, which has elevated to the level of a religious dogma the principle of "every man for himself"? Can private ownership of the means of production, the market economy, lead to anything but competition? Can competition, in a money economy, lead to anything but the desire to obtain the maximum income? The whole social climate, the whole educational system, all the mass media, the entire economic life, don't they inculcate in everyone, day and night, that what matters most, above all else, is to "climb the ladder of success"—if you have to step on the necks of others to do it?

That celebrated "freedom of the producer"—how can it be achieved under the iron rod of capital, which produces for profit and not for the self-realization of the human being? That celebrated "freedom of the consumer"—how can that be achieved under the rule of the advertising industry, behind which lurk the ten financial groups that control the economic life of the nation?

Gus Cool, Keulers, Dereau, and Houthuys don't want to abolish private ownership of the means of production. They don't want to get rid of capitalism. They don't want to eliminate national and international control of the economy by holding companies, trusts, and other monopolies. They don't want anyone to touch competition or the market economy, those beauties of the jungle.

But how will "participation" by the unions in the management of plants based on profit prevent shutdowns when profits are threatened or disappear? How will "participation" by the unions in the management of the economy prevent the concentration of enterprises, when these are precisely the result of competition? How will "participation" by the unions reestablish the "freedom of the producer and the consumer," when in the framework of capitalist economy, which is more and more automated, man more and more becomes simply an appendage of the machine, and the consumer more and more becomes a victim of television commercials, more and more manipulated?

The leaders of the CSC are inextricably entangled in a web of theoretical contradictions. They will not be able to get out of it, except by verbal gymnastics which serve only to reflect the lack of respect they have for their members.

But among these members, the number of those who will grasp these contradictions will not stop growing. To the extent that the members of the CSC experience class struggles, experience the contradictions of the capitalist system, they are brought to the point of asking themselves questions about the nature of that system, questions that the CSC heads seek only to dodge. And the more the members grasp the nature of the system, the more they will understand that their interests and their convictions demand that, far from collaborating with it or "participating" in it, they have to overthrow it and replace it with a Socialist system based on the collective self-management and planning of the workers.

In France, this idea has made enormous progress among the members of the CFDT (Confédération Française et Démocratique du Travail—French Democratic Confederation of Labor) during the last few years. This progress was further accelerated during the last few months, after the bracing experience of the May 1968 general strike. We can bet that Cool would like to avoid, at any price, such an explosion in Belgium, lest the members of the CSC draw similar conclusions from analogous experiences.

After having denounced the innumerable "violations of the human person" of which the capitalist economic system (excuse me, the present economic system) is guilty, the leadership of the CSC is satisfied with demanding passage of a law on bookkeeping records, extension of the rights of the plant councils, and constitution of a labor–management study commission with a view to reforming the plant. The mountain labored and brought forth a mouse—and the poor little animal seems pretty sickly and unlikely to survive.

Let's pass over the farce of the labor–management study commission for a reform of the enterprise that would eliminate all the sore spots mentioned above. Does anyone believe for a single minute that the employers can accept keeping surplus personnel on the payroll, given the laws of competition? But all the "progress" they boast of, including the famous "technological progress," has the exact aim of eliminating these workers. We can bet that the results of these talk-fests will not be the curing of the sore spots but the adoption of lots of bandages and sugar-coated pills, so that the patient won't suffer too much. That, of course, is right in line with the noblest of charitable motives, but it eliminates neither the ills nor their more and more frequent appearance.

The law on bookkeeping records constitutes a useful reform,

on condition that it serve a policy of workers' control. If not, it represents only a measure for rationalization of capitalist economy, which the workers should not get involved with, and which will, moreover, wind up being used against them.

But, of course, workers' control is not what the CSC has in mind.

The CSC talks a lot about layoffs and "groundless" shutdowns. But wouldn't the first thing to demand, in line with this, be the opening of the company's books? And not only those of the employers who went bankrupt, but those of all the employers, especially since the coal crisis taught us how holding companies and financial groups can manipulate their accounting procedures so that losses appear in all sectors that claim (and receive) public subsidies, while profits appear in all the sectors that "rely on private initiative," and where they want prices to rise on the stock exchange? Since these groups balance off, on an overall basis, "profit and loss" of the companies they control, it is therefore necessary to open the books of all these companies.

How can we determine which shutdowns are "justified" and which are not, without opening the books and eliminating secrecy in banking? But doubtless the leaders of the CSC don't like to "violate the rights of property," that is, of capital. They actually prefer, regardless of what they say, that capital constantly violate those famous "rights of the human person" that they do so much talking about—except when it comes to drawing some conclusions about the demands necessary to gain those rights.

The FGTB: Differences Between Theory and Practice

The problem of workers' control was reintroduced into doctrine of the FGTB by the "Rénard Tendency" during the fifties. It ripened in the aftermath of the great strike of 1960–1, the culminating point in the radicalization of the workers of this country since the 1932–6 period.

Inasmuch as "participation" is in fashion, and inasmuch as the CSC has several times taken up "reform of the enterprise," the FGTB cannot in all decency remain silent on the subject. It is, therefore, preparing a special congress on the problem of workers' control—the preparations for which are taking place, unfortunately, in secrecy, as if they were of no interest to trade unionists as a whole! The discussions on this merit very careful attention.

The FGTB obviously finds itself at an ideological crossroads. For a good ten years now, a more and more distinct cleavage has appeared between its theory, which is becoming more and more radical (at least in Wallonia as well as in Brussels and in certain Flemish regions), and its practice, which keeps turning to the right in Flanders and has also begun to deteriorate in Wallonia during the past few years.

For a problem as clearly defined and of such burning importance as workers' control, we must know if this doctrine will be interpreted as class collaboration in practice or if a new radicalization in theory will force practice to bend to the Left, as was the case, in part, between 1956 and 1962.

From the point of view of theory, all co-responsibility in capitalist management is excluded. We are thus talking only about control. When the demand for nationalization of the electric plants was abandoned in exchange for the establishment of a control committee, a great deal of care was taken to distinguish the latter from the "management committee," which was reserved for employers only.

Control under a capitalist system; co-determination under a Socialist system: that was the praiseworthy principle that was invoked. Let us see, however, how it worked in practice.

By being satisfied with a sham control, which respects the secrecy of company books and which, moreover, introduces a new secrecy in the relationships between union leaders and union members, one can in fact serve as a cover for capitalist management. It is a participation that doesn't dare call itself "participation," but which in practice is close to that principle of class collaboration.

Thus, after several years of the "committee of control of electricity," André Rénard and the comrades who led the Gazelco sector realized that they controlled nothing at all; they were running the risk of getting a capitalist management off the hook, in the eyes of the workers and consumers—a capitalist management that was more than ever imbued with the profit motive and not at all with the spirit of the "common good." They therefore began by demanding *real control over the calculation of cost prices,* which is inconceivable without opening the books and without an on-the-spot confrontation (right in the plant) of the employers' accounting figures with the economic and financial reality as directly perceived by the workers and technicians. They added to that, moreover, exact demands, calling for a kind of veto right over rate-fixing, investments, and rationalization.

None of this was obtained. They were satisfied with stretching the "Round Table" agreements to cover the gas business, at the time of the renewal of the agreement in 1965. As for the Gazelco sector, the union once again very opportunely put forth the demand for nationalization of the electric companies, but without ever succeeding in getting the FGTB to wage a genuine campaign on this demand.

Allocating the distribution of natural gas from the Netherlands to private industry compounded the scandal of profit from a public service monopoly going to the gas and electric trusts. But the FGTB put this scandal on ice. It doesn't even conduct an educational campaign any more for its members and for the public on the theme of nationalization under workers' control.

At the end of the brochure that it devoted in 1962 to nationalization of the electric companies, the Gazelco sector wrote: "Our joining the institutions of the 'Round Table,' the management committee and the control committee thus has a definite meaning. In a capitalist system the trade-union organizations have, in fact, to fulfill the mission of control. That mission cannot always lead them toward associating themselves with private management of industry and toward sharing the responsibility for it."

The authors of this brochure themselves call attention to the contradiction present in this doctrine, in this era. Actually, they do not reject every program of rationalization, but state: "We cannot lose sight of the fact that, in a capitalist system, rationalization is almost always accomplished at the expense of the working class." They are then led to add (in bold-face type):

"Also, never will we permit workers, manual or intellectual, to become victims of rationalization measures."

Several years later, the FGTB Metalworkers Federation was confronted with an analogous problem. Having gone astray in agreeing that the resolution of regional problems—independent of the class nature of the economy—be given priority, this federation decided to enter the Comité de Concertation de la Politique Sidérurgique (Iron and Steel Industry Policy Coordinating Committee).

It was inevitable that this committee would engage in rationalization. The FGTB trade union movement thus accepted associating itself with rationalization measures. Practice as well as theory had slipped a notch as far as the excellent principles of 1959 and 1962 were concerned. They *did* permit rationalization measures that victimized the workers (that is, a big reduction in employment). They were satisfied with demanding palliative social welfare measures, so that the workers wouldn't suffer too much.

Their practice slid from workers' control toward co-determination and that under the worst conditions: co-determination of a sector in relative decline, where the problem of cutting down employment was posed. Will theory follow practice? This is one of the things we shall learn at the special congress of the FGTB.

This is also one of the tasks of the militants of the FGTB: to prevent the introduction into trade union theory of the disastrous confusion between workers' control and co-determination (or participation). The latter transforms trade union organizations from instruments for the defense of the interests of the workers against the bosses into instruments for the defense of capitalist enterprises (including interest against those of the workers). If trade union doctrine continues to reject co-determination at the plant and industrial branch level, the same doesn't hold true, and hasn't for a long time, for its practice as far as the economy as a whole is concerned.

In the Central Economic Council, in the National Committee for Economic Expansion; in the Programming Bureau, and in numerous similar bodies, representatives of the unions amicably sit side by side with employers' representatives and together draw up analyses, diagnoses, syntheses, and programs. Sometimes their formulations do not agree. Often, they arrive at common conclusions.

An atmosphere of mutual understanding and collaboration—not to mince words, class collaboration—stems from this. It is this atmosphere that enabled Louis Major to exclaim, in the speech ending his career as general secretary of the FGTB (to start a new one as king's minister): "The relationships between unions and employers in Belgium are the best in the world."

We do not believe that knowing whether to sit on this or that committee is what matters. What is important is the *reason* you sit there, and what you do in practice. To take a seat for the purpose of gathering information useful for the day to day trade union struggle; to denounce short-changing and abuses on the part of employers; to bare the structural deficiencies of the capitalist mode of production, so flagrant and so visible throughout the country; to improve the quality of, the audience for, and the forcefulness of the agitation conducted among the workers—we do not see what would be wrong in such a tactic of challenge, to us a fashionable term.

But that is obviously not the tactic of the FGTB representatives. They don't challenge anything; they collaborate.

Speaking at the study weekend held by the André Rénard Foundation November 26–7, 1964, at Ronchiennes, Jacques Yerna commented about the Programming Bureau: "We have let neocapitalism absorb planning, just as it has absorbed so many other things in our program; and instead of going a step further, of forcing acceptance of our concept, the trade union movement was satisfied to pick what suited it from what was offered, and to reject the rest."

Note that at the regional level in Wallonia, the FGTB leadership is now running the risk of repeating the same experience but on a much bigger scale, and with repercussions that may be even more disastrous.

Haven't they associated themselves with the capitalists of the Wallonian Economic Council to formulate jointly all kinds of "regional programs," programs that cannot help but respect and enforce the capitalist profit motive? That is a far cry from "forcing acceptance of our concept." They are no longer even prepared for "rejecting the rest." They are content, humbly content, to beg for a minimum agreement with the "Wallonian" employers before defending the interests of X trust or holding company against Y trust or holding company, which is accused of favoring "Flanders." "Our concept" of structural anticapitalist reforms, especially the principal idea of seizing control of the economic life of the country from the holding companies, no longer serves as a guide to action.

When they study the documents on the subject of workers' control that someday will have to be submitted to them, FGTB activists will have to avoid three dangers:

1) That of seeking to adapt theory to practice, that is, of developing theory around, and accepting as doctrine, the concept of co-determination and participation. We shouldn't jump to the conclusion that such a thing is impossible. There is a temptation—especially among the Flemish leaders of the FGTB —to systematically align themselves with the positions of the CSC. And in other countries, such as West Germany, there are examples to show that an entire generation of trade union militants can become bewildered in the face of the confusion to which "participation" gives rise.

2) That of "whistling in the dark," that is, throwing a veil of modesty over the contradiction between theory and practice, and being satisfied with theoretical tinkering while doing nothing to change the practice (which obviously implies that such theory would be condemned to remain a dead letter).

3) That of deliberate confusion, which would consist in mixing "confrontationist" and "participationist" formulas and objectives, under the pretext of "unity," "realism," and "comradely compromise." This will only emasculate theory still more and accentuate the slide towards generalized class collaboration and intensified integration into the capitalist system.

FGTB activists, who are conscious of the workers' interests and of the crisis of the system under which we live in this country, will have to counterpose to the above three dangers a concrete program of workers' control, which, taking off from the immediate concerns of the masses and from the problems the country faces, tries to raise to a higher level the total challenge to the capitalist economy and the unitary state (that is, a centralized government which rides roughshod over the interests of the two nationalities combined in the Belgian state—the

Walloons and the Flemings). This is the only realistic possibility for assuring the future of the working class.

I must insist on the fact that the adoption of an action program would be just as important as the adoption of a program of demands going in that direction. Such an action program would signify a willingness to break with the practice of class collaboration and would outline a plan for phased mobilization of all the energies and all the fighting potential of the workers, with the perspective of winning workers' control by any and all means necessary.

Six Propositions in Conclusion

How can the theme of workers' control be integrated into real struggles waged by the workers? How can agitation for workers' control contribute to stimulating the combativity of the toiling masses, to raising their level of class consciousness, to triggering struggles that go beyond the framework of the capitalist system, that is, contribute to creating a prerevolutionary situation?

I have tried to answer these questions first by an analysis of the problem in general, refuting the current objections to this strategy and critically examining the timidity of the CSC and the FGTB in dealing with, if not a genuine struggle for workers' control, at least the problems raised by this slogan. Obviously, I don't pretend to close the question in this way. I want to set off a real debate. I hope especially that the rank and file, union activists, genuine representatives of the workers in the plants, will participate in this discussion.

The more that workers' control is discussed among the workers the more will controversy be aroused and the more numerous will become the blue-collar workers, the white-collar workers, and the technicians who will enlarge the horizon of their perspectives beyond the limits of reformism and neo-reformism.

But theoretical discussion, abstract discussion (it makes little difference if it is directed toward grasping the question as a whole) is not enough to stimulate the kind of perspective-changing discussion we refer to above. Something else is needed, a complementary factor, in the way of practical proposals, and I am anxious to end this series of articles with these proposals.

They must all correspond with the criteria set forth in the beginning of our analysis; they must be based on the immediate needs of the workers; they must be of such nature that capitalism cannot integrate them into a normal functioning of its system; they must thus create a situation of dual power which will tend toward a global confrontation between capital and labor; they must enlarge the workers' practical experience as to the fundamental nature of the capitalist system and the ways in which it can be challenged in its entirety, that is, they must prepare the masses to approach this challenge under optimum conditions of consciousness and organization.

1. Open the Books

Innumerable sources—most of them non-Marxist, indeed distinctly bourgeois in origin—attest to the impossibility of relying on employers' statistics to learn the truth about the economic life of the country (as well as all capitalist countries). The employers' balance sheets, their financial statements, their declarations of inheritance, falsify economic reality. These falsifications are not manufactured gratuitously. They have very definite ends in view, whether it be cheating on taxes; understating profits in order to justify refusing a wage increase; or deceiving the public about the real facts behind a particular trade union demand.

Every time negotiations with the employers are opened, whether they be on wage increases, an increase in productivity, or on the economic consequences of a trade union demand, we must routinely reply: "We refuse to discuss this blindfolded. Lay the cards on the table! Open your books."

The value of this demand as an anticapitalist structural reform, that is, as a transitional demand, will be all the greater if three conditions are added to it:

First, opening of the company's books must be done publicly and not be limited to a closed meeting with a few trade union leaders, whose tendency toward good fellowship with the bosses is well known. Secondly, analysis of the balance sheets and of the bookkeeping system should be facilitated by the adoption of legal measures for uniformity in accounting procedures. Finally, and especially, verification of the balance sheets and general accounts need not necessarily be made on the basis of the figures, but must be effected at the plants themselves, so that the mass of workers are in on this examination.

It is easy to doctor a balance sheet by undervaluing a supply of raw materials. But this value, although it has disappeared from the figures, cannot remain hidden from the workers who receive, warehouse, maintain, and regularly check this same merchandise. The objection is often heard that workers would be incapable of verifying balance sheets. We shall soon publish in *La Gauche* some of the Campaign for Workers' Control, that will facilitate study of balance sheets, and of capitalist accounting procedures by workers' representatives. Generally, these objections are greatly exaggerated by those who wish property "rights" to remain untouched. They are the identical twin of objections that used to be advanced by reactionary regimes to justify their denial of universal suffrage: the workers are too "ignorant," "badly educated," "unprepared to assume this grave responsibility," etc.

2. Right of Veto Over Layoffs and Plant Shutdowns

The major motivating force behind the workers' struggles for the past few years has without doubt been fear of unemployment, layoffs, and reduction in the volume of employment, in Wallonia and in many Flemish regions.

The reclassification and occupational retraining program has proved a failure. It has not been able to prevent a rapid decline in the level of employment in the target districts. As far as industrial reconversion is concerned, experience teaches that you can rely neither on big business nor on its unitary state, neither on various bourgeois governments nor on coalitions with the bourgeoisie, to make reconversion operational.

In these conditions, the workers more and more have the feeling that it is wrong for an economic system, for which they do not have the slightest responsibility, to make them bear the brunt of the costs of industrial changes. To obtain an effective guarantee of the volume of employment, what the workers must demand from now on is an effective veto right over layoffs and shutdowns.

This concrete application of the principle of workers' control involves the forcible reopening of plants shut down by their owners and the management of these plants by the workers themselves. It also involves making funds available, at the expense of the capitalist class as a whole, to enable these plants to operate during the transitional phase, before newly created modern plants, publicly owned and administered under workers' control, outdo these old rattletraps.

Our comrade Pierre Le Greve proposed a bill along this line when he was a deputy [in parliament]. It is useful to come back to this every time a shutdown or a layoff of workers occurs— not to encourage any illusions that that particular item of workers' control can be obtained through electoral or parliamentary means, but to stimulate the critical awareness of the workers and oblige the leaders of the mass organizations of the working class, which are making the demand, to take a position on these proposals.

3. Workers' Control of the Organization of Work in the Plant

The hierarchic structure of the plant seems more and more anachronistic, to the extent that the level of technical and cultural qualifications of the workers is raised.

In the most streamlined, modern industrial plants, where a high percentage of personnel is composed of technicians with middle or high level technical education, this anachronism is especially striking. But even in industry as a whole the growing complexity of production processes results, for example, in teams of maintenance workers often understanding the exact mechanics of manufacturing, and the bottlenecks that periodically arise, better than highly placed engineers—not to mention members of the board of directors!

To the many on-the-job conflicts that stem from the hierarchic character of the relationships between blue- and white-collar workers on the one hand, department heads and foremen on the other, must be added the stresses in the workers' life occasioned by the more and more frequent changes in organization of the work.

Changes in techniques often do away with trades and skills acquired through hard work and years of experience. Speedup increases workers' nervous tension and fatigue, and adds to the number of occupational accidents. The principal victims of these changes cannot be satisfied with the modest right to make suggestions, accorded them by legislation presently on the books, in the plant councils and the health and safety committees. They have to demand overall workers' control of organization of the work, a control that involves not only the right to be informed in advance of all proposed changes, but also the right to be able to oppose and prevent these changes.

When workers adopt the habit of answering each incident that set them against a department head or a foreman with the demand for workers' control, a big step will have been taken in the direction of overturning hierarchical relationships and of replacing the "heads" by workers elected by their fellows, recallable at any time, and responsible only to the rank and file, not to the boss.

4. Workers' Control of the Consumer Price Index

In Belgium we live under the system of a sliding wage scale, that is, automatic adjustment of wages to every increase in the official cost-of-living index above a certain threshold, which varies according to the parity agreements (generally, 2.5 or two percent). This system partially protects the workers against the erosion of the purchasing power of their wages and salaries. This guarantee is only partial for reasons explained many times in this newspaper. In this article it is sufficient to demonstrate one of these reasons: the lack of the representativeness and honesty in the retail price index.

The index is, of course, put out by the government. And the government is only too often tempted to give a bit of a push in the direction of its "index policy" (i.e., it's cheating), not only to please the employers, but also and especially to space the periodic adjustment of civil service workers' salaries—which weigh heavily on the budget.

It is true that the price commission has the right not to recognize the honesty of the index, to oppose this or that decision of the government concerning prices or price increases. But this right of opposition carries with it no power to enforce any changes.

A genuine workers' control over the consumer price index—an indispensable measure to efficiently protect the purchasing power of the workers against the permanent rise in the cost of living—would therefore involve some power of the trade union opposition to act (right of veto) on the government index. It also involves this control being instituted at the bottom, where teams of workers and housewives would regularly determine the real price increases in different parts of the country.

5. Elimination of Secrecy in Banking

Fiscal manipulation has been one of the bonanzas for all those who have claimed to rationalize management of the capitalist economy of this country in the course of the last fifteen years. This is reflected in one of the most striking swindles of the system, a swindle that results in wage and salary earners paying, at the same time, the major part of both indirect and direct taxes.

The proliferation of legal measures, fiscal reforms, administrative controls, is admittedly unable to eliminate this flagrant injustice. Elimination of secrecy in banking and introduction of workers' control on all financial operations, would quickly put an end to this scandal.

Actually, in the private property system, confidence between bankers and large depositors never prevails to the point that vast financial operations can take place without leaving any written traces. A workers' control over bank records—especially one exercised by bank employees devoted to the people—would quickly ferret out most of the guilty.

6. Workers' Control Over Investments

One of the most striking characteristics of neocapitalism is that there is a socialization of a growing part of production and overhead costs, a large part of long term investment has been financed by the state in the course of the last twenty years. The study of successive balance sheets of the Société Nationale de Crédit à l'Industrie (National Industrial Credit Society) is particularly instructive on this question. Sidmar as well as Chertal have in large part been financed with the help of public funds. It will be the same for the rationalization proposed by the Cockerill-Ougrée-Providence-Espérance merge.

But while an increasing part of the funds come from the pocket of the taxpayer (that is, mostly from the pocket of the workers), profits and stocks and bonds are not the only things that remain in the private domain. The right of decision on the regional distribution of investments and on their destination also remains in the private domain.

To demand workers' control over these investments is thus to demand not co-responsibility of union leaders for capitalist management of industry, but the right of union veto over these investments, as to the geographical apportionment, form, and destination projected by the employers.

It is clear that this kind of control opens the way to formulating a developmental plan for the economy as a whole, based on priorities established by the workers themselves. The MPW (Mouvement Populaire Wallon—Walloon People's Movement) used to speak about this a great deal, when the "Wallonian People's Plan" was being discussed. But this "plan" was discarded along with a lot of other things when André Rénard's successors trod the path leading to their reabsorption by the PSB (Parti Socialiste de Belgique—Socialist Party of Belgium).

The campaign for workers' control forms a whole which, without neglecting the day to day problems of the workers, acts in a definite direction: accentuating their distrust of the capitalist system, increasing their confidence in their own strength, and resolving to take their economic future into their own hands—by their own anticapitalist action.

A Slogan or a Movement?

It is no accident that the first two articles in this section come from Western European writers. What is a slogan in North America is a movement in Western Europe: workers' control in nearly every country there is a demand which at least part of the labor movement sees as critical, and it is an essential part of the European Socialist tradition. There is no such tradition, and no such experience, in the United States and Canada.

Yet this book is written for Americans and Canadians, and we must begin, however tentatively, to explore possibilities on this side of the Atlantic. David Tornquist's essay suggests some of the lessons we may draw from the European experience, past and present; in particular he argues that a North American workers' control movement should develop outside the structure of organized labor (though not wholly independent of it). Jack Rasmus, in the subsequent article, places the notion of workers' control in the context of present-day United States economic developments. Basing his argument on an extensive analysis of contemporary corporate and governmental policies, he foresees a growing potential for demands by which workers can extend their power over management.

Workers' Management: The Intrinsic Issues

David Tornquist

Advocating workers' management in the American context is something like taking a free fall. We say there is nowhere else to go, and yet we haven't located the destination very precisely and don't know the road. The workers' management solution—or posing of the problem—commends itself strongly to those seeking genuinely democratic answers to crucial questions of our society, but the workers' management arrangement isn't a way station or terminus on the path of predetermined historical development, and no surging social forces of the moment are impelling its creation. Advocacy of industrial democracy, then, is a bold salient that may have no supporting forces behind it. If though, as I think, industrial democracy is no less than a new dimension of economic life, then perhaps it is natural for advocacy to be the precursor rather than the outcome of a broad movement in that direction. I suspect that whatever aspects of the democratic ideal are eventually achieved in the workplace will depend rather exactly on an astute and resolute advocacy. The opinions that follow represent a diffident effort to make this advocacy sound more realistic to my own ear.

I want to use three stepping stones in stating my view. These were separate strands in my reading that began to twine. My most urgent interest was in the problem of Yugoslav workers' management, particularly the intramural difficulties of moving from workers' management as an institutional setup to management by the workers as a sociological actuality. As a sidetrack from this concern, I began to read Antonio Gramsci on the factory committees in Italy following World War I. Finally, and perhaps arbitrarily, Louis Adamic's chronicle of the 1928–38 period *My America* serves as a reminder that thirty years ago a man who hewed close to the bedrock of the American tradition could regard industrial democracy as the resolution of what he called America's "basic incongruity," the discrepancy between the democratic principles proclaimed in political life and the authoritarian principalities where people go to work.

Something more can be learned from Yugoslav workers' management if we look at it through a narrower glass than we usually aim in that direction. Let us forget all the whys and wherefores, and concentrate solely on the ways and means. Ignore all the laws and pronouncements that have been sluiced out in giddy succession over the last twenty years, and register what has actually been happening in the workplace. Doing this, we find that whether or not workers' management can in the long run provide the solutions expected of it, in the short and medium run it manifests itself overwhelmingly in the form of outstanding problems, dilemmas, and compromises. I don't mean to deny those important elements of the Yugoslav context that impede the progress of workers' management. The country's economic situation, for example, is fraught with overriding urgencies; there may, as some assert, be much ineptness and inexperience in the professional management of the Yugoslav enterprise; and the Yugoslav Communists do maintain, I think, a crucial ambiguity about the place of spontaneity in democratic process. But some of the agonies being discussed, confronted, or significantly evaded—as the case may be—in Yugoslavia today derive directly from the workers' management idea. Here is at least a partial list:

1. Premise: management and administration are professional specializations essential to the effective and efficient operation of any organization. What principles, then, are to govern the division of authority and responsibility between the professional management staff and the management bodies elected by the workers?

2. How can the internal goals of workers' management (independent initiative, worker identity, morale, disalienation, participation, etc.) be aligned with the external goals of the market-oriented business, of the social service agency, or of the public corporation?

3. Since the individual worker may be little affected in his attitudes by the existence of a workers' council at the front-office level, can managerial authority itself be decentralized enough to give rank-and-file workers access to real decision making?

4. Indeed, how much of workers' management can be direct, in the form of individual worker participation, and how much must be performed indirectly, through representation and delegation?

5. Since regularity and dependability of individuals are still necessary and cannot be taken for granted in the workers' management context, what are the sources and kinds of discipline appropriate to that context?

6. What guidelines should the worker-managers follow in deciding on assignment of corporate income to wages and salaries, enterprise community projects, and reinvestment?

7. Assuming fair material remuneration to be necessary as an incentive and a sound basis for intramural financial relations, what criteria should guide the workers in setting wages and salaries, in awarding bonuses, and in distributing whatever other money is set aside for remuneration?

8. What is the best compromise between technological dictates on the one hand, and human needs and relations on the other?

9. How much is work itself subject to humanizing changes that will not defeat the efficiency that comes from repetitiveness, routine, and programming?

10. It is self-evident that the workers' management system requires superb communication systems in both directions, upward and downward, but how can the completeness, objectivity, and accuracy of the information conveyed be guaranteed at a permissible cost?

11. What forms of organized intramural education can hasten the evolution toward more effective workers' management?

12. How can outside guidance be insured and outside interference avoided?

13. Given the indefiniteness and instability of the organizational framework in the initial stages of workers' management, ways have to be found of resolving conflicts and removing obstacles raised by trade unions, technocrats, bureaucrats, careerists, divergent political viewpoints, etc.

14. How can the democratic decision-making mechanism be streamlined to meet the need for enterprise responsiveness and maneuverability?

15. What place shall be given to individual autonomy, creativity, and dissent in the workers' management scheme, since it manifestly could increase, rather than decrease the over-organization that already prevails?

16. Finally, there is the broader question of the kind of society in which workers' management can flourish and in which the business entity can either broaden its purview to include overall social goals or can be induced to serve them.

I hope no further elaboration is necessary to demonstrate that this list does not bear a specific Yugoslav imprint, that these issues are inherent in the idea of industrial democracy. I submit that they are the challenges of that new dimension of economic life that workers' management opens up. Experts in American management techniques, even those sympathetic to the industrial democracy idea, advise the Yugoslavs to concern themselves less with these questions and institute tried-and-true management solutions that insure greater business efficiency. And in Yugoslav discussions of self-management theory quotations from Marx, Engels, and Lenin have been replaced by references to Gouldner, Roethlisberger, Simon, Lewin, and Likert. But the Yugoslavs are not taking over these theories as they stand. They have two very sound reasons for refusing to do so. Both are bound up with the inescapable evidence that both the theoretical and the practical development of workers' management is to be a lengthy and tortuous process. One of their reasons is the doubt that there is any point farther along the road—when the country is more prosperous, say, or the economy better balanced—where these issues will be easier to resolve if they are not grappled with now. The other is that workers' management involves an evolution of attitudes and social relations that takes place only in the attempt to make the system work.

There seems to be good reason to say in general that industrial democracy is not just a substitute system that brings large human rewards in immediate return for small readjustments and minor writeoffs such as some loss of efficiency, but is a protracted process in which the ideal of management by the workers offers itself up only through encumbered approaches. Industrial democracy, then, is not so much a set of answers in the back of the book to problems already stated, but a posing of new problems that have not been solved at all. Moreover, these problems are typically open-ended. The situations in which they are raised will offer more or less possibility of solving them, but there is a niggardliness about the problems themselves. They are governed by numerous specific, general, and cross constraints. They are apparently dynamic and perennial issues, subject to current resolution, but unyielding to permanent settlement. They embody the obstacles and opportunities of any thoroughgoing effort to set up industrial democracy. Indeed, to go even further, I suggest that if we are seeking the universality in the workers' management idea, we will come closest by defining it in terms of its issues, that is, in some such list as I have given. I take this to be the lesson of Yugoslav workers' management as it celebrates its twentieth anniversary. This view admittedly lacks the appeal of visions of immediate liberation and does not lend itself to sloganeering, but I think it does offer a sound footing for practical analysis and theoretical exploration.

How but with a long sigh can a Vermonter react in mid-January to postcards showing Mexican beaches? I have come to respond in much that same way to definitions of industrial democracy in terms of its noble goals or its promising formal structures. I favor the definition in terms of its characteristic issues because it seems to offer a next step. For if we give the name industrial democracy to what happens in the workplace when these issues are raised, to the evolution and exploration that alone can resolve them democratically, then we are justified in asking whether raising these issues directly in the workplace is not a way of making industrial democracy. It is Gramsci's fundamental idea that socialism could be made by raising issues in the workplace that makes him relevant here.[1]

Gramsci wrote about the factory committees at a time when there was still considerable New Left spirit in Old Left thinking, but for me his Marxism and his Leninism are still heavy-handed. In his scheme the political is so totally absorbed in the economic that when his poor Fiat worker casts his vote for shop steward he little realizes that he is exercising the only prerogative he will ever have and is in effect setting up the Communist International that will tower over the world's states and peoples. Gramsci offers greater interest and sounder views when he has the factory committee uppermost in his mind, and not governments floating on the hot air of political philosophy and agitprop. He can be quite exciting when he argues that the factory committee is the inherent institution of the working class, that as such it is the most appropriate and only reliable lever for achievement of worker democracy, and that it will be easier to create the worker committees before the revolution than afterward. This side of Gramsci's thinking is interesting, first, because he was the intellectual dynamo behind the Turin factory-committee movement around 1920 and, second, because he managed to sketch out a scheme of socialist metamorphosis in which the factory committee figures both as end and means.

Gramsci did not invent the factory committee, but hit upon it in a search for an indigenous worker institution that resembled the Russian soviet in the immediate post-October period. These factory committees, called Internal Commissions,

[1] Antonio Gramsci, *L'Ordine Nuovo* (1919–20) and *Socialismo e Fascismo: L'Ordine Nuovo* (1921–2), Turin: Einaudi, 1954 and 1966.

had originally been set up as grievance committees, and dated back to 1906 in Italy. In the first postwar years, of which John Cammett says, ". . . it is a wonder that no revolution took place,"[2] the workers had gained control over the committees and had beefed up their powers. In this sense the committees were worker institutions (not, that is, devised by radical intellectuals) and spontaneously revolutionary (reflecting in an immediate way the reactions and aspirations of the workers, not Socialist party or trade union policy), and these are the characteristics of the committees which Gramsci emphasizes most.

Gramsci fully accepted the precept that society will be ruled by that class which is most progressive in developing the productive forces. Revolution occurs by the nature of social dynamics when a submerged class becomes more progressive in this sense. Gramsci accordingly saw "the" socialist revolution as an incremental rather than an instantaneous event, a transformation dependent precisely on the workers' assimilation of the capacity to rule. Given his exclusively economic conception, ruling and managing were for him very much the same thing. At any rate, the first step toward control of the government was to take over management of the workplace. Since this bootstrap process within the workplace is the mainspring of the revolution, is indeed practically synonymous with it, the trade union and the political party compare unfavorably with the factory committee as the generator and vehicle of the advance toward socialism.

In Gramsci's view the patterns of the working class have been shaped by the configuration of industrial production, so that there is a point-by-point fit between the essential power in society, which for him is industrial or economic power, and the potential force that is to seize that power. In other words, the front line of the class struggle is drawn around the productive machinery and not down the middle of the contract-negotiating table or the parliament chamber.

We may well doubt that workplace confrontation, assuming even its greatest success, could be sufficient to bring about

[2] John M. Cammett, *Antonio Gramsci and the Origins of Italian Communism,* Stanford: Stanford University Press, 1967, p. 66.

democratic socialism in the social and political spheres of society. In any event, there is for me something repugnant and frightening in Gramsci's vision of a workers' state rising up by exponential indirection on the base of the factory committees. In his scheme politics proper would commence at the level of the ward council, consisting of delegates from local factory committees. These councils would culminate in city commissariats, and these in turn would erect the next stage of the scaffolding, the provincial or regional structure, and this process would continue on to the formation of the national state and a world government, all without further consultation, referendum, recall, vote, or any other form of leverage exercised by the worker.[3] We know enough now about totalitarian regimes to suppose that industrial democracy would not survive long in Gramsci's factories because the state that grew out of it would soon control and dominate not only the economy and its major interactions, but also the relations that prevail within the factory. The workers' management built up so carefully to accomplish the revolution would be vitiated by its own victory and vacated by the state it produced.

Some favoring political action—at the minimum something like Section 7a of the National Industrial Recovery Act—would seem a necessity to the ultimate success of confrontation in the workplace. But it cannot replace that confrontation in making industrial democracy. Just as we can doubt the capacity of workers' management to change the political system, we can also doubt the adequacy of the state in changing workplace relations. I suppose we all hold some pluralistic conception of how a more democratic society can be pressured into being, and industrial democracy is just one of the several components in that conception. It is logical to expect that each of these components, though aided by the others, has its own generative

[3] Regimes that posit the primacy of the economic over the political, recognizing the worker but ignoring the citizen, don't eliminate the political realm, but merely place a limit on its downward reach. The line of division is the level where representation becomes indirect. The rank and file vote on persons, and questions of public policy are put only to bodies of delegates, their importance increasing directly with the number of removes from the man at the bottom.

power. If we imagine that Gramsci is speaking solely to the point of how the impetus of and toward industrial democracy can be generated, then he can perhaps be useful.

Gramsci's factory committee, made up of delegates elected from the shops, is the practical mechanism whereby the workers begin to participate to the last man (in two senses: through involvement in factory issues raised or focused by the committee and by expanding autonomy at the work station), whereby they challenge management prerogatives by demonstrating their competence in and commitment to the production process, and through which they substitute their own forms and discipline for the instituted line-of-command authority. The factory committee, then, has the two important functions of altering worker psychology from that of the wage earner to that of the producer and of transforming relations in the workplace toward workers' management.

In the performance of these essential functions, he argues, the trade union and the workers' political party are inappropriate if not reluctant institutions. While militant trade unionists and Socialist party members would play an exceedingly important role in promoting the factory committees, the trade union and Socialist party would as organizations play a necessary but supporting role in Gramsci's version of the class struggle. They have been shaped, he says, not by the material forces of production, but by the laws of capitalist competition, and therefore they cannot go beyond the capitalist state. Themselves inappropriate and inadequate to organizing the workers for what Gramsci sees as the proletariat's revolutionary task, the trade union and workers' political party would become revolutionary only by responding to the pressures of the factory committee movement and by complementing it.

Before we take up Gramsci's elaboration of relations between the factory committees and the trade unions, let us consider for a moment the way things looked to Louis Adamic in 1938. I include him in these remarks because he represented a style and outlook of American radicalism which I find congenial and authentic. For me he provides a needed leaven of Americanism, of that chaotic and pragmatic American approach to social questions which strikes me still as the most resilient and promising. I am not convinced that the American consciousness has been absorbed by some sinister totality and all roads of social change routed back inward, but even in that case I would argue that direct, pragmatic ways are the most appropriate to that part of the socialist scheme which we call workers' management.

Adamic was born in Carniola, now part of the Yugoslav republic of Slovenia, and he came to the United States in his teens, but his Americanism is all the more profound, conscious, and communicable because he constantly held America up to two comparisons: the corrupt, unenlightened, and dictatorial Yugoslavia of the thirties at the bottom of the scale and the immigrant's pristine view of America's democratic promise at the upper end. Adamic kept a more level head than most in the America of the thirties: capital versus labor was the issue, he could see, but he constantly reminded himself that America approached its problems pragmatically, even in the person of its La Follettes, that the country's matrix of political democracy could override class divisions, and that labor, his special subject as a journalist, was inept in the mass, tended to bossism in its organization, and in those days at least harbored a firebug element. He paid the Communists what he thought their due for having raised important issues, but beyond that considered them daft; he offered a bemused cooperation in one or two New Deal schemes, but he became no liberal zealot; and in searching for the "long road," the authentic pattern of change by which America might realize her democratic promise, he took Arthur Morgan, the founder of Black Mountain College, a handful of obscure but exemplary newsmen, and the Wisconsin Progressives as pathfinders. Perhaps it is not whimsy to think of these figures as roughcast predecessors of the most inventive and clearheaded currents in the New Left.

In *My America* Adamic does not attempt to define industrial democracy, though he puts the query continually, notably to John L. Lewis himself, who was blathering about it in speeches at the time. Approaching from the negative side, though, Adamic knew that its tasks would include education of the worker to economic competence and citizenship within the industrial premises, humanization of work and thereby rehabilitation of the stultified worker, and penetration of democratic principles and broad social policy into the corporate kingdoms. Drawing a blank with Lewis on this question, he qualified his enthusiasm for the CIO with forebodings of what labor might become if it neglected these tasks, this transformation of the rank and file, and concentrated instead on building blocs of national power.

This is a point on which Gramsci had no doubts. In his view, the trade union was perforce a bargaining institution, one whose strength depended precisely on its centralization, on its bloc of power. He found it nothing strange that the trade unions were bureaucratic and remote from the worker. This type of organization, he thought, arose naturally from their inherent functions and, unlike Ernest Mandel, he issued no appeals for them to change their ways. Rather, he expected them to go on performing this important function of bargaining, of maintaining legality in industry. The only lever he saw for bending the trade unions toward a true transformation of the way society operates was the factory committee movement.

As we have seen, Gramsci was not fundamentally a decentralist. His factory-committee movement was diffuse only because he brought his focus to bear on the individual workplace as the key point of confrontation, the area of struggle not only between capital and labor, but also between the workers as they are and the workers as they must be if workers' management is ever to be realized. He saw the factory committee as the one instrument that can invigorate those areas of the worker's psychology benumbed by his having been treated grudgingly as a cost.

Gramsci's factory committee would depart sharply from the usual trade union attitudes. It would not eschew responsibility, but would avidly grasp for it; it would not oppose innovations on principle, but would strive to make its own contributions in this realm even though sometimes the benefits might accrue as much to the owners as to the workers. In other words, his factory committee would embrace the industrial process as its own territory and would strive to increase its control through superior performance. This view is hair-raising anathema to trade unionists, and they would seem to be right from their point of view. But workers' management requires that the workers shift at some point from hidebound trade union attitudes to initiative and responsibility in areas that are now the exclusive preserve of management authority. If workers' management is to be taken up as a means toward socialism, then that point must come before the workers are the owners and masters of the productive plant, and until that day comes there will be a need for the trade unions and for the attitudes they have found necessary in their struggle. Nothing in Gramsci's treatment is more useful than his recognition of the separate validity of the trade unions and the factory committees.

He believed, on the one hand, that the factory committee and the participation it implies and depends on would provide the worker with the tools of his liberation: first, from his wage earner attitudes, then from the rules and supervision that are not inherently essential in the production process, and finally from his passive attitude toward ownership and management by capital. Participation heightens the worker's awareness of his place in the production process, and thence of his place in the business of society as a whole, which Gramsci characteristically likens to a single large production complex. Such a worker, he argues, has a revolutionary potential which the trade union could never develop in its membership because of the trade union's relationship to its members and to capital.

Gramsci predicted a testy coexistence between the factory committee movement and the trade unions. The great achievement of the unions, his argument runs, is to have instituted legality in industry. But he sees this as a mere compromise, stable only until the balance of power goes against the working class. It is from the standpoint of legality in industry, to paraphrase him, that one can understand the relations that should prevail between the trade unions and the factory committees. He sees the committee as the negation of legality in industry; at every moment it is striving to destroy that legality and to bring the working class to seizure of industrial power. The trade union is an element of that legality and must strive for respect of it by its members. Because of its revolutionary spontaneity, the factory committee is precipitous in causing flareups of class war; because of its bureaucratic form, the trade union wishes to prevent class altogether. Relations between these two institutions, then, must tend toward a situation in which a capricious act of the committee will not force a step backward for the working class, a defeat for the class as a whole. The committee would accordingly accept and adopt a measure of discipline from the trade union, but the unions would in turn be influenced by the revolutionary nature of the committee, their bureaucracy would tend to break up as by a solvent, and the remote and isolated positions of trade union officials would be undermined. The trade union and the factory committee, Gramsci believed, would vie with one another, and yet not break, over the issue of legality, and this tension would guarantee that violations of that legality occur only at moments when the working class has at least that minimum of preparation that preserves it from permanent defeat. Relations between the trade union and the factory committee should be based on the single fact that most of the committee's electorate are also members of the trade union. Any attempt to link these two institutions by relations arising out of hierarchical dependence would weaken or destroy them both. If the trade union should rely exclusively on the committees and act only as their higher form, becoming imbued with the committee's inherent aspirations, it would no longer be able to assume its obligations in collective bargaining and would lose the features of a force that disciplines and regulates the impulsive forces of the working class. If the workers organized in the trade union do establish revolutionary discipline, a discipline that appears to the masses necessary for the triumph of the workers' revolution, then the committee would undoubtedly accept that discipline, and it would become a natural form for the action conducted by the committee. If the trade union office becomes a headquarters for preparing the offensive and the union is respected for its wise strategy, its exemplary people, and its effective propaganda, then the masses will see it as an indispensable ally and its action as a condition essential to the success of their cause.

America in the seventies bears little resemblance to any of the three contexts I have mentioned. Gramsci wrote about worker insurgency with the fact of it before his eyes. The occupation of the Turin factories in September 1920 was no ordinary event in the annals of labor. Even Adamic was present to record a fervor in American industrial workers which they have not shown since. And no need to dwell on all the conditions that distinguish the Yugoslav situation from the American. Nevertheless, I would like to speculate in the light of these three sources on what a workers' management movement might look like.

The development of workers' management in Yugoslavia suggests that industrial democracy is not just a different power setup from the usual pattern of industrial management, but adds a new dimension to economic life. Industrial democracy is an evolutionary process in two senses: it develops through recurrent raising and resolving of its characteristic issues, and it entails important and necessarily slow changes in social relations and psychological attitudes in the workplace. No matter what the external circumstances, then, when we talk of workers' management we imply the existence of pressures from below, within the workplace. The point is axiomatic. The attendant axiom is that worker aspirations can be properly awakened and attuned to the peculiar—and by no means immediately attractive—challenge of workers' management only via the way station of its rudimentary forms.

Antonio Gramsci grasped the evolutionary nature of industrial democracy, and he thought the energies to power that evolution could be found in the workplace, specifically the capitalist workplace. He saw the factory committee as the institution that could liberate and focus those energies, which he judged to be sufficient—to state his expectations at the minimum—to change the nature of production relations and to bend the trade unions and worker political party toward an effective socialist strategy.

I am drawn to Adamic not so much for his ideas as for the approach or attitude toward social change in America which he implies. One of the things that intrigued him most about America was that it didn't total up. Though he wrote in 1938 that the Communists, with their all-embracing program, seemed to offer more than anyone else in the Yugoslav situation, he noted, as have many others, that America has not tended or perhaps needed to solve its problems totally, but gets around to them one by one—usually, be it said, when every evasion has failed. The broadest generalization he risked about the country as a whole was that its democratic political principles would one day have to win out over the undemocratic principles of authority in the workplace. Adamic's last look at Yugoslavia came before the days of the workers' councils, and this is a particular shame because he had all the prerequisites to envision the implications they might have in the American context. I fancy he might have regarded the workers' councils in their most practical light, as a means whereby the decisive engagement between labor and capital might be brought about. At any rate, in urging that this approach be explored I am influenced by his message that if Americans are lukewarm toward grand schemes, even when they admit them to be right and handsome, they can on the other hand show great fervor and energy when confronted with "something that can be done." This assumption accounts for my bias toward the literal, the prosaic, the everyday aspects of workers' management.

How, then, do we get to workers' management? I think there is no detour around a workers' management movement in the workplace, a movement whose purpose would be to compete with management in detail, contest it at local points, and ultimately take precedence over it. The independence of this movement from the labor movement is important. The workplace movement would get its initial impetus by raising issues of rudimentary participation or by accepting the challenge to expand forms of participation that are proposed by enlightened management. Participation in Blumberg's sense would be its characteristic beginning in the workplace.[4] It is evident that direct participation can push its way only so far and its choices can be made with only limited wisdom unless some formal workplace organization is formed of worker representatives to face management at the shop and factory level. If this committee becomes bound up with the trade union, it will increasingly reflect overall trade union policy, rather than the

[4] Paul Blumberg, *Industrial Democracy: The Sociology of Participation* (New York: Schocken Books, 1969).

results and aspirations of direct worker participation in the shop or factory. If the committee does not speak for its own workers, but becomes an appendage of the trade union, then its activity will become sterile, and participation itself may stall or regress.

The fate of industrial democracy in any one locale will depend greatly on relations between the constituency of participating workers and the delegates representing them on the workplace committee. The committee has great potential as an institution, but detached from the workers it will either wither into a formality, be absorbed by management, or simply dissolve. Essential to industrial democracy is the process by which the workplace committee and the rank-and-file workers develop and enhance one another through dynamic interaction. Through the committee the workers develop their leaders, sharpen their focus, and penetrate the complexities of economic reality and of their own place in it. On the other hand, the position and the strength of the committee vis-à-vis management will always depend on this invigoration of the workforce.

I don't think the stance of the workplace committee should be fixed beforehand as one of blanket and adamant opposition. The scrutiny, surveillance, and veto Ernest Mandel speaks of would be important among its functions, and opposition to any single management decision would always remain open as an option. But the committee's deliberation ought to be selective. If it supports that alternative open to management that seems best from its own vantage point, then its outlook will increasingly become one of the important factors in the management decision. In time it would venture its own proposals and take due responsibility and credit for failure and success if they are adopted.

This approach need not be the same as co-determination. It would not mean that the workplace committee would countersign every management decision and thus be coopted. The workplace committee must be distinct from management, just as its position must be distinct from that of management. If they agree, let them share the responsibility and credit. This threat of possible concord between management and worker representatives will sound like collusion and capitulation to some people, and in the actual case there no doubt will be much of that, but matters are hardly improved by deferring the workers' assumption of responsibility to a time when the means of production have been nationalized in some socialist state. My judgment is that the prospects of workers' management are not essentially enhanced by nationalization. By lumping industrial power in the ministries of the state, nationalization does not guarantee or necessarily favor industrial democracy, but indeed gives rise to bureaucratic forces that will resist workers' management and deploy them in formidable order of battle. Workers' management means nothing more nor less than that the workers will directly organize their own work and indirectly perform the entrepreneurial and policy-making functions of the enterprise. The process by which they assume that role is what I have been calling industrial democracy. The further that process can be advanced in a capitalist or mixed economy, the more attractive and liberative nationalization will become.

Co-determination, some system of high level management–labor boards, does present itself as the all-too-possible institutional form whereby labor insurgency will be absorbed into the corporate system. Yet Mandel's workers' control would seem to be the same form with a different stance. In both cases the trade union would act on behalf of the workers; the only dispute is over the stand it will take: accommodation or opposition. In both cases the labor representatives would be remote from the workers. I would have no confidence in either one in the absence of a workplace movement alive to the doings of its delegates and able to call them to account. Certainly neither is a step closer to workers' management unless it is the culmination of stirrings in the workplace that can only be generated by direct participation at the work station. Moreover, it seems to me that Mandel's dog-in-the-manger opposition is based on a debatable view of the differences between late capitalism and early socialism. From the standpoint of workers' management the two are much alike because the old conception of the organization of work is being challenged and supported by forces that are similar in the two cases. To me it is dogmatic to suppose the capitalist system wholly intractable and the socialist system by definition liberative. Shouldn't we rather assume that both are basically intractable and unresponsive, but perhaps not entirely invulnerable to the motivations inherent in the workers' management idea? The question in both cases is whether a workplace movement can expand that area of vulnerability by directly challenging the organization of work and by raising issues of corporate policy.

My feeling is that the workplace movement should not so much raise the issues of socialism versus capitalism or of labor versus the employers, leaving them to the political parties and trade unions, respectively, but should discriminately raise the issues of workers' management which I have tried to suggest, should assert worker autonomy against established rules, should press for discussion of issues in anticipation of post factum directives, and should challenge the premises of hierarchical organization with the premises of industrial democracy—not abstractly, but in the terms of specific possibilities and the decisions that must be made concerning them. Admittedly, this is to project a chaotic and pragmatic—in short, messy—pattern of development for the workplace movement. Not that I think messiness is a virtue in itself, but I do take exception to those who think some doctrine is so important that preserving its purity becomes a major and sometimes overriding concern. Mandel, for instance, puts a limit on the workplace movement because of his doctrine of the class struggle and of its being decided in some violent clash, however muffled, outside the workplace. All that might well be, but it's no airtight proposition. And since the messy phase of workers' management must yet be got through after Mandel's decisive battle, I can't help but fear some new doctrinal purity will stand in the way of spontaneous insurgency in the workplace.

Gramsci did not stop so short as Mandel on the question of worker responsibility, but he did come to a point where he drew back from the implications of his own scheme. This was when the owners of Fiat offered to convert their shares to debentures, thus creating a kind of cooperative managed by the workers. Gramsci's arguments against acceptance of the scheme were that the Turin proletariat would thereby be cooperating with the bourgeoisie, would be rending the worker–peasant alliance, would be taking a privileged position vis-à-vis the remainder of the industrial proletariat, and would in any event be walking into a financial trap because their hands would be tied by the credit institutions. Gramsci fought tooth and nail against this Fiat proposal and a similar one at Reggio Emilia, referring to its supporters as reformists. He won the victory and expressed no second thoughts about his position when he reported the eventual outcome: "In April 1921, 5000 revolutionary workers were laid off by Fiat, the Factory Councils were abolished, real wages were reduced. At Reggio Emilia something similar probably happened. The workers, in other words, were defeated. But has their sacrifice been useless? We do not think so: rather are we sure that it has not been useless."[5]

Now it is unfair and presumptuous to second guess Gramsci about an event that took place fifty years ago, but the Fiat incident does evoke the general case. That is, where could the success of a workplace movement lead but to some such situation? Gramsci commends the workers' political maturity in having heeded the political philosophers and theoreticians and in having renounced this challenge which they had wrested from the Fiat directors. Myself, I wish they had shown more innocence of abstract political considerations and more plain curiosity about what would happen if they accepted. The pitfalls of the practical situation are obvious. Changing the shares of stock into debentures would not ultimately settle the question of ownership, income distribution, and financial backing, but the proposal would presumably have placed management of Fiat in the hands of the workers. Ownership could have come only after a lengthy period in which the workers paid interest on the debentures and eventually repaid the principal; meanwhile, we can assume that financial credits would have been a lever used to frustrate the workers' efforts. But I decline to reduce the practical risks involved to a set of class relations in which the workers betray their class if they accept the terms of the challenge, and must therefore doom themselves to the defeat which was not long in coming. The retribution that followed in April 1921 seems to me the one inevitability to be considered in deliberating such a decision.

I would prefer, as I say, a more pragmatic approach. Rather

---

[5] Antonio Gramsci, *The Modern Prince and Other Writings,* tr. Louis Marks (New York: International Publishers, 1957), p. 42.

than the moment to invoke precepts of political theory and philosophy, I think the workers' seizure of the chance to manage is when doctrine should be set in abeyance. It is after all based on past experience and can only be renewed by grappling with the uncertain. The challenge, I argue, should have been taken up precisely because the implications were not understood, because the outcome was in doubt, because the situation presented a potential for something quite new.

It can be argued that the terms on which workers' management was offered were bad. They certainly were not good. The situation of industrial democracy "within" and prejudicial financial relations "without" is not ideal. The directors' offer was presumably a gambit; they thought themselves so essential to the enterprise's operation that in the end the workers would implore them to return. Even had that been the outcome, the terms of their return could hardly have been worse than the settlement of the matter that resulted from the decision taken by Gramsci, Togliatti, and the other Turin leaders. At the least they would have left a more instructive legacy.

Workers' management is not likely to come about if its advocates are not prepared to take up this kind of challenge. Whatever workers' management means and whatever concomitant conditions it may imply, it means nothing whatsoever if the workers are not to assume the managerial and entrepreneurial role. The term "entrepreneurial" points up a dilemma. What the workers will manage is an enterprise, and the external terms, relations, and usages of that management are what we call business. Theretofore the victim of layoffs, disciplinary action, competition, and profit making, the worker-become-manager must now get sullied himself in these activities, at least until he finds other ways of dealing with the real conditions that capitalist management faces in resorting to them. So long as the worker was idealized as victim, he had an aura of innocence which he obviously must shed when he begins to act as manager and entrepreneur. From a certain angle the worker seems to be liberated in industrial democracy only to perform the distasteful role of an acquisitive businessman. He appears to be driven by the same self-interest, which has put on the clothes of collectivity, but has not become social.

I am aware of two ways out of this dilemma, neither of which satisfies me. One is to assume that business competition will vanish in the central planning of a socialist system. Calling such a system socialist is not enough to allay my fears that such a system would swallow up more freedom than it offered. If I read the economic experts rightly, there seem to be sound reasons why business and the market will survive a considerable while as necessities if not desiderata. As an advocate of workers' management, I take some comfort in the defects and difficulties of central planning schemes because the autonomy of the economic enterprise is that legacy of independence which workers' management must inherit for its own development. Not much will be left of the idea if one can take Gramsci's figure of society as a large production plant and then imagine the plant automated.

The other way out of the dilemma is to plug the public into business decision making by seating outside representatives on enterprise management boards. In the general case this approach is no substitute for legislation embodying public economic policy, establishing the rules of the market, and setting limits on economic enterprise. It is probably appropriate in the special case of the social services and public service enterprises. But even these services are so diverse that means of insuring the public interest may have to be devised from case to case. I doubt that it is a good approach in the economy; the element it would introduce into economic decision making seems too arbitrary and subject to pressure from special and local interests. It doesn't promise to be any easier to secure the broad social outlook of these public representatives than that of the self-managing workers themselves. However necessary it may be to establish a framework of controls to govern business relations— prices, bookkeeping, contracts, deliveries, penalties, mergers, takeovers, joint market actions, etc.—a workers' management movement that favors the admission of public officials to its councils is selling its own birthright. The controls that are imposed should be general and stable enough so as not to throttle business as a means of day-to-day economic adjustment. On the other hand, the controls can apparently be quite strict and enforceable, if only they do not change arbitrarily and too often, since in that case enterprises will turn to political considerations and short term interests for orientation in fixing business policy.

The workers' management movement I envisage, then, would develop from within the enterprise, and its primary goal would be to change the rules of the game within the enterprise. Extramurally, it would be more concerned with playing the game than with changing the rules. This is an important limit on what we can expect of it, but I suppose a realistic one. It seems to me wiser to rely on a broader social movement to curb the worker-managers once they have attained power than to incorporate public safeguards into the industrial democracy program from the outset. It is difficult enough to imagine a workers' management movement motivated by self-interest; I find it altogether impossible to imagine such a movement powered by the workers' concern for the public interest. Such a movement, if it materializes, will no doubt develop boisterously, unevenly, and pragmatically, and would pursue its goal of industrial democracy through compromises and on the best terms it can obtain. It probably wouldn't look much like nobility incarnate, but I for one wish it were there to see.

Workers' Control and the Nixon Economic Program

Jack Rasmus

With the announcement of his New Economic Program on August 15, 1971, Richard Nixon, in effect, served notice to organized labor and workers throughout the country that an era of relations between capital and labor in the United States had come to an end: an era of uneasy and mutually suspicious acceptance of a status quo in which the various relationships between these two major social classes were both "blunted" and "cushioned" by the Cold War and an exceptionally large social product.

But in order to understand the full significance of this crucial political development and, for the purposes of this article, its relationship to the idea of workers' control, it is first necessary to trace its origin from the deterioration of the United States economy and the failure of economic policies over the course of the last decade.

In the last ten years, in particular since 1967, the United States economy has undergone rapid and profound structural changes unequaled even in the 1890s or 1920s. These structural changes have assumed various forms: the rapid growth of totally new industries and markets, as well as the passing of many traditional ones; the rise and expansion of the conglomerate and international corporation; the increasing participation and integration of the state in the economy; significant changes in domestic and international patterns of finance; no less impressive changes in the size, composition, and character of the labor force; and the broadest and most rapid innovation and diffusion of new technology in all of social history.

Often a good barometer of the depth and extent of such structural change is the impact it has on various legal relations—relations designed in the past to accommodate previous economic conditions, but which now come into conflict with changed conditions and structures. And in U.S. society today the pressure on legal relations in general (and with regard to antitrust, labor, and tax law in particular) has reached a level of serious crisis.

To take just one example, the conglomerate corporation has seriously compromised the effectiveness of antitrust law (based in the past on now obsolete "vertical" and "horizontal" concentration criteria). It has produced a fundamental threat to collective bargaining structure. Last, but by no means least, the conglomerate corporation has created huge loopholes for corporate tax evasion. The impact of the conglomerate on legal relations is by no means the only example of pressures on social relations in general caused by present structural changes in the economy. For additional evidence one need only consult the numerous congressional hearings and reports on economic concentration, banking, small business failures, securities regulation, corporate disclosures, international trade, and so forth.

Of the various forces responsible for these great changes in the structure and condition of the United States economy, one of the most significant has been the impact of the Southeast Asian war. In fact, the war has acted as both a determining and a determinant element in these changes. And it is this dual, or mutually influencing relationship, which accounts for much of the acceleration of such changes since the mid-sixties and, consequently, the emergence of the Nixon "New Economic Program" in 1971.

It is not the purpose of this article to examine in detail the interaction between the structural changes and the war. But for the present we can focus, although in very general terms, on one factor that connects them. The nexus (both conceptually and in real terms) of this connection is the corporate profit margin. And while the complete interrelation between the changes in the structure of the economy, the war and profit margins is also a highly complex one, it nevertheless lends itself to a certain amount of useful generalization.

I.

Like most wars, the war in Southeast Asia has meant mixed blessings for big business. In the years of initial buildup it meant record production, sales, and profits for most industries. It also meant the securest of profit margins. The early years of the war brought expansion of profit levels and margins through special government tax cuts to business, accelerated depreciation allowances (which created an artificially stimulated capital goods boom), and the manipulation of organized labor into accepting "voluntary guideposts" on wages without corresponding guidelines for prices, profits, dividends, and other income earned from the ownership or control of capital.

Primarily by means of various tax and antilabor policies, the federal government between 1962 and 1965 in effect played the role of insurance adjustor for corporate profit margins. And what it could not insure on the side of subsidizing corporate costs, it more than made up for through fiscal policies as a "purchaser of the first resort" of corporate goods and services. For the first half of the sixties total federal purchases of goods and services remained remarkably stable. But from 1965 through 1970 a sharp departure from the pattern of the previous five years took place.* Under the impact of escalation, federal government purchases grew from $66.9 billion annual total in 1965 to $99.7 billion annual total in 1970. Of this average annual increase of about $27 billion, over $23 billion annual, on the average, consisted of war-related goods and services purchased from the private sector. Additional bureaucratic costs of running and operating the war must be added to the above figures if the full costs are to be determined. In short, official estimates that the war has cost the American people over $100 billion between 1965 and 1970 are extremely conservative.

It is important to understand that, while federal government fiscal, tax, and labor policies were the most important factors in expanding profit margins between 1963 and 1969, they were also directly responsible for generating the inflation which seriously threatened those same profit margins. For example: the United States money stock rose from a pre-1963 figure of $287.1 billion in 1964 to $445 billion in 1970 largely due to federal government war-related purchases. Much of this went for goods and services which would never circulate in the domestic economy but would rot instead in Asian jungles. Such overexpansion of the money supply without attendant real growth could only contribute significantly to inflationary pressures which, in turn, by the end of the decade would seriously cut overall demand, corporate sales and, consequently, profit margins.

In addition, as a direct result of the war and Johnson-Nixon monetary policies, general interest rates soared between 1965 and 1970 to the highest levels in well over a century. U.S. Treasury short term rates nearly doubled between 1964 and 1970. Average short term bank loans jumped from 5.06 percent

* All of the following figures are taken from the annual Economic Reports and Manpower Reports of the President.

in 1965 to 8.48 percent in 1970. Prime commercial paper rates went from 4.38 percent to 7.72 percent. FHA rates increased from 5.46 percent to 9.05 percent. Such record interest rates also increasingly cut into profit margins toward the end of the decade—first as a cost item directly affecting profits, and secondly as yet another of many factors generating administered prices, inflation, and a decline in demand and sales.

Another significant economic effect of the war and federal purchases of related goods and services was the failure of the federal government to provide adequately for purchases of much needed, and overdue, social and public services. This policy played a major role in the sharp growth of state and local government taxes, further inflationary pressures, and fiscal crises at the state and local levels (generating the need for "revenue sharing"). Between 1965 and 1970, federal purchases of goods and services associated with health, education, welfare, housing, and public transport grew only from $5.0 billion to $9.1 billion—at a time of sharper increase in the demand for such services. Faced with already large deficits and war-related expenditures, the federal government pushed off onto state and local governments the burden of financing social services and related investments. Thus, in contrast to the federal record, from 1965 to 1970 state and local government purchases jumped from $70.1 billion to $120.8 billion annually—the vast part of which went to supply (though still inadequately) the rising demand for social and public services. As a result of this major shift of financial responsibility, many state and local governments found themselves facing near-bankruptcy by 1971. But such financially depressed conditions did not occur overnight. And as the financial pressures steadily increased, state and local governments responded with corresponding increases in indirect taxes and other charges which the average worker had to carry. Chief among these were excise tax, sales tax, and other regressive taxes; local property taxes (with loopholes for local business) and, once these sources were squeezed to the near limit politically, the initiation in many cases of state income taxes (with attendant loopholes for the wealthy). This fiscal crisis played a key part in stimulating general inflationary pressures.

Federal tax policies also played a key role in changes in

corporate profit margins by the end of the decade. On the one
hand, the war-related surcharge undoubtedly contributed
heavily to higher administered prices and their eventual negative
effect on demand and sales. Even more significant, however, is
the role played by federal tax cuts and depreciation policies
generating over-investment, underutilization of plants and
equipment, and higher corporate fixed (and other nonlabor)
costs.

Stimulated largely by federal investment credits, faster depreciation rules, a general tax cut, as well as record corporate
profits during the war years, overall business expenditures for
new plant and equipment rose from $46.9 billion in 1964 to
$80.6 billion at the end of 1970—a record increase. In addition
to favorable tax policies, the availability of credit and internal
financing (due to record profits), and exceptional demand, the
record investment in new plants and equipment was also stimulated by the growth of new products on a previously unequaled
scale, the opening and expansion of many companies into international markets, and corporate anticipation of higher costs and
interest rates. In general, all these factors contributed to the
capital goods boom of the sixties which, in turn, led to over-
investment, underutilization of productive capacity and, thus, a
sharp rise in corporate fixed costs. As a result of the overinvestment and related developments the boom eventually turned to
a bust. At the end of the decade, under pressure of a now
accelerating inflation, many corporations got caught holding the
bag as the seemingly endless demand began to dry up—favorable taxation was temporarily suspended in 1969, foreign competition began to conquer the new international and domestic
markets, and a widespread corporate liquidity crisis took place.

As a result, by 1970 expenditures for new plant and equipment grew only slightly, and in 1971 actually declined. The
direct result of overinvestment was that by the end of 1970, for
example, the capacity utilization rate in manufacturing fell to
72 percent from 91 percent in 1966. Such a rate, for many
corporations, was well below the break-even point, and signified
a sharp increase in those fixed costs which cut heavily into profit
margins. This stimulated higher administered prices which,
consequently, had a negative effect on sales and demand. The

major contradiction faced by most corporations was how to protect that key indicator of corporate performance—the profit margin—by raising prices to cover rising costs when to do so would have a serious negative effect on demand, sales and, thus, profit margins.

In addition to the impact of all the factors discussed above on rising costs, prices, and declining demand (and thus profit margins), by the end of the decade still additional economic forces added their weight. On the cost side of profit margins were rising unit labor costs and, on the demand side, the conquest of many international and domestic markets by European and Japanese competitors.

Provoked by record corporate profits as well as by the inflation and rising regressive taxes which were also basically a result of the war, unions after 1968 began to renew demands for wage increases. It should be noted, however, that these wage increases were clearly a response to prior inflation, taxes, and corporate superprofits and only secondarily one of many other factors contributing to further price increases. For example, in 1965 the median annual rate of increase in wages negotiated through collective bargaining was only 3.3 percent. Not until 1968 did this rise to 6.0 percent, and to 8.9 percent in 1970. Moreover, these figures represent less than one third of the entire United States labor force. At least two thirds of the approximately 75–80 million workers in this period (1965–8) lacked the added strength of established collective bargaining rights and therefore had to settle for wage increases far below the above rates. As a result, in spite of higher wage increases at the end of the decade, wage earners in general could still not keep up with the much larger increases in prices, taxes, and profits. In 1965 the average weekly income for workers in private industry was $91.32; at the end of 1970 it had dropped to $90.16. In manufacturing the drop was from $102.41 per week to $99.66 per week.

But even though overall wage increases from 1968 on could not keep pace with inflation and taxes and as a result workers lost ground in terms of real income, higher wages still served to threaten corporate profit margins. On the one hand, they constituted an added element in rising corporate costs at a time of rapidly rising costs due to excess capacity and soaring interest rates. Furthermore, higher wages served to exacerbate prior inflationary trends, as the corporate practice of administered pricing simply added wage costs (like other costs) to the price of the product.

But by 1970 the rates of increase of various corporate costs had reached such a critical level that the practice of simply passing on such costs to consumers in the form of higher administered prices was becoming increasingly difficult. A limit was quickly being reached at which administered price increases were beginning to have a serious negative impact on demand. In addition, the higher prices were increasingly forcing United States products out of competition with European and Japanese challengers. By 1970 United States corporations in general found themselves in need of a new strategy that would protect and insure their profit margins against being squeezed, on the one hand, by rising costs and, on the other, by declining demand at home and the loss of markets abroad.

Nixon was reluctant to forge such a new strategy in 1969. His primary economic object was to cut inflation, but he chose to do this initially by creating a "controlled recession" with a "politically acceptable" rate of unemployment (5–6 percent officially). He did this mainly through the use of traditional fiscal and monetary means. No doubt he expected this approach would relieve the pressure on corporate costs and make U.S. products more competitive abroad. But he seriously underestimated the severity of the economic condition. And despite the engineered recession, the inflationary psychology provoked by war and overexpansion persisted, the rate of growth and productivity came to a standstill, and U.S. corporations continued to lose ground to foreign competitors. By the second half of 1970 Arthur Burns of the Federal Reserve Board (spokesman for U.S. banking interests and lobbyist for finance capital in general) and other spokesmen for the largest U.S. corporations began to pressure Nixon for a more direct approach and strategy for protecting corporate income.

Throughout 1970 corporate profit margins continued to be threatened by rising costs and declining demand. Equally important, corporations began to fear that to try to recoup the former by raising prices would only end up in depressing the latter. Traditional monetary and fiscal policies, it seemed, could not deal simultaneously with both horns of the dilemma; to grapple with one meant to be gored by the other. A new strategy was necessary that could control costs of U.S. goods produced at home while at the same time stimulating demand for these products abroad—and both on a large enough scale to insure the retention of acceptable profit margins. Out of this situation Nixon's economic strategy was to begin taking shape, emerging on August 15, 1971, as the so-called New Economic Program. This new strategy, which had been in the making since mid-1970, was to consist of direct suppression of wages at home, in conjunction with various measures designed specifically to expand the United States share of markets abroad.

Going back one step, it is clear that both the war and the overinvestment and overexpansion of the last decade were policies designed to artificially subsidize corporate profits, just as the emerging strategy of the seventies (based on wage controls, trade protection, and trade expansion with the Communist bloc) would also be designed with the same basic objective in view. The overinvestment and war policies of the last decade can be seen as desperate measures aimed at extricating the U.S. economy from the recession of 1958–61. Ironically, but understandably, the major fiscal and monetary policies responsible for helping end the 1958–61 recession were those same policies directly responsible for the present recession.

II.

The question that must be considered at this point is how the economic developments outlined above relate to workers' control.

In general, it can be said that the continuing inflation, recession, and resulting squeeze on profit margins established the economic basis and the necessity for Nixon's New Economic Program. In turn, this program, combined with certain shop level issues which also arose in conjunction with the inflation, recession, and squeeze, create conditions which make possible the raising of workers' control demands. Specifically, it is a situation of continuing squeeze on profit margins due to rising costs and declining demands which provokes, in a period of sharply reduced effectiveness of traditional fiscal and monetary measures, three important developments creating the *potential* for raising the issue of workers' control.

First, a general economic situation of continuing inflation plus stagnation sets off a corporatewide intensive effort to sharply cut operating costs all along the line. This, in fact, began to take place in the last half of 1970.

Second, such an economic situation also tends to accelerate an already high rate of displacement of labor with new technology and equipment. This takes place because in many cases it becomes cheaper for business to replace labor with new equipment and technology. And the primary reason why, in fact, it becomes cheaper is that government policies subsidize the replacement of labor with capital by accelerating depreciation allowances and creating more favorable capital investment incentives. Ironically, the cost of this subsidizing investment in new technology and equipment is passed on to the working public. In other words, the loss in tax revenues due to these special investment subsidies leaves working people paying taxes that pay for technology and equipment that will replace them on the job. To an important extent, therefore, a redistribution of income takes place in favor of business and capital and at the expense of working people. This redistribution of income is not so obvious as it is in the case of direct cost cutting practices which end up as layoffs and a decline in workers' real wages; but it is a redistribution just the same. The only real difference is that corporate accountants and financial directors execute the redistribution in one case while the corporate personnel directors and line management execute it in the other.

Despite the fact that as of 1971 approximately one half of all the plant and equipment in the United States was five years old or less, the trend of displacing labor with new technology and equipment has been an accelerating one over the last five to seven years. The trend itself is directly related to rising costs, the existence of federal tax investment subsidies, and more favorable depreciation guidelines and it is bound to increase as the inflation and economic stagnation persist or worsen.

Most important for the subject of workers' control, however, is the fact that both the present corporate cost-cutting effort and the accelerating trend toward the displacement of labor result not only in the direct loss of jobs and income for workers, but also signify a direct attack on real wages and working conditions.

The third important development which helps to create the potential for raising workers' control demands is the Nixon economic program itself. When corporate intensive cost-cutting and labor-displacement practices are no longer sufficient to subsidize profits at prior margins (and the usual fiscal and monetary means prove ineffective) then the Nixon program becomes necessary. In other words, when businesses are no longer able to protect and insure their profit margins through their own efforts at the plant, enterprise, or industry levels, they must call upon their political brethren in the government apparatus to do the job through direct emergency executive-legislative action. This action takes the form of an incomes policy—which is always essentially a policy to control and hold down wages, along with various empty gestures to control incomes earned from the ownership or control of capital. (An incomes policy may also contain measures to protect and/or expand the national business class's share of international trade. When it does, then the objective of the policy is to subsidize capital incomes at the direct expense of their capitalist cousins in international markets, as well as at the expense of the national labor force.) The U.S. version of such an incomes policy was being considered, planned, and experimented with throughout the last half of 1970 and the first part of 1971; it surfaced "officially" in August 1971.

As in the cases of corporate cost-cutting efforts and displacement of labor (and contrary to government propaganda), the real objective of an incomes policy is to redistribute income by subsidizing capital incomes at the direct expense of workers' incomes. It does this by holding the lid on the only source of workers' incomes—wages—while asserting only partial control over capital incomes by means of ineffective price controls and no controls over profits, dividends, interest rates, etc. The control of inflation is only secondarily the objective of an incomes policy. Controlling inflation is only part of a much broader strategy designed to redistribute income and thereby subsidize declining profit margins. Thus, the Nixon economic program should be seen as an executive-legislative extension of the corporate effort to protect and subsidize profit margins through intensive cost-cutting, displacement of labor in the production process, and other measures (such as exporting jobs abroad). Its function is both supplementary and complementary to corporate measures to protect and expand profits. Indeed, the Nixon program itself contains numerous elements designed to accelerate the displacement of labor and to aid corporate cost-cutting efforts, in addition to direct wage control and trade expansion.

So far we have set out the three key elements which create the potential for raising workers' control demands: the corporatewide intensive cost-cutting effort, the trend toward accelerating displacement of labor, and the Nixon economic program. All three represent a direct response by the capitalist class to the growing threat to profit margins. They have in common the basic objective of subsidizing corporate profit margins by directly attacking workers' real wages, jobs, and working conditions in general.

We should consider at this point how the first two, i.e., the corporate cost-cutting offensive and the trend toward increasing displacement of labor, together contribute to a situation favorable to raising the idea of workers' control. Following this we can consider the Nixon New Economic Program as announced in August 1971.

III.

As already indicated, with the beginning of the present recession and economic stagnation late in 1969 there began to emerge a corporatewide effort to cut operational costs. Management apparently expected that such action would "hold the line" economically long enough to sit out what was thought to be a temporary period of stagnation. This corporate cost-cutting was often translated into drastic changes in employment, work rules, and procedures, and working conditions and practices in general.

In many large enterprises a strong management effort was launched to eliminate many jobs and job categories, and to fragment and downgrade many jobs. Such practices almost always placed an increased burden on the existing workforce in the particular plant, shop, or office. It often meant the now decreased workforce had to produce as much as before, or even exceed the output levels of the previously larger workforce. In other words, speedups and increased emphasis on productivity were nearly always a direct result of cost-cutting measures. Management dependence on time-motion studies and other job evaluation techniques designed to force more productivity was often a part of this procedure. In industry, this frequently means new and harsher standards for the setup and speed of production lines and, in turn, increased hazards with regard to health and safety conditions. Developments such as these tend to bring out on the shop floor and in offices serious issues concerned with job security, job classifications and rates, work assignments, schedules, relative pay scales, job transfers, promotions and demotions, and innumerable additional changes in important and hard-won work rules. Furthermore, as workers rebelled under these pressures, the management offensive to increase productivity and cut costs at the expense of workers' real wages and working conditions frequently led to direct confrontation over issues relating to discipline (i.e., discharges, suspensions, fines, etc.). In many cases, such offensives meant extensive layoffs, plant shutdowns or relocations, and even the disruption of entire communities. Wildcats and lockouts often took place. Essentially the same kind of shop floor pressures and conflicts tend to occur when management policy in a particular plant, enterprise, or industry is characterized by a high rate of introduction and diffusion of new equipment and technology in the production process.

In other words, the more rapid the rate of introduction and diffusion of new equipment and technology (whether in the form of new work methods and procedures or new tooling and machinery), the greater the impact on the number and character of jobs within a plant. The issue of job security presents itself immediately, since many workers often become structurally displaced or are laid off. For those not laid off or fired, the struggle becomes one against management attempts to cut production costs even further at the direct expense of workers' real wages and working conditions.

Finally, issues and conflicts between management and workers multiply in number and frequency as workers respond to such deteriorating work conditions and greater exploitation in defense of their established rights and interests.

Perhaps one of the best examples where both cost-cutting and labor displacement have taken place is the steel industry in the United States. This industry has been characterized by an enormous rate of introduction and diffusion of new technology and equipment, especially in the last five to seven years. As would be expected, industry management has attempted to use such change as the leading edge of a policy designed to attack established work practices, conditions, and agreements. Increased use of job evaluation techniques, speedups, management attempts to manipulate job classifications, and the consequent health and safety hazards have all occurred. Along with such technological change and its pressure on work conditions and practices there has also been since late 1969 a heavy reliance on cost-cutting practices which has intensified the conflicts. As a result of both these developments, grievance bargaining in steel increased in frequency and militancy and ultimately the entire grievance system ground to a halt. Though traditional institutional and legal means for settling disputes became less available, the conditions in the industry creating the conflicts did not. The pressures on working conditions, jobs, and work practices continued to grow. The rank-and-file answer to this deteriorating situation was to raise the demand throughout the industry for the right to strike over local grievances—a demand and movement still very much alive.

The point is that all the above issues—job displacement, reclassification, job rates, job evaluation techniques and studies, health and safety, assignments, schedules, transfers, promotions and demotion, the regulation of production, discipline, and so forth—are *potential* workers' control issues.

But before discussing more specifically how the conflicts and issues outlined above relate to workers' control and to Nixon's economic program as well, it might be useful at this point to say something about the nature of workers' control itself.

IV.

Under existing conditions, the *form* that workers' control can take is one in which the kinds of issues and conflicts discussed above are injected, through practical shop level activity, with a broader meaning than they might otherwise assume. Under present conditions workers' control is basically the struggle, by whatever means proven effective, to restrain and to limit management. A workers' control demand is one which challenges the legitimacy of management's right to decide as it pleases regarding the issues discussed above. Workers' control is first a shop floor movement to protect workers' rights and interests. It is a struggle to check, to oversee, and when necessary to prevent the arbitrary exercise of management authority when it violates workers' rights and interests. A workers' control demand always raises the question of management's authority to act. In the present period workers' control does not include having workers directly make decisions themselves. Under present conditions management could easily sabotage such an effort at direct decision making and consequently discredit the idea of workers' control in general. The form workers' control must take in the present period is an "indirect" one: not direct control by workers over the actual decision making that determines production, but indirect control over the authority and ability of management to make those decisions as it pleases. It is the process of decision making that should be controlled, not the actual initiation of the particular decisions. Only in a period of economic collapse, when management's right to make decisions unilaterally has been seriously questioned, should workers attempt to assume authority to make decisions directly. In contrast, under present conditions and relations of production, workers can only control the decisions that determine their conditions of work by controlling management first, by controlling the intermediary force that stands between them and direct decision making, by controlling management in the process of making and implementing such decisions.

Workers' control is as much an offensive as a defensive strategy. It is not just the struggle for the protection of workers' rights and interests against present management and legislative-executive offensives, but it is also the fight for the extension and deepening of those rights and interests at the direct expense of management authority. In an ethical sense, workers' control is the struggle by workers themselves for self-determination and a bill of rights for labor at the place of work.

Some current demands that might be considered to be within the context of workers' control are:

1) The demand for the right of workers to appoint or elect a plant safety committee from among themselves; and for the right of the members of that committee to inspect plant safety and health conditions with no restraints as to the timing or the nature of such inspection activity; the demand for the establishment at management expense of a safety expenditures fund from which purchases of equipment necessary to insure safety could be made, and the right of the same safety committee to order whatever expenditures from the fund as it considers necessary; the right of the workers in general to draw interest from the fund; the further demand for the right of this committee to publish periodic reports to the workers in general concerning all inspection and expenditure activities, if any, and the right for committee members to review relevant company accounts in such case that the particular management in question should refuse to finance the above safety fund or in such case that it publishes reports or materials that contradict the various safety committee reports.

2) The demand for the right of the local union or workers' committee to full access to all job evaluation and time-motion study reports; the demand for the establishment of an all-worker job review committee from among workers of different shops and departments and for the right of this committee to review all management job evaluation reports and to call upon outside and independent sources to check upon the validity of any particular evaluation report; finally, the demand for the right of such a committee to veto any evaluation report and to refuse to abide by its conclusions if significant errors, inconsistencies, or prejudices in the evaluation can be shown.

3) The demand for the right to oversee all hiring, transfer, promotion-demotion, recall and work assignments, and to inspect all reports and written materials dealing with such; in addition, the right of workers or local union representatives to veto any man-

agement decision with regard to the above that can be shown to be threatening to the rights and interests of the workers in general.

4) The demand for complete and comprehensive union control of all pension, welfare, insurance, and other similar funds, including the right to draw full interest from such funds unilaterally.

5) The demand for the right to oversee all setups of production lines and the determination of production line rates; to have full access to any economic reports responsible for changes in such setups and rates; and to veto any particular setup or rate which can be shown to jeopardize the health and safety of workers involved.

6) The demand for the right to elect or to veto the appointment of all foremen, and to determine all issues relating to discipline by a two thirds majority vote of all workers in the particular work unit.

7) The demand for the right to have access to all economic, technical, or financial reports concerned with the determination of all work schedules, shifts, vacations, overtime, inventory shutdowns, and so forth; and the right to veto the implementation of any management decision relating to such.

8) The demand for the right to strike, by a two thirds majority decision of workers involved, over any local grievance or in case of management noncompliance with any worker's veto; the demand for the inclusion in every "grievance clause" of a section stating that failure to resolve any particular grievance within the agreed upon time limits automatically voids and nullifies that clause.*

9) The demand for the right to review and to veto, if necessary, all decisions relating to plant shutdowns, relocations, layoffs, and so forth, including eventually decisions concerned with pricing and investment.

As is evident in the above examples, three general principles fundamental to workers' control and any workers' control demand in the present period are: the right to information, the right to veto, and the right to strike in all cases in which management's response is noncompliance.

---

* Such an arrangement would serve to insure the prompt resolution of grievances by management or else would eliminate the grievance system altogether, thereby "legally" allowing for the resolution of grievances by means of sitdown strikes.

Under various management or liberal "participation" plans, which are essentially attempts to coopt workers' demands for real and effective control, workers' rights to information and veto are purposely restricted and formulated in a manner distinctly advantageous to management. Information under a "participation" scheme is almost always a one-way street where workers are allowed only the restricted right to offer "suggestions" to management. At the very most this might become that essentially useless arrangement called joint consultation. Consultation, whether joint or otherwise, means that the exchange of information goes on at a level beyond the control of the rank and file, and between management and workers' representatives whose loyalty to workers' interests is often compromised. Under conditions of participation the right to veto usually becomes a limited form of the right to register a protest. In contrast to all these characteristics of participation, the principles underlying workers' control are the *full* right to information and to veto. And it is by means of deepening and strengthening these principles that, given the limitations of present conditions, workers' control can be achieved up to a certain point, and in a way in which workers do not compromise themselves by assuming responsibility for management decisions at a time in which the chances of succeeding in such an endeavor are at a distinct minimum.

V.

Earlier it was said that the Nixon New Economic Program is best understood as basically an executive-legislative extension of present corporate efforts to protect profit margins by intensive cost-cutting and labor displacement programs. It was pointed out that the Nixon economic program became necessary once corporate efforts alone could not succeed in holding down costs and stimulating demand. Nixon's program was designed primarily to hold down wages (one of only several basic elements of corporate costs) while initiating various trade and taxation measures which would increase the U.S. corporate share of foreign markets and demand.

It was also pointed out, however, that Nixon's New Economic Program and subsequent related policies would exacerbate those shop level pressures and conditions that create the potential for workers' control. Thus, Nixon's economic program itself can also serve to develop further the potential for workers' control.

With the passing of the weeks and months since August 1971 it has become clearer that the basic objectives of Nixon's economic program have been the following:

1) To subsidize failing corporate profit margins by holding down wages and other corporate costs through presidential decree and other means, while simultaneously attempting to secure a bigger share of foreign markets for United States based corporations;

2) To seriously limit, and eventually to destroy, collective bargaining as it exists now in the United States by eliminating bargaining between labor and management based upon any criteria except that of "productivity": in other words, to eliminate collective bargaining based upon the traditional criteria of profitability, comparability, cost of living, low-wage, and so forth and to allow bargaining based upon productivity gains only;

3) To initially restrict and then to destroy, organized labor's rights to strike in the U.S. This, of course, would mean the end of the labor movement in this country and would signify as well the beginning of a new kind of "corporatism" between labor and the state.

The following evidence can be offered in support of these basic contentions:

Profit Margins and Income Redistribution

Beginning in late 1969 and extending into 1972, profit margins of many of the largest corporations in the United States fell to a level lower, in many cases, than experienced during the recession of 1959–61. The initial response to this by the Nixon administration was to attempt to alleviate the situation through the manipulation of traditional monetary-fiscal means. Throughout 1970 this mainly took the form of a legislative program characterized by vetoes of key social and public works legislation, along with strong presidential support for various laws establishing corporate direct subsidies.

For example, in the course of 1970 Nixon vetoed six key bills appropriating nearly $60 billion for various health, hospital, education, and manpower training programs. On the other hand, he also gave strong support to many bills designed to subsidize particular corporations and industries which were then feeling the squeeze on profit margins sooner and more seriously than others. The most prominent of these was, of course, the direct subsidy in 1970 to the near-bankrupt Penn Central Railroad. This pattern of vetoes and corporate direct subsidies was continued throughout 1971, the most notable case being that of Lockheed. Including funds appropriated by Congress at the rate of about $12–15 billion for housing and public works, the total amount of crucial job and income-creating funds withheld came to about $30–40 billion in 1971.

But as the squeeze on profit margins became more widespread throughout late 1970 and 1971, Nixon's program of selective corporate direct subsidies, financed at the expense of needed social and public legislation, became increasingly inadequate. As a consequence, new approaches and programs were explored and experimented with beginning in early 1971. One such approach was the initiation of an extremely "loose" monetary policy. Another was the sharp liberalization, by means of presidential executive order, of extant corporate depreciation rules and guidelines. A third was the introduction of selective wage controls.

In March 1971 Nixon imposed general wage controls upon the construction industry, and especially upon union collective bargaining and wage demands in that industry. A construction industry Wage-Stabilization Committee was set up to rule on proposed wage increases. In addition, an Interagency Committee was proposed to rule on price increases. By the end of 1971 wage increases in construction union contracts had declined by over forty percent compared to the previous year. On the other hand, the interagency or "Price Committee" was never activated and never reviewed any price increases in the industry. Largely on account of this the profits of contractors in construction increased by over twenty percent for the year. The direct result of wage controls in construction was the direct redistribution of income from workers to employers in the industry. To put it another way: As the methods of corporate subsidization became more direct, so did the process of income redistribution.

A second approach was to speed up the rate at which corporations could write off depreciation on their capital, and also to change the guidelines governing depreciation writeoffs so that corporations could have a freer hand in manipulating depreciation procedures and funds. With such an advantage corporate accounts could more easily be juggled in order to reduce figures representing total costs and, therefore, profit margins as well. Despite the fact that depreciation guidelines were liberalized sharply in the early sixties (which was a contributing factor to the capital investment boom of that decade), Nixon liberalized depreciation guidelines even further, by executive order, in January 1971. This was done not so much to stimulate investment, since the overall capacity utilization rate of U.S. industry at the time was only slightly more than seventy percent. Rather, Nixon's objective was to provide another direct subsidy to financially ailing corporations, especially those who had overinvested in the last five years and were feeling the squeeze of sharply higher corporate fixed costs.

After some slight opposition in Congress to the arbitrary manner in which the Nixon administration handed out such a fat financial plum to big business, the U.S. Treasury finally adopted the new rules on depreciation in June 1971. And Congress, in passing legislation later that year, made the same depreciation guidelines retroactive to January. It is estimated these new guidelines netted business about $3 billion in 1971 alone, and up to $39 billion for the next several years to come.

Nixon's third technique for protecting corporate profit margins was to artificially enforce lower interest rates on loans to corporations for investment purposes. Artificially lowered interest rates would mean correspondingly lower corporate total costs. Thus, by means of federal monetary measures, interest rates were forced sharply downward in the first half of 1971, with the expectation that such action would mean a decrease in corporate costs and therefore better profit margins as well. Unfortunately for Nixon policy makers, however, the desired effect was not forthcoming. Instead, the artificially lowered interest rates contributed heavily to the record balance of payments deficits and international financial instability which broke out in the spring and midsummer of 1971.

Wage Freeze and Productivity Bargaining

As already pointed out, by the summer of 1971 Nixon's previous programs designed to subsidize sagging corporate profit margins were proving to be insufficient. Neither selective wage controls, liberalized depreciation rules, or lower interest rates were having the anticipated impact on profit margins. This was partly because both the wage controls in construction and the new depreciation rules would have to lag several months before having the desired economic effect. Similarly, lower interest rates were having minimal influence in stimulating corporate profits. By the summer of 1971 more extensive and direct measures were needed.

Nixon's decision to proceed with more extensive and direct corporate subsidization measures was finally provoked by the record U.S. balance of payments crisis. The causes behind this crisis, and the shock to the international monetary system it produced, were several: excess U.S. spending to maintain military bases and wars abroad, in particular in Southeast Asia; the onset of the tourist season and private spending by Americans abroad; the sharp increase in U.S. short term capital movements abroad, especially direct investment by U.S. corporations. This latter factor of increased U.S. investment abroad—along with a corresponding decrease in foreign purchases and investment in the United States—was by far the most important element. The accelerating trend of U.S. corporations to set up production in low wage and low tax countries like Mexico, South Korea, Taiwan, Japan, the Philippines; the move by United States corporations to invest heavily in Britain as this country moved behind the tariff wall of the Common Market; the disincentive to foreign investment in the United States due to rising inflation and general economic instability, the higher interest rates in Western Europe in general—all contributed significantly to the U.S. balance of payments and international monetary crisis. In short then, Nixon's new depreciation rules and selective wage controls appearing in the first half of 1971 were too slow to be sufficient, and his monetary program actually made economic conditions worse, since his engineering of artificially lower interest rates in the U.S. did not result in more domestic investment, production, sales, and therefore profit. By midsummer 1971 emergency measures were called for. These measures were contained in Nixon's "Phase One."

If we look closely at Phase One it can be seen to be composed of three parts: the promise of lower unemployment; the freezing of wages and prices and, thus, inflation; a series of trade and taxation measures designed to rebalance the terms of international trade in favor of U.S.–based corporations. The overall program reflected, on the one hand, the existing U.S. balance of payments and international monetary crises and, on the other, the corporate pressure on Nixon to do something about the large union wage increases that were being demanded and obtained for the first time in nearly a decade. The crux of Phase One was to attack wages and give direct aid and support to U.S. corporations in their emerging struggle with foreign competitors. In both cases, however, the result would be the direct subsidization of U.S. corporate profit margins. First, by freezing wages and workers' incomes and not freezing profits, dividends, or interest rates (i.e., income of those owning capital), subsidization under Phase One really meant taking money from workers and redistributing it to employers and stockholders. Secondly, by arbitrarily giving U.S. corporations special and immediate tax concessions—such as the ten percent investment credit and repeal of the seven percent auto excise tax—in addition to the previously announced liberalized depreciation rules, and by initiating a ten percent import surcharge and floating the dollar, U.S. corporations would be able to regain many domestic and foreign markets lost to their European and Japanese competitors. This would mean additional sales and, it was hoped, increased profit margins as well—which, because of the wage freeze, would not filter down to the workers.

Phase One differed from Nixon's earlier programs in several important ways: it signified the beginning of an *integrated* and *systematic* (i.e., economywide) approach to subsidization. It constituted a much more *direct* and *immediate* (i.e., short-run) approach. Finally, it signified the beginning of subsidization via income redistribution, not only at the expense of United States workers but at the expense of foreign corporate competitors as well. Both this latter fact and the "directness" of the overall program made it an extremely important political development. Phase One signaled the opening round of a new international trade war; not less significantly, it announced the beginning of the corporate-Nixon offensive against organized labor.

In dollar terms the amount by which Phase One served to subsidize U.S. corporate profits probably ranges, conservatively, from $15 to $25 billion dollars. Roughly $2 to $4 billion can be attributed to the wage freeze alone. For 1971 in general, it is estimated the ten percent investment credit would yield U.S. corporations around $3 billion. Repeal of the auto excise tax would give U.S. corporations about $2.3 billion in the first year. (The investment credit would produce $4 billion in the next year and $2.5 billion annually thereafter, while repeal of the excise tax would mean about $2 billion annually thereafter.) This taxation income given directly to U.S. corporations by the Treasury was "debited" or replaced by the corresponding loss of workers' income which resulted from 100,000 additionally unemployed. Nixon proposed to finance much of his Phase One program by reducing the federal workforce by five percent. Thus, it was the average worker who ended up "financing" the greater part of the program. Finally, the ten percent import surcharge and floating the dollar would undoubtedly contribute around $5 to $10 billion.

This program of domestic wage restraints plus new trade taxation policy, which is the essence of the Nixon economic program, may eventually prove to contain some fundamental contradictions. To the extent that the Nixon trade taxation program proves too slow or too ineffective in regaining a greater share of markets and sales for U.S. corporations, the greater will be the pressure to subsidize profit margins domestically by attacking the wages of U.S. workers more directly. Thus, to a certain extent the future of wage controls (and ultimately of collective bargaining and the right to strike) in the United States depends upon the outcome of the emerging struggle between the Western capitalist nations for control of foreign markets and sales. Conversely, the extent to which wage controls and wage restraints fail domestically will contribute to the pressure to subsidize corporate profit margins by reducing other costs (i.e., interest rates, fixed costs, depreciation, taxes, etc.) and/or by improving the relative share of world markets for U.S. corporations. Profit margins are basically a function of sales and costs and can be protected or expanded by increasing the former, decreasing the latter, or both.

Phase Two, which went into effect in November 1971, was basically an extension of Phase One. The game was the same, only the cards were reshuffled so that the second hand dealt came from the same stacked deck. An important factor in Phase Two was the relatively little progress the Nixon administration was able to make in securing gains for U.S. corporations in foreign and domestic markets. Despite devaluation of the U.S. dollar and high level talks among the Big Ten Western capitalist nations, at the end of Phase One very little had been gained for U.S.-based corporations. This fact partly explains why controls on wages were progressively tightened at the beginning of Phase Two, and why price controls were progressively loosened over the same period. There is no need at this time to go into all the details of how the Pay Board's initial positions regarding retroactive wage increases, deferred increases, merit increases, substandard pay, "serious inequity" increases, catch-up increases, fringe benefit increases, and increases justified by productivity gains were "progressively" revised and tightened in the weeks and months following November 14, 1971. The record speaks for itself. The record is also clear regarding price controls, in particular with regard to rents, food, retail prices, insurance rates, taxes, professional fees, and corporate reporting where, for all practical purposes, price controls soon became effectively nonexistent. It was no coincidence that corporate profits and prices rose significantly in the first half of 1972 while wages and workers' real income hardly gained at all. Over the course of Phase One as well as Phase Two the relative distribution of national income clearly shifted from labor to capital.

The tightening of wage controls was not the only means by which the Nixon administration in the course of Phase Two sought to redistribute income from workers to employers and thereby to subsidize corporate profit margins. Holding down wages is only one of two basic ways of lowering unit labor costs for corporations. The other is to force greater productivity from the labor force for essentially the same rate of pay. Of course, higher productivity for the same pay is also a kind of wage restraint, since workers are made to produce more for less. In other words, their money income may stay constant but their real income falls.

As it becomes less possible during Phase Two and thereafter to hold down wages and workers' income by manipulating and tightening Pay Board rules and guidelines, the emphasis will begin to shift toward increasing productivity. In fact, long before the possibilities for tightening and manipulating Phase Two rules were fully exploited by the Pay Board, the way was being carefully prepared for the corporate-Nixon productivity offensive against labor.

This preparation began in June 1970 with the establishment by Nixon of a National Productivity Commission, designed mainly to consider and develop a program that could eventually become part of a Nixon economic strategy. The passing of the Productivity Act of 1971 (as an amendment by Javits of New York to the 1971 Economic Stabilization Act passed by Congress in December 1971) marked the second stage. An important aspect of this "productivity amendment" was that it called for the creation of Productivity Councils at all levels of industry, from the plant and shop level up. Such direct participation by government in all major collective bargaining contract determinations would, in effect, constitute eventually, if not initially, a kind of indirect and unofficial compulsory arbitration.

By March–April 1972 it appeared that the administration was heading more and more toward emphasizing increased productivity as the major means for redistributing workers' income to employers. Many high level public officials, including

Nixon himself, were beginning to make major statements on productivity. Phase Three will have begun when these productivity councils are fully established and actively in effect throughout the major areas of the economy.

At the present time the full administration emphasis on productivity bargaining has not yet become apparent. The productivity councils are not yet active, and the full corporate-Nixon productivity bargaining offensive is still to emerge. However, the pressures of increased emphasis on productivity are already beginning to be felt at the shop and plant levels as corporations themselves, in anticipation of future developments, have begun the productivity offensive at the local level. It is largely this offensive which has provoked the conflicts and wildcats over speedups and work standards that have occurred at places like Lordstown, Norwood, Fontana, and elsewhere. The outcome of such local struggles will probably have much to say in determining how, when, and in what manner the full corporate-Nixon productivity offensive will emerge.

But whatever the particulars of the strategy, one thing is certain: when it comes it will aim at nothing less than the destruction of collective bargaining as it now exists in the United States. At present, collective bargaining takes place on the basis of several criteria which justify union wage demands. These criteria are: the *profitability* of the particular corporation, enterprise, etc.; the *comparability* of wages in the corporation, enterprise, industry, etc., with wages in a similar or related corporation, enterprise, etc.; *cost-of-living* increases; inordinately *low wages* of a particular workforce, group, race, sex, etc.; and *productivity gains* made since the last contract in the particular plant, enterprise, etc.

According to the corporate point of view, collective bargaining as it now exists is proving to be too expensive for many U.S. corporations. It was suited to a period in which the corporations had free access to, and dominance in, world markets in general; a period in which there were, in fact, no major foreign capitalist competitors cutting into prize domestic and foreign markets; a period in which no nation could match the productivity of U.S. industry; a period in which there was no Southeast Asian war provoking record inflation at home and raising corporate fixed costs due to overexpansion. If and when the corporate-Nixon productivity offensive gets into full swing, it will be clear that its objective is to eliminate collective bargaining based on all criteria except that of productivity. In this way, an increase in wages will be allowed only if it yields a corresponding equal or greater increase in corporate income. Under productivity bargaining workers' money incomes may grow but real income will decline. In this way, collective bargaining will be transformed from a vehicle for increasing labor's share of national income (as originally it was to be in principle) into a vehicle for increasing capital's share—a vehicle for corporate subsidization and income redistribution.

The Anti-Labor Legal Offensive

Still another way of subsidizing corporate profits at the expense of workers and wages is to limit or destroy the right to strike. The ability to strike is labor's primary, and in the last analysis its only, weapon for securing wage increases. With this means effectively eliminated, controlling wages would be a relatively simple task. Moreover, at least seriously limiting the right to strike would make the institutionalizing of productivity bargaining a much easier task.

Establishing productivity bargaining, especially during a period of wage controls and wage restraint, can be expected to produce a revolt on the part of union rank and file. In anticipation of this, the corporate-Nixon offensive has begun making preparations for attacking labor's right to strike. (Such preparations would in any event have to go hand in hand with any attempt to destroy collective bargaining.) This preparation began back in 1970 with extensive congressional studies of the history of (anti)strike legislation in the United States. Following this there have emerged various bills designed to destroy the NLRB and establish labor courts, which would bankrupt most unions and effectively destroy protections granted under Section 8(a) of the NLRA which prohibit unfair labor practices. In addition, proposals for creating compulsory arbitration have narrowly failed passage in Congress and will most likely be on the agenda soon again. Legislation is being prepared to amend the Taft-Hartley Act to provide for extended "cooling off" periods and "regional" national emergency disputes injunctions. Not least, the federal courts, the Labor Board, and the Justice Department have joined the offensive and assumed an increasingly belligerent antilabor stance. Finally, the right-to-work movement has once more emerged nationally in anticipation of a new nationally coordinated legislative effort by the Nixon administration and its supporters.

It is not coincidental that this general antilabor and antistrike legal offensive has begun to emerge during the course of Phase Two. There can be little doubt that it is timed as an answer to the anticipated rank-and-file rebellion against the continuation of wage controls, the institutionalization of productivity bargaining, and Nixon's corporate subsidization program.

The Implications for Workers' Control

It was pointed out earlier in this article that the Nixon economic program, both present and future, would exacerbate those shop floor conditions creating the potential for workers' control and, consequently, would serve to further develop that potential. We will now attempt to summarize how this might occur and, in doing this, try to clarify the relation between workers' control as defined and the Nixon economic program in general.

1) Nixon's new, liberalized depreciation rules and the tax investment credit already in effect (as well as future plans to subsidize corporate R & D costs) will tend to accelerate the *trend toward displacing labor* with new technology and lead to an upsurge in capital goods investment in general. This will continue to put pressure on conditions of work, as described above.

2) Intensive *corporate cost-cutting programs* will continue throughout Phase Two and thereafter as long as inflation in the United States continues at current rates and foreign competitors continue their challenge to U.S.-based corporations. Moreover, to the extent price controls continue, and for political reasons are forced to become more effective than they are at present, the more the pressure will grow for more intensive corporate cost-cutting efforts as well. This too will lead to further deterioration of work conditions and work standards.

3) To the extent that *wage freeze* and *wage controls* continue and "tighten," the more workers will be unable to compensate for deteriorating work conditions with demands for higher wages as "payment" for accepting or tolerating those conditions. Workers will be forced to deal with the deterioration of working conditions and standards with more direct means. Conflicts and strikes over work conditions, standards, and rules will spread and intensify. Grievance systems will become increasingly ineffective and ignored. Grievances will be settled more and more by "direct" means. The right to strike over local grievances will become an increasingly popular rank-and-file demand.

4) As wage controls themselves prove to be ineffective and/or insufficient in restraining wages and subsidizing profits, more stress will be laid by corporations and the administration on developing and institutionalizing *productivity bargaining*. Squeezing greater productivity out of workers, without commensurate pay increases, lowers unit labor costs and, thereby, increases corporate profits. Wage controls and productivity bargaining become the two sides of the same vise squeezing workers' incomes. Productivity bargaining means the "trading off" of established work rules standards, and practices in "exchange" for additional money income for workers. This dual attack of wage controls and productivity bargaining will sharply accelerate the development of those shop floor conditions described earlier that create the potential for raising workers' control demands.

5) Wage controls, the increased emphasis on productivity and productivity bargaining, plus the introduction of new and more effective *antistrike legislation* together constitute a three-sided attack on collective bargaining in general. Eventually, the success of such an attack could lead to the elimination of all bargaining based on any criteria except that of productivity gains. With regard to workers' control, new antistrike legislation would have an effect similar to that of wage controls. It would make it even more difficult for workers to compensate for deteriorating working conditions by accepting higher wages. Moreover, it would seriously impair workers' ability to defend themselves against the productivity offensive. Antistrike legislation would be the hammer with which employers enforce the

reduction of unit labor costs and workers' real income through tighter wage controls and productivity bargaining.

6) To the extent that the various Nixon *trade and taxation* programs fail in their basic objectives of income redistribution and corporate subsidization, the greater will be the pressure for tightening wage controls plus intensifying and/or extending productivity bargaining. Consequently, the potential for workers' control demands will become greater. (Furthermore, it can be expected that the less effective wage controls become, the more emphasis will be placed on productivity, and vice versa.)

7) The greater the corporate failure to hold down unit labor costs by wage controls and productivity bargaining, the greater will be the necessity for the Nixon administration to underwrite other corporate fixed costs via more liberal *depreciation* rules, more investment *tax credits,* more subsidization of *R & D* costs, and so forth.

8) Finally, the less successful efforts are to hold down corporate costs in general (fixed and wage), the greater will be the pressure to protect and expand profit margins by *stimulating corporate demand and sales.* This may occur either by regaining a greater relative share of world markets for U.S.-based corporations at the direct expense of foreign corporate competitors, or by opening via diplomatic means the two great remaining world markets, China and the U.S.S.R. Extending and intensifying trade with the Communist bloc nations constitutes the core of Nixon's Phase Three trade policy; it was also the primary reason for his travels to China and the U.S.S.R. in 1972.

It is quite possible, however, that Nixon's success in expanding trade and the U.S. corporate share of world markets may prove successful enough in subsidizing profit margins (via increased sales rather than lower costs) that in the short run the need for an overall corporate attack on wages and workers' income may be relieved somewhat or even delayed. In the longer run, however, this direct attack on wages, collective bargaining, and working conditions in general must come. And with it will come renewed possibilities for workers' control. The same can also be said about corporate subsidization via tax measures and concessions such as more liberalized depreciation, tax investment incentives, underwriting research and development costs, and so forth. These measures may relieve the pressure somewhat in the immediate future, but they will eventually lead to a greater renewed attack on wages by means of new controls and productivity bargaining.

VI.

In conclusion, it can be said that at present the potential for raising the issue of workers' control is rooted in the increasing deterioration of working conditions, standards and practices plus the various social and economic forces which underlie and generate that deterioration.

The history of the last decade shows that the U.S. economy was able to extricate itself temporarily from the stagnation and recession of the 1958–61 period by directly subsidizing corporate profits by means of extremely liberalized tax and depreciation programs—plus an effective attack on organized labor in the form of the Landrum-Griffin Act and the introduction of "voluntary" wage guideposts up to 1965. This was accomplished also in no small part by the war in Southeast Asia and by the vast amount of federal spending it produced—expenditures which ended up mostly as corporate income.

Yet the seeds of the present recession and stagnation, which began in late 1969–early 1970, were sown by those very same programs and policies responsible for ending the 1958–61 recession, namely, the subsidization of corporate profits through the war spending and the various tax-depreciation–wage programs of the last decade.

Without a doubt, the war has been the primary cause of the high rate of inflation in the economy. But another important factor behind the inflation has been overexpansion and over-investment by most U.S. corporations in the last half of the sixties, and the sharp rise in corporate fixed costs this produced. (The war and the overexpansion as causes of the present inflation are not mutually exclusive, in fact, but are complementary developments.) Together the war and the overexpansion are responsible for the inflation which, in turn, has played a crucial role in causing the relative decline in demand and sales for U.S. products compared to those of foreign competitors—both domestically and abroad. The war and the overexpansion stand together as the primary economic forces responsible for generating the recession and inflation of the 1969–72 period, and the long run crisis in corporate profit margins underlying it.

It has been essentially this same corporate crisis which has provoked the various intensive cost-cutting programs and labor displacement practices since 1969. And in turn, these programs and practices have begun to create shop level conditions and pressures which can be conducive to introducing the idea of workers' control and the raising of workers' control demands.

As the corporate crisis continued and worsened throughout 1970–1 it became increasingly necessary to introduce more direct and extensive programs in order to subsidize failing profits. These additional programs aimed on the one hand at lowering corporate costs and, on the other, at expanding corporate demand and sales. (Both lower costs and greater sales would expand corporate profit margins.) At the center of the cost control program were liberalized depreciation rules, more corporate tax concessions, federal underwriting of R & D, and, most importantly, a direct attack on wage costs via wage controls. At the center of the "sales expansion" program were federal efforts to aid U.S. corporations in regaining a greater relative share of world markets (both in the U.S. and abroad) by means of floating the dollar, the import surcharge, subsidizing U.S. exports, the devaluation, and so forth.

Continued pressure on profit margins can be expected to produce: 1) more corporate tax concessions; 2) still more liberalized depreciation rules; 3) a general attack on collective bargaining by means of stronger wage controls, the introduction and institutionalizing of productivity bargaining, and a legal offensive against organized labor in general—especially the right to strike; 4) an increased competition and conflict between the United States and foreign capitalist competitors for a greater relative share of world markets, which may come in various forms; 5) sharp expansion of trade with the Communist bloc.

Which of the above approaches to subsidizing corporate profit margins is to be emphasized in the months to come will depend on the relative success of each. But to the extent that the various trade taxation approaches prove to be ineffective, too slow, or impossible for various political reasons, then the greater will be the possibility of a general corporate-government attack on wages. If this is the case, the average American worker will be made to pay the cost of subsidizing declining corporate income with his own income. Wage controls and productivity bargaining will constitute the essence of the attack on real wages, which will be supported as well by a general antistrike and antilabor legislative offensive. Collective bargaining as it now exists could be destroyed by such an attack, as could the right to strike.

But before developments reach this stage, the deterioration of established working conditions and standards fought for and secured over the decades will have accelerated sharply. In the meantime, the *potential* for introducing, extending, and developing the idea of workers' control will grow just as rapidly.

The Changing Nature of the Working Class

If a workers' control movement takes hold in the United States and Canada, it will be based on the needs and desires of real people in real situations—offices, schools, laboratories, and service enterprises as well as in factories—and not on the imaginary interests of a mythical proletariat. Bogdan Denitch's essay sketches a theme to which John Case's article returns: the changing nature of the "working class" in the United States. Case's article elaborates on this theme, reporting the few recent experiences with workers' control organizing on this continent and proposing some directions for the future. Though the approaches outlined can be only tentative at this point, we hope that Case's essay will serve as a starting point for debate among organizers, rank-and-file workers, and all those who look toward a more democratic and humane society.

Is There a "New Working Class"?:*
A Brief Note on a Large Question

Bogdan Denitch

Mass university education, in the advanced industrial countries,[1] is leading to a shift in the function and character of university-educated personnel. From an elite education for sons of notables preparing to assume leading roles, there is a turn to vocational training, and, also, to an imprecise rite of passage

---

* A major intellectual debt to Lucien Goldmann is gratefully acknowledged. The concept of the new working class used here relates primarily to the work of Serge Mallet and, to a lesser extent, to that of André Gorz.

[1] Recent UNESCO figures on the number of students per 10,000 inhabitants indicate that after the U.S. and U.S.S.R., both East and West European countries are among those with a relatively large number of students:

U.S.A.:	284	Yugoslavia:	105
U.S.S.R.:	183	France:	104
Canada:	164	Bulgaria:	101
Netherlands:	121	Denmark:	100
Australia:	116	Czechoslovakia:	96
Japan:	116		

That this is a matter of social policy, more than of the general level of industrialization and ability to absorb university-trained personnel, is underlined by the figures for some other developed countries:

West Germany:	44	East Germany:	62
Italy:	58	Switzerland:	55

designed to prepare technicians and white-collar workers for a bureaucratized economy. This trend has reduced many of the old style professionals to paid employees of institutions. The process has advanced farthest in the United States,[2] though a number of factors make awareness of it clearer in France and some East European countries. It is important to distinguish between the effect of *mass* university education, primarily a post–World War II phenomenon, and the older discontent of *unemployed* university graduates centered on status demands and often associated with right-wing movements.

The post–World War II expansion of universities has coincided with a growing demand for university graduates. Relatively high salaries and social mobility obtained through university education disguise their real loss of power and status. Students of working class or lower middle class origin tend to accept the university environment, since for them it does represent a major chance for social advance. But with them, too, promise evoked by higher education clashes with the result, which is often compartmentalized to a degree that an older generation of university graduates would find unrecognizable. Two results follow. Leaving the university after graduation comes to seem increasingly unattractive, since meaningful work *in terms of their own education,* particularly for students of the social sciences and humanities, is hard to find. And a fertile ground is created for hostility toward a society that seems incapable of assuring satisfying work even to university graduates.

The discontent is most clearly articulated in the social sciences and humanities, where the training one gets—the ability to critically analyze institutions and ideologies—has little relationship to the work one will end up doing. For what can one do today with an undergraduate degree in the social sciences or the humanities? The better situated students in those disciplines

[2] Martin Trow, "Reflections on the Transition from Mass to Universal Higher Education," *Daedalus,* Winter 1970, pp. 1–2. ". . . this sprawling system of some 2,500 colleges and universities enrolls over forty percent of the age grade, over fifty percent of all high school graduates and those proportions are steadily rising. In some large states like California, where roughly eighty percent of high school graduates go on to some form of higher education, our system of higher education begins to be very nearly universal."

increasingly accept the fact that their undergraduate degree is only a prerequisite for entering graduate schools. Yet, while graduate school postpones entry into the job market, it also increases the gap between the training one gets and the work one will do; not all graduate students, after all, choose academic careers.

II

This change in the role of universities reflects new needs of the economy: needs for increasing numbers of salaried people with technical and bureaucratic skills who will be dependent on institutions in which they hold no power. It is a process that can be observed in advanced industrialized societies, both East and West. Whole generations trained to think in terms of societal issues are offered roles as powerless, if well-paid, employees. Those with specific skills find their work compartmentalized and routinized. The shift in the authority of engineers and skilled scientists in industry also reduces them to a *new* highly trained working class.[3]

One root of student discontent lies in this shift of role. Students increasingly resent the fact that modern society seems incapable of providing meaningful work and participation in decision making. Far from temporary, the wave of student radicalism is neither localized in respect to political issues (an end to the Vietnam War might not reduce student rebellion in the United States) nor centered on the organization of universities. Nor is it in essence rooted in a conflict of generations. It represents instead the inchoate early struggles of "a class in the process of becoming," mostly unaware of its own needs and acting archaically or irrationally. Students have sometimes been called neo-Luddites. We should remember that the Luddites were an anachronistic expression of a then *new* working class in the process of being formed out of the old crafts: they were striking out in a socially irrelevant way at symbols of their *new* status marking the end of their old role. I would like to suggest

[3] The most cogent discussion of the theories of the new working class is to be found in Serge Mallet, *La Nouvelle classe ouvriere,* Paris: Le Seuil, 1969.

in a crude parallel that the direction of student discontent toward the universities is analogous. Not the university but their own new position in society is a major cause of student alienation, just as not the machine but the new social organization of work changed the role of the old craftsmen.

Student discontent, in my view, is only a harbinger of the discontent of a new and growing class. This discontent will probably reach students in the technical sciences later than those in the social sciences, if only because the latter have been trained to generalize ideas and societal issues. For those from the technical sciences a recognition of their real status may come only at work, where they will be joining portions of the old industrial working class whose skills and training also move them toward the creation of a new group of highly skilled technicians.

III

The process, which makes unskilled and semiskilled workers less powerful, makes many skilled workers more important. They are harder to train and replace. Because of their strategic position, small groups of highly skilled workers can often paralyze entire plants. Workers in process-flow industry who maintain the ever more complex machinery, skilled workers in communication industries, IBM, electronics, and even in some of the old trades—tool- and die-makers, plant electricians, and certain branches of the building trades—begin to converge with the technicians and younger engineers into a new working class. For them, too, the gap between capabilities and decision making becomes increasingly less rational, for often they are as competent to make day to day decisions as the foremen and management. Their skills are a key to modern production, and not the often archaic skills of the managers and owners.[4]

[4] This is even more striking in Eastern Europe where the political "skills" of the managers of nationalized enterprises are, if anything, more anachronistic than the training of their opposite numbers in the West. E.g., recent studies in Poland and Yugoslavia show that most managers who have a university degree tend to have a general law or economics degree.

The rationality of factory organization and the legitimacy of discipline are threatened when they seem based not on superior knowledge but on institutional power alone. In all the modern industrial societies, power, after all, remains in the hands of the old elites. It was always more difficult to be a foreman or supervisor, to exercise authority over highly-skilled workers than over the unskilled, particularly when the skill of the workers and their knowledge of the work process was greater than that of lower-level management. A traditional way of handling this problem in such trades as printing, tool- and die-making, etc., has been to have "working foremen" who were members of the union and organizers of tasks rather than managers of men. In many countries the highly skilled workers have developed a great deal of control over the work pace and process, eliminating lower management entirely. Thus the immediate authority faced by the worker was half voluntary, subject to his democratic organization and therefore legitimate. With the new working class, however, the skills of the workers, whether utilized or not, are so often superior to those of the lower, middle, and sometimes even higher management that authority derives from the organizational structure alone; it is neither reasonable nor legitimate.

A new working class, indispensable to modern economies, has a potential social weight greater than its actual numbers, which, in any case, are growing. Seemingly divergent strands— massive discontent among students in most industrial societies, a decrease in the independence of professionals, the "proletarianization" of many technicians and engineers, the increasing militancy of strategically placed groups of skilled workers (particularly in Western Europe)—are interconnected. They represent an early phase in the developing consciousness of a stratum in modern industrial societies which can be described as a "new working class." While this term has been used in the United States,[5] it is generally counterposed to the more traditional

---

[5] See Richard Flacks, "The Revolt of the Young Intelligentsia: Revolutionary Class Consciousness in Post Scarcity America," in *Revolution Reconsidered* (New York: Free Press); and Michael Harrington, "Whatever Happened to Socialism," *Harper's,* February 1970.

stress on the working class as agency for social change. There is a peculiar continuity between the New Left attempt to identify the young intelligentsia as the major group potentially committed to radical social change and the decades-old liberal stress on middle class liberals as the active political element. Both agree that the traditional working class is passive and will remain so. I say, however, that the new working class must help transform the labor movement and can become a significant social force only in alliance with sections of the old working class.

IV

In France in 1968 and Italy in 1970, the most militant strikers came from areas with the most advanced technology and the highest proportion of highly skilled or educated workers in electronics, chemistry, auto, aircraft, as well as from previously passive "middle-class" professions—teaching and journalism. Characteristic of these strikes is a stress on democracy at the point of production rather than mere traditional wage demands. Strikes of this kind indicate that relatively high wages do not succeed in buying off discontent. A sense of powerlessness is not sufficient for revolt; but a sense of powerlessness *at work* combined with a feeling of power *as a social group* provides an impetus toward organized militancy. This militancy expresses itself not only in regard to wages and working conditions but also in regard to problems of control in the work process. The demand for some form of worker's control increasingly characterizes the strikes in Europe—and it is raised by the most skilled workers and technicians, more often than not against the desire of the union leaders and parties of the Left.

This has profound implications for any analysis of student rebellions and "middle class" discontent, but even more for the trade union and socialist movements. For the latter, understanding and relating to this process is a matter of life and death. In Western Europe both the Social Democratic and Communist parties find that their bases of strength remain in the old working class, and these not only shrink numerically but become strategically less important. In France it was the previously Catholic trade unions (CFTU) rather than the Communist-led CGT that repeatedly took the initiative in strikes and alone related sympathetically to the students during May 1968. The CFTU's primary strength is in industries where the new rather than the old working class predominates.*

V

A major dividing line between Marxist and non-Marxist radicals has always been the insistence of Marxists that forces for social transformation had to exist in the society itself. Subjective desires of would-be revolutionists could never be enough. Around this issue center most of the polemics between Marx and Bakunin; it is the issue that led Kautsky to attack the Bolsheviks as neo-Jacobins. On the whole question of just how central is the presence of objective historical forces are waged bitter polemics between Guevarists and Marxists in Latin America.

In a way, both New Left utopianism and the increasing reformism of the mass working class parties in Western Europe are based on the same analysis of the role of the old working class. Each sees the industrial working class as passive and, if anything, conservative. They reach a pessimistic view of the possibilities for social change deriving from the action of the industrial working class, and therefore become either *de facto* liberal reformers or seek a different agency for social change. A theory of social change based on revolt of both the external colonies and internal marginal groups—either as yet unsocialized, as in the case of the students, or economically marginal, as in the case of the subproletariat—may sound extremely "radi-

* The author clearly refers to the Confédération Française Démocratique du Travail, which at its last (35th) Congress, for the first time, declared itself opposed to present capitalist society. It declared its aim to work for a socialist society based on democratic planning, self-management of enterprises, and public ownership of the means of production. The CFDT, with 700,000 members, is the second largest trade union in France. See *Links,* No. 13 (1970), p. 2.—Ed.

cal." But, implicitly, it rejects the view that *conscious and voluntary* action of the *majority* in its own name and interests is either a possible or, for that matter, desirable way to achieve a socialist society. Its central view is that at least in the advanced industrialized countries, "socialism" can and should be imposed by marginal revolutionary minorities on a generally reactionary majority—and particularly against the desires of a working class seen as the core of this reaction.

Two views are common in the New Left: first, a profound pessimism about the possibilities of mobilizing mass support, which sees the working class as bought off by the consumer-oriented society or even racist and reactionary; second, a view of student revolt as the symptom of a generational revolt rather than a reflection of major social shifts. These analyses combine to give the New Left an unreal, temporary, marginal charac-ter—to fixate it as a form of kamikaze radicalism without hope of producing major social change, yet determined to make the (necessarily only moral) gesture.

VI

What underlines the relevance of the growing layer of techni-cally and intellectually trained workers is that they are also to be found in the one-party "socialisms" of Eastern Europe where massive growth of the universities has an even more explosive potential—unless, of course, we assume an infinite capacity of those regimes to absorb and buy off their university trained cadres. The irrationality and inefficiency, not to speak of the brutality, of the East European societies is more "pure" than that of the welfare capitalism of the West. This is perhaps the reason why the demands there are so much clearer at this time: democratization of major institutions (the government, mass organizations, and party) or a multiparty system, and self-management or workers' control of enterprises. Few of the oppositionists use New Left rhetoric, and if some small circles of intellectuals may have absorbed the "new and modern" view that the working class is reactionary and coopted, it is an illu-sion that no regime dares have. In Prague in 1968 workers called for workers' councils and a real say in day-to-day decisions over production, while intellectuals centered on intellectual freedoms.

The reluctance of the Prague liberals to introduce workers' councils may go a long way to explain the relative indifference to the early phase of the Russian occupation by the same workers who, through massive slowdown, continued the struggle long after many intellectuals had left the country or had become silent.

Demands for workers' control or workers' councils are of course not new. They are to be found in early Marx, in Bakunin, Proudhon, and Kropotkin. They were present in the writings of some Bolsheviks and Rosa Luxemburg. Workers' control was not only central to the demands of the Workers' Opposition in the early Bolshevik period; it was the instinctive response of the working class in Spain at the opening of the Civil War. However, it is also true that most of the European Left parties, including Communists after the victory of Stalin, have borrowed heavily from the Jacobin tradition of revolutionary centralism. Though centralism was viewed not as antithetical to democracy but as an instrument against local, entrenched power, it did lead to neglect of the content and day-to-day organization of power. Nationalization of the means of production was seen by the Left primarily as depriving the old ruling class of its economic power, but not as fundamentally changing work relations inside the newly nationalized industry. Today, renewed demands for workers' control reflect not only dissatisfaction of the workers in the nationalized industries of both Western and Eastern Europe with the old authoritarian structures. The changing character of the workforce and mode of production further creates an ever larger pool of workers who believe that they are capable of running the industry and at least those social organizations most relevant to their day to day lives. A working though imperfect model of workers' control and decentralization in Yugoslavia gives the discussion some reality.

The fleshing-out of demands to control one's community and workplace can give radical intellectuals a focus. It also forms a platform from which the utopian and elitist views current in so much of the student New Left can be confronted. Democratic socialist critics of the irrational and putschist rhetoric of the student radicals have too often criticized them in the name of old platforms and unexciting vistas of endless drudgery for the demands developed in a different era. Today a new meaning can be given to demands to extend democracy to all aspects of social and political life—and the technical skills and education of the new working class equip it to challenge the monopoly of expertise of the old elites.

Workers' Control: Toward a North American Movement*

John Case

The last ten years have witnessed a rebirth of radicalism in North America. A series of social movements has come into being: of the young, the poor, the black and brown, the French Canadian—even, sometimes, of the white working man and woman. The movements focus their protest on the worst injustices of American and Canadian society. They demand reforms in social institutions from the primary school to the giant corporation.

Many in the movements for change in Canada and the United States—particularly among students—see themselves as social-

* Though this essay was written by one person, it is in a real sense a collective effort of the Cambridge Institute's task force on workers' control. Special thanks are due as well to Gerry Hunnius and other members of the Praxis task force on workers' control in Toronto.

ists, and consciously seek to overthrow or transform the capitalist social order. Most are of a less ideological bent. They sense rather than express the need for fundamental change, and protest what is rather than demand what might be.

Yet the sense is growing that there is something radically wrong with the way things are. When the May 1968 events broke out in France, the London *Observer* commented:

> The events of the past three weeks are of historic importance. For they have crystalized longstanding, nagging doubts not only about France but about the nature of government in all advanced industrial societies, capitalist and Communist alike. Something clearly is stirring under the surface of our inherited assumptions and conventional wisdom about the nature of our societies.[1]

The widespread discontent "stirring under the surface" by now seems to pervade both the United States and Canada. It represents a flood of energy whose momentum is growing with the beginning of the new decade. The radicalism which seeks to unite that energy is a new and potentially powerful political force. And it is a force which calls into question the very basis of our society.

At the same time, the labor movement—historically in the forefront of movements for social change—seems to have lost both radicalism and dynamism. The workforce remains less than one third unionized in both the United States and Canada. Few unions are initiating massive organizing drives in new sectors of the economy. (The exceptions, of course, are precisely those unions identified with the radical movements and/or ethnic liberation struggles of the past ten years: the independent CNTU in Quebec, for example, and Cesar Chavez's United Farm Workers.) Unions in organized industries are powerful, but well established and bureaucratic. Almost without exception, they emphasize higher wages and better working conditions to the exclusion of other social reform goals. The result, often, is not only that they have difficulty attracting new, younger members, but also that workers in

[1] May 26, 1968.

organized plants are increasingly disaffected from the unions which claim to represent them.

Though radicals today are far from complete agreement on goals, one theme pervades the many different movements for change: opposition to concentrated governmental and corporate power, and the demand for participation in the "decisions which affect people's lives." In a different setting, the same impetus gave birth to the labor movement. If the two forces are ever to come together, it may very well be around a concept which builds on that common base and extends it—directly—into the workplace: the notion of workers' control.

Our goal is democracy. We do not mean by this simply the system of representative government we now enjoy: we do not seek, in Herbert Marcuse's words, free election of masters by slaves. We seek *self-government,* in the economic and social spheres as well as the political. We believe that national wealth must be owned and controlled by the people. We think that both the economic and the political systems must be highly decentralized to allow the creation of a participatory democracy of workers and citizens. We look, ultimately, toward a radically decentralized cooperative commonwealth, in which equality and cooperation coexist with freedom and grassroots democracy.

What might a self-governed society be like? The question is no idle intellectual exercise. It can, of course, never be finally answered—and sometimes even asking it seems presumptuous, given the obvious need to work for immediate change and to broaden the base of our movements. Yet too often those who say "a better society will emerge from the struggle" or "make the revolution, then worry about the future society" are simply ignoring the lessons of history. The North American labor movements, for example, have a long, militant, and often violent past. Nor has their militance *per se* lessened much today, as the recent flurry of protracted strikes and wildcats demonstrates. Yet, in the absence of a clear radical vision, the militance has been easily channeled into wage demands: bread-and-butter, short-term reform issues, important in themselves but never really dealing with the basic problem. As André Gorz has pointed out, "the working class will not unite politically or mount the barricades to get a 10% wage increase or 50,000 more units of public housing."[2] Unless a vision of a better society can be made concrete, people will struggle for what they can get right now, and cast a justifiably skeptical eye on radicals who call for a "transformation of society."

Not only will ordinary people wonder why they should make a revolution at all, the revolutionaries may find themselves incapable of realizing the values they seek. In the Soviet Union, as in nearly all underdeveloped revolutionary nations, the imperative of immediate economic development was given precedence over other social goals. The result has been a sacrifice of democracy, equality, and the development of community—all in all, a distinctly unappealing image of "socialism" to North Americans, though our experience obviously could be quite different. Where socialist regimes have undertaken democratic experiments, as in Yugoslavia and (to a lesser extent) other East European countries, the result has at times been a tendency to adopt old capitalist forms (such as relatively autonomous investment banks) rather than trying to forge new socialist institutions.[3] Even in Cuba, so often held up by radicals as a model of what is possible, the economic system has been constantly reorganized and reoriented—simply because, as Fidel in effect admits, the Cubans do not have the experience which would allow them to realize their goals.[4]

Martin Buber has written that a better society must be built up gradually, be it before or after a political revolution. People's behavior and ways of thinking change slowly, and the changes can come only from new ideas and new experiences all along the way.[5] The idea of an event called a "revolution" begs the

---

[2] *Le Socialisme Difficile* (Paris: Editions du Seuil, 1967) p. 69. (My translation.)

[3] See, for example, Leo Huberman and Paul Sweezy, "Peaceful Transition from Socialism to Capitalism," *Monthly Review,* Vol. XV (March 1964), pp. 569–90, for a Marxist critique of Yugoslavia.

[4] See, for example, Fidel Castro, speech delivered July 26, 1970, excerpted in *The New York Review,* XV, No. 5, September 24, 1970. Interestingly, Fidel's speech suggests the introduction of a form of worker's control in Cuba.

[5] Buber, *Paths in Utopia* (Boston: Beacon Press, 1966). Buber drew on the work of the German anarchist Gustav Landauer, who once said: "The

question of the *process* by which the experiential base for a new society is created.

The problem of posing an alternative, then, must be faced sooner or later: if we are serious about the need for basic change, we must begin the discussion now. In Spain for forty years before the Civil War anarchist clubs and unions debated the nature of the society they sought to build. They asked—and began to answer—questions of how a producer-controlled economy might operate, how national planning and coordination could be accomplished democratically, how they would stimulate education and individual development.[6] When the Civil War brought the collapse of the old social order, anarchists in Catalonia were able to replace existing economic and political institutions with their own, which were established in accordance with the principles they had so carefully developed. And though the experiment was ultimately smashed by the Loyalist government and the Communists, it proved remarkably successful during its short life.[7]

The contrast with the present situation is obvious. In May 1968, the social order in France came close to collapse. Students battled police in the streets, students and workers occu-

---

state is not something which can be destroyed by a revolution, but is a condition, a certain relationship between human beings, a mode of human behavior; we destroy it by contracting other relationships, by behaving differently." (Quoted by Colin Ward, "The Anarchist Contribution," C. G. Benello and Dimitrios Roussopoulos, eds., *The Case for Participatory Democracy: Some Prospects for the Radical Society*, New York: Grossman Publishers, 1971, p. 287.)

[6] See, for example, D. Abad de Santillan, *After the Revolution: Economic Reconstruction in Spain Today* (New York: Greenberg Publishers, 1937).

[7] Noam Chomsky writes: ". . . workers' organizations existed with the structure, the experience, and the understanding to undertake the task of social reconstruction when, with the Franco coup, the turmoil of early 1936 exploded into social revolution. . . . All of this lies behind the spontaneous achievements, the constructive work of the Spanish revolution." "Notes on Anarchism," *The New York Review* XIV, May 21, 1970, p. 34. See also George Orwell, *Homage to Catalonia* (New York: Harcourt, 1952) and Lewis Herber, *Forms of Freedom* (mimeographed pamphlet, available from *Our Generation*, Montreal).

pied factories, revolutionary councils and soviets were established in several cities. Again, the government and the Communist party each did its part to crush the potential revolution. But this time the rebels themselves—as a mass movement—had no program, no ideas, no vision beyond the vaguest of slogans (though there were smaller groups who did). What was lacking was a coherent sense that the movement knew what it was about; the crisis had not been preceded by the slow, careful development of revolutionary force and vision which characterized the Spanish situation.

Finally, though we must learn these historical lessons, our situation is radically different from anything that has gone before. Never before have societies achieved so high a degree of material wealth, of technological development, of educational resources; never before has the potential for true freedom been as great as it is today in the United States and Canada. We are socialists: but to most of our fellows socialism means dictatorship, bureaucracy, and forced industrialization. We do not know what a humane, democratic form of socialism would look like in our advanced industrial societies. But if we cannot provide precise answers, neither can we avoid confronting the problem. The debate must begin.

Our vision, again, is of a self-governed, self-managed society, and this is why we speak of a strategy of workers' control. Self-management is a structural means of extending democracy to the workplace, where most people spend most of their waking hours for most of their lives. An enterprise in which workers collectively determine what they produce, how they produce it, and how to distribute the income they earn can better realize human values than a capitalist enterprise. Work is not necessarily subordinated to utilitarian efficiency, nor to facilitating authoritarian control. Jobs can rotate, providing everyone with a variety of skills and constantly changing tasks. Creativity, cooperation, and individual satisfaction can be encouraged rather than stifled. Participation itself reduces workers' alienation from the job and their product;[8] and a say in fundamental economic decisions can help direct economic resources toward human need rather than private profit.

It is in this context, then, that we use the term "workers' control." As we understand it, workers' *control* is a strategy, a series of demands aimed at extending popular control of the enterprise and the economy. Workers' *participation* is something quite different. It suggests a system usually introduced from above, in which workers share a partial responsibility for the operation of a capitalist firm, but management retains authority over fundamental production decisions. Workers' *self-management,* finally, describes a situation in which industry is socialized and workers are the primary governing body of the firm. (Yugoslavia is one example of this, although self-management there is compromised by a number of other factors.) Workers' control might be seen as a strategy to get from workers' participation—or undiluted management authority— to workers' self-management.[9]

Workers' self-management, of course, is not the only element of our vision. Pure workers' control could easily become a kind of "workers' capitalism" with an emphasis on profiteering and competition reminiscent of our present system.[10] Community self-government—including some level of community participation in economic decisions—is the second essential ingredient. One partial model, again, might be Yugoslavia, although the exact relationship between the self-governing commune and the self-managing enterprise within its boundaries is still in the process of being worked out. A second model might be the larger Israeli kibbutzim, where a single community assembly, open to all, governs the economic, political and social affairs of the kibbutz; workers' self-management functions within this

---

[8] This has been demonstrated by nearly every sociological study. For a summary of the research, see Paul Blumberg, *Industrial Democracy* (New York: Schocken Books, 1969), chs. V and VI.

[9] This definition follows Ian Clegg, *Industrial Democracy* (London: Sheed and Ward, 1968), pp. 7–8. Other writers in the present volume, of course, may use the terms somewhat differently.

[10] Huberman and Sweezy argue that in effect this has happened in Yugoslavia. See article cited Note 3.

framework, in effect as a committee of the assembly. In both cases, social services—education, health, etc.—are provided and controlled by the entire community, though the Yugoslav commune also allows for direct participation by social service workers (e.g., teachers) and those citizens most directly affected (e.g., parents of schoolchildren).[11]

The experiences of a small, developing nation or of primarily agricultural "micro-socialist" communities cannot be wholly transposed to the industrial societies of North America. The problem, rather, is to learn from them what we can and to propose and experiment with social institutions which reflect our own needs. North American communities—the neighborhood in the city, the county in the countryside?—might very well govern themselves and run, with the workers, their own economic enterprises. But what of the complex coordination and interdependence of the economy, and what of the governing of the national state?

Again, the questions can be raised more easily than they can be answered. On the economic level, history demonstrates that free markets tend to lead to competition, inequality, and the "collective egoism" of the locality or firm. Yet central planning can as easily lead to dictatorship, or at the least a bureaucracy which stifles community initiative and local democracy. Part of the answer may lie in the creation of regional socialist bodies, as William Appleman Williams in the United States and Robert Lafont in France have proposed.[12] Communities might federate on the metropolitan level as well: and the necessary economic coordination might be carried out, democratically, by a network of representative bodies with ultimate electoral power always remaining at the lowest level.

In the political sphere, our vision is of a truly participatory

[11] For more information on the kibbutz, see the article by Keitha Fine in this volume, p. 226, on Yugoslavia, see the article by Gerry Hunnius, p. 268.

[12] See Williams, *The Great Evasion* (Chicago: Quadrangle Books, 1964); Lafont, *La Révolution Régionaliste* (Paris: Editions Gallimard, 1967). This section of the paper closely follows the argument developed in detail by Gar Alperovitz in *A Long Revolution* (forthcoming), for which I am greatly indebted to him.

democracy at all levels. We do not mean by this that all the people would make all the decisions all the time. Rather, the principles of participatory democracy can be easily stated:

1) *Maximum decentralization of governmental power.* There should be no presumption that the national—or even regional—government should exercise any political function unless local communities are clearly incapable of doing it. Local communities which owned their own industry—and thus could establish a firm economic base—would be capable of providing most social services themselves. Education, health services, recreation, and a range of other current municipal functions could be largely controlled locally, without (as is presently the case) dependence on a private economic system. Regional, or state and provincial, governments might be responsible for functions such as intercity transportation, provision of utilities like power and fuel, and operating large scale industry like steel. They might also undertake to equalize communities' sources of revenue, to coordinate local production, and to stimulate growth in disadvantaged areas. In each case, of course, the workers of a given industry or service would democratically govern the operation of their workplace, within the guidelines laid out by the community or region.

2) *The greatest possible degree of direct democracy.* Primary communities would be small enough to allow regular assemblies of the citizenry, in the fashion of a New England town meeting. Factories and offices would be broken down to manageable units, thus allowing workers full participation in their day-to-day operations. Committees, executive agencies, and planning boards would hold regular open meetings, and would actively solicit the advice and consent of interested citizens. Where power was delegated to more centralized governmental bodies, it could be to delegates rather than to representatives—delegates subject to instruction and recall from below. The role and function of political parties, no doubt, would be radically different from what they are today, but an examination of this question is beyond our present scope.

Critical here is not so much the form democracy takes as the fact that it permeates social institutions at every level. As the English socialist G. D. H. Cole has argued, political democracy means little when there are vast social and economic inequalities—and when educational and industrial institutions "train to subservience" everyone who enters them.[13] Self-management on the shop floor and self-government in the neighborhood are the precondition for effective democracy on a larger scale. Without this grassroots experience, no amount of ballots, parties, and elections will make real democracy possible.

3) *Merging of the private (economic) sphere with the public (political) sphere to form a wholly new system of democratic control.* Suppose, for example, that communities were concerned about the destruction of the natural environment. The causes of the problem could be isolated—say, too much industrial pollution or too many automobiles—and attacked directly through a reorientation of production. If education needed reform—say, through greater involvement of the children in practical problems and direct experience with the world—the community could decide to make this a priority. Rather than fund a youth job-training program or start a vocational school and hope that industry would play along, the community and its workers would set up their own industries so apprenticeship, training and general education would be an integral part of the productive process.

The possibilities are endless; so are the problems. We have here only a sketch. But North Americans have given up too easily on the notion that a better society is possible, and radicals in particular refuse to take up the question of what an alternative to our present system might be. Yet if workers' control, or any other program for fundamental change, is to be significant, it must be as part and parcel of such an alternative. Workers' self-management represents a central part of our vision, and workers' control is therefore a critically important strategy for building the changes we seek.

A new society does not arise out of thin air. Still less does it arise full-blown out of the heads of radical theorists. The test of

[13] For a summary of Cole's views on this matter, see Carole Pateman, *Participation and Democratic Theory* (Cambridge: Cambridge University Press, 1970), esp. pp. 38–9.

an alternative vision is in practice, in the extent to which viable strategies can be developed which point toward the future. No vision is ever complete. We do not map out a blueprint for a socialist society, then demand that the blueprint be implemented as a whole. Instead we propose an idea, an alternative, and then work for its realization. If the goal is practical and speaks to people's needs, the strategy will make sense. If workers' self-management, as we believe, is a critical element of a better society, then demands for workers' control should, over time, have widespread appeal to workers on the job. But in the process the goal will be modified, its form discussed, and new proposals arise. We will be that much closer to a truly human alternative.

Most demands for reform—short of a total cataclysmic transformation of society—are often realizable in our present system, but only in bastardized form. Students demand control over their education, and get two representatives on a university advisory board. Parents demand control of the schools and get an advisory council made up of unrepresentative "community leaders." Workers' management is a prime example of this phenomenon. Right now, even in the absence of a workers' control movement in North America, employers are instituting worker participation schemes and job enrichment plans right and left. *Fortune* describes one such case:

> Until Corning [Glass Works, in Medfield, Massachusetts] introduced job enrichment at the Medfield plant, meters were put together on an assembly line basis. Now one individual learns the whole process, takes the entire responsibility—and gets all the credit. Profits are up, inspections have been reduced, and rejects are down.[14]

It is only a short step from this to the participation schemes of the Scanlon Plan[15] or the co-determination structures of West-

---

[14] Judson Gooding, "It Pays to Wake Up the Blue-Collar Worker," *Fortune*, Vol. LXXXII (September 1970), p. 133.

[15] For a description of the Scanlon Plan, see Charles Hampden-Turner, *Radical Man* (Cambridge: Schenkman, 1970), Chapter VIII, pp. 192–207.

ern Europe (see Section III of this book). Participation, in management literature, explicitly means no more than "the processes by which employees other than managers contribute positively toward the reaching of managerial decisions which affect their work."[16]

The problem is not that workers' participation, job enrichment and the like are bad in themselves, or that they cannot lead to demands for greater workers' control. It is simply that they are limited; and that a workers' control movement can be channeled into such schemes, leaving the prerogatives of private capital largely untouched, if there is no clear vision of self-management as the ultimate goal. What Gorz calls the "total alternative" must always be present, or workers' control strategies will never lead to fundamental changes in the worker's life.

At the same time, cooperation, a willingness to participate, a vision of equality and justice make sense only when they can be realized in practice. The idea of self-management itself may seem foolish to the average factory or office worker. Not only would he feel incapable of running the enterprise, he likely hasn't thought of how—beyond his own work situation, which he knows best—it might be run differently. A strategy of workers' control—in which demand builds on demand and the *autonomous* power of the workers slowly increases—can be a critical educating force which, one day, can help make democratic socialism a reality.[17]

It may be, of course, that any set of strategies we choose will require a cataclysmic collapse of society and a violent overthrow of the ruling strata. But as we have seen, it is never enough to try to bring about that kind of revolution—however much likelihood one ascribes to the possibility—without building up ideas and experience which can transform people's lives. And because the possibility of such a revolution seems so distant in our own societies, it becomes important to do something now that can establish some conditions of fundamental change.

[16] R. Sawtell, *Sharing Our Industrial Future?* (London: The Industrial Society, 1968), p. 1, quoted in Pateman, *op. cit.*, p. 67.

[17] G. D. H. Cole and the guild socialists argued along similar lines for a strategy of "encroaching control." See Cole, *Guild Socialism* (New York: Frederick A. Stokes Company, 1920), ch. XI.

How, then, might our vision be tested in practice? We believe that workers' control can be a strategy for labor: for the modern unionized industrial worker, for the expanding white collar–service sector of our economy, for the millions of unorganized workers in both private industry and public service.

Strategy: The Industrial Working Class

The North American labor force, as a whole, is not highly unionized. Indeed, unions represent only twenty-eight percent of nonagricultural workers in the United States (1968), and 32.5 percent in Canada.[18] These figures can be misleading, however, for unions are heavily concentrated in some industries and relatively scarce in others. More than seventy percent of the United States workforce in transportation, communication, public utilities and construction are unionists, for example, as are roughly half of United States mining and manufacturing workers.[19] Thus there is some truth to the commonly accepted idea that industrial blue-collar workers are normally union members.

Those who do belong to unions are better off than those who do not, as the introduction to Section II of this book notes. But even where union membership is predominant, the notion of the affluent, satisfied North American industrial worker is little more than a myth. In isolated instances—most notably skilled crafts and building trades—unions have won substantial economic benefits. For the rest, the problems remain.

In 1965, for example, 69.1 percent of U.S. union members earned between $5,000 and $10,000, and only 14.2 percent earned more.[20] At General Motors, where membership in the powerful UAW is virtually universal for blue-collar employees, the average annual wage is roughly $8,000. Yet the Bureau of

[18] Sources: Derek Bok and John T. Dunlop, *Labor and the American Community* (New York: Simon and Schuster, 1970), p. 42; and *Labour Organisation in Canada* (Ottawa: Economics and Research Branch, Canadian Department of Labour, 1969), p. xii.

[19] Bok and Dunlop, *op. cit.*, p. 44.

[20] *Ibid.*, p. 43.

Labor Statistics has stated that an urban family of four in America requires nearly $10,000 to maintain a "moderate" standard of living. And as a recent memo to the Secretary of Labor makes clear, the wage structure makes no allowances for increased income as expenses rise: the principle is "equal pay for equal work."[21]

Many of the problems, of course, are not purely economic, as some of the essays in this volume suggests.[22] The symptoms of discontent themselves often do not take the form of economic demands. Blue-collar absenteeism at General Motors, though pay is on an hourly basis, has more than doubled over the past ten years, to the point where the company tried offering the workers Green Stamps and monogrammed beer mugs for good attendance. Sabotage, drinking, and the use of drugs are all on the increase in large industrial plants.[23] Perhaps most significant, a number of studies have indicated an incredibly low level of mental health, on the average, for industrial workers, as Charles Hampden-Turner's paper documents. That this is closely tied to the nature of their work was demonstrated partly by the fact that mental health scores dropped dramatically with those whose jobs were the most routine and the most closely supervised.[24]

The issue is clearly fulfillment and satisfaction at work—or the absence of it, *alienation*. The problem has long been recognized, and a variety of solutions from revolution to suggestion boxes has been proposed.[25] For the moment, it is enough to note that the problem has not been solved, even where there is a

[21] Jerome M. Rosow, "Memorandum for the Secretary. Subject: The Problem of the Blue-Collar Worker" (Washington: mimeo, 1970).

[22] See, for example, Charles Hampden-Turner's article in this volume, p. 30.

[23] See, for example, Judson Gooding, "Blue-Collar Blues on the Assembly Line," *Fortune,* Vol. LXXXII (July 1970), pp. 69 ff. Also "The Blue-Collar Blues," *Newsweek,* May 17, 1971, pp. 80 ff.

[24] Much of the basic data on this can be found in A. Kornhauser, *Mental Health of the Industrial Worker* (New York: John Wiley, 1965).

[25] See Paul Blumberg, *op. cit.,* ch. IV, for a review of theoretical "answers" to alienation.

strong union. Interviews with Detroit production workers need hardly remind us:

"When you punch in, you wish it was go-home time."

"As it is, too many of us do one same thing over and over, and time drags."

"I don't want [my kids] to go through an assembly line like I have to."

"Every single unskilled young man in that plant wants out of there. They just don't like it."[26]

Unions, in their traditional role as collective bargaining agents, have been generally unable to deal both with the industrial worker's economic insecurity, and with his alienation at work. Workers' control demands—within or without the union, depending on the situation—may provide the starting point for a new strategy. Consider some specific examples.

A central aspect of the industrial worker's economic insecurity is management's complete control over shutdowns, layoffs, transfers of operations, and the basic organization of the plant where he works. In the past, these areas have been largely outside the scope of union concern. Today, there is some evidence that this is changing.

In Toronto in early 1970, a Dunlop Rubber plant closed down. The union local began to organize protests, and radicals working with the group found some support for the concept, if not the language, of workers' control. But the battle in this case began too late. Organizers were unable to reach the rank and file of the local to mobilize a broad base of popular support. The international union sent a telegram of encouragement but did little else. The Ontario provincial government stated firmly that plant shutdown decisions were management's prerogative.

When the Dunlop Rubber workers demanded that the company open its books to an impartial commission made up of labor, government, and management representatives, their demand was rejected by management and the Ontario government. With greater support from organized labor and community groups, the outcome of this struggle might have been different. Workers, with the backing of the community, might

[26] Gooding, article cited, Note 23, pp. 70–71.

have aimed at taking over the plant and running it themselves, demanding whatever technical help and working capital they needed from the government or the company.

In Italy, workers in a Reggio Emilia machine plant occupied their factory when it was due to be closed under the Marshall Plan. With widespread community aid—particularly in the form of money and food collected by the townspeople until the first tractor came off the line—they were able to operate the plant long enough to reorganize the process of production. Eventually the state decided to support the enterprise, due to pressure from working class parties. Similarly in France, the May 1968 events led to occupation of factories in Saclay, Vitry, and elsewhere. Though this action was short-lived, it may have provided the base for future developments; in fact the CFDT, France's second largest trade union federation, has recently gone on record demanding democratic Socialism and self-management in French industry. The CFDT was the only large union federation supporting any of the revolutionary demands of students and young workers during the May events.

In general, a workers' control strategy can lead to workers beginning to develop power over the functioning of their plant in the larger society: what it produces, how much the product costs, what the side-effects of production are. Already, the UAW, for example, has raised the issue of car pricing policies. Though these were not at issue in the 1970 strike, the possibility of affecting automobile prices—and thus the inflationary impact of a new wage settlement—represents a significant step toward workers' control. Similarly the Pulp, Sulphite, and Paper Mill Workers' Union in Canada has placed control of pollution on its bargaining agenda.[27] In both cases, the unions are in

---

[27] See André Bekerman, "Workers' Control: Toward an Offensive Strategy for Canadian Labour," in *Industrial Democracy and Canadian Labour* (Toronto: Ontario Woodsworth Memorial Foundation and Praxis: Research Institute for Social Change, 1970), p. 33. L. H. Lorrain, First Vice-President and Canadian Director of the Montreal-based IBPS & PMW, said in a speech to the members of the British Columbia Loggers Association:

"If we call into question management's right to unilaterally introduce technological change, should we not also challenge management's pre-

principle dealing with economic issues through workers' control demands. If the price of automobiles rises, or if working people are taxed more to pay for pollution control, union-won wage increases will go for naught. If the companies can be forced to absorb the cost of higher wages in reduced profits, the benefits accruing to the workers involved may provide the basis for more far-reaching demands.

Another issue of fundamental importance in this context is what the plant produces, and for whom. In the United States, this issue has direct and immediate relevance in the case of defense production. Many plants are wholly or predominantly dependent on defense production for their economic livelihood. But the defense business is wildly unstable: contracts come and go according to political ebbs and flows, and the needs of the Defense Department itself vary greatly with budgetary fluctuations and changes in the international situation. For workers in defense plants, the result is not only that they are made accomplices in an inhuman war machine, their jobs themselves can never be wholly secure. Demanding workers' control over choice of contracts and decisions about products can be a way of combating this insecurity.

In Minneapolis a local peace group has attacked the Honeywell corporation for its production of fragmentation bombs for Vietnam. Although the initial reaction of the workers was often hostile—understandably, because their livelihood seemed under attack—the situation allows for the development of alternative production plans and demands by union and workers that they help determine future product decisions.[28] In Bedford, Massachusetts, some years ago, organizers working with defense plant employees were able to raise this issue of product conversion.

---

rogative to make decisions about the use of natural resources and about preservation of the environment?

"We were especially disappointed this past year in our industry when our proposals to establish joint pollution-control committees were forcefully rejected by pulp and paper companies in Western Canada." (*Pulp and Paper Worker,* Jan.–Feb. 1971, p. 10.)

[28] See "Zeroing In on the Corporate Structure," *Liberation,* Vol. XV (March 1970), pp. 18–30.

They gained substantial support until the escalation of the Vietnam War made jobs seem secure once again.

Eventually, the critical initial economic demand—one which has characterized workers' control movements throughout the world—is to have the company "open the books." Whether the issue is plant closure, pricing and production policies, or choice of product, the workers are powerless to make effective demands if they do not have access to the same financial information as management. In their role as collective bargaining agents, unions have recognized this for some time: the UAW, for example, expends a good deal of effort keeping duplicate records of the auto companies' financial records. Workers' control struggles are even more dependent on the ability of workers to counter management's claims with information of their own.

But workers' control is not a strategy to deal with economic issues only. In fact, it must not be, for the evidence indicates that working conditions and the organization of production are equally important to the modern industrial worker. In the 1970 UAW strike, for example, the national union was bargaining primarily about wages and benefits; but the issue which most concerned many workers at the local level was their opposition to compulsory overtime work.

Control over working conditions and the process of production suggests many different demands. In Massachusetts, organizers have been working with union representatives on questions of industrial health and safety; eventually, such a project could lead to workers' councils responsible for overseeing the work safety aspects of production. Workers might also demand control over hiring and firing, as British dockworkers have done.[29] Or workers' control could take the form of reorganizing production itself. Thus the United Auto Workers has proposed "that teams of workers follow a new car down the assembly line, working on the car from start to finish." Such a change, the union claims, would make "the job of auto workers

[29] See Ken Coates and Tony Topham, "Workers' Control As a Strategy of Socialist Advance," in *The Debate on Workers' Control: A Symposium from Marxism Today* (Nottingham: Institute for Workers' Control, 1970), p. 46.

more interesting, and improve the quality of the product."[30] In general, workers' control over the job would mean, in the words of one union official,

> . . . direct control by workers over the scheduling of work, the speed of production, work methods, and the selection of supervision. It is also essential to establish veto rights over layoffs, discipline, and other management prerogatives.[31]

Is such a strategy viable? One answer is that every significant study has shown that participation in work process decisions and actually deciding on conditions of work substantially increases job satisfaction.[32] There is therefore every reason to believe that demand could build on demand, one leading to another, until workers are able to demand full control over the production process.

A second part of the answer is that unions and workers' groups must take the initiative in this area, or management will. Already, the "human relations" approach to management has gained widespread acceptance among large firms;[33] and a number of "enlightened" companies are introducing job enrichment and worker-participation schemes, as noted above. Unions have rightly been hostile to this process (though often for the wrong reasons), for it further integrates the worker into an economic situation which does not work to his benefit. But management is offering workers concrete rewards, and unless worker organizations can counter with an offensive that offers the same benefits *and* challenges management prerogatives elsewhere, they will continue to lose the support of their members. Workers' control can be a strategy for radical change only if the demand develops from the bottom up, and only if the strategy

30 "Unions Would End Car Line 'Boredom'," *Toronto Daily Star,* August 7, 1970.

31 André Bekerman, article cited in Note 27, p. 36.

32 See Paul Blumberg, *op. cit.,* chs. V and VI; also Charles Hampden-Turner, *Radical Man,* ch. VIII.

33 See, for example, Judson Gooding, article cited, Note 14; for a critique of the "human relations" approach; see Martin Oppenheimer, "Participative Techniques of Social Integration," *Our Generation,* Vol. VI (December 1968–January 1969), pp. 100–9.

does not aim at merely changing the work process while leaving management's power untouched elsewhere.

All of these situations at the moment, of course, represent no more than possibilities, fledgling attempts whose success cannot yet be determined. The point, however, is simple. The North American industrial worker—even where he is unionized, and many are not—remains in a fundamentally insecure economic position and is often deeply alienated from his work. Though traditional union demands can mitigate the economic problem, and can sometimes spell out desirable working conditions, a strategy of workers' control can go one step further toward a truly democratic workplace. The industrial labor force, far from being closed to issues of workers' control, may represent one strategic key for radical organizers.

Strategy: Service and White-Collar

The time is past, however, when the blue-collar industrial work-force made up the bulk of the working class. The North American labor force is in transition. Part of the shift is indicated by the relative growth figures for white-collar and blue-collar sectors of employment. In 1950 and 1966 alike, blue-collar workers made up roughly 55 percent of the workforce, while the white-collar portion rose from 29.7 percent to 38.8 percent. Broken down by occupational grouping, these figures reveal that professional and technical workers increased in number by 89.8 percent, clerical by 68.6 percent, and "operatives" (manufacturing workers) by only 18.5 percent.[34]

Within this shift another significant change was taking place: from manufacturing to service jobs, even within the blue-collar rankings. Commodity-producing sectors actually declined as a percentage of the workforce from 1950 to 1966, from 43.8 percent to 40.7 percent. Service-producing sectors, in contrast, rose from 40.9 percent of the workforce to 53.3 percent.

[34] Census data summarized in Jay Mandle, "Some Notes on the American Working Class," *The Review of Radical Political Economics,* Vol. II (Spring 1970), pp. 52–3.

Particularly important in this sphere is the growth of government employment at all levels. Economist Jay Mandle notes: "Between 1947 and 1965, nonmilitary government employment—almost totally service employees—grew by over 3 percent per year, far more than any other industrial sector."[35] Though the organized industrial sector of the workforce remains large and important, any movement for workers' control in North America must also deal with the expanding sectors of the labor force: white-collar, service, and government employees.

The development of workers' control strategies is perhaps most problematic in relation to privately employed blue-collar service workers: hospital workers, maintenance workers, waiters, and so on. Though this is a growing sector of the economy, few attempts have been made to unionize workers in this area, and their general low pay may make any demands beyond immediate wage increases seem superfluous. Nonetheless, at least two comments seem appropriate.

First, privately employed blue-collar service workers often work in economically marginal enterprises, or in nonprofit institutions such as hospitals and universities. The result is often greater than normal hostility to union activity. The small entrepreneur fears going out of business; the nonprofit institution, operating on a relatively limited budget, fears sacrificing "more important" programs to the wage demands of the low-skilled service worker. At the same time, the operation of the institution may be much less impersonal than that of a large corporation or government office. The worker feels himself not much different from the boss in the small, economically marginal shop. Or he feels himself part of the community directly affected by the education, health care, etc., provided by the nonprofit institution.

Second, much of the organizing in these situations in recent years has been done not by established unions but by independent radical groups. (This may be due to the organizing difficulties encountered.) Students on a number of campuses have

35 *Ibid.*, p. 66.

attempted to organize nonprofessional university employees. Radicals in several cities have initiated hospital worker organizing projects. Independent unions—such as New York's Local 1199 of the Retail, Wholesale, and Department Store Workers' Union—find that low-paid service jobs are wide open for organizing drives to expand their membership.[36]

Put together, these two situations at least raise the possibility of workers' control demands. On the one hand, workers can often perceive immediate benefits in having a say in the operation of their workplace. On the other hand, radical organizers can consciously undertake to put forward such demands. In Toronto, for example, the Canadian Union of Public Employees, an independent union, began to organize the nonprofessional staff of the University of Toronto. They then proposed a complete restructuring of the governance of the university, including participation from the service workers; and they proposed that the university's doors be open to all its employees and their children.[37] Similar demands in the field of health care have been made by insurgent hospital unions with roots in their local communities: not only should they (and the community) have a say in running health care facilities, the facilities themselves should be open for the benefit of all. Thus in Kansas, for example:

Members of the Kansas Health Workers Union (Local 1271: American Federation of State, County and Municipal Employees) recently put on a *Hospital Improvement Action* under the slogan *We Care*. For twelve hours psychiatric aides created their own model of how hospital wards should be run. Because they claimed that their work load was being increased to the neglect of patients, extra workers were added to each ward. Signs were posted stating

[36] See John Ehrenreich, "New Unions," *Hard Times,* No. 87 (September 7–14, 1970), pp. 1–4. Ehrenreich's article is reprinted from *Health-Pac,* published by the Health Policy Advisory Center of New York City.

[37] See "Brief to the Commission on University Government of the University of Toronto from the Canadian Union of Public Employees," (Ottawa: August, 1969, mimeo).

that this was a *Union Administered Ward*. Doctors and other professionals continued to function in their clinical roles. When the inevitable confrontation with city government and police came, community help began to pour in.[38]

Blue-collar service workers, however, may not be immediately responsive to workers' control strategies: again, when people are grossly underpaid, pure wage demands will necessarily take priority. White-collar service workers, in contrast, may be the most fertile ground for worker-control organizing. As a group, they have grown the fastest of any occupational sector of the economy. Moreover, as would be expected, they have the highest educational level of the workforce, and by and large the highest overall pay.

It is no surprise, then, that this group is the most concerned with questions of working conditions, job description, nature of the "product," and similar issues that are directly raised by the demand for workers' control. In Europe, evidence indicates that technicians and highly skilled workers have taken the lead here. In France during the May events, technicians led the occupations of the factories and raised demands for workers' control. Researchers in Naples occupied a laboratory, demanding full workers' participation in the operation of the lab. Journalists on the staffs of *Der Stern* in Germany and *Le Monde* and *Le Figaro* in France have recently demanded—and instituted— staff participation in the management and editorial policies of their newspapers.[39]

In the United States and Canada, young academics and professionals have begun to make clear that workers' control may be a real issue for many white-collar workers. Radical caucuses and organizations of doctors, lawyers, architects, city

[38] Gerry Hunnius, "Strategies for Change: Problems and Possibilities," in Gerry Hunnius, ed., *Participatory Democracy for Canada: Workers' Control and Community Control* (Montreal: Black Rose Books, 1971), p. 86.

[39] See *In Place of Management: The Press* (London: Free Communications Group, 1970), Appendices A and B; also Jean Schwoebel, "The Miracle Le Monde Wrought," *Columbia Journalism Review,* Summer 1970, pp. 8–11.

planners, social workers, economists, social scientists, professors, teaching assistants, and scientists have all sprung up during recent years. Among these organizations the demands have been for different kinds of work, for restructuring of the institutions which employ their members, for participation in decisions about policy. Sociologist Martin Oppenheimer describes this growth of radical caucuses and organizations:

> The caucus movement, like traditional trade unions, is organized both horizontally, as in the campus chapters of the New University Conference, and vertically, in professional organizations of sociologists, for example. It differs from trade unionism in that the caucuses question the nature of the product and the structure of the job, rather than being concerned solely with wages and working conditions. By "nature of product" is meant *what* is produced—whether a commodity, a service, an input of information, education, training, or an idea. By "structure of job" is meant the basic issue of decision making. The caucuses are united in seeking more participative structures. In Europe, demands for "worker participation" are now accepted by trade unions as equally valid as demands for better wages. Not so in the mainstream of trade unionism in the United States. But by questioning the nature of the product—in a sense, the ultimate decision governing the workplace—the American caucuses move beyond the European working class movement.[40]

Even beyond this narrow sector, there have been signs of similar activity among other white-collar service workers. Employees of a small computer programming company in the Boston area organized a union in objection to the hierarchical operation of the company. Media workers in Canada and the United States have organized, in places, to demand control over some portion of their enterprise's air time or printed space. The examples indicate that when a sector of the labor force is well educated and reasonably well paid, concerns are likely to turn to issues of workers' control. The possibilities for organizing in

[40] "White Collar Revisited: The Making of a New Working Class," *Social Policy,* Vol. I, No. 2 (July–August 1970), p. 27.

this context may thus be even better than in the context of the traditional industrial workforce.

A special but critical case demonstrating the growth of service workers in the North American economy is that of government employees. As noted above, this is the fastest growing employment sector in the economy: today some twelve and one half million people work for government in the United States—more than the total number of blacks in the American labor force. White-collar and clerical workers predominate, and pay scales, averaged out across the board, tend to be comparatively high.

Unionization among government employees has mushroomed in the last decade. Teachers' strikes, for example, are by now familiar in every major American city. United States postal employees shut down the mails for several days in 1969, while Canadian postal workers carried on a three-month-long rotating strike and slowdown in 1970. Sanitation men, transit workers, even police and firemen have gone on strike in New York, Chicago, Montreal, and elsewhere. Here too, there has been a good deal of hostility to public employee unionization, often leading in turn to greater militance.

While most of these strikes have been over wages, workers' control issues have appeared in a number of cases. Teachers demand control over class size, school policies, and hiring; police demand autonomy to "run their own affairs." Young professionals working in social welfare agencies or departments demand a say in departmental policies. Many of the points that apply to privately employed white-collar workers are equally applicable to their publicly employed counterparts. They are a growing sector, relatively well paid and well educated, and likely to be concerned about the quality and social implications of their work. Where political organizing does take place, demands for workers' control, in whatever form, may be able to take firm root.

Strategic Issues: Workers, Community, Unions

The problem of government employees, however, is but a microcosm of a larger strategic problem. When the residents of the Ocean Hill–Brownsville area in New York demanded control of their schools, the most vigorous opponents of the measure were not the Board of Education nor any governmental body—but the teachers' union. Community control, to many teachers, meant loss of whatever "workers' control"—particularly job security—they had been able to establish through their union. (And, of course, it threatened the power of the union leadership directly.) Similarly, police in large cities demand "workers' control" in the form of police department autonomy from civilian review. The result, again, is a conflict between workers and their demands on the one hand and the community on the other. Sanitation workers or transit employees can exercise a form of workers' control through strikes and similar actions; but it is the community that pays the bill, either in the form of reduced services or in the form of higher wages (financed through an inequitable tax structure).

In other cases, of course, "workers" and "community" demands have happened to coincide, or to reinforce each other. Social workers seeking a voice in the operation of their departments—as with the Social Welfare Workers' Movement—are doing so in order to work with, not against, protesting welfare mothers. Junior-level city planners demanding more of a say in the articulation of urban renewal plans demand the same thing for affected communities. Hospital workers and medical personnel organizing for greater control over health-care facilities often find allies in the community, and posit a goal of joint worker and community control.[41] But the strategic problem remains, for at any point where workers' interests and commu-

[41] This has happened in at least one instance in Montreal. For a review of the Montreal situation, see Ed Smith, "Community Control: The Montreal Experience with Some General Observations," in Gerry Hunnius, ed., *op. cit.*, pp. 53–57.

nity interests appear to diverge, the alliance can degenerate into the kind of conflict typified by Ocean Hill–Brownsville.

Nor is the issue limited, in theory, to the government sector. One of the more far-reaching developments of the last decade, for example, has been the movement for community control of economic development. As poor communities began to exercise their political muscle, they became increasingly aware of their dependence on the good or ill will of the large corporations and other economic interests governing their areas. In response to this, nearly a hundred U.S. communities have developed a vehicle for local control of the economy, the community development corporation (CDC).[42] The CDC, though it takes many forms—some, at this stage, no better than any private corporation—is based on the principle that the community as a whole should own and control the economic enterprises within its borders, and use the profits to provide local community services. Although most are just getting off the ground—and are only beginning to develop forms of real community participation—they clearly indicate the potential of community control movements, as much as workers' control movements, to move in the direction of a socialist vision. But where do the two movements intersect?

The issue need not be tied to the often problematic experience of existing CDCs. Wherever a community attempts to assert control of its economic institutions—by developing cooperatives, by opposing plant shutdowns, by setting up municipal enterprises, whatever—the possibility exists that community and workers will come into conflict. The case of Israel suggests the extent of the problem. There, the trade union federation (Histadrut) owns and operates its own businesses. But except for a small, cooperatively run sector of this "labor economy," the firms operate much like any capitalist enterprise. To be sure, the profits go to the federation: but in the absence of any

[42] For a description of a number of existing CDCs, see *Profiles in Community-Based Economic Development* (Cambridge: Center for Community Economic Development, 1971). It is worth noting that at least one—Operation Bootstrap in Los Angeles—is experimenting with worker self-management in the context of community ownership. See *Profiles*, p. 32.

mechanism for *community* control, there is no way that community interest in the production process can be asserted. The contrast with the kibbutz, for example, is evident.

In the long run, the problem will be to develop some form of joint worker self-management and community self-government, as suggested above. In the short run, the problem is less pressing, and may be as much a question of tactics as it is of ultimate program. Union teachers and poor black students have a common interest in better educational environments—if the issue is defined in such a way that that interest is apparent. Factory workers, the unemployed, and community residents have a common interest in controlling the corporations that govern their economic lives. Thus in Seattle, for example, organizers have made headway with workers at the huge Boeing plant and with community residents in demanding that Boeing convert to peacetime operation.[43] Unless such common interest—and joint organizing—is carefully developed, though, "workers" and "community" may time and again find themselves in opposition.

Another strategic problem which arises with demands for workers' control is what the role of unions should be. At this point in North America, no pat answers are possible. In Europe, André Gorz and others have argued that workers' control movements must operate outside the union structure arising spontaneously, demanding complete control of the workplace, and refusing to compromise with management (the union can then go in and pick up the pieces). The experience of the English workers' control movement has been quite different: there the shop stewards' movement and a number of the larger unions have provided vehicles for workers' control organizing. In the United States, workers' control demands may arise both inside and outside unions. The teachers' union in some areas, for example, has demanded faculty senates responsible for running the schools; on the other hand, a revolutionary union

---

[43] See Michael Lerner, "Conspiracy in Seattle," *Liberation,* Vol. XV (July 1970), pp. 36–42. "Retooling war factories like Boeing so that they would produce goods needed by people in the state rather than war matériel" was one part of a fairly comprehensive organizing program which centered on a tax petition.

movement like the League of Revolutionary Black Workers has found it necessary to work outside the structure of the UAW (and indeed in opposition to it). As is clear from the essays in this book, radicals disagree about the relative merits of the two approaches.

One can imagine a wide range of tactical alternatives. Working through the union may mean simply extending collective bargaining to new areas—for example, product pricing policies —without challenging the union's structure and function. Or, more likely, union-based workers' control demands can arise through a rank-and-file caucus, either local or national. In Canada, for instance, a reform caucus (though without a rank-and-file base) was instrumental in the Canadian Labour Congress's decision to support "industrial democracy."[44] And one can imagine local caucuses arising on any number of issues—health and safety, for example—when the union leadership fails to protect workers' interests. Finally, some form of nonunion worker organization may at times be necessary: an insurgent union to replace the old; a "workers' council" which remains separate from the union; or an extra-union political organization (such as the League of Revolutionary Black Workers). Even where no union exists, workers struggling for more control will face the problem of either forming a union or working entirely outside traditional union structures.

Choice of tactics can never be spelled out in advance. But at least two theoretical issues are relevant to the decision. First, what is the role of the union in capitalist society? Many activists argue that it can never present a challenge to the social order primarily because its functions (getting better contracts through collective bargaining) depend on maintenance of that order. A union struggling for workers' control—and thus for a radical redistribution of economic power—would, in this view, be almost a contradiction in terms. On the other hand, in the absence of a cataclysmic social change, there is a need to consolidate gains at any given point and to institutionalize new centers of power. The unions of the AFL-CIO may have turned

[44] See Policy Statement and Resolution, Canadian Labour Congress, Edmonton Convention, 1970 (mimeo).

into supporters of the status quo, but the IWW—which never signed a contract—is no longer with us. The answer may be that the union requires constant infusions of revolutionary spirit from below, whether this takes the form of insurgent caucuses *or* nonunion workers' groups. Both unions and insurgency seem to be necessary: the strategy, as the saying goes, should "walk on two legs."

Second, ultimate goals will have implications for tactical choices. In a socialist self-managed firm, the union does not necessarily become obsolete. In Yugoslavia, in addition to its educational role, the union serves the function of expressing workers' interests on the regional and national levels. More generally, as Paul Blumberg points out, it may be to the best advantage of the worker to have more than one representative (much as the citizen is represented, say, by the city council and the school board). The union, in Blumberg's terms, can represent the worker as employee, the workers' council his interests as producer.[45] Translated into strategic terms, this suggests the worker may very well want his traditional interests looked after by the established union, while he fights for new gains through caucus, council or whatever.

Unions, then, may serve as powerful allies or vehicles for insurgent workers' control movements—or they may be so entrenched as to fight local insurgency tooth and nail, much as the labor-based Communist parties of France and (to a lesser degree) Italy have attempted to quell most non-"official" labor uprisings, and as, of course, many North American unions do as a matter of course. The choice of tactics will ultimately depend on the local situation, the union, and above all the attitude of workers toward the union.

One thing seems clear: in all these settings—industrial, service, white-collar, governmental—the notion of workers' control will take on different strategic meanings. In a large factory, it might initially take the form of workers' councils setting

---

[45] Blumberg, *op. cit.,* p. 163. The union, in other words, would serve a protective function and the council an initiating/managing function.

standards and enforcement procedures for, say, health and safety regulations. In a public school, it might initially mean teachers' control of curriculum and methods. The *potential* of workers' control is that it provides a vision through which the specific demand can move to the general: demands for a say about working conditions or organizational policy right now can point toward the ultimate goal of popular control over the economic system.

This, in the end, must be what today's radical movements are about. Our ability to liberate ourselves and our society will depend on our ability to involve people in actively controlling their own lives—in building new forms of decentralized participatory democracy that can govern our society and its institutions in a way that meets people's needs. A decent society requires that equality, cooperation and community be built into the system; this in turn requires that self-management and self-government permeate our institutions from the bottom up.

In Noam Chomsky's words:

> If the present wave of repression can be beaten back, and if the Left can overcome its more suicidal tendencies and build upon what has been accomplished in the past decade, then the problem of how to organize industrial society on truly democratic lines, with democratic control in the workplace and in the community, should become a dominant intellectual issue for those who are alive to the problems of contemporary society, and, if a mass movement for libertarian socialism develops, speculation should proceed to action.[46]

Building a movement for workers' control, we believe, is one critical step in this long, difficult, but all-important struggle.

[46] "Notes on Anarchism," p. 35.

The Politics of Workers' Control: A Review Essay

G. David Garson

Recent years have seen a burgeoning interest in the concept of workers' control of the factory and office. This interest is shown in academic research, partisan debate, union demands, management experiments, governmental programs, and spontaneous revolutionary action. The present, selective essay alone discusses nearly four dozen books and pamphlets that have appeared on the subject, mostly in the last few years. The growing worldwide movement for workers' control may not be part of a convergence of social evolution toward labor-managed economies, as Jaroslav Vanek argues in *The Participatory Economy*, but it is at least the central issue of class struggle in our generation.

As the movement grows, the intellectual debate has moved to the left. Liberal schemes of joint consultation, human relations, and even profit sharing and nationalization have been proved shallow to all who are willing to examine the evidence. The controversy over whether workers' control "can work" has ceded to the question of "Under what conditions does workers' control work best?" Nevertheless, the politics of workers' control remains, in most countries, a politics of reformism, focused on the extremely limited possibilities of consultation and collective bargaining as modes for "whittling away" at management rights.

The scope of the movement is indicated by the number of

topics dealt with in the present essay. After discussing the general case for workers' control, articles bearing on its background in radicalism and relation to unionism are treated. These themes are illustrated in a discussion of the English movement for workers' control and its Canadian counterpart. Other experiments in Germany, France, Scandinavia, and Belgium are discussed in turn, followed by coverage of the less developed countries of Israel, India, and Algeria. Finally, movements for workers' control in the Communist countries of Poland, Hungary, Czechoslovakia, and Yugoslavia are examined. What emerges is a pattern of general failure of workers' participation without control, the effort of management and its allies to prevent genuine workers' control, spontaneous worker actions to achieve it, and the complex but hopeful results where it has been tried seriously.

The Case for Workers' Control

Paul Blumberg's *Industrial Democracy: The Sociology of Participation* (1968) is a useful starting point for the discussion of workers' control. After setting forth the failure of liberal alternatives of nationalization, joint consultation, and cooperatives, the author reviews the classic experiments underlying the human relations school of management, showing how these studies were misinterpreted to emphasize management concern and ignore the positive effects of worker participation. Blumberg's review of a host of sociological studies shows that increased participation generally leads to higher satisfaction and productivity, though the review is limited by the studies themselves, which are generally related to management concerns and to smaller groups. On the theoretical side, Blumberg devotes a chapter to a convincing polemic against the prevailing, conservative idea that collective bargaining unionism *is* industrial democracy. While radicals may find this trivial, many others will be helped to understand more clearly why unions are not like workers' parties and why the firm is not like a government in office. Blumberg concludes with a useful overview of the Yugoslav experience, rebutting arguments that Yugoslav workers' councils are ineffective, dominated by the League of Communists, and management dependent. Again, however, conclusive research is simply limited, and radicals will be disappointed by the professionally oriented thrust of the book, largely ignoring radical issues raised in a book like André Gorz's earlier volume, *Strategy for Labor: A Radical Proposal* (1964).

Gorz's work, while lacking the empirical dimension of Blumberg's, was more useful in outlining the *strategic* case for workers' control. Gorz argued that collective bargaining over wages was increasingly a deadend for labor, leading to cooptation of the unions on the one hand and to the failure to advance the share of the working class in the national income on the other. This spoke to concerns long heard among unionists, as in the Auto Workers, that wage gains are illusive, quickly taken away by price increases, speedups, layoffs, and technological changes in the workplace. Gorz's argument was also relevant to understanding the importance of shop-floor issues, the growing number of wildcats, and the formation of rank-and-file caucuses around what were, in essence, workers' control issues.

Blumberg's contribution was a sharp advance, however, over much of the earlier discussion of this issue in the United States. Illustrative of this earlier dialogue was a series of articles in the popular social science journal, *Trans-Action,* in 1965 and 1966. In these, Warren Bennis, a leader of the human relations school of management social psychology, defended the notion that educated labor combined with bureaucratic crisis was leading toward increased involvement, participation, and autonomy on the job. William Gomberg, a former director of the Management Engineering Department of the International Ladies Garment Workers' Union, criticized Bennis and the Harwood Company experiment on which it was based, charging this human relations approach was manipulative pseudo-participation. Alfred Marrow, a social psychologist and head of the Harwood Corporation, defended the experiment on the ground that workers experienced participation as genuine and neither they nor the union complained of manipulation in the twenty years of the project. In sum, much of the earlier debate was management oriented, concerned with management-initiated experiments that had limited success from that point of view but evoked labor memories of company union days.

In England, these issues were posed more sharply in Ken Coates' and Tony Topham's widely circulated pamphlet, "Participation or Control?" The authors, who figure prominently in the British movement for workers' control, developed the argument that nationalization is an essential part of the workers' control strategy, needed to connect control councils to the larger planning process, but also showed how nationalization has become a form of "businessmen's syndicalism." Coates and Topham rejected the Labour party's equation of industrial democracy with joint consultation common in wartime (the Whitely councils) and to attack modern counterparts to noncontrol "participation," such as productivity bargaining (discussed later). That Coates and Topham argue in these terms rather than those of Bennis and Gomberg highlights the importance of the politicization and radical traditions within British labor.

The more general case for workers' control has been ably stated by an English political theorist, Carole Pateman, in *Participation and Democratic Theory* (1970). After a critical review of participation and antiparticipation theorists from Rousseau to contemporary social scientists, with special attention to G. D. H. Cole and the English Guild Socialists, Pateman relied on empirical studies to argue that participation is a central means of attitude change. In particular, she cited a number of studies (those in Blumberg, Coch and French, Trist, Melman, McGregor, Likert) indicating that workplace participation generates general attitudes of political efficacy necessary to animate democratic citizenship, attitudes which have not been sufficiently developed by parliamentary democracy alone. While able to show rank-and-file motivation for worker participation in management, these studies are primarily at shop floor levels. The consultative (as opposed to control) nature of the higher-level studies (Glacier Metal, John Lewis Partnership, Scott Bader Commonwealth) merely show that consultation is a shallow experiment and are not informative about the effect on workers of participation at this level. Pateman concludes with a review of the Yugoslav experience, noting the considerable suc-

cess in spite of underdevelopment, wide nationalities antago-
nisms, illiteracy, and an agrarian workforce. She found the rate
of growth impressive in spite of inflation, relied on the work of
Kolaja to argue that workers' councils take positions independent
from the League of Communists, relied on the 1962 ILC study
to show that high management matters are dealt with regularly,
on Singleton and Topham to show frequent worker council
voting at odds with the firm director. On the other hand, she also
cited some negative evidence, such as a study by Stephen (unpublished) showing a shipyard workers' council rubber-stamped
complex decisions, concentrating on problems like worker housing. Similarly, Pateman found skilled workers overrepresented
on workers' councils and concluded that though Yugoslavia has
a long way to go, a participatory society is not only desirable
but possible.

Workers' Control, Radicalism, and Unionism

The conservative response to the case for workers' control has
been the argument that the Western pattern of unionism democ-
ratizes industry while avoiding the cooptation of consultative
and participative schemes, pointing to wartime experiences with
joint councils in capitalist countries and to the prohibition
strikes in Communist countries, including Yugoslavia. Books
which document this argument include Hugh Clegg's *A New
Approach to Industrial Democracy* (1960) and Milton
Derber's *The American Idea of Industrial Democracy* (1970).

Radicals have frequently taken the reverse tack, viewing
unions as a conservative, bureaucratizing check on the spontaneous potential radicalism of the rank-and-file. The anarchists
and "council Communists" have generally viewed both the
wartime capitalist and the Communist experiments as statist
maneuvers, not genuine tests of workers' control. Instead, they
have pointed to the spontaneous formation of workers' councils
in wildcat strikes, in the Spanish revolution, and more recently
in France and Italy since 1968. The case of Yugoslavia has
been divisive for this tradition, some rejecting it because of its

obvious statist and undemocratic elements, others giving it critical support because of its widespread grassroots support and
ideological commitment to reducing statism.

Among recently published or republished expositions of this
view is Alan Spitzer's article "Anarchy and Culture: Fernand
Pelloutier and the Dilemma of Revolutionary Syndicalism,"
printed in a special issue of the British review, *Anarchy*.
Pelloutier, an anarchist journalist who headed the militant
working class organized as the Bourses du Travail at the turn
of the century, led a fight inside the unions of his day for repudia-
tion of Socialist political action in favor of workers' control
organizing around the Bourses. While this example may provide
some support for radical arguments against seeking workers'
control through unions; it may also be interpreted in terms of
the failure of middle-class leadership of worker organizations,
similar to the "cultural uplift" period of nineteenth-century
American reformism.

Antonio Gramsci's tracts, "Turin 1920: Factory Councils
and the General Strike" and "Soviets in Italy," have been reprinted and widely circulated, adding fuel to the radical argument against unionism as the sole means to workers' control.
Gramsci outlined the unsuccessful General Strike of 1920,
showing how the factory council idea promoted by the L'Ordine Nuovo group spread quickly, especially in the engineering
factories, and served to replace the "impulsive, fortuitous character" of strikes by a coordinated, conscious, revolutionary
expression. The factory council movement drew support from
the Communists and the anarchists, with resistance coming
from the Socialists and union functionaries, leading Gramsci to
the lesson of "the necessity of fighting against the whole bureaucratic apparatus of the Unions." In the tract on "Soviets in
Italy," Gramsci set forth his view that unionism is a capitalist
form, and that two revolutions are necessary, one against the
bourgeois state aimed at establishing a proletarian, Communist
regime and the other against capitalist industrial forms aimed at
establishing liberated production.

A last representative of this tradition, also recently republished, is Anton Pannekoek's *Workers' Councils,* written in
Holland in 1942 during the Nazi occupation. In contrast to

versions in which workers' control is seen emerging from voluntary association or state action, Pannekoek sees workers' councils as a spontaneous development of increasingly important wildcat strikes. "These forms come up," he writes, "not through shrewd planning but spontaneously, irresistibly, urged by the heavy superior power of capital against which the old organizations [unions] cannot fight seriously any more." While this optimism about spontaneous action compared to the weakness of union and party organization partly reflects the wartime resistance perspective of the author, Pannekoek's arguments find their postwar counterpart in Gorz and in Jeremy Brecher's recent interpretation of U.S. labor history, *Strike!*.

The Workers' Control Tradition in the United Kingdom

The conservative, anarchist, statist, and other positions on workers' control are all present in one degree or another in the long history of the workers' control movement in Britain. The conservative approach is embodied in the experiment studied by Allan Flanders, Ruth Pomeranz, and Joan Woodward in *Experiment in Industrial Democracy: A Study of the John Lewis Partnership* (1968). This experiment, dating back to 1914, is representative of isolated participation experiments in England and the United States fostered by "progressive" employers, in part as an alternative to unionism. In essence, the John Lewis Partnership is a chain of department stores with a profit sharing and consultation system, where "in normal circumstances the Chairman's view of what is good for the business takes precedence over all other considerations," and where the remuneration system "accentuates the prevailing hierarchical structure" within the firm. Like the experiment in the Filene department store in Boston, concession of management rights to workers' control was in no way involved.

In contrast, Ken Coates and Tony Topham present a documented history of union approaches to workers' control in *Workers' Control* (1970). After brief treatment of the Owenites, the authors discuss the formation of the Central Labour College and grassroots movements (involving the classic workers' control pamphlet, "The Miners' Next Step") in the 1908–11 period, when prices outdistanced wages and precipitated a wave of wage demands and unionization. Arguments about workers' control were carried widely by these events, by agitation of Tom Mann's *The Industrial Syndicalist,* and various small groups. Among intellectuals, this trend was manifested in rejection of unitary, statist, Socialist collectivism by "pluralist" writers (Belloc, Figgis, Penty) who were contemporaries of the early guild socialists.

Coates and Topham trace the rise of the guild Socialists in the building trades, starting with the offer of allied unions to build 2000 units of housing on public credit for the city of Manchester. An earlier "Builders' Parliament" had been assimilated into the Whitely Councils (World War I era consultation bodies), but the new National Guild's initial success quickly fell apart as well in the face of withdrawal of government support and lack of capital. Gradually, G. D. H. Cole and many other guild advocates redefined their views until workers' control was excluded, with the approval of the Fabians. The authors argue, however, that the attraction of Communism was the key reason for the decline of the guilds, showing how "Communism won over syndicalists wholesale," presenting itself a hopeful, if problematic path toward workers' power in contrast to the proved failures of other approaches.

Coates and Topham then go on to document the shop steward movement that grew out of the 1917 strikes and its drift into the Red International of Trade Unions; the nationalization plans set forth for mining and railways; the rebirth of the rank-and-file movement starting with the 1935 Hawker strikes, partly through Communist support, and its dissolution during the period of Communist support of Churchill and the "war of production." When the Communists belatedly again encouraged rank-and-file militance after the start of the Cold War, "the climate had changed."

The authors conclude with a discussion of the modern movement for workers' control in the United Kingdom, partly as a result of the sheer increase in the numbers of shop stewards after World War II. Over the 1947–61 period, work stoppages rose twenty-three percent and working days lost by eighty-two percent, with emphasis on direct workshop negotiations and an increased stewards' role. Unemployment fights against redundancy layoffs were a central aspect of this movement and militance was reinforced by the emergence of a "New Left" which helped rediscover the workers' control tradition of the shop stewards' movement.

In the remaining section Coates and Topham trace the growth of the workers' control movement and its fight against government incomes policy and nonparticipatory labor relations policy. By 1968 an unprecedented five hundred rank-and-file delegates were attracted to a conference on workers' control, the Institute for Workers' Control was established, and some 1,100 delegates attended the 1969 conference. Among the early allies were Jack Jones, Assistant Executive Secretary of the Transport and General Workers' Union, and Sidney Hill, General Secretary of the National Union of Public Employees.

More background on the shop stewards' movement can be gained from articles written in 1964 by Peter Turner ("History and Role of the Trade Union Movement") and Bill Christopher ("Trade Unions v. the Law," discussing 1963 anti-steward court rulings). The debate in the New Left is illustrated in a rather abstract controversy over whether workers' control should be shop-oriented or should be part of a broad socialist movement (David Armstrong, "The Meaning of Work," written as a New Left Summer School paper; Dennis Butt, "Workers' Control"). A participant report on the 1967 workers' control conference, directed to the New Left, is Geoffrey Ostergaard's pamphlet, "Workers' Control: An Idea on the Wing" (1968). Descriptions of workers' control experiments with the "gang" or "free group contract system" as one aspect of the stewards' movement is contained in two other pamphlets, Colin Ward's "Workers' Control and the Collective Contract" (which discusses Melman's study of the Ferguson Tractor works) and James Gillespie's "Toward Freedom in Work" (which also discusses the Durham miners' system).

The early response among unionists to the workers' control movement can be gauged from another work edited by Ken Coates, *Can the Workers Run Industry?* (1968). This volume contains the outlines of worker control plans written for and by representatives of the fuel industry, health service, steel industry, dock industry, motor industry, and aircraft industry. Although the perspectives vary considerably, in general union contributors to this volume exhibited full awareness of the dangers of dilute forms of participation without control, but were also far more interested in relatively nonideological practical steps toward workers' control. Perhaps representative was the article by Ernie Roberts on "Workers' Control and the Trade Unions," the Assistant General Secretary of the AEF and founder of the journal "Voice of the Unions." Roberts argued for workers' control as neither only-for-after-the-revolution nor as Socialism-in-one-factory, but as a pragmatic, multipronged strategy for social change starting with demands for total control over hiring and firing but keeping the ultimate objectives of workers' control firmly in view.

The response of the Labour Party emerged in a 1967 "working party report," recommending nationalization, information disclosure (a key workers' control demand), and some minor reforms but opposing workers' councils or any dual channels of representation. This report, to which Jack Jones and some other unionists contributed along with industrial relations experts and academics, was criticized in an Institute for Workers' Control pamphlet by Ken Coates and Tony Topham, titled "The Labour Party's Plans for Industrial Democracy." Coates and Topham criticized the failure to condemn existing legislation (nationalization, abridgment of the right to strike), but welcome the positive steps.

In spite of some initial favorable response from the Labour Party, as a 1966 promise for docks nationalization with "a new, radical element of industrial democracy," by the end of the decade relations with the BLP had deteriorated considerably. This was true not only of the incomes policy, but in the actual plans for the docks, devoid of meaningful workers' participation, precipitating an historic one-day strike in 1970 for nationalization of the docks with workers' control. (The workers' plan for the docks was described in the *Workers' Control* volume; the docks crisis in the IWC *Bulletin,* Vol. II, No. 6–8.)

Workers' Control and Canadian Labor

Anthony Carew's pamphlet, "Industrial Democracy and Canada" (1968) reflects not only the influence of the British movement for workers' control, but also the nationalist influence which counterposes workers' control to American-dominated corporate concentration. Against the argument that workers' participation coopts unionism, Carew developed the thesis that strong unions continue to act independently regardless of workers' councils, independently paralleling the argument of Blumberg on this point.

The same debate nonetheless recurred in the spring 1970 conference on workers' control sponsored by the Ontario Woodsworth Foundation and the Praxis Institute. This conference, reported in Gerry Hunnius, ed., *Industrial Democracy and Canadian Labour* (1970), included academic, political, and labor representatives. Leo Roback's article defined terms and issues, citing increased disillusion with American-type bargaining and increased interest in worker participation, referring to Marcel Pepin of the CNTU and Fernand Daoust of the QFL. Jacques Dofny argued that workers' control requires both changes in Canadian unions and a vision of a future, liberated society, an observation ignored by the political and labor representatives.

The political representatives, from the New Democratic party, generally supported workers' control but pressed the argument for political action. They were, moreover, markedly split: one arguing that industrial democracy is best promoted simply by organizing the unorganized into unions, another supporting collective bargaining attempts to erode management rights clauses, and a third placing the issue as one among many (such as tenants, poverty, peace), admonishing the delegates to remember that political action "is where the decisive war must be fought."

Conservative unionism was represented at the conference by Charles Millard, Director of Organizations for the ICFTU, who called industrial democracy a "disembodied slogan," was pessimistic that much could be won, and, incredibly, pointed for hope to new allies, saying, "Shareholders, like workers in a factory, are citizens as well. They are both the beneficiaries and victims of manipulation." On the other hand, Chris Trower of the Steelworkers, André Bekerman of the Canadian Union of Public Employees, and Gil Levine, also of CUPE (not to mention unionists speaking from the floor), spoke in favor of extending workers' control, primarily through collective bargaining but also by pressing to the limit labor's role on public boards.

A second conference, also dealing with community control, was sponsored in fall 1970 and reported in Gerry Hunnius, ed., *Participatory Democracy for Canada* (1971). Attended by some forty unionists, the conference was addressed by André Gorz, who presented the arguments mentioned earlier on the stalemate of the collective bargaining strategy and cited numerous examples of worker militance emerging unexpectedly and rapidly. Gorz's theme was that "free discussion and exchange among the rank and file almost always lead up to violent outbursts of protest and unforeseen strike action," and that "normal times" are deceptive for during mass crises, militancy reappears, often around workers' control struggles.

Among the union participants, Bekerman cited the War Measures Act to warn that authoritarianism, rooted in the organization of production, is the dominant pattern of power in Canada. Trower supported Gorz's thesis that "by negotiating simply on economic matters, we have tended to get ourselves into a trap" Jim Tester of the Mine, Mill, and Smelter Workers disagreed with Gorz on the need for formation of dual organization, but also argued that shop stewards need to be strengthened to the point "where they constitute a power structure of their own." Harry Greenwood of the Steelworkers warned against expecting the rank-and-file worker to see himself as pioneering the Socialist takeover of industry; instead action should focus on immediate things like insuring that foremen are the popular choice of the workers (not necessarily elections).

In the section of the conference directed to community control, Howard Buchbinder, a community organizer later with the Praxis Institute, emphasized the lesson that an extrainstitutional approach was crucial to avoiding cooptation. For participation in a larger bureaucracy to work at all, the rank-and-file delegates need to be sustained by an ideological orientation that transcends a narrow grievance orientation. Other speakers also supported the priority of consciousness raising over immediate participation. These points, however, were criticized by others for underestimating the consciousness-raising effect of genuine participation (as Pateman argued, noted earlier). A concluding address by Gerry Hunnius on "Strategies for Change" called for building an alliance between the forces for community and workers' control, and urged a continuous interaction between theory and practice through conscious political self-education.

Workers' Participation in Europe

France has been among those nations experiencing a variety of approaches to workers' control: state-initiated tripartite joint consultation schemes, spontaneous workers' councils during the revolt of May 1968, and voluntaristic experiments growing up after World War II. The latter, described by Claire Bishop in *All Things Common* (1950), took the form of some four dozen "communities of work," mostly initiated by utopian capitalists, operating successfully and showing the relevance of community culture to work democracy, but spreading not at all into basic sectors of the economy and proving vulnerable to the state. The state-initiated works councils simply add to the list of failures of joint consultation schemes. As the report of the International Institute of Labor Studies states, these were initiated after spontaneous worker takeover of factories after World War II, when "From the point of view of both the employers and the Government, it seemed better to give some legal sanction to this movement and thus keep it within bounds rather than let it spill over into anarchy." Whether the spontaneous postwar worker council movement and that of the crisis of May 1968 form a deep enough tradition to prevail in the future, as Gorz believes, is the subject of intense speculation.

The IILS report on Germany discusses the growth of state-initiated worker participation since the Allied Control Council's

Works Council Law (1946) and the subsequent Works Constitution Act (1952) and Co-Determination Act (1951). The report attributes the prevention of "quite a few" wildcats to the operation of works councils, which are active in social and welfare matters but lack substantive economic powers. Unions in recent years have been pressing for the extension of co-determination, a more extensive scheme under which the unions name the personnel director and have fifty percent representation on supervisory boards, seeking to apply it to all enterprises. Although unions find utility in the system, the report notes that most studies show it to have little effect on the rank-and-file worker. Since 1965 "co-determination at the workplace" has been a union slogan addressed to this problem, but it remains unimplemented. Meanwhile, a diluted version of co-determination has been proposed as the basis for European labor law for the Common Market, a proposal which is anathema to workers' control advocates.

While this proposal might be construed as an advance over the Scandinavian pattern (see the managerially oriented studies of Rhenman, 1968; Emery and Thorsrud, 1969), it can also be construed as an attempt to forestall proposals by more militant groups like the Belgian General Federation of Labor (FGTB). The views of the latter are presented in Ken Coates, ed., *A Trade Union Strategy for the Common Market: The Programme of the Belgian Trade Unions* (1971). This program affirms a Socialist tradition, and calls for workers' participation at all levels with union autonomy. The issues of unemployment and workplace alienation are highlighted as two key foci for action. In the short run, the program calls for coordination of labor delegates to existing participative bodies in a campaign to achieve various reforms which are detailed. Bloch-Laine's view that "power cannot be shared" is endorsed, co-determination is rejected, and instead a call is sounded for workers' control, beginning with shop-floor affairs, worker training, and moving toward influence over consumers' groups, housing, transport, the media, combined with control of financial institutions through state planning.

Israel, India, and Algeria

While the kibbutz industries in Israel are among the more successful experiments in workers' and community control (see the article by Fine in Hunnius, Garson and Case, eds.), the most recent volume has focused on the union-managed Histadrut sector. In *Workers' Participation: Expectations and Experience,* Tabb and Goldfarb argue that the failure of worker participation in this sector is due to its being forced on an uninterested membership by an aging leadership as an attempt to preserve unity and ideological direction in a diversifying organization. On the other hand, the authors show that "most councils" sought to exercise powers beyond their minimal official ones, laying the basis for the alternative explanation that the failure in the Histadrut sector is part of the general failure of joint consultation committees with ambiguous "rights."

The equation of workers' participation with joint consultation also appears in Nabagopal Das's *Experiments in Industrial Democracy* (1964). Although a form of worker consultation has been a part of Indian governmental policy since 1957, Das labels the results "unimpressive." Thomas Blair's *"The Land to Those Who Work It": Algeria's Experiment in Workers' Management* (1969) illustrates a more extensive experiment under Ben Bella in 1962–5, albeit one immensely complicated by a struggle between revolutionary and workers' control forces on the one hand and owners, prefects, and local notables on the other. Ultimately, even at the height, the Socialist sector comprised only ten percent of agriculture and a much smaller proportion of industry. Blair evaluates the experiment as a symbolic success only, limited by lack of power and resources. "Autogestion," he writes, "far from breaking with the past, barely affected the structural imperatives and productive or human relations of the latifundia system." Even within autogestion, decisions tended to be handed from management down to the workers' councils. Juliette Minces' pamphlet, "Self-administration in Algeria" argues that many of the political problems of the experiment lay in a political battle at the top, with a primarily nationalist (not socialist) leadership which was threatened by workers' control. Ian Clegg's *Workers' Self-Management in Algeria* (1971) is a more sophisticated work arguing that Algerian workers' control was "a system of mystification" and a negative reflection, not on workers' control, but on the nature of the Algerian revolutionary process. These studies suggest that the failure of workers' control in Algeria cannot be construed as evidence against the feasibility or desirability of the system in other political contexts.

Workers' Control Under Communism

Adolf Sturmthal, in *Workers' Councils: A Study of Workplace Organization on Both Sides of the Iron Curtain* (1964), argued that councils may arise in Communist systems as a useful means of decentralization, a means which may, moreover, "wrest control of labor from unions." This dubious generalization perhaps best fits the case described by Jiri Kolaja in *A Polish Factory: A Case of Workers' Participation in Decision Making*. There Kolaja observed a council experiment imposed from above as a concession after the abortive revolt of 1956. The council failed, its most articulate worker delegate coopted by the Party and the rank-and-file regarding it as one more management tool. This perception, moreover, was essentially correct; the council never even got the elementary right of full information sharing, let alone significant control.

In contrast, Andy Anderson's *Hungary 56* (1964) and the ICFTU report on the workers' councils under Dubček in Czechoslovakia, both reveal powerful workers' council movements as a challenge to rather than a tool of the old regime, the former semispontaneous and the latter union-and-reform administration initiated. The smashing of both movements by Soviet power is one of the great tragedies of the struggle for workers' control.

Yugoslavia remains the leading example of worker self-management. Since the 1962 ILO report, *Workers' Management in Yugoslavia,* considerable attention has been devoted to this experiment. The ILO study, prior to the reforms of 1965 to

1968, concluded that worker participation is very extensive, that the legal powers of the workers' councils make it the focus of management decision making, that it must at least formally pass on key issues, and that the decisions were of such vital interest to the workers concerned that meaningful participation was likely. Economically, the report gave cautious approval to the view that self-management has increased productivity, at least in the area of trimming excess manpower, and in any event the growth rate has been high, reinvestment has been high, and payment of directors and skilled staff "comparatively low."

While many, including Huberman and Sweezy (1964), have noted the dangers of profit orientation and individualism in the Yugoslav system, strikes indicate growing worker independence while Tanic's 1961 study shows workers' councils evolving from personal issues to discussion of general problems.

Ichak Adizes' *Industrial Democracy: Yugoslav Style* (1971) reflects a 1968 Columbia doctoral dissertation arguing 1) there is some trend toward "management by exception" rather than routine participation in all decisions; 2) some council members preferred increased time for family affairs rather than opportunity to participate; but 3) the system was still marked by substantial worker influence which enhances productivity in at least some respects. Cast in business-school language, the work argues for limited participation though hardly "proves" this form is optimal. (The work also contains an efficiency study, but methodologically it cannot be used to test the efficacy of workers' participation one way or the other.)

Much of the most recent data on Yugoslavia is contained in Broekmeyer's volume *Yugoslav Workers' Self-Management: Proceedings of a Symposium Held in Amsterdam, January 7–9, 1970.* Yugoslav delegates to this conference presented a self-critical but optimistic presentation of recent attempts to develop self-management further. While the nationalities question was unfortunately downplayed, other interesting points were made. A number of speakers emphasized the sterility of the planning-or-market debate, asserting a growing recognition that both must be part of the Yugoslav solution, while at the same time it was asserted that the 1965 reforms made the market more important. Institute for Social Research (Zagreb) surveys indicate the model worker felt these reforms increased the influence of self-management in the life of the enterprise. Other studies indicating general support for the self-management system were cited, along with data showing some diminishing of the inflation problem, a trend on worker councils toward better-educated, higher-skilled delegates, and continued high level of investment. Jaroslav Vanek's *The Participatory Economy* (1971) provides a general summary of the argument for the Yugoslav system, a popular interpretation of his earlier work, *A Theory of Labor-Managed Economies* (1970). Vanek notes that Yugoslavia, in spite of unique problems, has had a rate of growth and level of investment and, more important, growth per investment comparable only to Japan and Israel and twice that for the United States.

Bibliography

Adizes, Ichak. *Industrial Democracy: Yugoslav Style* (N.Y.: Free Press, 1971).

Armstrong, David. "The Meaning of Work," *Our Generation* pamphlet, 3837 St. Lawrence Blvd., Montreal 18, Quebec, n.d.

Bennis, Warren. "Beyond Bureaucracy," *Trans-Action*, July–August 1965, pp. 31–5.

Bishop, Claire Huchet. *All Things Common* (Harper and Bros., 1950).

Blair, Thomas L. *"The Land to Those Who Work It": Algeria's Experiment in Workers' Management* (Doubleday, 1970; copyright 1969).

Blumberg, Paul. *Industrial Democracy: The Sociology of Participation* (Schocken, 1969; English ed., 1968).

Brecher, Jeremy. *Strike!* (San Francisco: Straight Arrow/World, 1972).

Broadbent, Ed. "Industrial Democracy" (New Democratic Party, mimeo, 1969).

Butt, Dennis. "Workers' Control," *Our Generation* pamphlet n.d.

Carew, Anthony. "Industrial Democracy and Canada," *Our Generation* pamphlet, n.d.

Christopher, Bill. "Trade Unions v. the Law," printed in *Anarchy*, No. 40.

Clegg, Hugh. *A New Approach to Industrial Democracy* (Blackwell, 1960).

Clegg, Ian. *Workers' Self-Management in Algeria* (N.Y.: Monthly Review, 1971).

Coates, Ken, ed. *Can the Workers Run Industry?* (Sphere, 1968).

——. *A Trade Union Strategy for the Common Market: The Programme of the Belgian Trade Unions* (Spokesman Books, 1971).

——, and Topham, Tony, eds. "The Labour Party's Plans for Industrial Democracy" (Institute for Workers' Control, Pamphlet #5, 1968).

——. *Workers' Control* (Panther Modern Society, 1970; orig. publ. MacGibbon and Kee, Ltd., 1968, as *Industrial Democracy in Great Britain*).

——. "Participation or Control?" (IWC pamphlet, reprinted in *Can the Workers Control Industry?*).

Dahl, Robert. "Workers' Control of Industry and the British Labour Party," *American Political Science Review,* October 1947, pp. 893–900.

Derber, Milton. *The American Idea of Industrial Democracy, 1865–1965* (University of Illinois Press, 1970).

Eaton, John; Hughes, John; and Coates, Ken. "Upper Clyde Shipbuilders, Ltd. –Workers' Control: The Real Defense Against Unemployment Is Attack" (IWC Pamphlet No. 25, 1971).

Emery, F. E., and Thorsrud, Einar. *Form and Content in Industrial Democracy* (Tavistock, 1969; in Norwegian, 1964).

Flanders, Allan; Pomeranz, Ruth; and Woodward, Joan. *Experiment in Industrial Democracy: A Study of the John Lewis Partnership* (Faber and Faber, 1968).

Gillespie, James. "Toward Freedom in Work," *Our Generation* pamphlet, n.d.

Gomberg, William. "The Trouble with Democratic Management," *Trans-Action,* July–August 1966.

——. "Harwood's Press Agentry," *Trans-Action,* September–October, 1966.

Gorz, André. *A Strategy for Labor* (Beacon, 1967; orig. 1964).

Gramsci, Antonio. "Soviets in Italy" (IWC Pamphlet No. 11, n.d.).

——. "Turin 1920: Factory Councils and the General Strike" (Moulinavant Press, n.d.; orig. 1920).

Huberman, Leo, and Sweezy, Paul. "Peaceful Transition from Socialism to Capitalism?" (New England Free Press, 1965; orig. 1964).

Hunnius, Gerry. *Industrial Democracy and Canadian Labour* (Black Rose Books, 1970).

——. *Participatory Democracy for Canada* (Black Rose Books, 1971).

Institute for Workers' Control, *Bulletin,* Vol. II, No. 6–7, special combined issue on the docks.

International Institute for Labour Studies. "Workers' Participation in Management: Country Studies Series," pp. 54–186, in IILS *Bulletin,* No. 6 (June 1969).

International Labor Office, *Workers' Management in Yugoslavia* (ILO, 1962).

Kolaja, Jiri. *A Polish Factory: A Case Study of Workers' Participation in Decision Making* (University of Kentucky Press, 1960).

Marrow, Alfred. "Gomberg's Fantasy," *Trans-Action,* September–October, 1966.

Minces, Juliette. "Self-Administration in Algeria," *Our Generation* pamphlet, n.d.

Ostergaard, Geoffrey. "Workers' Control: An Idea on the Wing," *Our Generation* pamphlet, n.d.

Pannekoek, Anton. *Workers' Councils* (Root and Branch Publ., 1970; orig. 1942).

Pateman, Carole. *Participation and Democratic Theory* (Cambridge University Press, 1970).

Rhenman, Eric. *Industrial Democracy and Industrial Management* (Tavistock, 1968; orig. 1964).

Spitzer, Alan. "Anarchy and Culture: Fernand Pelloutier and the Dilemma of Revolutionary Syndicalism," in *Anarchy,* No. 40.

Sturmthal, Adolf. *Workers' Councils: A Study of Workplace Organization on Both Sides of the Iron Curtain* (Harvard University Press, 1964).

Tabb, J. Y., and Goldfarb, A. *Workers' Participation in Management: Expectations and Experience* (Pergamon, 1970).

Turner, Peter. "History and the Role of the Trade Union Movement." *Anarchy,* No. 40.

Vanek, Jaroslav. *A General Theory of Labor-Managed Economies* (Cornell University Press, 1970).

——. *The Participatory Economy* (Cornell University Press, 1971).

The Editors

GERRY HUNNIUS teaches in the Department of Social Sciences at Atkinson College, York University (Toronto). He is a Fellow of Praxis: Research Institute for Social Change in Toronto and an Associate Fellow of the Cambridge Institute. A member of the Toronto editorial group of the international journal, *Our Generation,* he has published several articles on the Yugoslav system of workers' self-management.

G. DAVID GARSON is an assistant professor of political science at Tufts University. He received his B.A. from Princeton in 1965 and a doctoral degree from Harvard in 1969. He is author of a political science textbook and of several articles on social movements, particularly labor. He is a coordinator of the Labor Information Committee and codirector of the Seminar on Workers' Control of the Cambridge Institute and recently directed a field study of automobile workers' attitudes toward workers' control.

JOHN CASE has been a Fellow of the Cambridge Institute since 1969. Before that, he helped to found the New England Free Press and edited its now-defunct magazine, *The Paper Tiger.* At the Institute, he has been involved in studies relating workers' management to community-owned economic institutions and to long-term strategies for change.

Notes on Contributors and Sources

DAVID ELLERMAN was educated at M.I.T. and Boston University, where he earned a doctorate in mathematics and master's degrees in economics and philosophy. Aside from work in mathematics, his present research is directed toward a modern treatment of the labor theory of property (outlined in his article) and toward a critique of conventional economic theory from the laborist viewpoint. His article was written especially for this volume; a longer treatment of the same subject appeared in the *Review of Radical Political Economics*.

IAN ADAMS is author of *The Poverty Wall* (McClelland and Stewart, Toronto, 1970), from which the essay in this volume is excerpted.

CHARLES HAMPDEN-TURNER is a psychologist and author of *Radical Man* (Cambridge: Schenkman, 1970). He is currently writing a book on community-based economic development. His article in this volume is excerpted from an unpublished working paper written for the Center for Community Economic Development in Cambridge, Mass.

STANLEY WEIR has been an active trade unionist for over thirty years, mainly as a merchant seaman, auto worker, painter, truck driver, longshoreman, and teacher. He has been a shop steward, negotiator, and organizer and was editor of the *British Columbia Seamen's Union News*. Several of his articles on West Coast longshore and auto union conflicts have appeared in *New Politics* magazine. He is one of the contributors to the recently published *Autocracy and Insurgency in Organized Labor,* edited by New York labor lawyer Burton Hall, and he was one of the participants in the October 1971 Conference on Problems, Programs, and Prospects of the American Working Class in the 1970s sponsored by Rutgers University and *Trans-Action* magazine. He is now preparing a book on longshore work culture and teaching at the University of Illinois Institute of Labor and Industrial Relations (Champaign-Urbana).

STANLEY ARONOWITZ was born in New York City in 1933 and attended public schools. He dropped out of Brooklyn College as a freshman and subsequently worked as a lens grinder, truck helper, shipping clerk in the garment center; in New Jersey he worked as a turret lathe operator in a steel fabricating plant, and on the assembly line in a GM plant. After five years in a steel rolling mill and wire drawing plant he became steward and officer of the local union, participating in the 116-day steel strike of 1959. He was an organizer for the Textile Workers Union and ended up on the union payroll as assistant education director. Aronowitz ended his trade union career with the Oil, Chemical and Atomic Workers Union where he was organizing coordinator for the northeast region before being exiled to Puerto Rico because of his unpopular views on the Vietnam War. Since 1967 he has worked with the New York City manpower agency and with an antipoverty agency on the Lower East Side. He is now teaching and writing. His article was written for this volume.

DANIEL BELL, born in 1919, is professor of sociology at Harvard University. He has had a mixed career in journalism and the Academy. He has been managing editor of *The New Leader* and Labor Editor of *Fortune*. For ten years he was professor of sociology at Columbia University. He is currently (1972) coeditor of *The Public Interest*. Among his books are *Marxian Socialism in the United States, Work and Its Discontents, The End of Ideology,* and *The Coming of Post-Industrial Society*. The article in this volume is a shortened form of a piece that originally appeared in *Commentary*.

CHRIS TROWER is an international representative of the United Steelworkers of America, Toronto. His article is excerpted from a longer, unpublished manuscript.

PAUL BLUMBERG considers himself both a sociologist and social critic, and does not regard the two as necessarily incompatible. He was educated in California, receiving his Ph.D. from the University of California at Berkeley in 1966, and is currently Assistant Professor of Sociology at Queens College of the City University of New York. His most recent works include *Industrial Democracy: The Sociology of Participation,* from which the selection in this volume is taken, and *The Impact of Social Class: A Book of Readings.*

ED FINN is Research Director of the Canadian Brotherhood of Railway, Transport, and General Workers. He was Public Relations Director of the CBRT from 1963 to 1970 and has been labor columnist for the Toronto *Daily Star* since May 1968. Finn was a public relations consultant with the Canadian Labour Congress from 1959 to 1963. Before this, he worked for eleven years as a journalist on the *Western Star,* Corner Brook, Newfoundland, eventually becoming managing editor, and he also did reporting for the *Montreal Gazette.* His article originally appeared in the *Canadian Transpost.*

WILFRED LIST is the labor reporter for the Toronto *Globe and Mail.* His article is reprinted from *Task: News from the Ontario Department of Labour.*

LARS ERIK KARLSSON, thirty-one, is an active member of the left wing of the ruling social democratic party in Sweden. A graduate in business, economics, and organization theory since 1969, he has been employed by a special government commission to actively introduce the idea of industrial democracy into state industries. Karlsson's controversial book, *Demokrati pa arbetsplatsen* (Democracy at the Workplace, Stockholm, 1969) aroused great interest in the labor movement in Sweden. The essay in this volume is a slightly rewritten version of the first and last chapters of that book.

HELMUT SCHAUER is former president of the German Socialist Student Federation (SDS). His article was written for this volume.

KEITHA SAPSIN FINE holds a B.A. from Barnard College and an M.A. in Political Science from The George Washington University. Ms. Fine has been active in community organizing in the Boston area, has taught, and is a doctoral degree candidate at Tufts University. This paper was prepared for the Workers' Control Seminar at the Cambridge Policy Studies Institute. Her current research is on international Communist movements and their affiliated labor organizations.

ANDRÉ GORZ was born in Austria in 1924 and early in his academic career became a disciple of Jean-Paul Sartre. He has been a Paris journalist since the late forties and an editor of *Les Temps Modernes* since 1961. He is author of many books, among them *The Traitor* (1959), *La Morale de l'Histoire* (1959), and *Strategy for Labor* (Beacon Press, 1964). His article consists of the text of a speech given at a conference on workers' control and community control as strategies for change, Toronto, 1970. He was visiting fellow at the Cambridge Policy Studies Institute in the fall of 1970.

ERNEST MANDEL was born in 1923 and was active in the Resistance during World War II. He studied at Brussels and Paris universities, worked as a journalist, economist (member of the economic studies commission of the Belgian Trade Union Federation of the FTGB from 1954 to 1963) and teacher. At present he is professor at the Flemish section of Brussels University. Mandel is a leading member of the Fourth International and is editor of its Belgian section's weekly, *La Gauche*. He is author of several books which have been translated into many languages, among them *Introduction to Marxist Economic Theory*, *Marxist Economic Theory* (two volumes), *The Formation of the Economic Thought of Karl Marx*, *Europe vs. America?*, and *Workers' Control, Workers' Councils, Workers' Self-Management* (an anthology). His article in this volume first appeared in North America in the *International Socialist Review*.

DAVID TORNQUIST is a free-lance journalist and translator. He is author of *Look East, Look West* (Macmillan, 1966), a first-hand account of Yugoslavia's socialist experiment. He is currently gathering material in Yugoslavia for a book on workers' management and its problems. His article was written for this volume.

JACK RASMUS has been active in the labor movement in Canada, Britain, and the United States. He is presently employed with a large AFL-CIO union in the United States. His article was written especially for this volume.

BOGDAN DENITCH is senior staff associate in the Bureau of Applied Social Research, Columbia University. His article first appeared in *Dissent*.

VINTAGE HISTORY—AMERICAN